649.1097 Youcha, Geraldine.
YOU
      Minding the
       children.

39906000801004
03/10/1995

DATE		

ALSO BY GERALDINE YOUCHA

Children of Alcoholism: A Survivor's Manual
(coauthored with Judith Seixas)

Women and Alcohol: A Dangerous Pleasure

*Drugs, Alcohol and Your Children: How to Keep
Your Family Substance-Free*
(coauthored with Judith Seixas)

Child Care in America
from Colonial Times
to the Present

SCRIBNER

NEW YORK LONDON TORONTO

SYDNEY TOKYO SINGAPORE

Minding the Children

Geraldine Youcha

SCRIBNER
Rockefeller Center
1230 Avenue of the Americas
New York, NY 10020

Designed by Carla Weise/Levavi & Levavi
Manufactured in the United States of America

10 9 8 7 6 5 4 3 2 1

Library of Congress Cataloging-in-Publication Data
Youcha, Geraldine.
    Minding the children: child care in America from colonial times to the
present / Geraldine Youcha.
        p.   cm.
    Includes bibliographical references and index.
    1. Child care—United States—History. 2. Children of working
parents—United States—History. 3. Child rearing—United States—
History. I. Title.
HQ778.7.U6Y68   1995
649'.1'0973—dc20   94-33096 CIP
ISBN 0-684-19336-1

Picture credits are on page 415.

Title page photograph: "Jane Addams reading to the children of the Mary
Crane Nursery." Wallace Kirkland Papers, Jane Addams Memorial
Collections, Special Collections, The University Library, The University of Illi-
nois at Chicago.

For my children

CONTENTS

ACKNOWLEDGMENTS

This book could not have been written without the astute advice and guidance of Elizabeth Blackmar, the superb research of Jessica Kaplan, and the editorial acumen of Jan Lurie. My editor, Barbara Grossman, provided perceptive comments that helped shape the book and the enthusiasm and encouragement that kept the project going. Liz Darhansoff, my agent, has been a stalwart defender through the maze of the editorial process. Dozens of others across the country clipped newspapers, magazines, and professional journals, reported on conferences, scouted pictures, and asked probing questions. Still others offered their information and their time in extensive interviews. I thank them all. Most of all I thank my husband, Zeke Youcha, whose unfailing support made all this possible.

PREFACE

CHILD CARE IS A central concern of our time. Despite this intense interest, no systematic history exists of the ways Americans have cared for young children whose parents cannot or choose not to tend them full-time. This book is an attempt to begin to fill that gap by looking at efforts to grapple with this question from Colonial times to World War II and beyond.

The book came about because I nursed three children and became interested in the fascinating institution of wet nursing. That narrow focus broadened as I realized that women have always helped other women to be mothers, and I began to look at the ways American society has devised to provide substitute care for children, rich or poor, neglected or privileged.

This book is the result of that investigation. It is in no way comprehensive; many areas have been ignored or been given only brief mention, others have been explored in detail. What became evident as I wound my way through the research is that although we seem to be grappling with new problems, the Great American Experiment has been through this before. We live with modern counterparts of old systems. The myth of the full-time American mother as the eternal model does not fit the complex realities of the past any more than it does the practices of the present, and many of the options that exist today have had previous incarnations in only slightly different form. For example, Colonial apprenticeship was to a large extent male child care, part of a little-known tradition of men as nurturers. It was also an early form of foster care, particularly for poor young children whose families could not provide for them.

On the plantation slave children too young to work in the fields were dropped off in the morning to be looked after in groups, a situation oddly suggestive of today's day care for the children of working mothers. White children, with their legendary mammies, evoke a long legacy of shared mothering with more than one woman at the center of the picture.

In the mid-nineteenth century when the world seemed poised on the brink of Perfection, cooperative communities brought up children—their own and others—to be the hope of the better world that was surely coming. The seemingly radical communes of the 1960s were echoes of these solidly American experiments in communal living. Both kinds of communities believed that children could be trained to be better than their parents, free of competitiveness, hate, and possessiveness. In both cases, the dream proved illusory.

With the flood of immigrants from the Old World at about the turn of the century, day care for working mothers, often initiated by the new settlement houses, was a way to move the newcomers and their parents into the mainstream of American life and set them on the road to success in school and the New World. These are aims not too different from those of Head Start today.

The ancient institution of the extended family, alive today with particular power in the black community, also served the migrants and immigrants of the early part of this century as a way to care for children whose parents could not. But this small-scale solution was not enough, and institutions grew as the population increased: first dreadful almshouses, then orphanages that separated children from indigent adults and were hailed as "ideal." Today, the orphanage—or some smaller, more humane version of it—is being called for to deal with large numbers of children lost in the foster-care system, which itself had been seen as a more humane answer to children's needs.

Upper-class children with their nannies, governesses, and boarding schools between the two world wars experienced, along with their poorer contemporaries, shared motherhood and separation from home. Now, children of working couples are faced with similar solutions when neither busy parent is available to care for them. Even today's mother who works at home so she can care for her own children has her counterpart in the immigrant women of more than one hundred years ago who made artificial flowers or picked nuts out of their shells in dark tenements.

Comprehensive day care, called for today as a new approach, was tried during World War II, when almost-forgotten federally supported centers provided everything from health care to before- and after-school care to the children of women working in war industries.

There is also a curious amnesia for the role of the schools as baby-sitter as well as educator. This function was recognized as early as Colonial times, when two-year-olds went to dame schools run by neighborhood women and took their naps on a blanket in a corner of the room.

It seems that society, in large part, has tried everything before and, as Yogi Berra might have said, what seems new today is really "déjà vu all over again." In addition, we tend to approve what we need, changing what is seen as the perfect child-care solution as conditions change.

Often, the approval is supported by expert opinion. But this, too, changes in response to changing times, since even the experts are the products of the culture in which they live, not isolated in some scientific climate-controlled bubble. Clearly, what we consider basic truths about childhood and motherhood have changed over time, with each era buttressing its views with the latest respected theory.

In reconstructing this half-forgotten past, I have relied on a combination of archival research, reportorial fact-finding, and present-day interviewing. My sources include oral and written histories of slaves and slaveholders who provided early versions of both day care (for slave children) and care at home (for slave children by the planter's wife; for white children by nursemaids and mammies). Manuscript diaries and contemporary newspaper accounts of the nineteenth and early twentieth centuries clarified experiments in residential group care by the Shakers and the controversial Oneida community, both dedicated to producing perfect specimens for the future Eden in the mid-nineteenth century. To unearth the beginnings of kindergarten and modern day care I searched autobiographies of innovators such as Jane Addams of Hull House, who, in her efforts to serve the poor, rescued children tethered for hours to table legs as the only way their parents could keep them safe while they went out to work. I also listened to many firsthand stories from individuals who painted vivid pictures of what it meant to be brought up outside the mythical standards of perfect motherhood in an orphanage (originally hailed as "the perfect institution") or in the care of a nanny or in an all-day nursery.

My own experiences have provided a close-up view of child care in the recent past. As a longtime journalist I have been an observer of the social scene; as a parent and grandparent I have participated in the revolution that has moved more women out of the home and into the workplace than ever before.

When my first child was born I quit work on the editorial staff of a magazine to devote myself to full-time motherhood. My mother, on the other hand, had worked with my father in our small-town housewares store and juggled child care along with dressing the windows and selling pots and pans. By sixth grade I was left home alone after school, a latchkey child before the term was coined. At some point I must have made up my mind (although I never thought about it) that I would stay home with my children.

Predictably, my daughter swung the pendulum the other way. She decided that her children could be cared for during the day by other women while she worked. Of course, I was convinced by reading my early Dr. Spock that my grandchildren would grow up sucking their thumbs, having awful nightmares, and feeling deprived. Nothing of the sort occurred. I watched the two girls move smoothly and happily from a baby-sitter at home to group care to after-school programs. It seems that each generation discards the patterns of the past only to have them reappear in the future.

By listening to the voices from our neglected past—those of children, their parents, their caretakers, and the makers of public policy—we can track these shifts and learn not only what happened but the emotional impact of all these possible alternatives. In addition, today's psychological insights can illuminate what has gone before and offer a fresh perspective on the present, as long as we recognize that in any form of child care some children will be neglected and harmed and some will be loved and nurtured. By placing earlier efforts in a historical context, I also hope to stimulate debate on where we as a nation dedicated to the improved care of children want to go in the future, and how we will respond to the pressing challenge of "who's minding the children?"

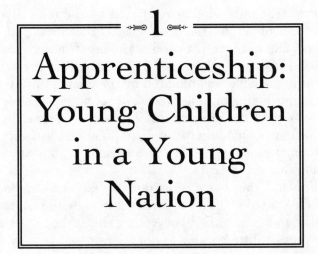

1
Apprenticeship: Young Children in a Young Nation

Fatherhood, history reminds us, is a cultural invention.

—*John Demos, historian*

IN COLONIAL TIMES what we think of as childhood—a carefree period of being coddled and cared for without having to do serious work—often ended at the age of today's second grader. Children were expected to work early and hard; idleness was a sin. Yet, as Sir Francis Doyle pointed out in the nineteenth century, "It is the intention of the Almighty that there should exist for a certain time between childhood and manhood, the natural production known as a boy." The boy existed in Colonial America as well as in Doyle's day and our own. It is the definition of when childhood ended that has been transformed.

Children assumed adult responsibilities in early America when they could hardly lift a bucket; today dependency can stretch beyond graduate school. Seven was a pivotal age in Colonial times. Boys and girls both wore long robes until then, and after that time dressed as miniature adults and were expected to work. This arbitrary cutoff point has also been seen by later philosophers and psychologists as a reasonable time to expect more of a child. Rudolf Steiner, the Austrian educator and philosopher, proposed in the 1920s that children be taught to read only when they started to lose their first teeth—about the age of seven. And Jean Piaget, the Swiss psychologist, found important changes in a child's thinking, from magical to logical, occurred at about the same age. In early New England the father of an illegitimate child was required by the court to pay something toward his upbringing until he was six or seven, presumably because he was too young to be of much use. These observations, before and after the insights of modern psychology, point up the reality that basic developmental changes form the backdrop for many attitudes about children and child care.

In England, the source of wisdom for Colonial America, Lord Chesterfield started writing cautionary letters to his illegitimate son when the boy was six: In 1741 he wrote, "This is the last letter I shall write to you as a little boy, for tomorrow you will attain your ninth year; so that for the future I shall treat you as a youth. . . . Childish toys and playthings must be thrown aside, and your mind directed to serious objects. . . ." By fourteen, a child could sign his own indenture as an apprentice. At that age, according to English common law, he could marry without parental permission. A girl could marry at twelve. At sixteen in Plymouth Colony a boy became legally responsible for his own actions, whether they involved being "Stubborn or Rebellious" or untruthful and slanderous. (Today, a child stops being legally a juvenile in many states at the same age.) Yet a boy who seemed to have achieved the rights and privileges (or disadvantages) of adulthood as a young teenager could be kept under the thumb of his master until he reached twenty-one.

The Apprenticeship System

From England the colonists imported a three-tier apprenticeship system. At the top were the sons of merchants who paid fees for their teenagers to be qualified to become lawyers or doctors or silversmiths. Then there were the craft apprentices and servants, voluntarily placed by their parents (or if they were old enough, usually fourteen, by themselves) into a contractual arrangement that transferred the duties and obligations of a father to the master or mistress who would instruct them in morality as well as practical skills: At the bottom were the poor children, bound out by the parish or overseers of the poor, with their parents (if they were around) having little or nothing to say about what happened to them.

Although the apprenticeship system was ostensibly designed to train adolescents in trades such as carpentry and printing, more than half the eleven hundred poor apprentices in Boston between 1734 and 1805 were five to nine years old. The master's job was not only to teach but also to act as a substitute father and ensure the proper moral development of his charges. He was responsible for children barely out of toddlerhood as well as those in their teens, and he served as "father" until the children in his care were old enough to be on their own—usually twenty-one for boys and sixteen to eighteen for girls, or until they were married. Childhood, then, lasted until seven, and youth gradually merged into independent, responsible adulthood in the late teens and early twenties.

Very young children sometimes worked outside the home long before they became apprentices. Thurlow Weed was apprenticed to a printer in upstate New York when he was twelve years old, but his first job, "when about eight years old, was in blowing a blacksmith's bellows for a Mr. Reeves, who gave me six cents per day. . . . I stood upon a box to enable me to reach the handle of the bellows." He was next a boy of all work in a tavern, and then cabin boy on board a sloop. For carrying a trunk for a passenger he received the first shilling he had ever owned and "purchased with that shilling three two-penny cakes and three oranges for my brother and sister."

Whether they acknowledged it as their primary task or not, the masters and employers of these young children were engaged in child care. They may not have blown runny noses or heated bath water, but every day they acted as stand-in parents, supervising, chastising, and influencing their immature charges. They were among this country's earliest answers to "who's minding the kids?"— socially approved and economically indispensable surrogate fathers.

Apprenticeship was a system that evolved along with the country. In early Colonial America's harsh environment, the family unit was virtually self-sufficient, acting as factory, school, and moral preceptor. The colonists were this country's original "do-it-yourselfers," building houses, planting crops, weaving cloth. Even very young children could stuff pillows with feathers or scrape wood smooth. But as settlements grew into towns and cities at the start of the eighteenth century, a child had to be placed outside the home if he was to learn a specialized trade that was marketable in the wider world.

Consequently, the more fortunate youngsters were apprenticed as a way of providing vocational training. But parish apprenticeship for both boys and girls—under the sponsorship of the church or overseers of the poor—was chiefly a way to take care of orphans, indigent children, and those whose parents could not care for them for one reason or another at little out-of-pocket expense. It was early America's version of foster care. With its help, "poor children and others were transformed from social liabilities to social assets," according to Lawrence Towner, whose master's thesis about the poor apprentices of Boston is a landmark study. The system was not just a method of poor relief; it was also designed to furnish at least a minimal education in both book learning and practical skills for all the young people of the new country. Single mothers—widowed, deserted by their husbands, or unmarried—used the system to provide child care that they were unable to supply. In Connecticut in 1746, Abram Finch, "aged 1 year, 10 months, child of single-woman Rose Anna Finch of Norwich, [was] bound to Nathaniel Phillips of Windham until Age 21."

Children were also sold into apprenticeship, with the overseers of the poor or those who had charge of them reaping the profit. One ad in the *Pennsylvania Gazette* for April 3, 1760, read: "To be sold by Thomas Overrend, at the Drawbridge, Two white Boys and a Negro lad; all about fourteen Years of Age. Also very good Lime juice, by the Hogshead or Gallon." In New York in 1750, Peter Jacobson, "a free Negro," was apprenticed to Gerardus Stuyvezandt by a standard indenture (rather than by sale), and after the Civil War large numbers of deserted and orphaned black youngsters were apprenticed in what was many times a continuation of the exploitation of slavery. In at least one case, however, an agent of the Freedmen's Bureau required that a planter who took five children, aged five to thirteen, have them "taught the rudiments of an English education" and given "four or five dollars per annum for each year that he serves," a revival of old requirements when the institution was almost at its end.

Abused and neglected children could be apprenticed to save both their souls and their bodies even if their parents were solid, taxpaying citizens. In Virginia in 1748 a law declared, "To prevent the evil consequences attending the neglect or inability of poor people to bring up their children in an honest and orderly course of life . . . where any person or persons shall be . . . judged incapable of supporting and bringing up their child or children in honest courses, or where it shall appear to the court that he, she, or they neglect to take due care of the education of his, her, or their child or children, and their instruction in the principles of Christianity . . . by order of their county court [they shall] bind every such child or children apprentices, in the same manner, and under such covenants and conditions as the law directs for poor orphan children." Entertaining unwholesome company and neglecting religious duties were valid reasons for taking a child from its parents. Living in ways that offended public morality was as subject to scrutiny then as now.

Apprenticeship for both rich and poor had a long history in the mother country, beginning in the Middle Ages. In the sixteenth century, English parents who could not provide proper training for their children were required to apprentice them to a trade, thus keeping them from wandering from place to place and becoming dissolute.

Although the apprenticeship system was transported across the ocean, the strictness and organized guilds designed to keep English goods profitable were left behind and the American version tended to be less rigorous than its English counterpart. The circumstances were different. Until the middle of the nineteenth century most Americans lived on farms. Apprenticeship in these circumstances was for many a way to learn farm work and perhaps during the slow winter months a craft useful on the farm, such as blacksmithing or coopering. The demands were different from those in cities. City apprenticeship, on the other hand, more closely resembled the English model.

The Poor and Neglected

In 1735 Boston revived an earlier requirement insisted on by both the Pilgrims and the Puritans a century before: instruction in at least the first two of the three Rs as evidence of parental competence: "where persons bring up their children in such gross ignorance that they do not know, or are not able to distinguish the alphabet or twenty-four letters, at the age of six years, in such cases the overseers of the poor are hereby impowered and directed to bind out into good families, such children, for a decent Christian education, as when parents are indigent and rated nothing to the publick taxes." There is no way of knowing how often this measure was put into effect—the involuntary apprentices for whom records remain were largely children of the poor, derelicts, illegitimate, orphans, or abandoned with no means of support. Whether their parents provided them with that basic Protestant skill, literacy, is impossible to determine.

For very young children the system was more pure foster care than apprenticeship, animated by the expectation that the child would eventually become a useful member of society. It was generally recognized that a good, Christian family was the best place for a child to grow up, and if his own was not "good" enough he was shifted to another in a kind of moral equivalent of the place-changing game of musical chairs. Poor children were apprenticed to keep them from being public charges and costing the community money, but also to provide them with the kind of care they needed to grow into respectable adults. There was also the hope that, with wholesome role models, they would learn how to act within a family and would take better care of their own children than their parents had taken of them. If a family judged to be unfit tried to keep its children with it, it faced formidable legal obstacles. Robert Lyman and his wife, of Northampton, Massachusetts, went to court in 1680 "showing their earnestnes that their children should not be put out." Despite their protests, the court ordered that the two youngest boys and one girl be apprenticed because "what the Parents Spoke [was] more out of fond affection and sinful Indulgence than any Reason or Rule."

A century later Maryland enacted unusual legislation sensitive to the concerns of parents. The law gave the standard recitation of the need for apprenticeship to care for children who might otherwise grow up to become "useless or depraved members of society" but followed it with "provided always, that when any child is about to be bound out, the parent or parents of said child, if living in the county, shall be summoned to appear before the said justices, and the inclination of the said parent or parents so far as is reasonable, shall be consulted in the choice of the person to whom the said child shall be bound out."

Parents acting on their own often placed their children with relatives as a way of keeping them close to home, sustaining family ties, and exposing them to what was, in essence, a "family business." On the other hand such actions also limited vocational choices and kept children mired in the setting in which they had had their start. Parents may have hoped that family affection would mitigate the harshness of apprenticeship, but as Benjamin Franklin found out, a half brother was as likely as any other master to beat the child in his charge. Sending children to grandparents to learn their trade had its hazards, too. This practice was frowned upon by John Robinson of

Plymouth Colony, who warned that grandparents were "more affectionate towards their children's children than to their immediates" and prone to "too great indulgence." This same warning was repeated more than a century later by the Shakers and the Oneida community, who feared grandparents as a corrupting influence on the children they were bringing up communally.

Well and Faithfully Shall Serve

The indenture document hardly changed over centuries. It got its name because it was originally written in duplicate on one sheet of paper, then torn or cut apart irregularly, forming indentations, with one half given to the master, the other to the apprentice or his family. That the two parts fit perfectly together made clear who was apprenticed to whom. Isaiah Thomas's indenture to Zachariah Fowle on July 7, 1756, is typical. Boston's overseers of the poor bound out the eight-year-old until he was twenty-one and stipulated:

> *During all which said Time or Term, the said Apprentice his said master and mistress well and faithfully shall Serve, their Secrets he shall keep close, their Commandments lawful and honest every where he shall gladly obey; he shall do no Damage to his said Master etc. nor suffer it to be done by others, without letting or giving reasonable Notice thereto to his said Master etc. he shall not waste the Goods of his said Master etc. nor lend them unlawfully to any.*

Personally, he was to lead an exemplary life.

> *At Cards, Dice or any other unlawful Game or Games he shall not play: Fornication he shall not commit: Matrimony during the said term he shall not contract: Taverns, Ale-Houses, or Places of Gaming he shall not haunt or frequent: From the Service of his said Master etc. by Day or Night he shall not absent himself.*

If Isaiah accepted this constant more-than-filial subservience, he was to be "taught by the best way and means he [the master] Can the Art and Mistery of a Printer also to Read write and Cypher." In addition he was to be given sufficient food, clothing, and lodging, have his clothes washed, and at the end of his time be provided with "two good Suits of Apparrell [*sic*] for all parts off [*sic*] his Body One for the Lords days the other for working days Suitable to his degree."

His indenture was eventually inscribed on its face, "Free January 8th. 1769." He grew up to be one of the most influential and successful journalists in this country's early history.

A child could sign his own indenture (or make his mark) at about fourteen, the age at which he was deemed competent to know what he was doing. Before then his guardian or the overseers of the poor had to sign the document and keep it safe.

A wide variety of conditions were written in to customize the standard form. The clothes Isaiah Thomas received as his freedom dues were a bare minimum; some apprentices were given tools, others received guns, books, money, or a horse or other animal in addition to the essential two suits. Some indentures provided that if a child had been bound out early, he could choose whether to remain with his master when he reached the transforming age of fourteen. Others stated that he had to give his consent if he were transferred (or, in today's terms, sold) to another master. For twenty pounds, John Galway's remaining term of eleven years and three months was transferred to William Dugdale and John Searle of the City of New York Reapers in 1719 by his original master, Peter Colvell. In the new indenture, John was said to be "well Contented and doth Give his full Consent."

Craft apprentices were cordwainers (shoemakers), cobblers (shoe repairers), cabinetmakers, bakers, shipwrights, chandlers, or one of a dozen more. They were taught all the trades that made the country work. Benjamin Franklin's father, fearful that he would follow an older brother to sea, walked him through the streets of Boston so he could see bricklayers, turners, joiners, and braziers at work. This early vocational counseling, making vivid the variety of choices available to a biddable boy, set Franklin's feet firmly on land. The choice was not necessarily irrevocable. Some boys who learned one trade later switched to another, or went on to college or established themselves in politics or in business. For example, Daniel Clapp started as apprentice to a carpenter and became the register of deeds and then representative of Worcester in the state General Court in the early 1800s. He was a feisty young man who served on a defiant grand jury that ignored British regulations in one of the earliest overt acts of the Revolution. Benjamin Heywood of the same city served his apprenticeship to a "housewright," became a carpenter, studied hard, and in two or three years entered Harvard in 1771. Apprenticeship clearly could be a route to upward mobility as well as a way of cementing class position. For some boys, however, it represented a downward slope as their families fell upon hard times and had no choice but to send them away from home to learn a trade.

Craft apprentices were said to have been exclusively boys, with masters acting as their fathers. Girls were bound out, often to women, to learn "housewifery." This was seen not just as sweeping and scrubbing, but, as Dr. Johnson's eighteenth-century dictionary puts it, "Domestick [*sic*] or female business; management." In its way, it, too, was recognized as a trade that had to be formally learned. A few girls were actually apprenticed to be taught more specific womanly skills: Elizabeth Burgess of Baltimore County was nine years and ten months old in 1779 when she was to be taught "Needlework to make wolland [*sic*] shirts." Others learned candlemaking or embroidery or mantua (cloak) making or dressmaking. But it is not quite true that only boys were taught manly trades while girls were confined to feminine pursuits. An occasional girl escaped the stereotype. In an unusual provision, Mary Mariot of New York, aged eleven, was apprenticed to a joiner (carpenter) who was required to provide her at the end of her term with "A New Cupboard worth three pounds and a Chest worth fifteen Shillings and also three pounds in Money." It seems likely that she was one of the rare girls who learned a craft and was to keep something she had worked on. Judith Shields was another exception. In November 1771 she was apprenticed to John Vanderen in Philadelphia to be "taught the trade of a spinning wheel and chair maker, to read in the Bible, write a legible hand." She was twelve years old.

A fee was standard before a master took on an apprentice, particularly if the craft was a prestigious one or, like silversmithing, required costly materials. The fees ranged from mundane agricultural products such as corn or beans to an amount of money that could go over one hundred pounds. One eighteenth-century Boston merchant required a hundred-pound fee plus a bond of five hundred pounds before he would trust a young man to serve him. Benjamin Franklin's father refused to pay what he judged an exorbitant fee and took his son back home before his trial period with a cutler was over. In England, a valid apprenticeship lasted seven years, time enough to become skilled at joinery or sailmaking.

In this country, apprenticeships often varied according to the age of the child. Poor children put out early were apprenticed for ten years or longer; George Beckwith of Lebanon, Connecticut, was bound out for seventeen years to Henry Otis "to learn habits of obedience, industry and subordination." Between 1734 and 1751 in Boston, some poor apprentices served fifteen or sixteen years, and more than half served more than nine years. Older children might serve only two or three years before they were entitled to the seal of approval that apprenticeship conferred, but some crafts did stick to the seven-year standard. Once an apprentice had completed his term he could work for wages as a journeyman anyplace he chose. When he had saved enough (about fifty pounds in Colonial Philadelphia to set up a print shop, for example) he could go into business on his own. Sometimes the apprentice was given a trial period before formal papers were signed, to see if master and child were a good fit and if the child was teachable. Samuel Seabury, who eventually became a leading Episcopal minister, evidently was not. "The truth is," he recalled of his time as a fourteen-year-old apprentice cabinetmaker, "I had a most astonishing inaptitude for all mechanical employment." In frustration one day he threw down his saw and jackplane, packed his clothes, and left before his trial period (usually six months) was over.

Apprentices passed on, like property, to the heirs of the master for the fulfillment of the rest of their term. Unlike slaves, who were required to continue to serve for life and whose children were also heritable, apprentices were bound only by the terms of their indenture. What was inherited was time, not the person himself. Slavery and apprenticeship shared another similarity with a difference—the term "master." As W. J. Rorabaugh, author of *The Craft Apprentice*, has pointed out, "God was master of the world; the father was master of his family; the teacher was master of his pupils; the skilled craftsman was master of his apprentices; and the planter was master of his slaves. 'Master' was a term both familial and hierarchical." Under apprenticeship, the master's superior position, unlike the father's or the planter's, was limited by time rather than by life. When an apprentice's time was up, the indenture was his to prove that he was qualified to practice his trade and had not run away or violated the contract (it had been held by his parents or guardian until the end of his term).

The Family

The family, not the individual, was the building block of society. That's why apprenticeship, which placed children within families, suited the tenor of the times. Within the household, wife, husband, and children formed an almost self-sufficient miniworld.

Men have a long-neglected history as the caretakers of young children. They were in contact with even very young children all day every day and routinely performed what would now be considered domestic tasks. As Mary Frances Berry points out in her book *The Politics of Parenthood,* once children had been weaned it was the father who had primary responsibility for them. He played with them, decided what they were to eat, and tucked them into bed at night. A typical example was Cotton Mather, the New England preacher, who was comforted at night when he was sick by his father, not by his mother.

Final say in what happened to children was in the hands of men, whether they were fathers, masters, or guardians. When Creek Indian Agent Benjamin Hawkins in 1797 was thinking of marrying a Creek woman, he felt it necessary to explain this European view to her mother: "The ways of the white people differ much from those of the red people," he said. (Indian women had absolute control over their children.) "White men govern their families." He would therefore require that his wife agree to raising all children (even those she, as a widow, already had) "as I please, and no one of her family shall oppose my doing so." The match did not go through. His prospective mother-in-law "would not consent that the women and children should be under the direction of the father."

Most societies entrust the mother with exclusive care of the infant because of the requirements of breast-feeding, but after that, power passes to the man. In a very few communities, fathers have played an active role even with very young children. For example, when the anthropologist Cora DuBois visited the East Indian island of Alor in the late 1930s, she found women going back to work in the fields when their babies were ten days to two weeks old. The babies were left with their fathers or older siblings or grandparents, and often went hungry on makeshift feedings of gruel. The father's primary job was to handle the political, financial, and ceremonial life of the island, and DuBois discovered that "it is definitely the less busy— that is, the less important—father who has time to be a good mother substitute."

Clearly, the definition of "fatherhood" is closely tied to the society, culture, and customs of its time. Today, too, as the idea of the nurturing father has become popular, fathers are expected to be more involved with their children but, like the fathers of Alor, are likely to be exempt if their work is significant and time consuming.

My Master, My Father

If the master, contractually and in the eyes of society, had the obligations of a father, the apprentice, on his or her part, had the obligations of a son or daughter—to follow the master's bidding, to act responsibly, to respect his privacy, and to be industrious. Love, however, did not play a specific part at either end of the equation. Isaiah Thomas's master promised his mother that he would treat him "as his own," since he had no children, and give him a good education, and that when he reached the age of fourteen he could choose whether to remain or not. But when Isaiah was formally apprenticed and his master "had absolute power," these promises were ignored.

The transfer of authority and responsibilities from biological father to master suited the needs of an American society looking for ways to expand the bounds of the family and provide the training and moral indoctrination needed in a new, growing nation. As in the early seventeenth-century home, where young boys were largely in the charge of their fathers, apprenticeship provided for male child care with the master, like an attentive sheepdog, watching over and correcting a flock of apprentices. It also ensured that girls, apprenticed often to women, were still under the control (and care) of the head of the family.

The available instruction books on child rearing (most imported from England) were addressed to fathers (masters) who were charged with the duty of producing good Christians, mindful of their manners and obligations. *A Father's Gift to His Son on His Becoming an Apprentice* was an anonymous tract published as a kind of Polonius's advice to Laertes for the 1750s. The author reminded his son that though he was an apprentice now, he would be a master later. When he reached that position he should behave well toward his apprentices because "for them you stand in the parent's place; they are to receive the treatment of sons, and to be considered as future masters, whose credit and respectability will in some measure shine upon your memory."

Even the law lumped masters and fathers together. A New Plymouth Order of June 1671 stated that the officials of every town were obliged "to see that all Parents and Masters do duely Endeavor, to teach their children and servants [a word used interchangeably with apprentices] as they grow capable, so much learning as through the blessing of God they may attain, at least to read the Scriptures [a basic need on the road to salvation] . . . and further that all Parents and Masters do breed and bring up their children and apprentices in some honest lawful calling, labour or employment." Otherwise, the children could be removed from the home and placed with a master or moved from one master to another. A good master, like a good father, had a lasting influence on his "children." For many youngsters, as Rorabaugh pointed out, "The wisdom of the master was of more importance than the actual learning of a trade." A man who had been apprenticed to a bricklayer remembered his master as a kind of latter-day Socrates: "When he had all his boys at home and seated around his winter evenings' fire, we constituted a sort of debating club."

Education such as this young apprentice recalled with gratitude continued to be mentioned in mid- and late-eighteenth-century laws and indentures, sometimes in a desperate attempt to keep the system humane rather than merely pragmatic. But by the end of the Revolution, apprenticeship was losing its force as a substitute family system. Society had changed. The need for labor was not so pressing, the spirit of independence had infected young people who wanted to be free to make their own way, skills could be acquired through books and courses as well as personal instruction, and industrialization was changing the nature of craftsmanship. In this changing climate, masters were permitted to arrange for someone else to handle the book learning, and night schools grew up especially to meet the needs of apprentices.

As the eighteenth century progressed, apprentices were also frequently boarded out and, removed from the master's intimate household, they became more like employees than like sons. The legal and traditional fiction continued that they were to be treated with filial concern, but both parties neglected their obligations as circumstances changed.

Apprentices often complained, even in the early days, that the master's obligations were being neglected. Isaiah Thomas wondered how his master, who could hardly read himself, could teach him. "I was left to teach myself," Thomas wrote. "He never once attempted to learn me either to read or write or caused it to be done." This is all the more remarkable because his master was a printer. Thomas felt

compelled to learn punctuation after the master, who was typeset-
ting a new ballad that was without periods or commas, put them in
by placing at the end of each line whatever had been used to punctu-
ate another, quite different poem. He also complained, as did Benjamin Franklin and almost every other apprentice who wrote about
the experience, that "he put me to all the servile employments of his
family that I could perform." But this was part of the tradition. The
newest apprentice did the sweeping up and other household chores
until he became senior enough to merit real instruction.

Apprentices were not always thorough in carrying out their
part of the bargain, either. A Massachusetts law passed soon after the
colony was founded opined, "Forasmuch as it appeareth by too much
experience, that divers children and servants do behave themselves
disobediently and disorderly towards their parents, masters and governors to the disturbance of families and discouragement of such
parents and governors," magistrates were given permission to whip
the delinquents. Again, no distinction was made between fathers and
masters.

Influences, Good and Bad

Just as children were taught by the Bible to honor their fathers and
mothers, Cotton Mather, the Puritan preacher, charged apprentices
with "Whatsoever *Service* you do for your *Masters* [or Mistresses] do
it as a Service unto the Lord Jesus Christ." Later, as apprenticeship
declined, Benjamin Franklin suggested that the service be done to
get ahead rather than as a gift to the Lord. Success, not salvation, became the aim of life.

Apprenticeship was often the key to higher social standing, a
more reliable trade, and a brighter future. But for some, such as
Samuel Seabury III, the son of a struggling minister, it represented
downward mobility. Although he expected to go on to college, family
fortunes made this impossible, and his father, who "wished to do the
best he could for his children . . . had but little choice of opportunity," and placed him with a furniture maker at the age of twelve. He
never forgave his father, although he cloaked his resentment with
praise for his wisdom when faced with a difficult decision. Since the
father could not afford "a liberal education," he "determined himself
to bring up his children as *mechanics* in which capacity he thought
they would have the least temptation to forfeit the virtues of sobriety

and honesty and stand the best chance to reap the advantages of frugal and industrious habits." But for Samuel, "It is a most unreasonable—a most cruel thing—to take a boy who has been brought up
with some degree of moral delicacy and place him among a set of
semi-savages who are utter strangers to the refinements of social
life." It not only affronted compassion, it went against a fundamental
tenet of the new country's philosophy—that children would do better than their parents.

For Samuel Seabury, the influence of his fellow apprentices and
journeymen was degrading, but for others, it was as vital and benign
as that of a loving older brother. The journeyman Samuel Draper, "a
good printer and a kind man," rescued Isaiah Thomas from the worst
aspects of life with his master and helped him become an expert
printer. Another journeyman, Tobias H. Miller, was credited by
William Lloyd Garrison, the abolitionist editor, as his model for
later life. Garrison was a boy of twelve when, without a father and
with an older brother who was alcoholic, he found Miller as his
model. "I was drawn to him magnetically from the beginning," he
wrote. "He was a very Benjamin Franklin for good sense and ax-
iomatic speech, and in spirit always as fresh and pure as a newly-
blown rose . . . from his example I drew moral inspiration and was
signally aided in my endeavors after ideal perfection and practical
goodness." If things went wrong he would say, "Patience and perseverance!" or " 'Tisn't as bad as it would be if it were worse!" Garrison
later recalled. "They made a deep impression upon my memory, and
through all the subsequent years of my life, in all cases of trial, have
been of invaluable service to me." Miller's axioms sound like the ones
English nannies passed on to the children in their charge a century
later. Perhaps they reflect venerable attitudes that survived the sea
change from the old country to the new. What seems like timebound
wisdom, as far as child care is concerned, often turns out to be old
precepts recycled for a new age.

Day by Day

Trying to discover what it was like, day by day, to be an apprentice in
the care of a man who was not your father is like trying to assemble a
jigsaw puzzle with only half the pieces. Neither apprentices nor masters were likely to keep heart-searching diaries, and the few details
we have come largely from men who became printers. They were a

special breed, of necessity most often literate, and we can only assume their experiences were typical. The recently rediscovered journal by a boy apprenticed in the early 1800s, as the institution was declining, to a cabinetmaker he dubbed sardonically Mr. Moneygripe adds a confirming voice to these earlier accounts. It is clear that apprentices woke early, worked hard at least six days a week, and grew up fast.

Isaiah Thomas started inking type when he was just six years old, standing on a box to reach the press. His job was to beat the form with an inked ball—an old-fashioned method even in those days. He was so tiny he had to grasp the ball with both small hands. By the time he was eleven years old he could run the whole business, from buying supplies to setting type to printing finished broadsides. He neither liked nor respected his master, but he does not seem to have been particularly ill-treated. The print shop was his only school.

William Lloyd Garrison's print shop experience was a happier one. Apprenticed later, at the age of thirteen, he was at first intimidated by the speed at which the more experienced boys were setting type. "My little heart sank like lead within me," he later recalled. "It seemed to me that I never should be able to do anything of that kind." But he learned very quickly, even though he, too, was too small to reach the table and had to stand on a fifty-six-pound weight to pull proofs.

Three years earlier, in 1815, he had begun his working career with a shoemaker and had an even harder time physically. He was thin and frail, burdened by a heavy leather apron and the leaden lapstone, and hardly able to pull the waxed thread through the tough sole. Luckily, he escaped this bondage as soon as he had finished his first pair, when his mother moved the family to Baltimore. He was so homesick there, however, that he moved back to Newburyport to live with friends and eventually was apprenticed to a printer.

With both his apprenticeships Garrison was fortunate to have understanding masters and mistresses with whom he lived, and who took him in as if he were one of their own children. He repaid the favor by "caring for the younger children of the family as if he were an elder brother, and making himself always helpful," his own children declared in the biography they wrote of their eminent father. He decided to stay in the printing office even when his mother asked him to rejoin her in Baltimore, and she reluctantly agreed to the continuing separation, reporting that his master "is very partial to you and says he never had a better boy."

The most detailed account of daily life as an apprentice comes from Samuel Seabury III, who was sent to work and live with "Mr. Moneygripe" in New York in the early 1800s. A gentle boy, genteelly brought up, he was dismayed by what he found. His mother had told him she thought he would have a room of his own and gave him strict instructions for keeping it neat. Instead, he helped carry his trunk to "a small garret room under a sloping shingled roof. . . . On the floor, which certainly had never been washed—lay two large beds—covered each with a filthy looking blanket and black spread." Six apprentices slept there. Samuel, as the newcomer, was assigned the center part of the corner bed, with a fellow apprentice on either side. Their meals were the leftovers from the master's table, eaten in a dismal room with the uncouth servants.

Every morning before breakfast Samuel opened the doors and windows in the warehouse and rubbed down the furniture. After he had eaten, he made glue, carried heavy joists on his shoulders down the street to be made into bedposts by the turners, and on and on until he was tired enough at night to fall into his filthy bed and sleep. When he told a fellow apprentice how surprised he was by these realities, he was told that "those who got such a place as we had were pretty well off—they had good fare and though old Moneygripe was as cross as the Devil yet he took it all out in jaw—and never beat or abused them."

Other apprentices were not so lucky. Conditions were hard and runaways were common. Benjamin Franklin called his running away "one of the first errata of my life," but his later success emboldened other boys to leave unhappy placements and try to make their way in the world without completing formal training. Rorabaugh called the legacy Franklin left "an example of wrongdoing richly rewarded."

Cruel treatment propelled apprentices to look for a better life elsewhere, but they faced legal risks as well as the dangers of the open road. The laws decreed that, if caught, they might have to serve double their time with a master who would then be even more likely to abuse them. So widespread was mistreatment of servants, slaves, and apprentices that Virginia passed a law in about 1700 aimed at their protection. Servants (and this term was used interchangeably for any bonded labor, including apprentices) were free to petition the court without cost, and if the case went against the master he was to pay for everything. Masters were also admonished to provide what they had contracted for; "good and wholesome diet, clothing, and lodging." Clearly some did and some didn't, just as some fathers were kind and others vicious.

Apprentices also ran away because they were just plain homesick. Forced to leave their families at an age when today's children are hardly expected to go farther than the local elementary school, these youngsters were often sent to strangers in a strange town. In 1643 in Plymouth, the parents of Joseph Billington, age five, were threatened with confinement in the stocks if they offered him shelter again when he ran away from his master. Evidently the court thought he was too young to punish, although he was not too young to work.

Newspapers carried ads searching for runaways day after day. One of them packs a brief biography of the relationship of the master to his apprentice in a few telling lines: "Blanchard, James, ran away from Silas Chapman of Hartford (Conn). James is short, thick set, thick dark complextion, aged 13. Took with him 3 months old black dog. Reward 3 shillings, 6 pence. Return of dog only, reward 3 shillings." Runaway ads usually cost three to five shillings for the first ten lines, and one to three shillings if the ad was repeated. They were a costly investment, an indication of how much an apprentice was worth whether or not he was well-liked.

Another "short but unhappy life" was detailed in verse in the *Pennsylvania Gazette:*

> *This present instant on the fourteenth day,*
> *My apprentice boy did run away: . . .*
> *He has always been a vexatious lad,*
> *One reason why he is so meanly clad:*

[retribution for misbehavior was often a cut in rations or in clothing]

> . . .
> *Of apple pies he took with him but five,*
> *For to preserve himself alive;*
> *Three quarter dollars are missed of late,*
> *Which perhaps he took to pay his freight;*
> *Believe him not if you be wise,*
> *He is very artful in telling lies;*
> . . .

For which I whipt him, I thought severe,
But did not make him shed one tear:

. . .

Of a reward they may be sure,
Six-pence at least I do propose
To give for him and all his clothes;
Or clear me of him forever and mine.
And his indentures away I will sign;
Now to inform you further still,
I keep a saw and fulling mill;
In East-Fallowfield township
and Chester County is the place of my abode,
I subscribe my name unto the same, and that is
William Moode.

For Which I Whipt Him

Many apprentices were exploited by their masters to provide the most labor at the least cost. Their difficult condition was only temporary, though. In typically American fashion that foreshadowed the egalitarian philosophy of later years, it was assumed that through their own efforts they could make their fortunes. They would be judged not by their origins, but by their deeds. Apprenticeship of the poor and not so poor not only saved money, it fit right in with the American dream that success was possible for anyone who worked hard enough. The apprenticeship system also shared attitudes about physical punishment with the society at large. The rod was necessary child-rearing equipment.

Child abuse is as old as childhood. But in Colonial America some parents and masters, distorting the dictates of the church, cloaked cruelty with righteousness. Cotton Mather, the fire-breathing Puritan preacher, said, "Better whipt, than damned." Children were punished for the good of their souls. They were also punished for the good of their character. John Robinson, another preacher, reminded parents that "there is in all children (tho not alike) a stubbernes and stoutnes of minde arising from naturall pride which must in the first place be broken and beaten down." This doesn't mean that parents and masters routinely beat children cruelly; it suggests only that the rod, used in anger, could be justified as an instrument of the higher good. Even the Reverend Mather, who saw children as inherently evil, cursed by original sin, presented himself as an example of moderation in his booklet of advice on child rearing: "I would never come to give a child a blow; except in case of obstinacy or some gross enormity. To be chased for a while out of my presence I would make to be looked upon, as the sorest punishment in the family."

Outside the family, and even inside it, apprentices were exposed to punishment ranging from sadistic to kind. Sometimes even though these chastisements were relatively mild, the sting lasted long after the event. Benjamin Franklin never forgave his half brother, who was "passionate and had often beaten me, which I took extremely amiss. I fancy his harsh and tyrannical treatment of me might be a means of impressing me with that aversion to arbitrary power that has stuck to me through my whole life." Isaiah Thomas, too, recorded much later in notes for his autobiography that he was "twice whipped when a child by my master, and made to confess crimes I never committed."

Excessive punishment, like child abuse and neglect, could be brought before the courts, and the records are as grisly as any that make the front pages of today's supermarket tabloids. In 1660 in Maryland, John Ward, an orphan apprentice, appeared in court "with a most rotten filthy, stinking, ulcerated leg that even loathed all the beholders therof, his apparel being all ragged and torn and his hair seemed to be rotted off with ashes." He was released from his indenture to Master Arthur Turner. Another apprentice was so terrorized by this treatment that he "did constantly wett his bedd and his cloathes, lying in them, and soe suffered by it, his clothes being frozen about him." The boy was crushed when he fell carrying a log that was too big for him. Then, "being down, [he] had a stripe or two" (a whipping) and "in respect of cruelty and hard usage he died." His master was convicted of manslaughter. This is an extreme example of sadistic behavior, but other apprentices were hung by the heels, whipped, and treated with inhuman severity for what today seem minor infractions.

Apprenticeship sometimes served as a way to remove a mistreated child from a home in which it was abused and place it in another, more benign family, much as foster care does today. Michael and Charles Deinvert in Philadelphia were bound out as apprentices in 1758 because their father, a chairmaker, "made a practice of chaining them at Night by the Neck and Heels in a Cellar where he worked, leaving them there alone without anything to Sleep on but

Chips and Shavings, and for fear the said Chips should wear out their Shirts, he always Stripped them Naked."

The Parents Left Behind

Some women, left without a husband, made every effort to keep their children with them. Isaiah Thomas's mother tried to make ends meet by opening a small shop with money provided by friends, but it was not enough to keep her family together. She was, however, one of a large number of "she-merchants." Colonial women were more likely to run businesses such as taverns or shops than women in 1830, when the "true woman" was supposed to stay out of the workforce and at home. Women alone made all sorts of desperate efforts to help their children without relinquishing them completely. In New York, another eight-year-old whose mother was a widow was apprenticed to a wigmaker, who agreed that the child was not to leave the state without the mother's consent.

Some mothers sent their sons and daughters away from home secure in the knowledge they were doing the best they could to give them a good start in life. If the children were in the same town, the wrench was not great, but if the child went even a few miles away, the difficulties of travel made the separation seem irrevocable. Samuel Seabury was the first of four sons to be apprenticed. He was sent on the ferry from Brooklyn to Manhattan in 1815, when he was thirteen years old, but his mother reacted as if the harbor were the China Sea. "My mother set about the task with varied emotions," he later wrote, "and awaited the arrival of the day fixed for my departure as the most trying season of her life. . . . She regarded her separation from me as the first gash in the severance of her domestic duties." Samuel realized how different his own reaction was—although he didn't look forward to working when he had hoped to be able to go to college, he was setting out on his first adventure. "My heart was beating with vague expectation!" he recalled. "One thing only weighed heavily on my heart and that was my mother's dejection. . . . She clung to me as if we were about to part forever: and as I took my last embrace my heart sickened and some such vague presentiment seemed for a moment to paralyze my soul." Seabury had different feelings about his father. Although he recognized that he was in many ways admirable, he never felt close to him. His mother, to whom he was devoted, did not, as he had sensed, live long after her separation from him.

Neither did the mother of William Lloyd Garrison, who was far away in Newburyport while his ailing mother was in Baltimore. She, like other fathers and mothers of apprentices, kept up a steady stream of advice, clinging to her parental role even though her child was growing up in another home. "I do long to see you," she wrote. "I will do everything for you I can; it will be my greatest happiness to make you happy." For his part, he said, "I always feel like a little boy when I think of Mother." In a letter years after her death he wrote, "I had a mother once, who cared for me with such a passionate regard, who loved me so intensely, that no language can describe the yearnings of her soul." Discounting the hyperbolic rhetoric of the time, this is still a moving tribute to a woman who had been forced to separate herself from her son in order for him to grow up successfully.

Mothers had less competition from the substitute family than did fathers. A lucky child might find himself in a home where the master's wife was kind and helpful to the apprentices who lived with her, but she was not central to their lives; a master was expected to move into all the rights, duties, and privileges of fatherhood. As one father reminded his son, who was then an apprentice but would eventually be a master, "Consider well how many calls there are upon your tenderness and watchfulness [when you become a master] over those who are placed with you; and remember that the hopes and future joy of a good father are lodged in your hands." Essentially, for children whose fathers were concerned with them (and this often excluded the children of the poor whose fathers were dead, had deserted, or had never married their mothers), apprenticeship provided for multiple fathering. The master might be in day-to-day charge, but the father kept an eye on things.

Fathers bombarded their sons with letters and, if they were close by, acted as ombudsmen if there was trouble with a master. Benjamin Franklin, who was apprenticed to his half brother, often appealed to his father for help. "Our disputes were often brought before our father, and I fancy I was either generally in the right or else a better pleader, because the judgment was generally in my favor." Franklin's father also acted as his writing instructor, and Franklin "saw the justice of his remarks and thence grew more attentive to my manner of writing, and determined to endeavour to improve my style." Where the master failed, the father stepped in.

On more serious occasions, fathers took masters to court. Hugh March, Sr., of Newbury charged his son's master with not caring for him properly when he was sick, and also "for not teaching him his art or trade according to indenture." The boy hurt his leg and was in such pain "the continual hearing of his doleful crying out night and day for a long time was a great distraction to the family" when he was finally taken home to be cared for. His father asked the court for reimbursement for his medical expenses, since the master was legally responsible for them.

When apprentices ran away home, fathers were called to court if they protected them from the master who had rightful claim to their time. And one father brought the master before a judge because he had left his son idle. Partly this was the standard complaint that he was not being taught his trade, but it was also a reflection of the still powerful Puritan view that idleness was a vice.

When parents were not in the picture, the legal bonds of apprenticeship sometimes became loving bonds, and a child was, for all intents and purposes, adopted. Since common law did not recognize adoption (it was not until 1851 that straightforward adoption became possible in Massachusetts, and gradually in the rest of the country), those who wanted to keep the ties that had been nurtured by long, affectionate association found other ways to formalize the relationship. A will could transfer property to the apprentice who had become a true member of the family, and the Massachusetts General Court sometimes passed private laws providing for a change of name.

Childhood—Considerably Condensed

Childhood was short not only because children worked early, but also because it was so often ended abruptly by death. In New England in the seventeenth century in relatively healthy areas, one in ten infants died before their first birthday; in unhealthy areas, the rate was three in ten. Today, it is less than one in one hundred. Parents who believed that even infants were tainted by original sin were understandably more concerned with their children's souls than with their psyches.

This high death rate led some historians to conclude that Colonial parents stayed unattached to their young children as a way to protect themselves from the inevitability of loss. This "detachment" would make more understandable the treatment of children as interchangeable parts, equally able to live in one family or another, rather than as unique, precious human beings. Children were sent to relatives or to masters, cared for by whoever happened to be around, and seen in economic rather than emotional terms. The care could seem casual by today's standards: Children fell into boiling caldrons or unfenced pits, watched or unwatched by older sisters or brothers or the frantically busy parents themselves.

But to conclude from tragedies such as these that children were not loved and seen as individuals would be to ignore the growing accumulation of personal evidence. In one of the rare diaries kept by a woman in the early eighteenth century, Mary Cooper, living on a farm at Oyster Bay, New York, carefully recorded her sorrow at the anniversary of the birth and death of each of her lost children. On May 8, 1771, she mourned: "This day is eleven years since my dear son Iaac [Isaac] departed this life. Sorrow, sorrow and loss unspakabel." Isaac had lived only four years.

Attachment was not confined to mothers. A New England minister saved the notebook of his "dearly loved child" and wrote on it, "Fifty years ago died my little John. A child of promise. Alas! Alas! January 10, 1805." Even without the later romanticization of childhood that deified the mother and her selfless devotion to her innocent babes, men and women were deeply tied to their children.

By the late eighteenth century, attitudes toward children approached those of modern times. Paternal authority weakened, and children were not seen in strict, orthodox terms as depraved creatures who had to be saved from themselves. Gravestone markings shifted from death's-heads to cherubs, reflecting the growing sentimentalization of childhood.

In addition, in the cities and towns children were paradoxically becoming more important as they became less important in an economic sense. With industrialization, there was less for young children to do to earn their keep. In the new republic, mothers rather than fathers were entrusted with the moral lives of their offspring, and it became a mother's duty to devote herself to her children. If something bad happened to them, it was her responsibility. Of course, this view of motherhood applied largely to the upper and middle classes. Poor women and farm women could not afford such single-minded devotion.

The new, central importance of children arose in part because the birthrate declined, not only in the cities but all across the country, starting in about 1800. Children became fewer and precious rather than expendable. Why this happened is still a mystery. There were no great technical developments in contraception to account for it. Perhaps the emergence of a middle class aware of the expenses of caring for and educating a child had something to do with it. Perhaps, too, women were more able to insist that their husbands practice the standard method of birth control—coitus interruptus. Whatever the reason, by the middle of the nineteenth century many women had ceased to be perpetual childbearing machines and children were less likely to be placed out of the home. The semipermeable family that took in children not born to it and sent out its own was no longer the norm.

As the republic grew, so did opportunities and alterations. Clearly defined male and female roles emerged as society began to take over many of the functions formerly performed in the cramped quarters of the Colonial house: education, religious training, vocational instruction. The family became less and less the center of the economic world, women became more dependent on a husband's ability to earn cash, and children became more independent of their tight-knit family. Women were also less likely to work at trades inside and outside the home and to need apprenticeship to act as child care. The decline in women's independence and occupations laid the groundwork for discontent that led to the flowering of the women's rights movement of the mid-nineteenth century.

It is fashionable today to bemoan the decay of the family and the damage to children whose lives are torn by divorce. But in Colonial America, children were much more likely to die or be orphaned, and to be switched from one home to another. We know very little about what being separated from a father does to a child in modern times; the emphasis on the mother in psychoanalytic thinking has made fatherhood a neglected state. And we certainly know nothing about how it affected development three hundred years ago.

Modern research has focused on mothers, not fathers, a legacy of the view that children must have one-to-one care by a mother in order to thrive. The father hardly exists. In psychiatrist Daniel Stern's influential book *The Interpersonal World of the Infant: A View from Psychoanalysis and Developmental Psychology*, published in 1985, the word "father" does not even appear in the index.

Times seem to be changing. Fathers have been discovered as important figures even in infancy. In what has been hailed as a revolutionary movement, as many as 62 percent of fathers are now present when their babies are born. This can be seen as a radical step forward only if one forgets that in some parts of preindustrial America, fathers were routinely present at births. The woman in labor squatted on the man's lap to deliver, with his strong legs serving as a "Father chair," the living equivalent of today's birthing chair. The father also participated actively in the process, pressing down on the woman's abdomen during contractions. Even before the supremacy of the male doctor in the nineteenth century, birth was not always a process of women helping women and excluding men.

Preliminary research on the role of the father has disclosed the surprising finding that children are connected as much to their fathers as to their mothers, whether or not they were present at the birth. For example, a study of nine-month-olds shows that they protested separation from their fathers just as often as they did separation from their mothers.

Although the "nurturing father" has come into the lexicon, and a few men do provide primary care for their children, we do not yet have the kind of male child care that apprenticeship represented. It reflected a wider family practice. After infancy in Colonial America, boys spent more time with their fathers than with their mothers. This was reflected in the language: Men spoke of "my son," and mothers referred to "his boys."

Today's social reality is starting to have its effects on contemporary society and on science. But as William Kessen of Yale pointed out in his 1978 speech to the developmental psychology division of the American Psychological Association, "It would be difficult to defend the proposition that the recent interest in the place of fathers or the possibilities of out-of-home child rearing grew either from a new theory of development or from striking new empirical discoveries. Rather . . . fewer and fewer American women have been willing or able to devote all of their work time to the rearing of children. It will be instructive to see how much the tasks assigned fathers and daycare centers reflect the old ascriptions to essential maternity. Psychology follows culture, but often at a discreet distance." What seem like newly emerging patterns are really as old as the country. They served a need then, and they serve a need now.

It was not only the fate of children in early America that was similar to conditions today. The family in the new country faced living conditions very different from those in England, and worriers predicted then, as now, that it would not survive. The old hierarchical systems were failing to meet the needs of the new wilderness, and the older generation, which knew nothing except the clear-cut distinctions that had existed since medieval times, was certain the family would be destroyed as the keeper of social order.

Apprenticeship was part of the old hierarchical system, and its decline was heralded early as youngsters began to act above their station. In 1760, an ad for a runaway described him wearing clothing more fit for a gentleman than for a worker: "Had on when he went away, a light coloured Cloth Coat and Breeches, with yellow carved Metal Buttons, black Jacket, check Shirt, and a pair of Silver Buckles on his Shoes." By the nineteenth century masters and apprentices both were evading the strict legal requirements of the indenture agreement. The "binding" was much looser, allowing for freer movement, and apprentices often boarded away from the master's house and were thus emancipated from his strict parental influence. Only the Quakers in Pennsylvania, as Ian Quimby has pointed out in his study of Philadelphia apprenticeships, clung to the old idea that masters were obliged to act as good fathers and fought to keep the institution from degenerating into nothing more than another kind of employment.

Despite their efforts, conditions in Philadelphia in 1795 prompted Matthew Clarkson, the city recorder, to lament the attitudes of both masters and apprentices. The masters neglected their duty to provide moral training and a firm disciplinary hand, and the apprentices were "insubordinate." Crowds of unruly youths roamed the streets, attacked innocent children and teenagers, stole, and made city life (Philadelphia was this country's largest city through the 1780s) unbearable. The decline of traditional apprenticeship, which had provided a way to control the behavior of young people, had played a role in what we would call today a rise in juvenile delinquency. Clarkson sagely pointed out what reformers have continued to emphasize for more than a hundred years: "It must no doubt be conceded as a fact, disagreeable however in itself, that the disorders in question can never be wholly banished from a place so populous as Philadelphia. But it will not follow from this that endeavours ought not to be used to *mitigate* that which we cannot perfectly cure."

Apprenticeship was not perfect, but in a young nation in which women were sorely burdened in the best of families, schooling for most youngsters was rudimentary, and no other formal system outside the home provided training in making the goods necessary for daily living, it was probably the best that might have been devised. It was, says Lawrence Towner, who studied the poor apprentices of Boston, "a valuable and workable social institution . . . that seemed to fit the needs of a free society."

With the Revolution it began a slow decline, and by the Civil War it persisted only in pockets here and there. Its value was eroded by a host of social and economic changes: As industrialization took hold, crafts became less important, the need for labor ceased to be so great that very young children had to be put to work, independent youths were reluctant to give up all personal freedom in exchange for training, and how-to books began to take the "mystery" out of many skills. It was no longer necessary to become an apprentice to acquire the training to be economically independent. Apprenticeship had met the needs of its time. It supplied a trained workforce for an expanding economy while keeping adolescents supervised and busy and caring for poor, neglected, or deserted young children in a way that served both them and their society. It prefigured what we now call foster care, which, when it began, also expected that the child taken into a family not its own would work to pay at least part of its keep.

When it placed children firmly in families apprenticeship set a pattern that has been overlooked, then revived, throughout the history of American child care. In the early nineteenth century the idea of the family as the ideal place for children—any children—gave way to the idea of the orphanage as the most practical way to care for large numbers of them. Institutional solutions replaced personal ones.

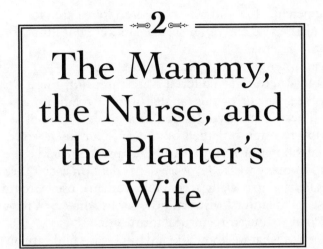

2

The Mammy, the Nurse, and the Planter's Wife

If black Mammies and nurses usually delivered the white babies, white mistresses sometimes delivered the black and more often helped look after both mother and infant. If Mammies and nurses raised the white children, mistresses helped raise the black.

—*Eugene Genovese, historian*

WHILE THE APPRENTICESHIP SYSTEM flourished and faded, slavery, that "peculiar institution," evolved its own innovative child-care practices, which prefigured today's attitudes and options. As Deborah Gray White points out in her book *Aren't I a Woman?*, "Neither the slaveowner nor slave society expected the biological mother of a child to fulfill all that child's needs. Given the circumstances, the responsibilities of motherhood had to be shared." They were shared so that black women could fulfill vital and potentially conflicting roles—to bear children and to work in the fields alongside men— and white women could perform their managerial and social functions. Yet no matter how much plantation care resembled today's arrangements, there were distinctive, bone-chilling differences.

For one thing, slave children belonged to their master, not to their parents—a unique situation. Slave parents had no control over what happened. How and where children were cared for and whether they would be sold and never seen again were questions for the master, not the parents.

Even when parents—white parents this time—could decide by whom and where their children were cared for, there were special tensions arising out of the tangled web of relationships woven by slavery. The normal rivalries and resistances between servant and mistress were often inflamed by the self-contained world in which they lived. Sometimes they shared the same man, and the care of his children. In many ways they were dependent on each other, with the mistress having no socially acceptable woman close by to turn to. For the most part planters' wives and the slaves who cared for their children lived in an uneasy reciprocal intimacy.

Much of what we know about day-to-day child care on the plantation (large or small) comes from reminiscences of planters and their wives written after the Civil War or from oral histories collected from former slaves during the Depression of the 1930s. These accounts must be treated with compassionate caution. Memory is a good editor, deleting some things and heightening others. Then, too, stories told by black former slaves to attentive white interviewers (interviewers were often white) may have suffered from a desire to please and make things sound better than they were. And some important questions may never have been asked or answers may never have been recorded. As one former slave said, "If your head is in the lion's mouth, it's best to pat him a little."

Even the language of the slave oral histories is suspect. Some of them are recorded in sanitized, schoolmarm English—evidently an effort by the interviewer to produce a smooth, readable narrative. Others are in heavy dialect that seems to today's ear to be racist caricature, and these, too, may not be completely authentic. The interviewers were instructed in how to reproduce local speech, and they tried to follow these guidelines. One Mississippi interviewer protested, "I have not used 'mammy' as of your correction because none of these negroes have used the word. They say mamma and mother, daddy and father interchangeably." Despite these problems, the oral histories remain the best record we are ever likely to get of what it was like to be a child under slavery.

As for the planters and their fond characterizations of the black women who cared for them, it's important to remember that these black women were their surrogate mothers, and we tend to idealize our mothers, no matter who they were. There is no way to get a picture of what the roles and relationships of black women and white children or white women and black children really were; the best we can do is preface any generalization with a silent "sometimes."

White Women as Caretakers of Black Children

The role of the planter's wife in caring for black children is one of the neglected chapters in the annals of the South. Yet when there was no old or incapacitated slave to look after the babies and toddlers while their mothers worked, the mistress moved into the job of caretaker, often assisted by slightly older slave children. Some of the children the mistresses cared for might be the offspring of their husbands or sons.

Upper-class Southern white women tended to ignore the tangled sexual liaisons of upper-class white men and black slave women. What they got in return, according to *A History of Women in America*, by Carol Hymowitz and Michaele Weissman, was the guilt white men felt at producing black sons and daughters born into slavery (since the status and ownership of the child followed that of its mother). The guiltier the men were, the more they placed white women on a pedestal as superior to nasty, brutish males—and supposedly promiscuous black females.

Sometimes these noble women could not bring themselves to disregard the existence of café au lait evidence of infidelity, and this had serious consequences for the child and his or her mother. Louisa Picquet wrote that her mother "was fifteen years old when I was born. Mother's mistress had a child only two weeks older than me. Mother's master, Mr. Randolph, was my father. So mother told me. She was forbid to tell who was my father but I looked so much like Madame Randolph's baby that she [Madame Randolph] got dissatisfied, and mother had to be sold." Louisa and her mother were sold together to a Georgia planter, and her mother suckled the new master's baby along with her own.

Other mistresses restrained their revenge and helped rear light-colored children, usually as house servants in deference to the ambiguity of their origins. These women cared for the children of field hands, too, and watched over the health of all the slave children, who, they hoped, would grow up to be valuable property. Despite the myth of the aristocratic plantation mistress who had nothing to do but make social calls and occasionally tend to the medical needs of slaves, she was more often hardworking and harried.

One former slave remembered that "sometimes they's as many as fifty cradle with little nigger babies in 'em and the mistus, she look after them. She turn them and dry them herself. I'd blow the horn for the mudders of the little babies to come in from the fields and nurse 'em, in mornin' and afternoon. Mistus feed them what was old enough to eat victuals."

"The white folks was crazy 'bout their nigger babies," another former slave said, "'cause that's where they got their profits."

The care often continued long after the babies had grown out of their cradles. "I stayed with my ma every night but my mistress raised me," reported one man. "Ev'y eve'nin at three o'clock [evening was any time between noon and sunset] ol' mistress would call all us litsy bitsy chillun in an we would lay down on pallets and have to go to sleep. I can hear her now singin:

> *Hush-a-bye, bye, mammy's pickaninnies*
> *Way beneath the silver shining moon*
> *Hush-a-bye, bye mammy's pickaninnies*
> *Daddy's little Carolina coons."*

There were times when the mistress even acted as wet nurse to free the mother to return to more productive labor. Rube Montgomery was born in October in Choctaw County, Georgia. There were only two slaves on the place, his mother and a field hand who was not his father, and "my old Miss made Mammy wean me in March an' she [Old Miss] suckled me. I was jus' two weeks older 'n her child. Course I don't have to tell I was raised in de white folks' house. My white folks was sho' good to me; specially Missus."

Children who were reared in the big house understandably became attached to that way of life and to the substitute mother who treated them with kindness. This burdened the black woman with the pain and rivalry often felt by women whose children turn to another, particularly since the black mother had had no choice in the matter. Sara was a slave child who went as a young girl to live with her mistress. When the Civil War ended her mother came to claim her as her own. Sara said, "I didn't want to go; I wanted to stay with Mis' Polly. I begun to cry and Mammy caught hold of me. I grabbed Mis' Polly and held so tight dat I tore her skirt bindin' loose and her skirt fell down about her feets.

" 'Let her stay with me,' Mis' Polly said to Mammy. But Mammy shook her head. 'You took her away from me and didn't pay no mind to my cryin', so now i'se takin' her home. We'se free now, Mis' Polly, we ain't gwine be slave no more to nobody.' "

The health of their valuable young slaves was of great concern to masters and mistresses, who might not have day-to-day contact with them. Babies died at an alarming rate, but black babies died at twice the rate of white ones and only one out of three survived until the age of ten. They died of a long list of diseases—lockjaw, tetanus, "worms," convulsions, and "teething" among them. The last two can be symptoms of tetany, mineral deficiencies caused by inadequate diet.

The owners devised a variety of methods to check on and ensure the health of their young charges. In Mississippi, John Foxworth set up a "summer camp" for children too young to hoe cotton. The camp was in the hills, to avoid malaria, since "he didn't wan any o' his li'l niggahs to die." Although slaves adapted more successfully than their white owners to the hot, humid lowlands, many still succumbed. (We now know the blacks were protected from malaria in part by the sickle cell trait, a blood disorder found in people of African descent that can have serious health consequences but makes contracting malaria less likely.) Once a week "Marse John" would ride out with lump sugar in his pockets for all the youngsters and use the treat to set the stage for his health examination. "He sho did set on his horse and laugh t'see us scamblin' fur dat sugar. Den he'd 'samine us all," Elias Spencer told an interviewer, "an' look at our tongues, an' watch us set round a big wooden pan o'clabber and eat till we nigh 'bout busted."

Appetite was a measure of health on other plantations, too. "It was a rule" on one plantation "that all the little colored children eat at the great house every Sunday morning in order that Marster and Missus could watch them eat, so they could know which ones were sickly and have them doctored."

These slave children "all carried a mussel shell in their hands to eat with. The food was put on large trays and the children all gathered around and ate, dipping up their food with their mussel shells, which they used for spoons. Those who refused to eat or those who were ailing in any way had to come back to the great house for their meals and medicine until they were well."

It would be easy to dismiss these efforts as little more than the solicitude of an owner for the vitality of future workers—much like that of an old-time farmer for his workhorses. But it would not be fair to see this concern as only monetary. There were often genuine attachment and affection or, at the very least, a sense of noblesse oblige.

This continued even after Emancipation, when some former slaveowners found themselves with the children of those who had fled the war or gone off in search of a better life. "When peace was declared," Emaline Watts told her WPA interviewer, "my mother and father went to Vicksburg with the yankees and left four of us poor little children. Old marster brought us up to the 'big house.' Lots of children were there who had been deserted by their parents. Asa Watkins was Provost Marshall and he said, 'Will anybody here take these poor motherless children to raise?' Not a soul answered; nobody would take us, so the only mother I knew was my marster. He brought us up and was good to us."

Black children cared for by white plantation owners were often taught to speak and behave in ways that would make them superior house servants. The earlier the training started, the better. Lucy Kimball, whose "language and manner was that of an educated person," had been a dining-room servant on an Alabama plantation. She distanced herself from other slaves with, "Honey, you don't believe I am like these other negroes, who still cling to all that before the war nonsense? I might tell the children a rabbit foot brings good luck because it is an old custom for superstitious persons to carry one. But, honey, you'd have just as good luck if you carried a lot of brick-bats in your pocket. My white folks . . . never brought me up to believe in superstitious things."

The children were also socialized in subtle and not-so-subtle ways to become good slaves. I. E. Lowery grew up in the big house and became his master's "waiting boy." Once a month he was taken to Sunday school and services, and he remembered all his life the dreadful sermon he heard warning that running away was a sin that could never be hidden from God. Other former slaves remembered the emphasis put on the commandment "Thou shalt not steal."

Slave children brought up in the big house had privileges as well as the obligation that they behave themselves. Unlike the field hands, they had a backstairs taste of the life of the white plantation owner.

Child-Care Centers—Plantation Style

To free able-bodied women to work in the fields most slave children were cared for by other slaves, usually in groups. Individual care was a luxury that disappeared after the first two or three months, during which a baby might be nursed by its own mother until she was strong enough to do at least half a day's work. Sometimes the group care was day care that foreshadows today's; sometimes it was a system vaguely anticipating the communal child rearing of the Israeli kibbutz, with children living in a separate house and visiting their parents from time to time.

George Kye was one who lived night and day in a children's house. "I didn't live with Mammy because she worked all the time and us children all stayed in one house. It was a little one room cabin chinked and daubed, and you couldn't stir us with a stick."

The old or incapacitated men and women who had primary care of the children were often assisted by boys and girls too young to hoe or plow. (They were usually kept out of the fields until they were ten or twelve years old.) Barney Alford was one of these boys. "Ole Mammy 'Lit' was mity ole en she lived in one corner of de big yard an she keered fur all de black chilluns while de old folks wurk in de field. Mammy Lit was good to all de chilluns en I hed ter help her wid dem chilluns en keep dem babies on de pallet." But despite the fact that cooperative motherhood was an accepted part of plantation life, Barney preferred his own mother and knew where to find her. "Sum times I wuld run wa en go ter de kitchen whar my mammy was at wurk en mammy 'Lit' wuld hafter cum fur me en den she would whip me."

While no account is typical, Jennie Webb's story of her childhood has elements that appear again and again. She said, "De fus' things I recollect is living in a slave cabin back o' marse's big house along wid forty or fifty other slaves. All my childhood life I can never remember seeing my pa or ma gwine to wuk or coming in from wuk in de day light as dey went to de fiel's fo' day an' wuked 'till after dark." Jennie was born someplace between the fields and the cabin as her mother returned from a regular workday. When she was old enough to help, Jennie looked after the younger children, keeping them quiet and getting them to go to sleep.

She also helped feed them from the large wooden bowls that held all the food. She and the other bigger children scooped the food out with their hands. The bowls were never washed, and "after we got through eatin' in 'em de flys swarmed over 'em and de dogs licked 'um an' dey sho' did smell bad." Finally, the big children virtually stopped eating and "we began to git skinny." One day the master stopped by, saw Jennie hand-feeding a toddler, and asked why she wasn't eating herself. She told him. He scolded the cook (who was Jennie's aunt) with "Adeline, how do you think I can raise de little niggers an' you feedin 'em lak dis?" and after that "we wuz fed right."

On other plantations, too, the children were fed more like animals than like human beings. The mass feeding was a way to make child care easier, but for the youngsters there was lasting resentment. One said, "Deed, chile, you ain't gonna believe dis but it's de gospel truf. Ant Hannah had a trough in her back yard jus' like you put in a pig pen. Well, Ant Hanna would just po' dat trough full of milk an' drag dem chillun up to it. Chillun slop dat milk jus' like pigs."

The children were usually called to eat by the blowing of a horn—the same horn signal that called nursing mothers in from the fields to feed the babies too young for the pot liquor left over from cooking greens or the milk and bread that were the usual fare. Sometimes a distinctive horn blast sounded for each mother when her baby needed her. More commonly, the horn blew at stated intervals rather than when the baby cried. The mothers were given only a few minutes to nurse, then had to trudge back to the fields. One mother recalled, "My master would make me leave my child before day to go to the canefield; and he would not allow me to come back till ten o'clock in the morning to nurse my child. When I did go I could hear my poor child crying long before I got to it. And la, me! my poor child would be so hungry! Sometimes I would have to walk more than a mile to get to my child, and when I did get there I would be so tired I'd fall asleep while my baby was sucking." Another mother realized she could not get back to her baby and feed it within the time allotted, so she would just sit somewhere and hope that the baby would die.

No one can know what effect this kind of feeding at the master's demand rather than the babies' had on these children. Given what we know about child development, however, we can speculate that these children were often undernourished, both physically and emotionally. A New York psychotherapist who has worked with people who report they were left crying for long periods as babies says they grow up with feelings of powerlessness and futility. "Nothing helps" is often their attitude. They turn against themselves, chiding themselves to "grow up. What are you complaining about?" and have difficulty feeling compassion even for their own children. Some, according to this observer, bury the rage at having been neglected and turn it against the outside world when they are no longer helpless infants.

Some nursing infants were taken to the fields with their mothers and perhaps a youngster only four or six years old to look after them between feedings. Ebenezer Brown of Alabama said babies were put on a quilt at the fence corner and when the mother got to the end of a row she would put her hoe or plow down and nurse her crying infant. "Sum of de wimen had bigger chilluns, dat day wud put dar to watch de babies," he explained.

Despite the variety of possibilities, the kind of care infants received depended to a large extent on the size of the plantation or farm and the number of nonworkers available to act as nursemaids. There were times when babies died of neglect. One mother had no one else to care for her infant and was not permitted to take it with her to the fields. This was probably a plantation so small there were very few slaves and no provision for child care. She told her interviewer, "Yes, Missus, [I left him] 'lone, couldn't help it, bliged to. Hang it up dere in de basket an' boil some flou' for it. It cry all day and I cry all day, an he died, 'cause he cry so."

Another mother did not leave her child either at home or to the care of others in the field. In a kind of anticipation of today's baby carriers, she twisted a piece of linen cloth into a backpack and put her baby in it. She carried him all day as she hoed her rows.

Despite these occasional individual efforts, the general practice was for children to be cared for—well or indifferently—as a community effort. Some babies in the children's houses were nursed by wet nurses while their mothers were in the fields, perhaps avoiding long periods of hungry crying. And women cooperating with other women also provided a way for babies to survive the deaths of their mothers at a time when maternal mortality was distressingly high. Charles Davenport lived after his mother died because "dey turned me over to de granny nurse on de plantation. She was de one dat attended to de little pickaninnies. She got a woman to nurse me what had a young baby, so I didn't know no difference. Any woman what had a baby about my age would wet nurse me, so I growed up in de quarters and was as well and as happy as any other child."

This sense of a supportive community network, some historians believe, gave slave children a feeling of security that helped mitigate the terrible possibility that their families might be torn apart. The children called almost all slave adults Aunt or Uncle or Granny and were looked after in one way or another by any of these. The system was approved of and supported by both whites and blacks; it was not (as some modern arrangements are) merely tolerated or disavowed. It provided a safety net of "fictive kin" for children who were part of the "family" of many of the slaves. Since women were sold less often than men, family life centered on them, and it was their chain of relatives and pseudorelatives who provided continuity. It is a system that survived slavery and provided a helping network after freedom.

Within the slave community, traditions, folklore, and practical everyday knowledge were passed on from one generation to the next through this communal system. Slave children learned about herbal remedies, how to wash clothes with battling blocks and battling sticks, how to cook. They learned to say "ma'am" and "sir" and, some psychotherapists suggest, to curb their aggression in order to survive. They also learned the basics of child care, since they, as well as adult or teenaged black women, looked after children on the plantation.

Black Children as Nurses

Black children and white children, too, were cared for by baby-sitters only slightly older than they were. As a result, some of the earliest work a girl or boy did was "nursing." Mattie Curtis said, "When I was little, I had picked up the fruit, fanned flies off the table with a peafowl fan and nursed the little slave children." Parker Pool of North Carolina remembered, "We got up at light. I had to do most of the nursing of the chillun 'cause when chopping time come, the women had to go to work."

Sometimes the nursing started in childhood and went on into adulthood. Ellen Betts of Louisiana said, "With all the colored children coming 'long as fast as pig litters, I didn't do nothing all my days, but nurse, nurse, nurse." (Estimates of the number of Africans imported into the United States range around four hundred thousand; by Emancipation there were ten times that number, the result of phenomenal natural increase.) "I nurse so many children," she went on, "it done went and stunted my growth, and that's why I ain't nothing but bones to this day." She began tending white and black babies when she was so young that "some them babies so fat and big I had to tote the feet while 'nother gal tote the head."

These children watching children missed out on their own childhoods unless they used stratagems to resist the system. One old woman remembered that as a child she helped her mistress watch the babies: "When I was tired I would just ease that baby over [ease the cradle over and dump the baby out] and Mistress would slap me so hard; I didn't know a hand could hurt so bad, but I'd take the slap and go out to play. She would slap me hard and say, 'Git on out of here and stay till you wake up,' and that was just what I wanted, 'cause I'd play then."

Cheney Cross of Alabama had an unusual role as the child nurse of children: "I was brung up right in de house wid my white folks. I slept on a little trundler bed what pushed up under de big bed, during the day. I watched over dem chillen day and night. I washed 'em and fed 'em and played wid 'em. One of de babies had to take goat's milk. When she cry, my mistis say, 'Cheney, gon and get dat goat.' Yes, Lord! And dat goat sure did talk sweet to dat baby. Just like it was her own. She look at it and wag her tail so fast and say, 'M-a-a-a.' Den she lay down on de floor whilst us holds her feets and let de baby suck de milk. All de time de goat be's talkin', 'M-a-a-a,' 'till dat baby got satisfied." Goats as wet nurses were well known in sixteenth-century Europe. Michel de Montaigne, the French essayist, reported, "It is an ordinary thing in my part of the world to see the village women who cannot feed their children at their own breasts calling in the aid of she-goats. . . . These goats are quickly trained to come and suckle the little ones; they recognize their voices when they cry, and run up to them. If any but their nursling is brought to them, they refuse to feed it, and the child likewise will refuse a strange goat." Goat's milk is naturally homogenized, and nursing directly from the animal eliminated the problems of contamination and spoilage that could have occurred if the animal had been milked and the milk put into a bottle.

In addition to the individual attention of an older child to a younger one, on some plantations there was a group expectation that older black children would look after the younger ones. This practical system resembles today's teenage baby-sitting for family or neighborhood youngsters.

The cook who "seed to all the chillen' " would call them after the grown-ups had eaten. "All the children that were big enough would come to the cook shack. Some of them would bring small children that had been weaned but couldn't look after themselves." After the meal the older children would "go back to see after the babies. If they were awake, the large children would put on their clothes and clean them up. When there was one woman who had two or three small children and didn't have one large one to do this, they'd give her a large one from some other family to look after her children. If she had any relatives, they would use their children for her."

Asking more of children than they could reasonably be expected to do sometimes led to tragedy, particularly when punishment for minor neglect of duty toward the white child was the standard method—whipping. Here is part of the transcript of a trial in Alabama during Reconstruction. It highlights the horrors of the legacy of the slave system under which a child was killed by her mistress. A witness was asked:

> *"How long after the whipping did she die?*
> *"In eight days."*
> *"How old was she?"*
> *"She would have been ten years old on the 26th of next August."*
> *"What was she whipped for?"*
> *"She was hired out as a nurse to see to the baby. She had taken baby out to the front yard among a parcel of arbor vitae; and being out there, the baby and she together she was neglectful so as to leave the baby's cap out to where it was not in place when the mother of the child called for the cap."*

The mother of the child whipped the girl, who died later of internal injuries.

Often there were more subtle effects on the children who cared for other people's children, just as there were effects on the black children of mammies who were not able to be with them. One woman recalled sadly, "I 'member dat big ole joggling board dere on de front piazza dat I use 'er ge' de chillun to sleep on eve'y evenin'. I be dere singin' one uv dem baby song to de child en it make me hu't lak in me bosom to be wid my ole mammy back up dere in de quarter. I wuz jes a child den en yuh know it uh child's happiness to be raise up wid dey mammy."

Mammies, mourning this separation from their children, sang in a minor key to their white charges the lullaby that begins, "Hushabye, don't you cry/Go to sleep, little baby," and included a second verse recognizing their slave children's anguish at being deserted:

> *Way down yonder*
> *Down in the meadow*
> *There's a poor little lambie,*

The bees and the butterflies
Pecking out its eyes,
The poor little thing called Mammy.

The Mammy—Real and Imagined

Some black mothers had no choice but to leave their own children to care for those of the master and mistress. The prototypical picture of this mammy is of a "gentle old woman completely dedicated to the white family, especially to the children of that family. She was the house servant who was given complete charge of domestic management. She served also as friend and adviser. She was, in short, surrogate mistress and mother."

This legendary mammy had one of her great incarnations in Margaret Mitchell's *Gone with the Wind:* "Mammy emerged from the hall" in her first appearance, "a huge old woman with the small, shrewd eyes of an elephant. She was shining black, pure African, devoted to her last drop of blood to the O'Haras. . . . Mammy was black, but her code of conduct and her sense of pride were as high or higher than that of her owners. . . . Whom Mammy loved, she chastened."

Like the exemplary nanny of mid-nineteenth-century England, the mammy adopted and enforced the standards and attitudes of her master and mistress and even passed on their way of defending their view of their world. When one little girl asked her mammy the inevitable question, "Mammy, who made you black?" the answer was a recitation of the biblical story of Noah's ark that would have made any apologist for slavery happy: "Ham was disrespectful to his pa and laughed at him and Gawd told Ham he and his children should be always servants; so He made him black, and dat's where we all black people come from."

As far as correct behavior was concerned, mammy often went parents one better. Mammy Harriet kept her charges out of the kitchen because "nobody but niggers go in thar. Sit in de parlor wid'er book in y'or hand like little ladies." During the Revolution, Lucy Carter's Mammy Betty, who took care of her and her sister after their mother died, "knew how young ladies ought to behave and she kept them rigidly up to her own and her Master's requirements. Dressed in silks, with their hair powdered, they were carried around by her in state to pay visits of ceremony to the neighboring gentry."

Mammy snobbery survived Emancipation. In Mississippi, Mammy Rose, who worked only in "quality families," lamented the passing of the old days with "The white folks don't raise dey chillen now. Day jest let 'em come up."

Along with instruction on how to behave, white children absorbed from their black mammies and nurses the wisdom and superstition of the slave quarter, as all children take in the teachings of their early caretakers. Ollie Fraser, brought up on a plantation in Virginia, learned from her mammy that the devil threw all bad children into a tub of some molten mass that was placed over a roaring fire. If one of the children dared try to escape, the devil would push it back into the tub with his pitchfork. But Ollie was told not to worry too much: Parents, not children, were responsible for their actions until they were seven years old (that magic number of maturity again), and she was younger than that. Ollie checked this out with her mother and was relieved to learn that the story was "just one of Mammy's sayings," and even more relieved when she was reassured that the detail about being safe until you were seven years old was correct.

White children not only absorbed theology and superstition, they also developed an appreciation for the music of the slaves, their foods, and the depth of their devotion to their charges. The devotion was reciprocated.

This love of the white child for the black nurse has been expressed eloquently by William A. Percy, who grew up after the Civil War but proudly cherished the standards and attitudes of his slave-holding forebears. "Southerners like to make clear," he wrote, "especially to Northerners, that every respectable white baby had a black mammy who, one is to infer, was fat and elderly and bandannaed. I was a respectable and a white baby, but Nain was sixteen, divinely café-au-lait, and she would have gone into cascades of giggles at the suggestion of a bandanna on her head. I loved her devotedly and never had any other nurse. Everything about her was sweet-smelling, of the right temperature, and dozy. Psychiatrists would agree, I imagine, that I loved her because in her I found the comfort of the womb, from which I had so recently and unexpectedly been ejected and for which I was homesick. The womb may be comfortable, but I have my doubts and, without a little first-hand information, I will continue to believe I loved her for her merry goodness, her child's heart that understood mine, and her laughter that was like a celesta playing triplets. Chiefly, I remember her bosom; it was soft and warm, an ideal place to cuddle one's head against." A song Nain sang brought him to tears, and the effects stayed with him the rest of his life. "If her music opened vistas and induced contemplations, unbearably poignant and full of pity, I should perhaps thank her . . . for certain Bach chorales and Negro spirituals that, awakening kindred compassions in the core of my being, have guided me more surefootedly and authoritatively through life than all ten of the Commandments."

When a mother died, a mammy often moved quickly to take her place, filling all the maternal roles. F. D. Srygley tells in his *Seventy Years in Dixie* how his mammy took over and continued to care for him until he was eighteen, when she herself died. Although mammies were ubiquitous, probably the most common answer to "who's minding the kids?" when children were left motherless was the stepmother. What are now called "blended families" were commonplace. The high rate of maternal mortality, a shortage of women in the Southern colonies and states, and a dismal death rate among men as well made it inevitable that widows and widowers would remarry, often bringing with them children from both previous families. Surprisingly, in Charles County, Maryland, during Colonial days, widows took new husbands three times more often than men took new wives. Although the threat of death in childbirth was real, the male-female ratio was also skewed by the emigration patterns of the colonies.

It was the stepmother (perhaps aided by a mammy or nurse if the children were young) who took care of motherless children, then and later, and it was this possibility that, in the nineteenth century, worried Sarah Gayle, whose health, like that of many young mothers, was precarious. She gave her husband instructions in case of her death: "No stepmother for my poor girls—she may be an Angel for you, but very different for them." For this woman a devoted mammy seemed a more reliable caretaker.

The mammy's devotion enveloped her charges. "Mother Tid," as she was called by her neighbors in Warren County, Mississippi, had been nurse to a small boy whose father was notoriously cruel to all his slaves. Once this master slapped her face unjustly, and she ran away and hid in some bushes, planning to make a break for freedom. Before she could go farther she heard the master's four-year-old son calling her, "Tid, Tid, come back to me. I won't let you get hurt any more." Her love for him was so great, she said, that she went back and stayed until he was grown.

Mammies as Wet Nurses

Mammies and nurses sometimes wet-nursed (as well as "dry-nursed") white children, so the stories of being "suckled at black breasts" in the diaries and biographies of white Southerners are accurate evidence of one way a society grappled with infant feeding in a time without reliable alternatives. Medical thinking at the time discouraged mothers' feeding of their own infants (although many disregarded this advice and complained of sore nipples and exhaustion when they did the job themselves), and black and white wet nurses were sought after. Even Sojourner Truth suckled a white baby at one breast, a black baby at the other. Sarah Louise Augustus, interviewed in Raleigh, North Carolina, said, "My grandmother . . . was called Black Mammy because she wet-nursed so many white children. In slavery time, she nursed all the babies hatched on her master's plantation and kept it up after the war as long as she had children."

Ellen Betts, too, wet-nursed after Emancipation. She said, "Two year after the war, I git marry and git children of my own and then I turn into the wet nurse. I wet-nursed the white children and black children, like they all the same color. Sometimes I have a white one pulling one side and a black one the other."

During slavery a planter's wife wrote to her sister-in-law describing the situation of a mother who recognized that she could not compete with a caretaker for the love of her child: "I would not hesitate about coming to see you if I could bring my servants, but I could not bring my baby without assistance. She is a great deal fonder of her Mammy than she is of me. She nurses her and it would be a great trial to go without her." Foreign visitors were amazed to find black women nursing white children and recognized the dangers of the attachment that might develop: "It may be incredible to some that the children of the most distinguished families in Carolina are suckled by Negro women," wrote one. "Each child has its *Momma*, whose gestures and accent it will necessarily copy, for children, we all know, are imitative beings. It is not unusual to hear an elegant lady say, *Richard always grieves when Quasheebaw is whipped, because she suckled him.*"

The milk a child received from a wet nurse was widely thought at the time to endow the baby with its nurse's characteristics—her red hair, her temperament. It is curious that no one worried that white children nursed at a black breast would turn black—or, for that matter, that the infant nursed by the goat as a substitute for a human being would grow up to bleat.

Babies were usually nursed for a year or more—but many of them died before that point was reached. Although the death rate for white infants was distressingly high, it was twice as high for black infants (as it still is today). Even those who were nursed by their mothers who worked in the fields were sometimes malnourished because laboring in extreme heat dehydrated the mothers, cut down on the milk supply, and diminished its nutritive value.

When a white child who had been suckled by a black nurse grew older, there were often the genuine, warm feelings that many Southern whites expressed in their memoirs. Sometimes, however, there was ambivalence and even hostility. What did it cost a white person, emotionally, to be mothered by a black woman and feel for her all the natural love of a child for the one who succors it, yet be just as deeply attached to the institution that enslaves her? Ellen Cragin of Mississippi told her interviewer of the time her mother was at her loom and fell asleep. She was awakened by blows from the young master she had nursed and cried out, "These black titties sucked you, and then you come here to beat me." She, in turn, grabbed the stick and beat the young master.

What happened to their own babies when black women suckled white children? Sometimes the two were fed together without any problems. Yet mammies have been accused of neglecting their own infants and children in favor of those of the planter, and as in all myths, there is some truth to this. What is not examined is what the mammy or nurse felt when she had to pay attention to the needs of someone else's children—and what her children felt as far as their own self-worth was concerned if they saw themselves as second on the nurturing list. Harriet Brent Jacobs reports in *Incidents in the Life of a Slave Girl* what happened to her own mother. Although this was in town, not on a plantation, it probably represents what happened from time to time wherever wet-nursing took place. "My mother's mistress," she wrote, "was the foster sister of my mother; they were both nourished at my grandmother's breast. In fact, my mother had been weaned at three months old, that the babe of the mistress might obtain sufficient food."

Mammies were sometimes midwives or attendants at births as

well as wet nurses. Lewis H. Blair of Richmond wrote in 1889, "Most of us above thirty years of age had our mammy, and generally she was the first to receive us from the doctor's hands and was the first to proclaim, with heart bursting with pride, the arrival of a fine baby. Up to the age of ten we saw as much, perhaps more, of the mammy than of the mother, and we loved her quite as well."

It is interesting to reexamine this account in light of what we now know about infant bonding—the tie of the mother to the child, and the child to the mother. In the 1970s Dr. Marshall Klaus, who studied this interaction for twelve years, found there was a period of a few seconds to about one hour after birth when the infant was awake and alert, and during which a primary attachment was formed. This was so even if the person was not the biological mother. He tells of a "remarkable accident in an Israeli hospital [when] two mothers were inadvertently given and consequently took home and cared for the wrong babies. At the time of the two-week checkup, the error was discovered and efforts were made to return the babies to their own families. Each mother had become so attached to the baby she had cared for during the first fourteen days that she was reluctant to give him up. . . . In other nursery accidents where the wrong baby has been presented to a mother for the first feeding or to be held for a brief period, we have been greatly impressed by her lingering thoughts about that baby."

Klaus also found that observers of the labor and birth became more closely attached to the baby than other relatives or caretakers who had not been present. Klaus has since backed off a little from his first statement that bonding soon after birth has to take place for development of the child to be optimal and concedes that bonding takes place over time, rather than in an instant, but his observations nevertheless add a valuable dimension to any understanding of the black mammy (or nurse) and her white charges. They also illuminate the identification of the black child with the white mistress who was present at the birth and may have nursed or cared for him or her.

Since Mammy was often present at the delivery (as midwife or helper), often first held and made eye contact with the baby, often gave it its first feeding, and was chief caretaker for a long stretch of childhood, it is no wonder she was remembered as being deeply attached to "her" white children. The attachment was real and elemental. And the white planter's "myth" of the mammy may have been hyperbole rather than fiction. "This original mother-infant [or can

we say mammy-infant?] bond is the wellspring for all the infant's subsequent attachments and is the formative relationship in the course
of which the child develops a sense of himself," Klaus insists. Others
question this categorical statement but agree that early infancy can
be important. One can only speculate what this kind of basic attachment did to relations between the races when the baby grew up to be
the master or mistress. Certainly it produced an identification with
the black person. "If there's one thing I understand, it's the black man
[or woman]" was a common statement made by white Southerners.

John W. Blassingame, in his *The Slave Community: Plantation
Life in the Antebellum South*, saw other effects on the white male. "Often he internalized the love ideal of the black mammy but later
learned that she was a hated black thing. His intimate relation with
the mammy, his observation of the casual sexual contacts among
slaves, the idealization of white women and the pursuit of black
women by white males, convinced him that sexual joy lay in the arms
of a black paramour. The white male frequently resolved his love-
hate complex by pursuing the allegedly passionate black woman. At
the same time, he exaggerated the sexual prowess and desire of the
black male for liaisons with angelic white women and reacted with
extreme cruelty to any challenge to his monopoly of white women."

Blassingame missed what may have been another important
component in the attraction of the white male to the black female.
Since (if one believes psychoanalytic theory) we all on some level
marry our mothers, it is possible that the white planter's amorous
tendencies may be due, in part, to his basic attachment to his black
surrogate mother. This kind of psychohistory may be farfetched, yet
it is hard to dismiss the long-term consequences of what we now recognize as a fundamental tie. The effects on the black child of having
been nursed by a white woman have not even been considered in the
speculations about the complex relationships that were nurtured on
the plantation.

Attachment to a mammy on the plantation had one special feature that cannot be minimized: the potential for betrayal. There was
no guarantee that the black mothering figure would not be sold—although the children's attachment to her could and did make it less
likely that this would happen. Nevertheless, a mammy or nurse was
still a slave, still subject to the will or whim of a master. And especially after his death (or the death of his wife), she was in danger of
being treated like any other piece of property.

There was another tie that was also close to kinship—that of the white baby and black baby suckled at the same breasts and brought up together. Here, too, betrayal was always a possibility. Although it is not a plantation story, the events Harriet Brent Jacobs recounts poignantly illustrate this possibility. Her mother and her mother's mistress had been brought up as "sisters," nursed by her grandmother. While the mistress lived she promised that her black "sister's" children would always be cared for. Jacobs's mother assumed that when this mistress died, she would be set free. But when "the will of my mistress was read, we learned that she had bequeathed me to her sister's daughter, a child of five years. So vanished our hopes." She commented, "We all know that the memory of a faithful slave does not avail much to save her children from the auction block."

The Myth Reconsidered

The black mammy on the plantation has been a victim of mythmakers and myth bashers. Once enshrined on the Aunt Jemima pancake box as the essence of motherly warmth, she has now been reduced to a shrunken head in the upper-left-hand corner of the package. Rejected by race-conscious blacks and embraced by race-conscious Southern whites, she is currently in the midst of a historical reassessment. This reassessment is taking place even in the black community, where memorabilia celebrating the stereotype are collectors' items. Some of the collectors say they are preserving history; others, black and white, agree with Benjamin L. Hooks, Jr., then head of the National Association for the Advancement of Colored People, who said, "We still denounce them [Sambo dolls, Mammy cookie jars] and I don't have anything good to say about them."

Jamaica Kincaid, a black West Indian writer, while understanding the objections to the mammy as objections to the system that produced her, is nevertheless sad that "black people do not like the image of the Mammy anymore." She was, Kincaid feels, to be admired because, among other things, she "loves you for no reason at all. A Mammy is fair, loving, loyal, nurturing, supportive, protective, generous, and devoted." American blacks are not so quick to accept the stereotype.

Historically the figure of the mammy has been associated in the black community with the evils of slavery. When, in 1923, the Daughters of the Confederacy proposed erecting a monument in Washington, D.C., to honor the memory of this mythic figure, the black press was against it. They said it would be better to make practical changes in the status of blacks—discontinue lynchings, for example.

To many white Southerners the opposition was bewildering. To them, according to Jessie W. Parkhurst of Tuskegee Institute, who surveyed the memoirs of planters and their wives, mammies (although not other slave women) were seen as loyal, affectionate, sensible, dignified, and warmhearted, among their other laudable attributes. A monument seemed only fitting tribute. But the project died in the House of Representatives.

Recent myth bashers have pointed out that mammy as the head black woman on the plantation appears only occasionally in reliable records and certainly existed only on large plantations. Many white Southerners who reminisced about their mammies were referring to the far more common black child nurses, who lacked the practical power of the mammy. Nevertheless, they (and the mammies) played a crucial role in the upbringing of the Southern white, a role that had far-reaching consequences and that is yet to be investigated with rigor and psychological sophistication. Whatever may come of such an investigation, there is enough evidence now to see this relationship as often glowing with deep, warm, and enduring feelings. In the slave cemetery on Sapelo Island, Georgia, there is a tombstone to the memory of "Baba" (an African name found among the Hausa tribe).

> *IN MEMORY OF BETSY BEAGLE*
> *BORN JULY 1796*
> *DIED JAN. 30, 1890*
> *SHE WAS THE FAITHFUL LOVING*
> *NURSE FOR THE SPALDING CHILDREN*
> *FOR TWO GENERATIONS*
> *"MY BABA"*
> *MAY SHE REST AS PEACEFULLY AS THE*
> *LITTLE HEADS SHE PILLOWED TO SLEEP*
> *ON HER BOSOM*

Today's children, brought up by nannies or baby-sitters or maids, may also be tied by invisible bonds to the woman who pillows them on her bosom. They may also, like the slave children in group care or exposed to multiple mothering by women in the community, learn to attach themselves to several caretakers without losing or diluting their attachment to their own mothers. But there is one vital difference. The uncertainties and changes in today's methods that expose children first to one, then another, surrogate mother depend on individual decisions. Slavery, on the other hand, made shifts in caretakers the sole province of the master who had the power to sell them at will.

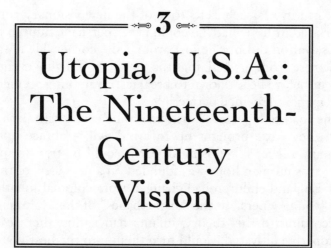

Utopia, U.S.A.: The Nineteenth-Century Vision

Sectarian utopias represent the impossible possibility without which very little is possible.

—David Martin, *professor of sociology, London School of Economics*

A CONTAGION OF REFORM swept through the country in the mid-nineteenth century, challenging, among other truisms, the sanctity of the cult of motherhood and struggling to free women from the burdens of child care. Industrialization hammered at the old agrarian society, the frontier was wide open, and God seemed to be waiting in the wings for the establishment of his kingdom on earth. The depression of 1837—the worst in this young nation's history—threw society into a state of flux in which old ideas and standards lost their sovereignty, and the chance to turn revolutionary theories into reality beckoned. The nation bubbled with utopian ferment—socialist, agrarian, pacifist, communist, millenarian. The seemingly radical social experiments of the 1960s were really echoes of these earlier American experiments in communal living. A Transcendentalist at

Brook Farm in Massachusetts (one of the new visionary communities) declared in 1841 that "he could never persuade himself that the world's salvation did not lie just around the corner. He always felt, when he rose from his bed, that the 'one far-off divine event' might well occur before he sat down to breakfast." Anything seemed possible, and mankind seemed perfectible.

The road to a perfect world had to be paved with perfect children. If they were brought up to avoid evil, embrace good, and squelch any flicker of selfishness, earth could be transformed into heaven. This utopian hope was founded on a new view of the child. In New England children had changed from colonial Jonathan Edwards's "young vipers" to the "divine babes" of the Transcendentalists. According to this theory, infants had within them capacities that, properly cultivated, would turn them into the best that human beings were capable of, producing a new Eden in which possessiveness and hate had no place.

The Shakers, whose communities began with the beginning of the nation, provided a model for all the perfectionist experiments that followed. With each wave of religious revivalism that swept the country in the 1800s, Shaker membership increased. Men and women who believed they had seen the way to avoid the world's corruption fervently joined the Society and willingly separated themselves from husbands, wives, and children. After the last great revival of the 1840s, membership crested at six thousand men, women, and children in eighteen Societies made up of fifty-eight Families.

Both the Shakers and the Oneidans in upstate New York shared the view that children could be taught to avoid the pitfalls that produced adults who made wars, lived meaningless lives, and shirked responsibility for their fellow men. Their attitudes were an amalgam of Locke's tabula rasa—the child as a blank slate—and Rousseau's romantic view that the child in its innocence is closer to God's ideal than the adult. If society could preserve the innocence and write on the slate only what would make for a better world, perfection was within reach.

Along with high optimism for the future came discontent with current hidebound institutions—the church, the family, the state. By the 1840s about one hundred intentional communities had popped up in places as far apart as New England and Indiana. Like the Shakers and Oneida, they offered order when traditional hierarchical patterns imported from the Old World were crumbling. Many of them were based on innovative religious ideas, and all of them were determined, like the avant-garde poets and artists of the 1920s, to "make it new" and make it better. Only a very few lasted beyond the lives of their charismatic leaders.

Some of the utopian enthusiasts were outsiders, on the fringes of society. Fredrika Bremer, a Swedish traveler who wrote her impressions of America in 1853, saw the Shakers this way: "There will always exist the need of places where the shipwrecked in life, the wearied of life, the solitary and feeble, may escape as to a refuge, and where their good-will and their powers of labor may, under a wise and affectionate management, be turned to account, where the children of misfortune or misery may be brought up in purity and love. . . . And this is the case here."

On the other hand a surprising number of utopians were solid, thinking people, looking for a better way. For the groups—such as the Shakers and Oneida—that included men, women, and children, the children were seen as bearers of the flame, to be brought up to create the ideal world of the future. The Shakers, although they had started much earlier, reached their peak during this mid-nineteenth-century time of ferment. The Oneida community began then, and so did the Mormons—and they all flourished in western and central New York State where the Second Great Awakening of religious revivals in 1842 ignited a grab bag of unorthodoxies among middle- and lower-class Protestants. Whitney Cross, author of *The Burnt-Over District*, has pointed out that western New York State was to that time what California was in the 1960s—the place where all the eccentrics gathered.

One of the eccentricities these groups shared was their recognition that they had to crash through the conventional boundaries of family life in order to build a new world. The Shakers were celibate, the Mormons polygamous, and the Oneida Perfectionists practiced what they called complex marriage, a unique combination of polygamy and polyandry. They, and other groups, rejected the traditional position of woman and her role as mother in a nuclear family.

A member of an early, influential community based on the ideas of the French social reformer Charles Fourier summed up the new thinking with: "Very many women find other employments more attractive than the care of their children, and consequently the children receive comparatively little attention from them. Now, this seems to me to show the plan of Nature, who does not form every woman to take care of children, but only a certain proportion of women. You will, perhaps, say that these are not good mothers, and that they *ought* to discharge so interesting an office. But is not this to substitute for the method of Nature certain notions which you have formed for yourself, and which Nature does not at all recognize? I think it is, but granting that every mother *ought* to take charge of her children, the fact remains that many do not, and will not, to say nothing of the majority who absolutely cannot. Should the children, therefore, suffer? The associationist says no! Let them be cared for, not by menials whom accident furnishes, and who may be the most corrupt persons in the world. Let them be given to the charge of persons of high character and education, in whom the maternal instinct is so largely developed that they discharge with delight the duty which the mother of the child does not, and which Nature may, perhaps, have unfitted her for, in bestowing upon her the most brilliant talents in other spheres."

This strikingly modern assessment was written in 1844. It was shared by the Shakers and Oneida, both groups developed methods for caring, round the clock, for children who came to or, in the case of Oneida, were born into, the community.

THE SHAKERS

The example of the Shakers (in particular) has demonstrated not merely that successful communism is subjectively possible, but that this nation is free enough to let it grow.

—*JOHN HUMPHREY NOYES, FOUNDER OF THE ONEIDA COMMUNITY*

SHAKER RELIGIOUS BELIEFS and practices came to America with Mother Ann Lee, who led a small band in a perilous trip across the ocean from England to what they hoped would be a more hospitable land. In 1776 the first community was established at Watervliet, New York. Mother Ann was a mystic, and her beliefs were founded on visions and, like other utopian ideas, on the particular circumstances of her own life. She had given birth to four children, all of whom died in infancy, and she then refused to have sexual relations with her husband, seeing "lust" as the cause of all evil. This conviction formed one of the pillars of the Shakers' distinctive belief system, compelling them to live lives of complete celibacy. Mother Ann's grief at the deaths of her babies also led her followers to take in other people's children to care for as their own. Another of their singular tenets was that God was both male and female. The male was exemplified in Christ (whom the Shakers saw as just a man), the female in Mother Ann. Both were recognized as Divine Saviors, with the male aspect representing power, the female, wisdom. The Second Coming (or millennium) had already occurred with Mother Ann, they believed, and "the earth is [already] heaven, now soiled and stained, but ready to be brightened by love and labor in its primeval world."

One broadside summarized the ideals of their philosophy in these terms:

> *Equality of the Sexes, in all departments of life,*
> *Equality in Labor, all working for each, and each for all,*
> *Equality in Property—No rich, no poor, Industrial Freedom, Consecrated*
>   *Labor, Dedicated Wealth, A United Inheritance, Each using according to*
>   *need, Each enjoying according to capacity,*
> *Freedom of Speech, toleration in Thought and Religion. Often persecuted,*
>   *Shakers have never been known to persecute,*
> *Abolition of all Slavery—Chattel, Wage, Habit, Passion, Poverty, Disease,*
> *Temperance in all things,*
> *Justice and Kindness to all living beings,*
> *Practical Benevolence. Thou shalt love thy neighbor as thyself.*
> *True Democracy, Real Fraternity, Practical Living of the Golden Rule*

It is no surprise this Shaker broadside sounds suspiciously like Marx's "from each according to his ability." Friedrich Engels, coauthor with Marx of the *Communist Manifesto*, knew of the Shakers and applauded their views on the abolition of private property. He called them the first people in the world to create a society based on common property. Shaker influence was more widespread than that of any other utopian movement at home and abroad. They were so well known that Abraham Lincoln specifically exempted them from service in the Civil War, placing them among this nation's early conscientious objectors.

Like all ideals, the Shakers' were somewhat tarnished in real life. Although they professed equality of the sexes and the duality of the deity, the Shakers did not, after the very early days, have women in top religious posts. Men and women were separate, if technically equal, with women taking on the customary female tasks in the communal kitchen and men doing the farming. As for their view of contemporary feminist ferment, Eldress Harriet Hubbard praised Lucy Stone and Elizabeth Cady Stanton, but said she thought women had their own particular sphere, and it did not include politics.

Nonetheless, the Shakers did accord women more equal status—in making community decisions, in being coleaders of each Family (into which communities were divided)—than did the outside world. And, like most other utopians, they freed women from their drudgery, isolation, and concentration on child rearing by making communal arrangements for the care of children, cooking, and cleaning.

The Shakers lasted longer (from 1776 to remnants in one community today) than any of the other utopian experiments that flourished in the mid-nineteenth century. They survived the death of their charismatic leader and her immediate successors, but could not survive their celibacy. One of the last sisters at the Canterbury community in New Hampshire observed sadly when she was in her nineties, "Our great mistake was that we did not have children." And yet, that may have been what kept them going for so long. Other communitarian societies that flourished and faded within a generation or two were often destroyed as the grown-up children rejected the philosophy of their parents in an age-old pattern of rebellion. The Shaker children did not often have parents to rebel against.

The Shakers took children into each of their celibate societies, seeing them as their hope for the future. Some came from orphanages; others were waifs they themselves had found on the streets, those placed by relatives or guardians, occasional foundlings, and those who came along with one or both parents. No distinction was made in the care of the children, and parents often tempered their attachment to their own children, sometimes even sending them to another family. Children of immigrants were welcomed along with the others. As one old Shaker sister put it, "They loved you, and they took you in."

Holy Mother Wisdom, the spirit who represented the feminine side of the deity, sent down instructions through a medium during the great revival of 1842 and instructed her adherents about the nature of the child: "Its capacities are small, but it is ready to grasp at whatever comes within its reach. They are as a rich soil, ready for planting, the first seed that is sown, will yield a thrifty growth, hard to be uprooted if suffered to ripen."

Given this malleable material, the Shakers in their utopian zeal felt they could shape the child in the way it should go. Their blueprint for the perfect child, published in 1823 to counter criticism about their practices, declared that at the Mount Lebanon, Massachusetts, village:

All are carefully taught to regard the principles of honesty, punctuality and uprightness, in all their conduct; to keep a conscience void of offense towards God and all men; to be neat, cleanly and industrious, to observe the rules of prudence, temperance and good economy in all their works; to subdue all feelings of selfishness and partiality; to let the law of kindness, love and charity govern all their feelings towards each other; to shun all contention and strife, and be careful never to give nor take offense; to conduct themselves with civility, decency and good order before all people; to promote the happiness of each other as the only sure way to enjoy happiness themselves, and to bless one another as the best means of securing the blessings of God.

The assumption was that children brought up in this way could not help but be cooperative, self-sacrificing members of the community chosen to light the way for the rest of the world. The virtues to be inculcated were those that would make group living pleasant and possible. Totally missing was any recognition that children also need (by today's standards, at any rate) an opportunity to develop their own individuality and creativity. To survive in Shaker society, a child had to learn to put aside "me" in favor of "us."

This does not mean that life for them was solemn. At Canterbury, New Hampshire, in the 1870s they enjoyed all the delights of country living. The girls had gymnastics as well as flower gardens. The boys played ball, went fishing, and farmed their own individual garden plots. They had fun berry picking, ice skating, and sledding, and although they were forbidden "worldly toys" in the early days of Shakerism, attitudes later changed to allow them musical instruments and simple playthings such as marbles.

Shaker religious dancing, too, provided them with a physical outlet as well as pleasure. Boys at the Enfield, New Hampshire, village in 1850 collaborated on this exuberant song:

We love to dance. We love to sing.
We love to taste the living spring.
We love to feel our union flow
Around and round and round we go.

Although Charles Dickens, that ubiquitous observer who visited New Lebanon (also known as Mount Lebanon) in 1842, saw the Shakers as "grim," Elizabeth Chandler, who, with her husband and son, "concluded to try the Shakers," wrote to a friend, "They are a jolly set of them, always some joke agoing. Bub [the son] likes them first rate they are most of them very fond of children."

They were not only fond, they were remarkably perceptive. Purportedly the word of Mother Ann (who told the medium through which her words were transmitted long after she had died, "At most of the time, my spirit was in a measure satisfied, save with the children"), *Mother's Word to the Caretakers* would be approved by today's psychologically sophisticated advice givers. Written in a clear hand in an unlined beige paper booklet "copied by inspiration by Mother Ann's desire March lst 1841," it includes these astute instructions:

"You should always, in all serious labors and conversation with them, speak words of entire truth, and well considered; such as which will by no means vary, nay, not in the least, from the true meaning, or from that which you intend they should understand."

"Never by any means, make known their failings and weaknesses to the members of the family, or delight to make sport of their odd ways at any time."

"You need to be at all times clothed with a mother's love, patience, charity, meekness, forbearance, true knowledge and wisdom."

"Be very careful, always to learn, if possible, the whole truth on both sides of a disagreement between them before you attempt to settle it."

"Never keep a child on its knees over 15 minutes for correction."

The instructions went on to give guidance to teachers and others who might spend time with the children:

"Never make promises to little children that you cannot fulfill according to your word." (It added that they were to be given privileges, not presents, for a job well done.)

"And the present time is ever the best time to correct a child for a fault, even while it is fresh in its memory, and can realize the justice of the correction."

The children themselves were not left out of these wise counsels. After all, the Shakers were concerned not only with their responsibility to bring up children ready to live in the millennium they believed had already occurred; they had the practical need of all caretakers to have some of their own wants attended to.

To this end, children were admonished, "Always be lively, cheerful and industrious in the mornings, but learn to be still, if you get up before the common time." When followed, this rule endeared the youngsters not only to their caretakers but to the other children as well. With their generations of experience in bringing up children in a group setting, the Shakers were wise in the ways of avoiding unnecessary friction.

The ideal child would be respected, but corrected if he or she strayed from the prescribed path. Corporal punishment was prohibited, "except the use of small twigs applied to extremely contumacious children a dozen years of age." Verbal reproofs were swift and unbending, yet tempered by understanding. The Shakers knew that public humiliation could curdle a child's heart. "Avoid calling them liars and thieves, or filthy, nasty, stinking creatures, and the like, in the presence of the class of children," the Spirit said. "But if you have occasion for such words for mortification, let it be in your private labors." Another rule that, if followed, would avoid one of the pitfalls of communal living cautioned against using one child's accusation as the reason to punish another: "Never accuse any one of a crime, great or small, that you are not entirely confident, or have not a proof that you can rely on, that they are guilty or to blame. Never correct a child upon the word of another, unless you have some proof of your own."

The last injunction was particularly important. The children were kept to proper behavior, to a great degree, by the Shaker institution of confession. Modeled on the confession of the primitive Christian church, the ritual consisted of once-a-week recitation to a caretaker in private of unworthy actions and thoughts. One Shaker characterized it as a "heart to heart talk," with the child receiving wise advice from a concerned adult. There was no absolution—only God could offer that—but there was a purification that came of having things out in the open. The first step "toward walking in the light" was to bring sin "to the light."

In practice, confession may have been less benign than it sounds. Nicholas Briggs, who entered the East Canterbury, New Hampshire, village when he was ten years old and stayed until he was fifty, remembered that confession was on Sundays, with all the boys sitting in a silent row waiting their turn, forbidden to talk to each other until the ritual had ended. They were not pressed to confess falsely (although other accounts indicate that "sins" were sometimes fabricated because they were expected), but they were encouraged to report on others. This is a chilling precursor of the thought control practiced by Chinese and Russian communists, whose loyal citizens were trained to inform on their neighbors. Among the Shakers, the accused boy was called in and asked to admit his wrongdoing, but Briggs reports that, just as in other authoritarian settings, false accusations were sometimes used as revenge. The strict injunction to the caretakers in 1842 to have independent confirmation of any accusation may have grown out of this unpleasant reality.

"A bad feature about this business," Briggs wrote, "was that warm personal friendships were discouraged and practically tabooed." Institutionalized tattling effectively interfered with trust, and "stickiness" was discouraged wherever it was found. The attachment was to be to the group, not to one individual or another. "If two boys were supposed to especially love one another they were stigmatized as being married which to a Shaker was a very reproachful term. There was, to be sure, some reason for this attitude, as boys thick together might influence each other in wrongdoing, but the baleful effect resulting was to destroy the pleasures of companionship, and tattling assumed the place of conscientiousness." The problem was, he added, worse among girls and sisters and "savored strongly of woman's inhumanity to woman."

History has sentimentalized the Shakers, seeing them as kind, unsophisticated men and women who produced strikingly simple, beautiful furniture and left a legacy of "hands to work, hearts to God" that might well be emulated by today's troubled society. They took in children who needed a haven and treated them with unusual understanding. Missing from this largely accurate, admiring picture is the reality that this was a celibate society in which sex was the great sin underlying all evil. What was it like to grow up in such a setting? Observers have noted that in repressive societies in which sexuality is strictly regulated for adults, it is even more strictly clamped down on in children. The fear seems to be that if the genie gets out of the bottle, it will tempt the grown-ups who have tried so hard to subdue it in themselves. The Shakers were different from other celibate groups who brought up children—nuns and monks, for example—since many of them had, in their worldly lives, been married and had children of their own. They had personal knowledge of what they were trying to quell in the children of the sect.

Masturbation was to be avoided at all costs. An early rule declared, "When children are put to bed, they ought to be made to lie straight, to prevent them from growing crooked." This may well be what it seems—a health measure to encourage unbent bodies—but when it is placed against the everyday experience of an adolescent boy it takes on additional meaning. Briggs remembered that at East Canterbury, New Hampshire, "The boys must lie back to back in bed [several boys shared a bed] and go to sleep with hands pressed together near their faces, and the caretaker was supposed to inspect the rooms to see that this was attended to before he retired for the night." Victorian society, which put pantaloons on piano legs out of excessive modesty, also guarded against masturbation, which was said to cause insanity, blindness, and other dreadful evils. In 1870 a "masturbation lock" was even patented. The inventor described it as "a device for so covering up the sexual organs of a person addicted to the vice of masturbation, from his own touch and control that he or she must refrain from the commission of the vicious and self-degrading act." The Shakers were particularly vigilant because they believed the practice was not only "degrading" but would lead, step by step, to hell.

Caretakers not only watched to see that hands did not wander where they were not supposed to be; they were told to "use no words in your public or private labors that will excite the young minds to desire a still further knowledge of the influence of their own carnal passions." If children did indulge in "filthy and vicious practices" the wise spirit of Mother Ann advised caretakers to "deal with them in private labors and corrections as far as possible."

Perhaps the cruelest rule—although unwittingly so—was the one that stated, "They should never be left entirely alone, even half an hour," unless important duties carried the caretaker away. This may have kept the boys and girls sexually pure, but an entirely public childhood was a childhood deprived of the necessary luxury of solitude.

Some children blossomed in the bosom of purity; others were desperately unhappy. For Eleanor Fairs, an orphan who came to the Shakers with her two sisters when she was ten years old, her experience with the Believers (even though she eventually left) gave her a chance to escape the label of the weak one in the family. She was given increasingly responsible jobs and recalled, "Maybe I didn't go in so strong but I came out of it with a better appreciation of my own worth." Nicholas Briggs, on the other hand, was desperately unhappy although "I never received an unkind word from my caretakers nor teacher, nor do I recall even a word of reproof . . . yet in spite of all favorable circumstances I was not thoroughly contented. Why not? . . . I think a fair answer will be that I was in an institution rather than a home."

The institution was in some ways like others of its period, in other ways quite different. Unlike children in large orphanages, Shaker children slept two or three in a room, often with a caretaker, a closer approximation of home living. Villages had at most twenty or thirty children at a time, making it possible to give them more personal attention than larger settings could provide. Yet the children followed the usual patterns of group living and, like many other institutionalized youngsters, went to school "on grounds" to learn what was thought suitable for those in their position.

The Three Rs

Shakers were simple people. Most of the early Believers had been farmers or artisans, dedicated to working hard with their hands. The education they offered the children they took in was simple, too. They were not intent on producing scholars, just good Shakers. As one man put it, "Erudition was not strongly favored." The teachers were community members, limited by their own training and philosophy, but some, such as Eldress Dorothy of Concord, New Hampshire, read widely, including novels. One of her students who finally left the order commented, "Human nature crops out in Shaker Village as elsewhere."

At first, the children were taught only the rudiments of reading, spelling, and writing for just twenty minutes a day. Later, schoolhouses were built and staffed with Shaker teachers who led the children through arithmetic, geography, and grammar in addition to the basics. They were also coached in proper behavior and manners.

Boys and girls were strictly separated, just as their elders were. For some children, this single-sex living, in school and outside it, was hard to bear. Briggs, who lived with the Shakers from the time he was ten years old, lamented, "My companions from morning until night were boys. From one week to another and from one month to another boys, only boys. . . . Girls sometimes wish they were boys, but I never heard a boy wishing to be a girl, yet when I saw those girls at the church, in the dining room, in the door yard I wished I could be a girl just a little while for a change."

In general, boys went to school for four months in the winter, girls for four months in the summer. This allowed the boys freedom to help with the farming and time in the cold months to concentrate on a trade. Both boys and girls were taught a practical skill. With time, the Shaker schools surpassed those in the communities near them and some received public funds so that local "worldly" children could attend.

Charles Nordhoff, the Yankee writer who visited several villages in the mid-nineteenth century, was favorably impressed. "In the school at Shirley [Massachusetts] physiology was taught, and with remarkable success as it seemed to me, with the help of charts; the children seemed uncommonly intelligent and bright. The school is open three months in the summer and three in the winter [villages differed in their schedules]—two hours in the forenoon and two in the afternoon; and the teacher, a young girl, was also the caretaker of the girls. Singing-school is held, for the children, in the evening."

Nordhoff found in another village that the children's instruction in music was enhanced by an organ that one of the families brought with them. A Shaker brother from New Hampshire provided the lessons, although "instrumental music . . . has been opposed by the older members, and here as in some of the other societies it has been introduced only after prolonged discussion." Despite their seeming rigidity, as the years passed the Shakers accommodated to the needs of the children they nurtured. Society on the outside was embracing superfluity—hanging fringe on every piece of velvet, eating and drinking with abandon, cluttering surfaces with knickknacks—while the Shakers embraced simplicity. But the simplicity was modified in the case of the organ music and for practical reasons in the frilly pincushions and sewing kits they made for sale to the outside world.

The struggle to maintain a way of life minimally tainted by the world's goods and desires was a hard one. So was the struggle to provide an education particularly suited to the needs of the community and to the children in it. The Shakers recognized that not all children were alike. In the 1790s Joseph Meacham wrote "Education of Youth and Children in the Church" and advised, "[it is not right] to give one of a Lesser ability the same measure of Instruction as one of a Greater—A Vessel Cannot Contain any more than its measure—a man Cannot Contain any more useful Knowledge than is Equal to his Ability and calling." Along with his suggestion that his brethren follow the "from each according to his ability" dictum, Meacham cautioned that it was not easy to tell who would excel and who would not. Therefore, since "some of a Lesser ability may be sooner Ripe than others of a greater it would not be Prudent for them to Labour to make any Great distinction in that Respect But to Class and Instruct them Chiefly according to their age and make no more distinction in Relation to their abilities and Callings than is clearly manifest and may be done with wisdom and Prudence according to their age."

Despite their best efforts to lead children into choosing Shaker life, the Believers lost all but about 10 percent of those they had taken in. Perhaps they left because, as the English literary critic V. S. Pritchett has pointed out, "Extreme peculiarity in a religious sect is exciting, even stimulating and enlarging to a child; it isolates him, and in doing so gives him a heady importance. . . . But the experience is too fierce. It creates that 'chaffiness'—so quickly burned out—which the early Quakers were always talking about."

Some withdrew when, at close to the age of eighteen, they were given the choice of leaving freely or becoming Shakers. Others finally wrenched themselves away years after they had "accepted the cross." Eleanor Fairs left when she was seventeen although she felt she had been well taken care of and loved the Eldresses. "It wasn't I was unhappy," she told an interviewer gathering oral histories of people who had known the Shakers, "I just didn't want to be a Shaker. There wasn't anything wrong about that, if one wanted to be. But I have nothing but praise of anything as far as the Shaker movement goes." She later married.

Marriage and its lures led many young people out of the community and into the world. Mabel Russell eloped with a hired man (the problem increased as the Shakers declined in numbers and became more tied to local communities for laborers) and left Sabbathday Lake, Maine, for New Hampshire, where they were married. Mabel was only fifteen years old. Had she been older, she might not have had to sneak off. The *Cincinnati Gazette* of 1878 mockingly told the story of a Shaker romance that was not hidden: "Louis Robbins, 31 years old, for 17 years has been working as a broom-maker at the Shaker village at Whitewater. He lived in contentment until he met Luella Carpenter, one of the sweet women of the community, and his heart fluttered to a music that is tabooed by Shaker rules. She returned his love, and, after slyly exchanging vows they informed the elders that they wished to marry. They were accordingly permitted to depart, he receiving $10 and she $5."

The departure may have been permitted, but it was not sanctioned. Mother Lucy (a successor to Mother Ann) sent word during the last Great Revival warning the children, "If you ever get tired of being reproved and instructed by your Elders, and turn to the world for rest, you will have to go to hell, never to be redeemed; for the privilege which you now have is great, and will prove a savor of life unto life, or of death unto death." Anna White, an Eldress at New Lebanon, mourned "in spirit when I see or here [hear] of youthful minds turning to the beggardly elements of the world, selling their holy birthright grasping eagerly at delusive pleasures and vain pursuits."

Briggs stayed with the Shakers for forty years before he had the courage to risk perdition. He later admitted, "Yes, it was fear that held me. . . . There was little of joy in it for me. Year after year I longed for death, but wanted to die a Shaker."

He noted that other boys were unhappy, too, and occasionally two who had revealed their discontent to each other would run away. A particularly enterprising boy might strike out alone. Boys were constantly coming and going, and only a few remained. "Of the twenty four boys of the company there with me, the last one had left more than thirty years ago [by the time Briggs left after forty years] while probably a hundred more, old and young, had come and gone within that time in the Church Family alone."

Some children were reclaimed by friends or family, even though indenture agreements surrendering them had been signed. The Shakers were scrupulous about getting permission to keep the children from some responsible relative, friend, or official. Nevertheless, as Sister Ada S. Cummings recorded in her diary, "Sunday Fannie goes with her grandfather. How badly she felt. I must say I felt sorry to see the poor unfortunate go with that horrid man."

Sister Ada was twenty when she became a caretaker of the girls. They were the only children she was likely to have, and she became deeply attached to some of them. When Ada was twenty-four she was given the child who became, in her mind at least, her own. On December 4, 1883, she recorded, "Edwin Smith and little girl came here to live. We take care of the girl." Lulu (also spelled Loulou and Leulu in the freewheeling orthography of the time) endeared herself to Sister Ada. A month later she wrote she had new clothes to make "for my Loulu." The attachment seems to have been mutual. The child "seems very grateful for everything we do for her and tonight when we were fixing the girls in bed for the night she says 'How good it seems to me to have you fix me in bed and kiss me good night. I have not had anyone so kind to me and I thank you ever so much.' "

The next year, when Lulu's father left the community, deciding that he didn't want to be a Shaker, Lulu stayed behind. "She feels very bad, but said it was no more than she expected." The Shakers permitted parents to visit children who had been left in their care (some accounts say this was only once a year, in the presence of Shakers, but there was clearly some flexibility), and Lulu's father came to see her in February and brought her a pair of rubber boots. A year later he decided to remove her from the village at West Gloucester (also called Sabbathday Lake). "I do not know how things will turn out . . . I am sure," Ada wrote. The next week Lulu's father did what many other parents tried to do when they wanted to take their children back: He saw her and a friend privately and "talked awfully about the folks here." The slander "worked like poison upon their souls. Eldress Lizzie came out here and talked with the girls but they did not seem to heed it much. May God send down conviction to quicken them."

The conviction did not come, and when Lulu's father and the woman who had cared for her before she went to the Shakers (her mother was evidently dead) turned up at the village, she went with them. Sister Ada was devastated. "She was glad to go did not even bid me goodbye. Oh how sadley [*sic*] I feel tonight. What a lovable child she has been to me until lately and now glad to leave me. I shall probably never see her again." The next night she recorded the classic lament of caretakers whose charges are torn from them by circumstances beyond their control: "I miss Lulu more than tongue can tell." That winter, the world exacted its toll. "I hear that Leulu Smith my dear child that left me so coldly the first day of June was found dead in her bed. It is supposed she suffocated by the gas [used for heating and light]. So this is the sad end of *one* of my girls." She did not record what happened to any of her other charges.

The Outside World

The Shakers filled a need that was becoming more and more pressing. As cities grew larger, poverty became more concentrated and more evident. Prostitution was a growing problem—there were few other ways for a lone woman to support herself—and the filthy streets were crowded with increasing numbers of people, natives and immigrants, who could not find a place in the changing economic world. Even in the countryside, dramatic evidence of hard times became unavoidably obvious. In 1841 Charles Dickens saw a village of railroad workers in upstate New York with "clumsy, rough and wretched . . . hovels. . . . The best were poor protection . . . the worst let in the wind and rain through wide breaches in the roofs of sodden grass . . . some had neither door nor window; some . . . were imperfectly propped up by stakes and poles, all were very . . . filthy. Hideously ugly old women and very buxom young ones, pigs, dogs, men, children, babies . . . dunghills, vile refuse, rank straw, and standing water, all wallowing together in an inseparable heap, composed the furniture of every dark and dirty hut."

Gradually economic rather than religious reasons prompted most people who joined the Society, and most of the postrevival converts were women. They joined with their children because there was no way they could provide a home for them on the outside.

Even earlier, women had turned to the Society as a haven. One of these was left alone with four children to support after her husband died of consumption. In the bitter February of 1837 Elder Daniel Hawkins led the destitute family from Albany to Watervliet on a desperate odyssey: "The Hudson River was frozen over at the time so she [the mother] with her Shaker guide crossed on foot the Elder walking faster would occasionally call back to her to hurry up, but as she did not care to have the public know she was going to leave Albany and go with the Shakers she purposally moved slowly, but they reached the good Elder's sleigh in happy spirits and drove to the South family where she lived for some years."

Although there was reluctant respect for the Shakers' industry, craftsmanship, and benevolence, there was from the first ridicule of their strange ways that made this mother's fear of disclosure understandable. Their celibacy was both laughable and laudable. It was laughable because it went against the laws of nature; it was laudable because it was the logical exaggeration of Victorian society's view that women were passionless. If passion did enter the picture, it was safer to have it directed to God rather than man. Celibacy was also a threat to a world in which the large family was the ideal. Given this ambivalence, *The New York Times* called the Shakers "kindly, but remarkably eccentric" in an 1869 story, and went on, "no one can look upon the most astounding doctrinal prodigies of the Shakers with anything more than good humor." Their strange religious practices made them fair game. A woman who had recently come to the Shakers wrote to a friend about Sunday services, "They go in order around the room two by two. The Trustee in the first family is a man weighing about 240 lbs . . . it is laughable to see a man as that going round the room something as children hippe to hop."

After the Civil War and criticism of the Shakers as pacifists, their numbers declined. Aware that celibacy carried with it the seeds of their own destruction unless they could continue to attract new converts, they ran ads such as this in a New York newspaper: "Men, women and children can find a comfortable home for life, where want never comes, with the Shakers, by embracing the true faith and living pure lives. Particulars can be learned by writing to the Shakers, Mount Lebanon, New York."

Early on they preferred young people in their twenties who had had some experience of the world and were ready to subdue their sexual desires in exchange for economic security and the joys of an ecstatic religious fellowship. Later they were happy to get whoever would join.

The Shakers—like the Oneidans—were most often New Englanders or transplanted New Englanders, of Anglo-American stock. In their zeal to distinguish themselves from the prejudices of the world, the Shakers accepted into their midst immigrants, American Indians, blacks, and Jews, without discrimination. The accepted view of society was that all these groups were genetically inferior and threatened the survival of Protestant America. The Shakers' broad benevolence was unique for its time. They were against slavery and required that any slaveholder who entered the order set his slaves free. They also sheltered runaway slaves, and after the Civil War took in many freed blacks. Charles Nordhoff noticed that Watervliet, the very first Shaker community, "had formerly a good many colored members; and have still some, as well as several mulattoes and quadroons. One colored sister is ninety years of age." The South Union, Kentucky, village had a colored Elder, head of a family of colored Shakers. When that Family became too small to exist as a separate unit, its members were taken into the white Families, without segregation or discrimination. Slavery was so abhorrent that Shaker children absorbed this loathing along with the other basic tenets of their belief. Girls speaking as mediums through which the holy spirits of Shakerism came to earth saw visions of slaveowners writhing in the flames of hell.

The New Order

Although they gradually accepted some of the ways of the world, Shakers recognized that their way was not for everyone. They were the elect and lived by a higher rule, since they were the people of the resurrection, and they alone knew that Ann's coming had removed Adam's sin. Elder H. L. Eades, of the South Union Society of Kentucky, in the 1870s explained it this way: "We Shakers are up-stairs, above the rudimental state of man, which is the generative. The other Communities are down-stairs—still in the rudimental." He said the Shakers saw the world as a house: Those on the first floor marry and have children, those on the second floor are above the temptations of the flesh and are celibate, and those in the basement are inferior and should be discouraged from reproducing. William A. Hinds, who reported this explanation in his book *American Communities*, and was himself a member of the Oneida community, could not resist adding a good word for his own doctrine: "Now it is conceivable that the house should have more than two stories and a basement; that there should be at least a third story, in which love and parentage are exercised without sensuality or idolatry, and in the spirit of true science for the good of humanity."

When parents and children sought refuge from the world together in the Shakers' "second floor" they had to adhere to the strict requirements of celibacy. Husband and wife separated and lived as brother and sister, and as a sign of total rejection of the married state, the woman resumed her maiden name. Children were housed with the Children's Order, often a room attached to the shop where they learned a trade.

Joseph and Betty Stone and their son Solomon and daughter Mary were early converts and lived in their own home at Sabbathday Lake before the community was formally established and separate buildings erected. One stormy night they could not get out to the public meeting, so they held services themselves, carefully observing the separation of the sexes. As Sister Aurelia Mace told it, "Joseph took the little boy on one side of the room and Betty the little girl on the other, and they turned their backs to each other and sung and danced. They were both good looking and feared being tempted if they faced each other." Later the boy and girl were sent away by their parents, to the community at Alfred, New York, "for fear they would love them better than they did the other children." "Stickiness"—unseemly attachment—had to be avoided in Shaker villages as it was in other communal societies. But the Shakers were not intent on completely severing the ties. Mother Ann's spirit told the children, "Ever remember to regard and respect your natural parents, always behave as becomes dutiful children to them."

Caretakers, too, had to avoid the evil of partiality. Nicholas Briggs, who was often sickly, remembered that "one of the nurses quite adopted me as her son, and told me she 'loved me particularly.' Once she gave me a great big hug, which would no doubt have elicited a reproof from the Eldress if known. Very likely she confessed it and received her reproof, as I never received a second hug."

When parents disagreed about joining the Shakers, a separation had to be worked out by both husband and wife. A man joining the Society had to give his wife who stayed behind her share of his possessions; if there were children, they had to be provided for in the outside world or taken care of within the Society.

Bitter custody battles sometimes erupted when husband and wife could not agree. The Shakers were accused of kidnapping children, or hiding them, or holding them against their will when one parent joined and the other did not. The evidence indicates that they sometimes did hide youngsters to protect them from being thrust back into the evil world. One of the most celebrated cases was that of Eunice and James Chapman and their three children. Eunice claimed that James, a drinking man, had deserted her and the children, who ranged in age from two and a half to six. A year later, in October 1812, James became a Shaker. Rather than provide for his family on the outside, as the community required, he was determined that they join his new religious fervor and new life. At his insistence, Eunice visited the Society at Watervliet overnight, but decided the simple life was not for her. For a year, they argued over the children. Finally she went to Watervliet to discuss the matter in person, leaving the children with her sister. When she returned much later than expected, after she had been deliberately (she said) given the wrong directions by the Shakers, she learned James had kidnapped the children and taken them to Watervliet. Undeterred, she demanded their return and finally marshaled influential friends in the political life of New York State.

Still, she was stymied in her attempt to divorce James and regain custody of the children by the strict law of that time. Judges were very reluctant to give custody to a woman and required first that she produce the children in court to testify that James was an unfit father. But the Shakers denied knowing where they were.

At the prodding of Eunice and her friends, a report of a special committee of the New York State legislature in 1816 struck back at the Shakers, claiming, "They hold the marriage contract to be unlawful and immoral, and place the relationship of husband and wife, and of parent and child, on a footing which absolves them from the legal, moral and religious ties and duties which have always been considered of the utmost importance to the peace and welfare of the community." A new law should be passed, they suggested, declaring married men or women who join the Shakers as "civilly dead," their property to be disposed of as if they really had died. The resulting bill was hotly debated, revised, and passed, but eventually was vetoed.

Eunice tried again, providing evidence that James was an unfit father, while witnesses on his side characterized Eunice as unseemingly bold. Finally, on March 14, 1818, the legislature passed a special act giving Eunice her divorce—the only legislative divorce in New York State history, according to Nelson M. Blake of Syracuse University, who has studied the case. (In other states, legislative divorces were not uncommon.) The decree also gave any parent the right to go to court to pry loose children held by the Shakers, and imposed stiff penalties for anyone who hid a child or spirited it across state lines. Although the penalties were erased in 1896, the other provisions stayed in force for more than a century and were finally dropped in 1975.

Armed with the divorce, Eunice followed up on rumors that the three children had been concealed at Enfield, New Hampshire, and undertook an arduous journey in an open wagon to get there and snatch them away singlehandedly. Although she tried to hide her identity, she was recognized. After the townspeople rallied to her defense, the Shakers reluctantly agreed to let her see the children they had denied having and whom she had not seen for more than three years. She reported the boy and two girls "appeared inflexible, undutiful and unnatural." When she tried to lift Julia, the youngest, into her lap the child pulled away saying, "It is against order to sit in lap." The children had obviously absorbed Shaker teachings. They had, in modern terms, been "brainwashed" by a cult.

Once more, the children disappeared. Desperate that she would never get them back, Eunice arranged to have George, the eldest, kidnapped by local townspeople from the isolated barn in which the Shakers had hidden him. He was miserably afraid to be with the woman he had been told was "common and base," but he soon came to love her. On the strength of his information, she got a court order to give her custody of the two girls as well. The bitter battle was over. Eunice's struggle to gain custody of her children is a painful precursor of more modern attempts that involve cults, kidnappings, and the use of children as pawns in parental struggles.

The Shaker Children

At first, the Shakers took in whatever children came to them. But it soon became clear that many of these were not suitable to remain in the order and quickly left the society. Gradually, the Shakers became more selective. Yet in some villages, they were hard pressed to keep their membership up and were willing to take chances. Said an Elder at Enfield, "We want a good kind; but we can't do without some children around us." After the Civil War, children who came into the Society with their parents were preferred, although the South Union, Kentucky, Elders adopted twenty children of Civil War widows. A member of the Harvard, Massachusetts, village told Charles Nordhoff in 1875, "Yes, we like to take children—but we don't like to take monkeys"—an indication that the benevolent Shakers were beginning to learn what other child-care institutions have learned through the generations: If you can select your population, refusing the troubled and those with serious behavior problems, you have a greater chance of success. An Eldress at Watervliet put it this way when explaining why they no longer took children from orphanages: "We stopped doing that because 'one rotten apple will spoil the barrel.' "

Children who went with the Shakers were formally apprenticed, not to the whole community, but to an individual member, long after craft apprenticeship was in decline. In this way they hoped to avoid custody fights, and they were scrupulous about having the document signed by a parent, guardian, or some other responsible person. Some of the apprentice papers were standard printed documents, other were handwritten or revisions of the standard version. One, completed for two-year-old Lydia Merriner by her father in 1816, signed her over to "learn the art, trade or mystery of Common womens work." But in accord with the Shaker view that women were equal to men, added to the printed form in pen and ink was "and also to read and write."

The children were expected to work, just as their Elders did.

Work was a seamless part of experience, glorifying the eternal order and leading to harmony in everyday life. A *Book of Orders*, transcribed in January 1842 at New Lebanon, declared, "The shop where children work, should be swept and put in order, three times a day, before breakfast, again before dinner, and when their days work is done at night. If this order is kept, the good spirits will delight to come into their shops, and into their dwelling rooms."

Girls were expected to help the sisters, boys the brethren. In this way they were socialized for their future roles, just as they would have been had the girls helped their mothers, the boys their fathers. They lived in rooms adjoining the shops in which they worked and shared rooms (and sometimes beds) with their caretaker. One sister noted in her diary, "Laura S. sleeps with me tonight out to the shop and by taking Morphene pills I get a little sleep." Narcotics were then freely available, and women, in particular, used them with no awareness that they might be dangerous. Noted herbalists, in their early years the Shakers harvested much of the domestic opium used in America to produce morphine and other derivatives.

The day began at 6:00 A.M. "As far as I am concerned," Eleanor Fairs remembered, "you work hard—physically you work. Everybody was supposed to work. . . . You'd run downstairs and have your breakfast and whatever your chores would be, you would do them right away and when you have finished all the things you know you were gonna have to do, then we girls would go to Mary Dahm's. She was in charge of the girls and then you'd get what you were supposed to do next. Now I helped the Shaker that did canning—peaches, you name it, you know, in jars. I did that for every year. I got tired of it—but I learned a lot." She and her sisters worked so hard that the Shakers at first refused to accept the nominal payment her uncle, who had placed them, offered for their care, saying they had earned their keep. The guardian of another child gave the community one dollar a week.

When Eleanor first started at the age of ten, she set the table, then cleared it every morning. She went on to dusting and keeping the floors clean in a routine in which work and devotion were inseparable parts of the whole. Breakfast was at six, dinner at twelve, and supper at six again. A bell rang to announce each meal.

Unlike children in other institutional settings, the Shaker children did not complain about the food. They helped grow, cook, and preserve the bounty that all community members shared. Eleanor's first introduction to the Shakers was favorably colored by their cooking. She and her two orphaned sisters had been met at the train (it was 1910) by two community sisters, and "we got there [to Watervliet] when it was dusk and it was after the Shaker supper was over, but none of us had eaten, so the table was all set up for us and the two sisters that came to meet us. And . . . we had the most delicious ice cream."

After supper and a religious meeting, the day ended. Nicholas Briggs said the boys had kneeling prayers, all in a line, and after that, climbed into bed. There was to be no talking until morning.

Simplicity and order in all things meant that the children's clothing was strictly regulated. They dressed as miniature adults. No ornaments were allowed, and the style did not change with the changing fashions of the large society, a reflection of a view of children that saw them as capable of living by the same confining rules as their elders. They dressed like them, danced like them, and worked like them. Their conspicuous dress protected them from temptation when they encountered the children of the corrupt world in town, or when worldly children visited the Shaker village. They looked too odd—the boys in long black frock coats, the girls in skirts and capes, their hair cut shorter than a man's—to be approached child to child.

More boys than girls left the Shakers when they were of age. Each boy had been taught a trade, and those who had not been convinced to join the order felt they could make it on the outside. They had been taught habits of industry, morality, neatness, and precision that served them well in newly industrialized America.

The Spirit World

Along with a practical view of life the Shakers had an abiding faith in the reality of the spirit world. Ann Lee herself set the tone. She saw visions, "spoke in tongues," and responded to orders from an unseen force. Many Shakers were converted by experiencing visions themselves, and the lively dances and songs that characterized their religious services were all first seen in "dreams and reveries." Children were as susceptible as adults to the influences of the spirit world, and the past and the present blended imperceptibly into one.

Shaker spiritualism reached its height in 1838, a time when strange happenings were animating other groups, too. Just ten years before, the Angel Moroni had revealed the golden plates of Mormon to Joseph Smith; shortly after the Shaker revival, the Millerites were moved by visions to expect the imminent end of the world. Belief in the occult, if not part of mainstream society, was at least acceptable enough to keep the faithful from being seen as deranged. It was as much a part of the atmosphere of the time as today's interest in New Age crystals and horoscopes. The Spirit of Mother Ann chose this time and this method to chide her followers for allowing the corruption of the world to creep into their lives. America was developing a "dog eat dog philosophy" as increased competition went hand in hand with increased industrialization. Simplicity was threatened by superfluity. And the Shakers seemed in danger. Something had to be done.

Children played a leading role in the strange Shaker phenomenon. First, a group of girls reported hearing celestial singing as they walked on the banks of a creek. Some of them were chosen as mediums for the spirits, reporting their words to the community at North Union, Ohio. They knew that, in Watervliet, the spirits had already been active in the person of four young girls, and they waited for more marvelous manifestations in their own midst. They came one August Sunday morning when the girls, aged ten to fourteen, were holding their own meeting apart from the grown-ups. A messenger hastily called the Elders to witness the astonishing phenomenon, which one of them recorded: "When we entered the apartment, we saw that the girls were under the influence of a power not their own—they were hurried round the room, back and forth as swiftly as if driven by the wind—and no one could stop them. If any attempts were made in that direction, it was found impossible, showing conclusively that they were under a controlling influence that was irresistible. Suddenly they were prostrated upon the floor, apparently unconscious of what was going on around them. With their eyes closed, muscles strained, joints stiff, they were taken up and laid upon beds, mattresses, etc."

The girls then began to speak, bringing messages from the spirit world. "This was only the beginning of a series of 'spirit manifestations,' the most remarkable we ever expected to witness on earth," the Elder concluded. By morning, the girls were themselves again. The ecstasies and whirlings were in marked contrast to the measured, placid flow of daily life. Although Shaker meetings had been traditionally marked by vigorous "shaking" and dancing, these were usually carefully programmed. The current visitations were unexpected and uncontrolled.

A skeptic might point out that these girls were on the threshold of adolescence, buffeted by sexual feelings that were not even acknowledged in the world in which they lived. Although the outside world grudgingly accepted the existence of sex publicly and enjoyed pornography privately, girls in Victorian America were faced with their own variety of repression. As the sentimental view of the untouchable, passionless woman gained power, sexual conflict sometimes expressed itself in fainting, helped along by the unbearably tight corsets that were part fashion, part protection against "loose" behavior. The frenzied dances, convulsions, and insensibility of these Shaker girls could just as easily have been their culturally correct releases of sexual excitement as manifestations from another world. In the adults, sexuality contained seemed to result in enormous energy that could be channeled into productive activities as well as intense spirituality. The Shakers were creative inventors (the clothespin, the washing machine, the circular saw) and industrious entrepreneurs. But for the children, such repression sought other outlets, and these manifestations were among them. The frenzy spread to other communities, and the Shakers, who had done an excellent job of public relations by inviting outsiders in to see their services and sample their food, felt compelled to close themselves off from the world for seven years. They feared they would again be persecuted as they had been at first in England and then in this country.

The immanence of the occult affected children in another, benign way typical of the Shaker sensibility to the needs of the very young. Sister Aurelia G. Mace (of Sabbathday Lake, Maine) took it on herself to explain to the editors of the *Lewiston* (Maine) *Journal* how Santa Claus had been admitted into the canon. "I know not what may be the opinion of all Shakers," she wrote in 1896, "but our little ones generally expect Santa Claus to bring them some little present at Christmas. . . . The occult exists all around us. The child is taught to thank God for its blessings. Because we cannot see God with material eyes would it be right to tell the child that there is no God?

"Santa Claus really exists in the occult. It is the Spirit of the Yuletide Season. . . . I do not consider Santa Claus a myth. . . . Therefore I would continue to teach the child to thank Santa Claus for filling its stockings from the beautiful reindeer chariot which exists in the realm of the occult. . . . We cannot take the mystery out of the child-life. Almost everything is mysterious to the child, and why should it be deprived of the mysteries that give it happiness."

One of the mysteries of utopian communities had been solved by the Shakers—how to combine spirituality and practical success. Their fame was worldwide, their influence pervasive. John Humphrey Noyes, the founder of the Oneida community, declared, "It is no more than bare justice to say, that we are indebted to the Shakers more than to any or all other Social Architects of modern times. Their success has been the solid capital that has upheld all the paper theories." At the height of their influence there were eighteen communities in places as far apart as Kentucky and Massachusetts.

THE ONEIDA COMMUNITY

The child is best brought up in an open Community element, and not in a closed circle of family relatives.

—The Oneida Circular, JANUARY 29, 1863

IMAGINE A COMMUNITY of three hundred men, women, and children that persisted for forty years and had "NO orphans, NO widowed, NO loneliness, NO economic insecurity, NO unemployment, NO divorce, NO unwanted children, NO venereal disease, NO child abuse, NO drug abuse, NO oppression of women, NO crime, NO alcoholism, NO illiteracy, and NO hunger." This is the somewhat idealized picture of the Oneida Community painted by Imogen Stone, granddaughter of the founder, John Humphrey Noyes. Yet, for the most part, she was accurate. Noyes envisioned a community in which selfishness would be replaced by unselfishness; in which all things—human beings as well as property—would be shared in common. At Oneida in upstate New York he established his society of Perfectionists in 1848, and they set about living in harmony, inspired by his vision and fused together by the force of his personality. All assets were held in common. Children were reared together and were considered the property of the community. Jobs rotated, so that no one was stuck in a boring routine. Men and women worked together with little regard for the usual sexual stereotypes. And through the practice of "male continence"—intercourse that stopped short of orgasm—succesful birth control freed women from perpetual pregnancy. It was the only communist society with its roots in American soil—others, such as the Shakers, the Fourierists, and the New Harmonists, had originated overseas. And it became an enormous financial as well as communitarian success.

The founder of this astonishing utopia was, according to one of his descendants, "a powerful man with powerful appetites." The community reflected the conflicts and solutions of his own life. John Humphrey Noyes was born in Brattleboro, Vermont, in 1811 of a solid New England family. His father represented Vermont in Congress, and he followed the standard route of going to Dartmouth to study law. But he was swept up in the great Finney Revival, a religious movement that led him to question the course of his life and his beliefs. He studied theology at Yale but could not fit into the straitjacket of traditional beliefs. He believed that the Second Coming of Christ had occurred within a generation of the Crucifixion; that it was possible to be free of sin (and so declared himself) in this world; and that he was a representative of Christ on earth. He gathered a group of followers—called Perfectionists—around him at Putney, Vermont, and elaborated his philosophy to justify his life. When he found himself attracted to one of the women in the group, he persuaded her and her husband as well as his own wife to agree to a share-and-share-alike arrangement. This became institutionalized later as "complex marriage," in which all were married to each other, and a woman could accept or reject the sexual advances made by any man—including the one who had been her husband. His wife, like Ann Lee, had had a terrible time with childbirth. Only one child survived her five pregnancies in six years, so Noyes developed "male continence" to protect her. Like the Shakers, Oneida built on the experience of its founder and recognized selfish sexuality as the basis of society's evils. But the Shakers chose celibacy as the solution; Noyes chose complex marriage, an extension of the principles of socialism to human relations. A woman could have as many partners as she liked without tarnishing her reputation, and sex was seen as not only normal but delightful—and pleasing in the eyes of God. Oneida's view of sex as a sacrament was the flip side of the Shaker view of sex as evil. But both turned to the Bible to prove that in the resurrection state, which both believed to have occurred, "They neither marry, nor are given in marriage."

In 1848, fearing public retaliation against his unorthodox views, Noyes took his small band of followers, including his wife and son, to Oneida in western New York State, where a tiny group of Perfectionists was already established. There they flourished, attracting lawyers and craftsmen as well as merchants and farmers. By the end of the community's first year, twenty-nine men, twenty-nine women, and twenty-nine children had renounced the errors of the world to strive for perfection. Oneida reflected Noyes's intellectual interests and achievements, with a library of one thousand volumes (which are still on the shelves of today's Mansion House), subscriptions to as many as forty newspapers, and concerts, plays, adult education classes, and lectures to keep the minds of his followers alert. Noyes himself provided the magnetism that kept the community alive. Seen as a saint by his followers and as a sinner by the outside world, he was clearly a genius whose vision led him to put into practice ideas that were far ahead of his time.

Stickiness

By the time the community had been established in the mid-nineteenth century, motherhood as the popular press saw it was enthroned on a newly polished pedestal with room at the top only for a mother and her children. (Father was out of the house working in a newly industrialized society.) The idealized mother devoted herself to her children, cut off from the evils of the world. Her love and undivided attention redeemed them; her absence doomed them. With maternal power came maternal responsibility: Too much mother love could interfere with necessary discipline, but it was the burden of the mother to produce the perfect mix. For the first time in history, motherhood was enshrined as a full-time job. Noyes set about knocking this pedestal down by organizing a system of multiple mothering, freeing women for work, education, and love of both men and God. Children, reared communally, were the responsibility of the community, not the parents, and their destiny was taken out of the sentimental hands of their mothers.

In 1863 the community formulated principles to guide parents. The rules were clearly meant to ensure that the revolutionary ideas on which Oneida was based would not be subverted by remnants of worldly individualism. Among the rules were these startling commandments:

> 1. *The love and care of children in parents should not supplant or interfere with their love as man and woman. Amativeness takes precedence of philoprogenitiveness [love of children]. . . .*

6. Rearing children should be carried on in connection with self-culture, and the appetite for universal improvement, and not be allowed to seriously encroach upon them. . . .

7. The transition from the mother's care to the Children's Department should be made easy, and to this end each child should be early accustomed to recognize as friends and parents those whom it meets in the family.

Grandparents (and there were some in the community) were to be avoided, since they above all others were prone to lavish too much affection on their grandchildren. "Philoprogenitiveness," the *Circular*, the community's newsletter and bearer of official policy, warned, "is so strong a passion, particularly in women, that one who has had a family of her own needs rather to devote her after life to recovering herself from the disorders which it has brought upon her, than to continue the cultivation of it by taking possession of the second generation." Bronson Alcott, father of Louisa May of *Little Women* fame, who, at about the same time as Noyes, developed a philosophy for producing perfect children, also warned against grandparents who might toss and rock and fondle the children and disturb them. They were also to be avoided because they might be behind the times, relying on outdated folklore and customs instead of the latest advice on child rearing. In the modern age child rearing was to be scientific rather than instinctual.

But breast-feeding encompassed both values, being superior in the eyes of science as well as natural in the eyes of society. Women at Oneida nursed for varying lengths of time, from six or seven months to a year or more. This time of closeness and exclusive care is now thought to bond the child to the caretaker, and the caretaker to the infant. Loosening the bond was wrenching, at first, and for some women, remained a problem for years. But community mores—and Noyes—demanded it. Children had to be separated from their mothers to meet the needs of the new society. The babies stayed with their mothers until they were weaned and could walk. Then, until they were three years old, they were in a toddlers' department. From there, they moved in stages into school-age groups and continued to live in the Children's House until they were eleven or twelve years old.

With the building of the new brick Mansion House in the early 1860s, a wing was set aside as the Children's House. Now they were segregated but not isolated as they had been when they lived in a separate building at the start of the community. Their seven spacious rooms connected to the main building. Older children could move freely back and forth with permission, but younger ones were kept strictly within bounds so that they would not disturb adult tranquillity. Thirty children (an average over the years) were cared for by women who volunteered for the task, as well as by a changing group of mothers. All told, 193 children were reared at Oneida. At the community's height in the middle of the century there were a head and from six to ten helpers. They worked rotating shifts, so that each of them had half a day for study or recreation. At least one man—and sometimes two or three—formed part of the child-care team. The men in the department seem not to have been involved in diaper changing or hair combing. Their chief role was doling out discipline and keeping order. Order was important, and both boys and girls were whipped if they were recalcitrant. The severity and frequency of this punishment varied with the men in charge, and in general, discipline in the Children's House was kept to a level not much different from that on the outside. Although he remembered the discipline as generally benign, Pierrepont Noyes also recalled one Children's House father whose "smart raps with a ruler—one, two, three—left many a sore hand. I am sorry to say that he was often guilty of that maladroit Victorian exaggeration: 'It hurts me more than it does you.' "

Children did not usually go back to their mothers at night. A few stayed round the clock in the children's department, with regular evening and brief daytime parental visits permitted. Others were parceled out to community members for the night (not their parents, and not any one person for more than a week, to avoid creating an untoward attachment). In later years of the community, twelve- and thirteen-year-olds slept in "halfway house" dormitories, one for boys, another for girls, until they joined the adults.

The day began at 6:00 A.M. for the school-age children. They grabbed their clothes off hooks in one of the children's rooms, dressed, and ate breakfast in the large dining room of the Mansion House. The center of each table had a lazy susan, a revolving surface that held large bowls of food and had been invented at Oneida. Then there was "Morning Meeting," where the Bible was read aloud and the children were given moral lectures. Everyone was expected to work, and this was often in New England–style working bees, children and adults together shucking peas or picking strawberries. After work came school until noon, then dinner and school again. Older children studied Latin and history; the younger ones played with blocks and toys much like those in a modern nursery school. In their perceptive way, the Children's House mothers noticed that the children soon became bored with the same toys day after day. To keep interest high, they set aside one set of toys for each day, whisking them away in the evening to be replaced with the "new" set the next morning. This kept the children contented and avoided the possibility that a child might become especially attached to any one plaything—the sin of "stickiness."

After school, the youngsters could visit their mothers or play in the playrooms or outside on the spacious grounds. Boys played with boys, girls with girls in the segregation of the sexes that not even a utopian experiment could erase. Then there was a light supper, more play time, and while the parents were off at their evening meeting in the Big Hall, story time and bedtime. This routine varied during different times of the year and changed as the community evolved, and by 1872 the Children's Meeting had been shifted from morning to five o'clock in the evening.

For Pierrepont Noyes, this was "perhaps the darkest spot in our daily routine." Papa Kelly of the Children's House did the reading and lecturing and occasionally "spoke in thunderous tones until Jonathan Edwards' hell yawned at our feet. My soul still bears the scars made by one or two of his dramatic revelations of eternal fire and brimstone." But religion, although a daily duty, did not permeate the lives of the children. Wrote Pierrepont, "We were Biblically educated, but not morally precocious."

Despite its aura of religion, Oneida's communal child care—particularly of the very young—was sharply criticized by nineteenth-century middle-class America, which was firmly convinced that only a mother could successfully rear a child. The *Circular* rebutted the charges with "Do you think it is cruel to put our babies into the Children's House at fourteen or fifteen months? We pity a mother who has no such place for her child at that age. . . . We have proved it over and over again, that the mother's care is like hot-bed warmth, while the Children's House care is like the open air and sunshine; and that about fourteen months is the judicious time to transplant. When a mother takes her child away for an hour, you should see how pleased it is to get back."

If a child benefited at fourteen months, why not even earlier? In 1873 babies were put into the Children's House as soon as they had been weaned—as early as seven months. Their mothers brought them at 8:00 A.M. and retrieved them at 5:00 P.M., although they could stop in and visit during the day when they had a break from work. If the mothers' testimony is to be believed, this was on-site day care at its very best. The children were in the hands of women who had chosen this job and stayed with it; they were good at it; and the parents had community approval and support for placing their children—all factors cited today as contributing to superior day care. The *Circular* solicited comments from the mothers on this revolutionary arrangement. Read on the surface, these are universally in favor of the scheme and seem like repetitions of a party line. Read between the lines, they give a vivid account of the emotional cost of the new plan until both babies and mothers adjusted. One woman reported her doubts and her hopes: "Although my heart ached at the thought of separation, I had a secret feeling that it would prove a relief in the end." Her eleven-month-old boy "seemed quite homesick, pining and worrying and watching the door whenever it was opened" when he was first put with the other children. To cure him of his discomfort, his mother, in accord with community custom, turned him over at night as well as during the day to one of the other women and stayed away from him completely for a week. At the end of that time, "He was as happy a child as you could wish to see . . . the old claiming, sticky spirit (which made us both miserable) is gone." She was again able to keep him with her at night, but suggested that his age made him take "the change so much more to heart." She suggested that "the sooner children learn to love a great many beside their mothers, the surer they are of health and happiness."

Once the babies had adjusted, mothers reported, they did not cry when they were left in this early form of on-the-job day care, and one commented, "The benefit to me is very great; it relieves me of a care that was too great for my strength; it gives me time and opportunity for other occupation, it chastens my affections and frees me from absorbing distractions." The *Circular* for July 3, 1871, summed it up with "The babies do not love their parents less, but they love some of the rest of us just as well."

Along with his advanced theories on child rearing, John Humphrey Noyes had advanced ideas about diet. Like today's health food enthusiasts, he banned alcohol and tobacco, allowed sparing use of meat, and concentrated on carbohydrates and fresh fruit. Babies who had just been weaned were fed "bread and milk, baked potato, and mush made of coarse wheat flour dressed with cream and sugar. All the weaned ones eat strawberries lustily and are not hurt." In 1873 a new regimen was instituted for the youngest children. They were fed only two meals a day—breakfast at eight, and dinner at three. "Much of the ease with which they adapt themselves to this method is doubtless due to their diet, which is largely composed of coarse wheat flour and fruit. They go to the table with splendid appetites and are allowed to eat all they wish . . . they never tease for food between meals . . . they certainly are far less restless at night and rise in the morning bright-eyed and buoyant."

The older children, too, did well with unusual regimens except when parental ambivalence clouded the arrangement. "Children who are committed heartily to the Community are easily subjected and readily controlled, but the double-mindedness of the parents shows itself immediately in the disobedience of the children," an early report complained.

Since the children belonged to all men and women of the community, the "sickly, maternal tenderness" of one woman toward her own children was an evil, not a virtue. "Stickiness" and ambivalence had to be avoided at all costs. It wasn't easy. "Having so recently left ordinary society, with its old traditions, it is not surprising that occasionally a melodramatic scene should occur," Harriet M. Worden, who grew up in the society, observed. Corinna Ackley Noyes, one of the daughters of the founder, created just such a scene after she was forbidden to see her mother for two weeks: When "I caught a glimpse of [my mother] passing through a hallway near the Children's House [I] rushed after her screaming. She knew—what I was too young to know—that if she stopped to talk with me another week might be added to our sentence." The mother tried to disappear into a nearby room, but Corinna "flung myself upon her, clutching her around the knees, crying and begging her not to leave me, until some Children's House Mother, hearing the commotion, came and carried me away."

Self-denial was a virtue. Jessie Catherine Kinsley remembered "my mother praising me for letting her go from me, and going from her room back to the children's rooms by myself without crying." She also remembered another girl's "passionate wails for her mother."

Too much attachment could result in fewer visits or even banishment for a time to one of the satellite communities, such as the one at Wallingford, Connecticut. In an atypical threat for this reasonable society, women were warned that excessive love could cause the sickness and even death of the child who was the victim of such "idolatry." Jessie Catherine Kinsley was sent away for the sake of her health after she had been particularly successful in lifting her mother's depression after a serious injury, and they had grown too close. "Alas!" she recalled, "the powers in the Children's House and my Father Hatch felt sure that some passing illness of mine was due to Mother's 'bad influence' "—or excessive emotional dependence.

Excessive emotional attachment also led to Pierrepont Noyes's banishment to a satellite community. On his return, "There stood my mother, waiting and eager, but suppressing her eagerness and struggling to keep her demonstrations of affection within approved bounds." He remembered throwing a raging tantrum when he was refused permission to visit her, but nevertheless felt the arrangement was harder on mothers than on children. "Whenever I was permitted to visit my mother in her mansard room—once or twice a week (I have forgotten which) [evidently, they were rationed because of too much "stickiness"]—she always seemed trying to make up for lost opportunity, lavishing affection on me until, much as I loved her, I half grudged the time taken from play with those toys which she had—I think somewhat surreptitiously—collected for my visits."

Despite this sensitive understanding of his mother's position, it is clear from other comments in his chronicle of his boyhood that Pierrepont suffered, too. The effort to focus love on the deity and the community, rather than on individual human beings, took a terrible toll. "A child has little capacity for loving that which it can neither see nor touch. Hence the pressure to elevate the love emotion reacted with us as a suppression and, at least in my own case, oriented my interest toward material things. Whether or not this orientation prevented my greatly missing the parental love and tenderness that commonly surround children, I am not sure." The men and women in the children's department, although kind and skilled, could not make up for the closeness that was lacking. They, too, were bound by the prohibitions against "stickiness." Calling this "a paradoxical blessing" because it meant the children were free of constricting attention, he added, "None of those fathers and mothers of the Children's House had, I am convinced, any great affection for us individually."

The war against exclusive affection was even waged in relationships among the children themselves. For a while Pierrepont and his cousin Dick were "inseparable"—a cardinal sin. They were forbidden to speak to each other for several days. Being resourceful but obedient boys, they followed the letter of the law by taking another boy with them when they went outside to play, and using him as a verbal go-between.

Individual affection was banished from playroom possessions, too. It was important to stamp out "idolatrous" attachments early. Mary Cragin, one of the first "mothers" in the Children's Department, gave each of the girls a "handsome wax doll," and provided two or three large ones as community playthings. The girls became so enamored of their dolls that they spent time talking to them, dressing them, and acting as little girls do in the noncommunal world. The community discovered that "we were idolaters, workshiping our little waxen images," Harriet M. Worden recalled, and decreed that they should be banished. The girls met to discuss the matter in a miniature version of the adult meeting, and agreed. Then, "Suiting our actions to our words, we all formed a circle round the large stove, each girl carrying on her arm her long-cherished favorite, and marched in time to a song; as we came opposite the stove-door, we threw our dolls into the angry-looking flames, and saw them perish before our eyes. We were all hearty and even enthusiastic in making the sacrifice, and yet it was some time before we could think of this wholesale slaughter without a slight emotion." After this ritualistic doll burning, no dolls were ever again permitted at Oneida. The girls had been saved from practicing to be mothers before they could become people. Such concern about the influence of dolls on the little girls may seem outlandish, yet, today, the Barbie doll is acknowledged as one way society educates girls to accept the standards of beauty, popularity, and material possessions that are so much a part of our own culture.

From all accounts of life from the inside, Oneida's children were as bouncy and happy as those on the outside. But Charles Nordhoff may have sensed the dulling effect that Pierrepont Noyes described when, as a generally approving outsider, he noticed that they seemed "a little subdued and desolate, as though they missed the exclusive love and care of a father and mother. . . . [I would] grieve to see in the eyes of my own little ones an expression which I thought I saw in the Oneida children . . . perhaps I might say a lack of buoyancy, or confidence and gladness. A man or woman may not find it disagreeable to be part of a great machine, but I suspect it is harder for a little child."

Jessie Catherine Kinsley thought it was harder only for a certain kind of child. "I cannot say that our individuality was much studied," she wrote. "Some energetic, mischievous children suffered. I was timid and anxious to please."

Mothers suffered, too. "Stickiness" was a female affliction. None of the fathers seems to have been concerned about it or punished for indulging in emotional possessiveness. As a matter of fact, it is very difficult to assess what the role of the father was in the community. John Humphrey Noyes, who fathered at least nine children during his long reign, was a distant figure. "I owe immensely more to my mother, in the warp and woof of character, than I do to my father. He never seemed a father to me in the ordinary sense. I revered him, but he was much too far away, too near to heaven and God" was the way Pierrepont put it. Corinna Ackley Noyes, another of the founder's children, did not even mention him in her memoirs.

The community was not ignorant of the importance of the role of the father, however, and went about supplying it in its own peculiar fashion. After Edith Water's father died, her mother chose one of the men in the community to take "a kindly and special interest in her." Another girl was an "accident"—born without community approval, and because her mother thought her sexual companions were practicing male continence. For seven years she was fatherless. Then one of the men became convinced that he had sinned, and that such an accident would be "just his luck." He claimed her as his daughter and her mother, though doubtful, acquiesced. She changed her name from Baker (her mother's name) to Hatch, since the children commonly took the name of the father as theirs. Visitors to the community often wondered if the children knew who their fathers were. The standard reply was "They have no more proof than other children— only the testimony of their mothers."

Like mothers, fathers were permitted to visit the children whenever they liked. They often stopped by in the evenings to toss the little ones in the air and play games with them. But they stayed essentially uninvolved and thereby avoided any danger of stickiness. One father wrote in the *Circular* for January 25, 1875, that he liked to play with his baby daughter but "to take care of her for a whole hour especially if she be fretful, I have found it real hard work." He commented, "It is very lucky for us 'lords of creation' that women are so fond of such chores as to relieve us almost entirely. We are willing to do a fair day's work in the shop or field, but we want to eat our meals in peace, and sit down undisturbed to the evening paper when the day's work is over." Women at Oneida may have been equal, but not as equal as men.

The Power of Mutual Criticism

The children at Oneida seem to have been healthier than those on the outside. Perhaps this was due as much to their inherited constitutions as to their eccentric diet, but during the first twenty-one years of the community's existence the mortality rate for children from birth to fifteen years was almost half that for children in Philadelphia, for example. And although they suffered from colds and fevers and even diphtheria, community members would point out that they recovered quickly because of the power of mutual criticism—a method that anticipated modern sensitivity training and group encounter sessions and was used as a cure for illness and its psychological aftermath as well as a way to encourage personality change and keep the community in line.

Noyes brought the system with him when he moved from Putney to Oneida. Something like it had been practiced in the primitive church and was carried on in other utopian communities of the time. Noyes put his personal stamp on the Oneida version, which, with the adults, acted to maintain the communities' peculiar sexual arrangements as well as cure sickness and foster personality change. A person could request criticism or be asked to submit to it. He or she then went before a group, which enumerated his or her faults while the subject kept quiet and listened. In the pamphlet on the subject that is generally attributed to Noyes, he wrote, "Let it always be remembered that the object of criticism is not that the critics may unload themselves of grudges, but to help the person criticized—to tell him the truth in a good spirit—to improve his religious experience—to bring him nearer to God—to give him a new enjoyment of life." In recognition of what today's behavior modification experts summarize as "You can catch more flies with honey than with vinegar," the session was to begin with praise. Murray Levine and Barbara Benedict Bunker, psychology professors who examined Oneida's scheme of "interpersonal feedback," felt it demonstrated "shrewd insights into the dynamics of the process."

Children were not exempt from subjecting themselves to being improved, personally, religiously, and physically. When a severe influenza outbreak hit, "Acting on our faith that disease comes in and goes out through the spirit, we commence the course of exhortation and criticism with the children who are most affected, advising them to confess Christ as their physician, and invite criticism as their medicine." (G) was criticized for hardness of spirit, which had come in by being petted. He was in his place the next day among the children at work and at their play. Illness was seen as evidence of lack of faith, at the very least, and sin at the very most. Samuel Butler, in his 1872 utopian novel, *Erewhon* (an anagram of "Nowhere" and the literal meaning of "utopia"), took this view one step further, and recounted the criminal trial of a man accused of having developed consumption. He may have been influenced by Noyes.

The secondary gains of illness—special attention, staying in bed, parental concern—were dealt with firmly, too. When a mild epidemic of whooping cough affected eighteen of the children, they were told "at the beginning of the cough to resist it—not give way to it nor cough any oftener than they could help. A good, hearty 'indignation meeting' was held, and the next day most of the children were outside sleigh riding."

Noyes, in his wisdom about illness, even anticipated Norman Cousins and his laughter cure. Miss A., the head nurse, developed this system: "If the children are a little ailing—have the headache, etc.—she gives special attention to their diet, keeps them quiet and above all cheerful. . . . Miss A. says that many an apparently grievous pain is entirely dissipated by getting the little ones to stop crying, and diverting their attention with a pretty picture or a story. The children when ailing are always encouraged to confess Christ, say they are not going to be sick, and will scarcely ever admit anything of the sort."

Even children as young as four acted successfully as critics. Among the older children, "We find that criticism does away with the need for whipping, keeps them soft-hearted, and in good relations with their superiors, teaching at the same time the most perfect sincerity among companions." Despite this mechanism for mutual correction, the children could not quite shake the code of childhood that forbids "snitching." "We were taught that 'telling' represented the highest virtue" (since Christ knew anyway, and criticism was helpful), yet, Pierrepont Noyes recalled, "I remember on more than one occasion children surrounding a boy, pointing their finger at him and reciting jeeringly, 'Tattletale, tattletale, hang him on the bull's tail.'"

Adults saw the children's participation in criticism as an unmitigated virtue; for the children it was a difficult but often rewarding ordeal. "I remember the mental chaos I would find myself in when, after a criticism, I would leave the friendly group of critics, which I myself had requested to convene, and go away by myself to take thought and cry a little," Jessie Catherine Kinsley recalled. She had been criticized for not standing straight and toeing in, for hurting someone else's feelings, and for her unruly temper. She had also been comforted by Miss Emily, who told her she seemed more careful, and Miss Harriet, who said she had improved control of her tongue. "There was great relief in prayer, in the *hope* that 'Christ within' might thus be helped to shine through the faulty cover of the 'outer man.' " This concept of an inner, true self that has been obscured by a false outer shell turned to face the world is one that has only recently come into modern psychological thought through the work of the English psychologist D. W. Winnicot and the "object relations" school. The Oneidans believed that mutual criticism could release the true self—or, in today's terminology, "the inner child."

Prefiguring another modern concept, they also saw mutual criticism as a way of building self-esteem. One of the boys was criticized because he liked to play the clown. This deficiency was seen "to arise mainly from a deficiency of self-respect. . . . His love of approbation descends now to the boys' answering laugh. With more self-respect, it would lead him to please the Community by manly, praiseworthy conduct." It was thought he "needed to be encouraged by praise and an appreciation of all that is good in him. As to his propensity, let it be civilized and elevated, and who knows but it will find an edifying sphere. Perhaps there is a place for a clown in such a Community as this."

Despite their unusual upbringing and the fine-tuning of mutual criticism, children at Oneida were very much like children elsewhere. Taught to substitute "ours" for "mine" and share all toys in common, they were nevertheless "very competitive" in producing the length of metal chain each was required to complete every day. The view inside and outside the community was that work was good for children—it taught them to succeed in the adult world. Oneida's children vied with each other to see who could finish first, throw off his apron, and run outside to play. The chain was used in manufacturing the innovative animal traps, sold all over the country, that provided the community's main income. Oneida, through the years, also developed successful canning and silk-spinning businesses, and came to be among the largest employers in the area. Its members were seen as "peaceable and industrious citizens" by those who benefited from their commercial enterprises.

Role of Women

The position of women at Oneida was, in theory and in most cases in practice, far ahead of most of the thinking of the time. The community began in 1848, the same year the first conference on the rights of women was held at nearby Seneca Falls, New York. A member of the community declared that women at Oneida "have all and more than all that is claimed by the women who are so loudly asserting their rights." He answered a hypothetical question from a visitor on the equality of women by saying, "We believe that every man, woman and child should be surrounded with circumstances favoring the best development of heart, mind and body, and that no one should be excluded on account of age, sex, or race, from engaging in any occupation for which he or she is adapted by nature or culture." Women helped in the harvest, did accounting, used lathes, and worked in the print shop. Men did not do the cooking, but they did take turns cleaning the house and doing laundry. In the present-day Mansion House museum is a self-wringing mop bucket invented by the men to ease their drudgery. Despite the lofty ideals, women still did the sewing and cared for the community's children.

Nevertheless, the reply to the "visitor" continued, "Communism emancipates [a woman] from the slavery and corroding cares of a mere wife and mother; stimulates her to seek the improvement of mind and heart that will make her worthy of a higher place than ordinary society can give her. Freed from forced maternity, a true and holy desire for children grows in her heart. Here no woman's hand is red with the blood of innocents, as is whispered so often of many of her sisters in bondage. . . . And through it all they have not ceased to love and honor the truth that 'the man is the head of the woman' and the woman's highest, God-given right is to be 'the glory of man.' "

The system of male continence was a remarkably successful form of birth control. In the community's first twenty years, only two children a year were born. Ascending fellowship—the hierarchical concept that placed certain men and women above the others, usually on the basis of age and spiritual development, also kept the birthrate down. Young women were the sexual partners of older men experienced in avoiding orgasm, and young men were paired with older women, usually those past menopause and at no risk of pregnancy. Theoretically, women were as free to initiate and refuse sexual advances as men. Actually, most of the approaches were made by men, who passed them along through a third party, usually an older woman, to avoid personal confrontations and hurt feelings. Since this was a scientific process, all the matings were recorded in a ledger. Women were particularly privileged over their counterparts in constricted Victorian America: Male continence was designed to provide them with orgasms through a sex act that was a spiritual as well as a physical experience, without exposing them to pregnancy. Women had two to four sexual encounters a week, with several men. As a result, the community lived in a state of constant courtship.

Noyes believed in the great influence of the first male on the offspring of the female, a concept borrowed from animal breeding. This led him to appoint himself "first husband," and until age made it impractical, he initiated most of the girls at Oneida. Women interviewed in later life by an obstetrician who visited the community in 1877 at the request of Noyes's son, who was himself a doctor and wanted to counter criticism of its sexual arrangements, reported cases of girls starting sexual activity as early as ten and twelve years of age. The obstetrician did careful interviews and examinations of the women who volunteered, and concluded that an early, active sex life, continuing past menopause, had not harmed them.

To go with their extraordinary sexual arrangements, the women wore unusual clothes. They cut off the bottoms of the voluminous dresses commonly worn at that time and made them into pants, at about the same time Amelia Bloomer scandalized society. What was left of the dress became a kind of tunic. The women at Oneida were following the practical lead of other utopian communities in which women worked alongside men, adopting the orthodoxy of the avant -garde. In the 1820s the women of New-Harmony, Indiana, wore pants, as did those of Brook Farm in the 1840s. The Oneidans not only discarded skirts—horror of horrors—they bobbed their hair. The new fashion was devised because, Noyes wrote, "The present dress of women, besides being peculiarly inappropriate to the sex, is immodest. Women's dress is a standing lie. It proclaims that she is not a two-legged animal, but something like a churn standing on casters!" The distinctive dress was a mixed blessing, and later feminist critics have seen it as paradoxically freeing women to perform men's work, yet keeping them confined within the community. For a time there was only one conventional dress, borrowed by anyone who had business on the outside, and tied and tucked to fit women large and small. Men had no such strictures, wore conventional suits, and traveled freely. The scandalous tunic and pantaloons outfit on two women traveling to New York City almost caused a riot; police had to be called when they stepped out of the train at Grand Central Station. As the fashion historian James Lavery has pointed out, "Clothes . . . are not merely the covering of the body, but the vesture of the soul." The uncorseted, unconventional dress of the Oneida women proclaimed their sexual freedom in public and threatened the moral order.

A feminist critic, writing in 1975, pointed out that women at Oneida were not really fully free and were confined by sexual stereotypes: They continued to be the ones to care for the children and work in the kitchen; they hardly spoke up in meetings and mutual criticisms; they were bound by the rules of a patriarch. On the other hand, she grudgingly concluded, "Oneida women were rather satisfied with their lives. . . . Given the realities of nineteenth-century social mores, Oneida women were probably correct in their assessment of the 'deliverances' which Bible Communism offered them."

One of the burdens from which they were delivered was the constant care of their own children. The question of whether these youngsters—and those that have followed—would have done better if they had remained in the care of their mothers is still being debated today as more and more mothers of very young children enter the workforce. Modern research, taking off from the work of John Bowlby, who, in the 1950s, examined research on institutionalized children, has focused on documenting the damage done to the child under three years of age who is separated from his or her mother for a large part of the day. This research has been criticized as assuming incorrectly that institutional care can be equated with day care. Dr. Louise B. Silverstein, a psychologist at New York University who surveyed myriad recent studies, concluded, "No consistent pattern of significant differences in the quality of attachment to mother between home-reared and child-care-reared groups has emerged. In some studies, the child-care-reared group has been rated as insecurely attached, and in the other, the home-reared group has been so rated."

The adherents of John Humphrey Noyes were convinced that

the child-care-reared child had a better life. His granddaughter Imogen Stone put it this way: "If a child is subjected to the hangups and neuroses of just two people, it has a hard time. There is something spacious and good about having many caretakers." The Oneida caretakers were a special group, since the children knew them as part of their "extended family". Nevertheless, some evidence that, in the long run, attachment to the mother, seen as the prototype for all future attachments, may be affected by communal care comes from a twenty-year follow-up of children reared in a kibbutz. They were cared for, round the clock, by women of the community and spent only a few hours a day with their parents. A. I. Rabin and Benjamin Beit-Hallami compared them with children reared in a cooperative community in which the nuclear family remained the focus of child rearing. The researchers found the kibbutz children were not more disturbed or less able to function, but they did document that in the areas of friendship and relations with parents "members of the kibbutz group show a lower level of closeness and attachment." No one studied the Oneida children in later life, but Imogen Noyes's experience with her own parents, who had been born in the community, may offer a clue to the long-term effects of that system of child rearing on the next generation. She recalled her father as "very loving, but remote. I don't remember having very many human conversations with him." And neither of her parents, she felt, "really took in the emotional requirements of young growing girls." Both her mother and father had been born by design, as part of a unique experiment in breeding human beings.

Stirpiculture

A perfect world needed perfect children, and these could not be left to chance. As a man educated in the latest scientific ideas—Darwin's *Origin of Species* appeared in 1859, placing mankind firmly in the animal kingdom, where breeding could be controlled—Noyes wrote, "We are opposed to *random* procreation." He promulgated his ideas almost twenty years before Galton coined the term "eugenics," and he believed the time would come when "involuntary and random procreation will cease, and when scientific combination will be applied to human generation as freely and successfully as it is to other animals." He also adopted the animal breeder's maxim, "Breed in and in"—in other words, "incest." In 1869 he instituted what he named "stirpiculture"—the mating of the best with the best. The word was derived from the Latin *stirps*—a stem, root, or source. As George Bernard Shaw pointed out, "The existence of Noyes simplified the breeding problem for the Communists, the question of what sort of men they should strive to breed being settled at once by the obvious desirability of breeding another Noyes." During the decade of the experiment's existence, fifty-eight children were born to forty fathers and forty-one mothers and Noyes fathered at least nine of them.

Breeders were chosen for their health, intelligence, and moral qualities by a committee of Elders, with Noyes as their leader. Some couples applied together for approval, while others were selected by the committee. Women were deemed best suited to bear the leaders of the future when they were between twenty-five and thirty years old; men were usually ten years or more older. Borrowing from Lamarck, whose ideas on the inheritance of acquired characteristics had preceded Darwin's natural selection, Noyes believed that mankind would avoid the problems of the past when "wisdom and righteousness are fixed in the blood, so that the lessons which the parents have learned by experience, the children will have in them when they are born." Adding Darwinism to this, one member of the community declared, "Education is not enough, it must be accompanied by an intelligent system of love relations, so that when through education or other means a desired brain development has been achieved, it may not be lost by injudicious mingling with undesirable strains, but be intensified and made permanent by an infallible intuition which will surely follow any intelligent attempt to improve humanity by looking for the best conditions and traits most desirable for transmission."

Even the best scientific intentions sometimes went awry. One of the "stirpicults," as they were known, was stillborn. Another evidently had learning problems. But the rest were bright, healthy children. Were they the geniuses and spiritual masters it was hoped they would be? Pierrepont Noyes, who was one of them, did not think so. He wrote, "From what I have heard I am led to suspect that the desire of our elders to discover moral superiority in us 'stirpicultural' children was disappointed, that those who lived closely with us acknowledged, at least to themselves, that at the age of four we were much like other children of the same age." In later life they were "especially able," according to Imogen Stone. Many went on to college and were successful in business and the arts. They lived longer than the average adult of their time. But there were also casualties. One man became drug addicted and "others had problems. But no more than the general population." One generation is not enough to allow an assessment of the benefits of selective breeding, and perhaps whatever advantage the stirpicults did display was, as Milton Jannone, a sociologist who has studied the community closely for fifteen years, believes, due "not to scientific breeding, but scientific upbringing." Noyes's bold experiment did not provide a clear answer to the question that continues to plague behavioral scientists—the relative importance of inheritance and environment.

This experiment also contributed, inadvertently, to the end of Oneida. In order to be sure that superchildren would be conceived, couples had to sleep together again and again during the woman's fertile period. This led to the kind of attachment the community had worked so assiduously to avoid. The outside world had also gained a foothold within the Mansion House. Hired men, visitors to the community, and young men who had been sent away to college (usually Yale, where Noyes had been a student) and returned brought with them whiffs of a different life. The young women began to rebel against being paired with older men, and the young men wanted to choose their own mates. In 1874, the *Circular* warned, "As we value the future of Communism, we must see to it that our children—the rising generation—are brought up in 'the nurture and admonition of the Lord,' else they will some day rise up against us and become a curse."

They did rise up. Rebellion in the ranks was coupled with Noyes's aging and decline, and renewed, fierce attacks by clergymen and ordinary citizens. In 1873, a letter writer to *The New York Times* objected to the railroad extending its tracks to Oneida with "Do the directors of this great enterprise know . . . that the Oneida Community is most thoroughly a 'free love' establishment, where all may follow their 'affinities' under a conveniently arranged formula?" Its continued existence was a threat to the fabric of conventional life. On June 2, 1879, Noyes, fearing he would be indicted, fled to Canada, taking with him a few of his staunchest supporters and some of his children. He lived in exile for six years. First he advised his followers to abandon complex marriage. A rush of monogamous marriages resulted, partly for sentimental reasons, partly to protect children who were about to be thrust into the world from being called "bastards." Finally, the community metamorphosed into a joint stock company, with the financial interests of all the participants protected. The socialistic utopian experiment ended as a capitalistic success. Noyes died on April 13, 1886. His descendants continued until recently to play a major role in the Oneida Silver Company, started in 1877, shortly before the final dissolution. It is now the world's largest producer of stainless steel flatware.

Utopia's Children

Shaker and Oneida children were alike in many ways, different in others. The most striking similarity was in the prohibition in both communities against "stickiness"—close emotional attachment. In societies that were determined to stamp out exclusive affections, children were deprived of closeness to other children as well as to the adults who cared for them.

Both the Shakers and the Oneidans saw children as "trailing clouds of glory" from heaven—to be respected, protected, and kept as close to their early innocence as possible. Both abhorred masturbation and sexually suggestive language, but the Shakers taught celibacy as the road to redemption, and the Oneidans favored strictly regulated sexual fulfillment. Despite these advanced views, the children in the Oneida community did not, according to Pierrepont Noyes, have precocious sexual interests. On the contrary, he felt they were less involved than those outside in trying to unravel the mysteries of sexual behavior. Among the adults, flirting was frowned upon and public displays of affection were prohibited, although discreet signaling of interest was acceptable. Perhaps it was because Oneidans saw sex as a sacrament—something to be enjoyed as a kind of religious experience—that youngsters grew up expecting to participate in it as a wholesome, pleasurable activity when they were old enough. This time came very early. Some girls were initiated at the tender age of ten. When boys began full sexual lives is not clear, but they did not have to repress their sexuality for years after puberty, as the Shakers and even the proper, outside world required. It is possible that this early accepted consummation defused the interest that seems to increase in proportion to its prohibition.

Both communities stretched thin the ties between biological parents and their children—whether the parents were in the community or outside it, as was sometimes the case with the Shakers. Only children of members of the community lived at Oneida's Mansion House. Some of them grew up in the midst of relatives—aunts, uncles, cousins, and grandparents—who were forbidden to treat them with any special affection. Nevertheless, the children were part of a network—related and unrelated—that supported their communal upbringing. Shaker children—some of whom came into Families with their parents—were a more isolated lot. Sometimes one parent and not another became a Shaker, and the children were torn in their loyalties. The orphans, some of whom were placed by family members, had to deal with that rejection. All in all, their experience was likely to be more conflicted than that of the early Oneida youngsters.

Both groups treated children as benignly as their philosophies allowed and were part of a cultural climate that found corporal punishment a necessity—although usually a reluctant one. Both communities avoided some of the evils inherent in the congregate, institutional living that was seen at the time as "ideal" for poor children. Both gave the youngsters the security that comes of living surrounded by people who shared their religious and moral views, protected from the pressures of dissent. But, despite their best efforts at rearing unblemished children, they succeeded only in producing human beings much like any others.

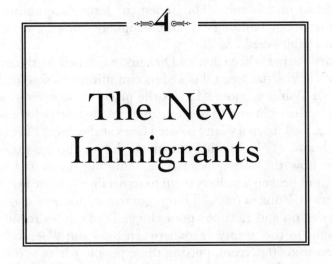

The New Immigrants

WORKING MOTHERS, WORKING CHILDREN

[They] toiled and suffered and died that their children might inherit the promise.

—JOHN CLARK RIDPATH, HISTORIAN

THE STREETS OF the Promised Land—the utopia the immigrants had dreamed of—were paved with horse dung and garbage and held such throngs that a newcomer from Galicia in eastern Europe marveled, "The people were so thick, like you could walk on top of them." One man, in this country for three years, was moved to admit, "Sometimes I am homesick for the America of my hopes."

Crowded, stinking, and dark, New York's tenements were excoriated in 1903 as "indescribable in print . . . vile privies and vile sinks; foul cellars full of rubbish; . . . dilapidated and dangerous stairs; plumbing pipes containing large holes emitting sewer gas throughout the houses; rooms so dark that one cannot see the people in them; cellars occupied as sleeping places; . . . pigs, goats, horses and other animals kept in cellars; dangerous old fire traps without fire escapes; . . . buildings without adequate water supply—the list might be added to indefinitely." The Tenement House Committee called these apartment buildings "infant slaughter houses," since one in every five babies died.

Fifty years earlier Charles Dickens, hardened by the misery of London's slums, had been shocked by conditions in New York's infamous Five Points section: "This is the place; these narrow ways, diverging to the right and to the left, and reeking everywhere with dirt and filth. . . . The coarse and bloated faces at the doors have counterparts at home. . . . Debauchery has made the very houses prematurely old. See how the rotten beams are tumbling down and how the patched and broken windows seem to scowl dimly, like eyes that have been hurt in drunken frays." Things got worse, not better, as the century moved on and Europe's poor clogged the city's already swollen underbelly. In the twenty years between 1864 and 1884, the population increased 50 percent, putting three people where two had been before. It was then (as Dickens had said in his time) more crowded than London, which had 170,000 people to the square mile, while New York had 290,000. "One block contains 52 tenements with 2,360 occupants, or 45 to each house," the annual report of the New York Society for the Improvement of the Condition of the Poor noted in 1884.

A tenement was, by law, a building with at least three "tenants" and common hallways. Dumbbell tenements, shaped so as to allow a five-foot-wide airshaft between buildings, began as a reform in 1880 and ended as a horror. Families, relatives, and boarders crowded into three-room apartments with windows only in the front and rear rooms. (The middle room got dim light from the airshaft.) Wealthy landlords such as William Waldorf Astor increased their profits and the crowding by cutting apartments into two, then jamming people into each half. Where three or four might have fit comfortably, as many as twenty-five were packed. One boy turned up at the newsboys' home looking for a place to sleep because, he said, "There's seven in the bed already and I couldn't get in." The Lower East Side of New York was the most densely populated area in the world, more congested even than Shanghai or Bombay.

What had been a trickle of immigration from northern and western Europe in the eighteenth and early nineteenth centuries, easily absorbed and necessary for an expanding country, became a wave and then, between 1881 and 1890, a flood. In the early 1800s one in every twenty-five Americans lived in a city. By 1900, the figure was one in three, with much of the increase coming from immigration.

The 4,737,046 men, women, and children who arrived in America in the last years of the nineteenth century came chiefly from Italy and eastern Europe, edging out the northerners from Germany, Ireland, Scandinavia, and England. Between 1901 and 1910, the flood virtually doubled. Cities such as New York suffered from urban indigestion, unable to assimilate the strange people with strange ways, languages, and religious practices, who settled in ghettoes within ghettoes. They were so numerous and so different that those who had arrived earlier were fearful the hard-won American way of life would be overwhelmed. They complained that countries were dumping their paupers and their misfits and they would infect this country.

Warnings against "race suicide" were sounded as early as 1870 in Massachusetts where the foreign-born (chiefly Irish) produced children at a higher rate than the native-born. The wealthier and better-educated a family was, the fewer children it had, and alarmists predicted that if the trend continued, sturdy American stock would soon be overwhelmed by inferior foreign elements. The responsibility for averting this disaster lay with Protestant, old-stock women, who were, the critics said, mistakenly limiting births and living an "unnatural life style" that made childbearing less likely. "Race suicide," commented Charles E. Rosenberg in his book *No Other Gods: On Science and American Social Thought*, "seemed a problem in social gynecology." Approaching the problem from another angle, worried observers proposed limiting immigration itself. Peter Finley Dunne's "Mr. Dooley," who used Irish dialect to poke fun at the foibles of immigrants and native sons, observed in 1903 (after paupers had been specifically excluded in 1891, and while agitation to keep out anarchists gained momentum after the assassination of President McKinley), "As a pilgrim father that missed th' first boats, I must raise me claryon voice again' th' invasion iv this fair land be the' paupers an' arnychists iv effete Europe. Ye bet I must—because I'm here first. . . . 'Tis time we put our backs again' th' open door an' keep out th' savage hordes."

The "savage" newcomers lived in a different world from the uptown swells. They brought with them survival skills, determined that their children would thrive in the New World, but they were beyond the reach of the latest thinking. Children worked, as they had in the old country; philosophies of child care hardly extended beyond avoiding starvation, when possible. Uptown, parents were burdened with the newly popular idea that children, far from being depraved, were innocents to be cherished. If they flourished it was because their mother brought them up properly; if they faded it was her fault. God's grace and motherly devotion, not original sin, were what counted. Downtown, parents were too burdened to consider what might be best; children were essentially economic assets, not ornaments, often making it possible for the family to pay the rent. This does not mean parents had no tender feelings. But privacy and self-fulfillment were luxuries no immigrant child could afford. John West, an English shoemaker, wrote home that "a man can do better here with a family than with none. For children at 6 years old can work and get some money." Child labor had a long history as a "righteous institution." In the Middle Ages, children of even wealthy families were put to work as soon as they had some sense and manual dexterity, and children of nobles were sent as pages to other noble families at about the age of seven to learn diligence and cement alliances. And as we have seen, American children were often apprenticed at the same age in the seventeenth and eighteenth centuries.

Homes as Factories

The immigrants brought with them memories of the days (no longer alive in the industrialized Europe of the nineteenth century) when families had worked together for the common good. In the dismal tenements, they revived family labor. Often deprived of the extended family networks that might have provided child care for women who went out of the house to work, and faced with seasonal and uncertain jobs for men, women had no choice but to work with their children at home. Necessity kept mother and child together, rather than, as in other child-minding systems, wrenching them apart. Mothers working alongside their children to earn enough to live fit right in with the new country's religious conviction that poverty was a sign of God's displeasure and that, above all, poor children and adults should shun the sin of idleness.

Among the newly rich, though, idleness became a virtue, symbolic of a man's success. If a woman could afford to stay home as an ornament, her husband had fulfilled his mission. Thorstein Veblen's "conspicuous consumption" replaced thrift. James O. S. Huntington, a Catholic priest, saw the sham in this double standard and said bluntly at an 1892 conference on philanthropy and social progress, "We belong to the House of Have: they belong to the House of Want;

and the rules of one family are not the rules of the other . . . while the duty of working for a living is always emphasized when the poor are in question, the charitable societies with remarkable unanimity disregard, and thereby practically deny, the existence of any such duty on the part of the rich.

"I only ask that . . . we will be just as outspoken against idleness and dishonesty in the mansions and business offices of the rich, as in the tenement rooms and attics of the poor."

In the tenement rooms of the poor, working at home to earn money became popular when the piecework system, originated by German tailors, made it possible for parts of garments to be sewn at home, then delivered to the factory. Men, women, and children toiled ten to fourteen hours a day sewing, basting, and pulling out stitches. By the turn of the century these were largely Jewish families, most likely of all the immigrants to have brought their wives and children to the Promised Land. Italian immigrants in New York worked at making paper flowers; Bohemians (from what became Czechoslovakia) in the cigar trade. Each group had its specialty, passed on within its community. Homework for immigrant children did not mean schoolwork but paid work to add a few pennies to the family income.

Children from four to eight worked all day with their mothers. (In a departure from the rest of this book, this chapter considers child care by mothers and, at times, fathers themselves—although under extraordinary circumstances.) In a tiny room on Hester Street, a mother and two children sewed overalls. "I couldn't do as well if it wasn't for Jinny and Mame there. Mame has learned to sew on buttons first-rate, and Jinny is doing almost as well," the mother told an inspector. Jinny was a stunted black-haired six-year-old who looked as if she were only three. She reached for the string tying a bundle of overalls ready for finishing and was quickly reprimanded. "Me and Mame was going to play with it," she said. "There's small time for play," the mother replied, "there'll be two pair more in a minute or two, an' you're to see how Mame does one an' do it good too, or I'll find out why."

In this era of high mortality, when tuberculosis and measles were plagues that carried off parents and children alike, men were often left alone to care for their brood. Next door to Jinny's family a tailor made coats. His five-year-old daughter sat on the floor and picked off the surplus threads. "Netta is good help," he said. "So fast as I finish, she pick all the threads. She care not to go away—she stay by me always to help." There was one other surviving child in that family, who sold newspapers on the street. "Last year is five," he said, "but mother and dree [three] are gone with fever. It is many that die. What will you? It is the will of God."

Parents recognized that this kind of life was not what they would have chosen for their children. One mother of a seven- and an eight-year-old acknowledged, "It's hard on 'em. We work till ten and sometimes later, but then they sleep between [while waiting for the next corset cover on which to sew buttons] and we can't; and they get the change of running out for a loaf of bread or whatever's wanted, and we don't stir from the machine from morning till night."

In Providence, Rhode Island, an investigator for the federal Children's Bureau found a family of a mother and five brothers and sisters setting stones in jewelry. This family had added an American touch to their immigrant labor. One of the girls was sent by the mother to the movies every afternoon after school. Then, at night, "When we would sit down and do the work, I would tell my brothers and sisters about the movie I saw. . . . I used to tell them the whole movie." Movies not only provided a way to survive the tedium of homework, they were a window onto the world the immigrants hoped to enter.

This girl was lucky. She went to school. But so many children were kept out of school illegally that benevolent organizations such as the Society for the Improvement of the Condition of the Poor eventually provided "scholarships" to replace what the family lost when a child's hours were curtailed by education that seemed to have no relevance to his or her real world.

Small as the income was, homework had one advantage over going out to work in a factory—a mother could watch her children. Said one immigrant mother, "I have two children and would rather be home to get them something to eat at mealtime." But the work was sometimes so taxing, and the conditions so debilitating, that child-care needs were overwhelmed by filth and fatigue. An 1887 study of women and poverty described "one room a little less than twelve by fourteen feet holding a family of seven persons, three of them children under ten, all girls. Tobacco lay in piles on the floor and under the long table at one end where the cigars were rolled, its rank smell dominating that from the sinks and from the general filth, not only of this room but of the house as a whole. Two of the children sat on the floor stripping the leaves, and another on a small stool . . . all alike had sores on lips and cheeks and on the hands . . . a number of women often club together, using one room, and in such case their babies crawl about in the filth on the wet floors, playing with the damp tobacco and breathing the poison with which the room is saturated. . . . Yet because an entire family can find occupation in it, with no necessity for leaving home, it is often preferred to easier employment." Girls under ten years of age regularly spent ten hours a day stripping the tobacco leaves. "Even the factory child-worker fares better," the researcher wrote, "for in the factory there is exercise and the going to and from work, while in the tenement-house cigar-making the wornout little creatures crawl to the bed, often only a pile of rags in the corner, or lie down on a heap of the tobacco itself, breathing this poison day and night uninterruptedly." (The researcher was ignoring the reality of factory work with its twelve-hour days and limb-mangling machinery.)

Cigar making was the most noxious of the immigrant occupations. But as the National Child Labor Committee noted, "Home industry demands the toil of the tiniest fingers. For it the mother will neglect her home, herself and her children. . . . The mother nurses the baby while she sews and eats her scanty, unwholesome food with the work still on her lap." Lewis Hine, photographing working children for the committee at the turn of the century, found a family of stair-stepped children sitting around a table where their mother was "nursing a dirty baby while she picks nuts [pecans]. She was suffering a sore throat." They made a dollar-fifty to two dollars a week. Rent was about ten dollars a month, consuming an exorbitant proportion of their income. Only private charity, not a government safety net, existed to make life bearable.

The well-meaning charity workers who visited the tenements and deplored the filth and disorder came of a world the new magazine *Good Housekeeping* was prodding toward a fresh standard of domestic perfection. In 1889 an article called "The True Home Life" declared: "Nothing can take the place of neatness and order. These depend much upon good management, for one can always be cleaning, yet never clean, always arranging yet never in order. Sometimes one's own spirit is restless, which is the secret cause of the lack in the divine part of true home life."

The author was unexpectedly perceptive about the restlessness of the woman charged with guarding "the divine part" of homemaking, but the homemaking of immigrant women hardly came up to these standards. Women in the tenements who tried to maintain any semblance of order and cleanliness often had to cart water five flights up. Privies were in the backyards. There was no "outside" as there had been in the small European villages from which most of them had come. Here, all life—birth, eating, sleeping, dying—took place in three rooms into which were crammed families and boarders and relatives. The only "outside" was the street, or the air space between buildings over which laboriously hand-washed clothes could be hung on lines like flags of defiance against the dehumanizing conditions.

Men's work was often irregular. Another picture by Lewis Hine shows a man sitting in a rocking chair, his wife and children at the table working. He called it, "A common scene in the tenements." The father explained, "Sometimes I make $9.00, sometimes $10.00 a week on the railroad; sometimes nottin." This family made about four dollars a week picking nuts out of their shells.

Although there was a compulsory education law, it required attendance for only fourteen weeks a year and was often flouted. Even when they did go to school, the children worked many hours each day, before and after classes. Annette, nine years old, told an observer of the National Child Labor Committee, "I earn money for my mother after school and on Saturday and half-day Sundays [by crocheting slippers]. I get up to work at 4 o'clock in the morning. I go to bed at 9 o'clock." Children survived these as well as other horrendous conditions in the tenements. Not that they were healthy—a doctor who worked with the poor found only sixty healthy children among the 535 she saw during 1886. But many did, amazingly, live through circumstances that seem unbelievably harsh. In one family this same doctor found four-and-a-half-year-old twins sewing on buttons from dawn until ten at night.

Women as well as children lived lockstep lives. Anna Kuthan, from Bohemia, told an oral historian, "If they didn't have nobody to mind the small children what they did, when the husband came home from work the wife went to work. So she did all the housework during the day, do the cooking, send the kids to school, and he has to take over. He just eat the supper, everything was ready, and she just put her coat on and run on the subway to work night shift in the offices. It was cleaning women cleaning in the office."

Tenement rooms that were really factories, and apartments in which the beds were always warm, serving both day and night shifts, were in stark contrast to the prevailing middle- and upper-class tenor of the times. Home, the newly popular ladies' magazines proclaimed, was meant to be a refuge for the family. Here the tired husband relaxed from the struggles of the wage-earning day, and smiling children played under the benevolent eye of a loving mother. Home was no longer the center of work for the whole family as it had been in Colonial days, and motherhood was the purpose of life for women. Of course, some women were beginning to question their confinement to a golden cage and to stand up for women's rights. A small number entered the professions and were economically independent.

But for the woman of the working class, the world, "so far as her measure of opportunity goes, [remained] very much as her great grandmother left it," Edith Abbott concluded in her 1910 study of women in industry. The women and children of the poor were condemned to live in tenements "where the home had ceased to be sacred—those dark and deadly dens in which the family ideal was tortured to death, and character was smothered; in which children were 'damned rather than born' into the world," wrote Jacob Riis, the crusading journalist.

Women had always worked, and continued to do so, usually at lower pay than men. Their duty was not to preside over a serene home, but to work and contribute economically to keep the family together and, incidentally, to avoid that earlier but still dreaded sin— "eating the bread of idleness."

Romantic attitudes about children, too, did not apply to the poor. Middle-class children were cherished as noble innocents, to be protected from the realities of life until they had been prepared by time and education to cope with them. A new understanding was dawning that they had emotional as well as physical needs, and that play was an important part of their development.

Poor or immigrant parents had neither time nor energy for such niceties. As one immigrant put it, in the old country "people got old faster." By the age of seven (that number again marking the end of childhood) "children somehow knew without being taught that they should help the family." Emotional awareness was a luxury few could afford. The psychotherapist and writer Lillian Rubin remembered that after her father's death her overburdened mother told her "angrily, or so it seemed to the child—'You're lucky you're not in an orphanage.'" Although she was terrified at the time, Rubin later understood her mother's frightening statement as a distorted expression of how much she cared. "Keeping the family together represented a deep manifestation of love."

Poor children were seen as threats to the common good if they were not kept busy at work. Of course, diligence and hard work were virtues for all children—but for the children of immigrants these virtues were expressed in unremitting labor. The labor was approved because it fitted in with a long tradition that began with the start of the colonies when children were actually recruited to come to this country to work, and was reinforced by the religious views of both the Puritans and the Quakers. Early philanthropists, too, were almost universally in favor of child labor, warning of the "vice and immorality" that lay in wait for children "exposed by a career of idleness."

"No, I Don't Play; I Got to Work"

It is impossible to know, except through a rarely recorded conversation with a concerned adult, how these working children felt. They were not the ones to enter history. Immigrant children who did write about their early lives were the successful ones, not those who had worked twelve hours a day and been kept home from school, or made to work before dawn and then after school until ten or eleven o'clock at night. The ones who made it were more likely to have worked part-time in the streets—hawking newspapers, making deliveries— rather than in the sweatshops and tenements. The streets offered freedom, the chance to snatch time to play, the place where children found companions for the time-honored youthful task of forming a separate society. All biography is as much fiction as fact, and immigrant children who have written their stories often say they never knew they were poor and never felt they suffered—everyone else was in the same boat. City life was exciting and challenging, and America was the land of opportunity. Yet the accounts of concerned charity workers at the time paint a grim picture of neglect, exhaustion, and hopelessness among the children. The few stories they recorded do not sound like the "Up from Poverty" men and women who became succesful actors, writers, and musicians—and wrote autobiographies.

Rosa Peccaro was one of those who never wrote her story. When she was eleven years old, she got up every morning, swept out the three dark rooms of her family's tenement apartment, helped get breakfast, did the dishes, and then went off to school. When she came home, she studied for an hour, then made flowers at the kitchen table along with her sisters, her cousins, her aunt, and her mother. "We put the yellow centers into forget-me-nots. It takes me over one hour to finish one gross [144 flowers] and I make three cents for that. If we all work all our spare time after school, we can make as much as two dollars a week between us," she told a visitor from Greenwich House, a New York settlement house.

In the summer, Rosa became full-time mother to her baby brother, Danny. "Sometimes I go to play for a little while at night on the street with the other children, but I must mind Danny then, too, because he does not like to go to bed until we do. Then he gets so tired he goes right to sleep on my lap and I carry him up. I think my brother is a very good little boy, but I get tired minding him sometimes."

Danny was what the comedian Sam Levenson called "the bundle"—the ubiquitous accompaniment to older children, who sometimes put "the bundle" down to jump rope or play ball. Tenement girls didn't have dolls to play with—they had the real thing. But when they took care of the younger children in the family full-time so that their mothers could work, they became burdened "Little Mothers," sacrificing their own childhoods. Lewis Hine photographed a wide-eyed seven-year-old in the dark hallway of a tenement, holding a baby and clutched at by two other children. "Mother in shop sewing. Father out of work, bartender," he jotted down with the picture.

In a shift from the dark picture painted by social reformers and favored by earlier historians, the tendency in recent years by some writers has been to minimize the difficulties and focus on the fun, just as the autobiographies did. Children are children even under dreadful circumstances, and David Nasaw, in his book *Children of the City: At Work and at Play*, emphasizes that youngsters who worked part-time were a special group. They were not responsible for vital contributions to the rent or the food supply, in his view, and, "Work for the part-time child laborers of the early twentieth-century was far from the routinized hell that had destroyed generations of working children. It was, on the contrary, almost a pleasant interval between a day's confinement in school and an evening in cramped quarters at home." The life of the newsboys has even been romanticized in a Disney musical. But this picture may be as skewed as some of the others, both rosy and bleak. Here is just one example: At the Third Avenue El station on the Bowery a twelve-year-old girl was found selling candy at the head of the stairs leading to Track 6 every afternoon. Her mother kept on eye on her from the outside entrance where she sold newspapers. The Society for the Prevention of Cruelty to Children had the mother arrested and brought to court. For a few days, the mother kept the gum and candy (and the girl) with her at her newsstand, but business dropped off. Soon, the girl was back at her old place. In self-defense, the mother said that "she cannot pay her rent without the money that the little girl brings in." This hardly sounds as if the girl's part-time work was an unnecessary addition to the family's income. Rather, it reinforces the view that women and children had to work—and work together—to combine child care with scratching out a meager living.

One pamphlet circulated by reformers pointed out that child labor was not only evil—it was an affront to nature: "No fledgeling feeds the father bird," it declared. Children were not meant to work to support their parents.

Middle-class families with the father as sole provider were closer to the natural order, as the reformers saw it, than the working families of the poor. *Good Housekeeping* magazine in March 1889 admitted that "the idea of a child receiving everything it needs directly from its parents, with no forethought on its own part, and no more notion of commercial values than the budding blossom has of a sunray, is invested with much poetic charm. Parents . . . enjoy the typical relation they sustain toward their children—giving, ever giving, out of a resource that to the little one seems illimitable." The new magazine, while recognizing the allure of this traditional view, boldly published an article about a mother who rebelled against it and trained her children to keep their rooms tidy and pay for their clothes and school supplies from an allowance. She did this while remaining a model wife and mother, "preparing her daughters and little son for the actual work of life, and preserving the while her own youth, freshness, and sweet temper; having time for social enjoyment, time to dress and to read, time to entertain her husband in his brief intervals at home, time to look after and relieve cases of poverty and suffering in her neighborhood; time, in short, to be a useful member of society." Of course, children had long been encouraged to be tidy. Catherine Beecher in 1841 suggested it would be good training for them to be helpful around the house. What was new in this mother's attitude was the demand that her children learn to spend (as well as save) the money their father had provided, preparing them to take their place in the consumer society that would transform America.

The Gilded Gap

While tenement children crowded the streets and middle-class women dressed and read, Lillian Russell was riding her gold-plated bicycle with its bejeweled wheels and diamond-and-emerald monogram around the reservoir in Central Park. When she dressed for the evening, her hats were decorated with sweeping plumes that had been shaped in the tenements by taking a feather in one hand, a knife in the other, and drawing the knife smoothly over the fronds as if they were ribbons to be curled. With hard work, a whole family could earn forty cents a day at such labor. Mrs. William Astor (whose husband was what we would now call a slumlord) set the social tone with her annual balls on the first Monday in January. She greeted guests wearing a triple necklace of diamonds, another chain of them across her waist, and a diamond tiara in her hair. One observer described this New York of contradictions as "a lady in ball costume, with diamonds in her ears, and her toes out at her boots."

The downtown immigrants did not venture uptown. The Gilded Age—from about 1865 to 1900—was one of the times in American history when the gap between the urban rich and the urban poor yawned most widely. "Our country has grown great and rich. . . . But in the back streets multitudes huddled in ignorance and want," Jacob Riis chided. But Riis also pointed out—true to his belief in progress—that the waves of immigration had changed from Irish to Italian to Jewish, with each one labeled in turn as lazy, dirty, and corrupt. Yet, "All alike they have taken, or are taking, their places in our social phalanx pushing upward with steady effort."

As the immigrants pushed upward, men's lives and women's lives continued to be pushed farther and farther apart. De Tocqueville, who visited the United States in 1830–31, noticed the change that became even more firmly established as time went on: "In no country has such constant care been taken as in America to trace two clearly distinct lines of action for the two sexes. . . . American women never manage the outward concerns of the family, or conduct a business, or take a part in political life; nor are they, on the other hand, ever compelled to perform the rough labor of the fields, or to make any of those laborious exertions which demand the exertion of physical strength. No families are so poor as to form an exception to this rule."

Poor women were invisible to de Tocqueville, yet immigrant women—the most overburdened members of the family—struggled to be both wage earners and mothers, muddling the supposedly universal "separate spheres." To the middle-class charity workers imbued with the importance of the separation of home and work, poor women were outside the social order. "The social and moral life of a smaller family where the father earns enough to support wife and children, and where the mother can devote her time to the care of them, and where neither she nor the children go out and help in the support of the family, is superior to that of a family with a large number of children where the wife and often the older children must slave," one wrote. Of course, they understood it was sometimes economically necessary for women and children to work, but that situation had no uplifting moral value.

A few women were able to see beyond the limitations of their cultural background. Mary Simkhovitch of New York's Greenwich House recognized that the woman who "slaved" often had some advantages over her more fortunate, ornamental "sister." "The position of the mother was a strong one," she wrote, "much stronger than often obtains in families of a higher economic order. . . . The family economy depends on her interests, skills and sense of order . . . in her humble status, her position is thoroughly dignified."

Goblins in the Mills

Outside the big cities some immigrant children and their mothers worked nights as well as days—not at home, but in the New England and, occasionally, Southern textile mills, taking the place, in the North, of the young women who had organized reading clubs and asserted their rights as workers while toiling thirteen hours a day. When they went on to marry or teach school, desperate immigrants filled their jobs.

In the South, mothers and children from the back country worked alongside the immigrants. Edwin Markham, whose poem "The Man with the Hoe" was seized on as exemplifying the plight of exploited workers everywhere, described the scene at one Southern cotton mill this way: "We find a gaunt goblin army of children keeping their forced march on the factory floors—an army that outwatches the sun by day and the stars by night . . . a spectral army of pigmy people." As at home, older members of the family were expected to work with and supervise the "goblins," whether they worked at night or during the day. In New England, the immigrants were chiefly Irish or French-Canadian; in the South they were likely to be European, supplementing the lean and hungry hill people who came into town to substitute one hardscrabble life for another.

Mill work had a long tradition. Samuel Slater, who started the first American spinning mill in 1790, listed a mother, father, and two children among his first workers. The Mouton family, which included six children, was paid $58.62 a month for a minimum of twelve hours a day in 1827. Most child workers in the early mills were between seven and twelve years old, and the system of allowing mothers to have "helpers" put children as young as three and four to work. Although the toddlers were not paid, they increased the mother's output and thereby the meager family income. Keeping them with her meant they had at least minimal care.

Child labor was justified not only because it kept idle hands occupied and was therefore a moral good, but because it was economically necessary for the nation. A report of a Massachusetts commission in 1830 reflected the economic view that was as respectable as the moral one and cast a long shadow down through the years, perpetuating child labor even when common human feeling deplored it: "Labor being dearer in this country than it is in any other with which we are brought in competition in manufacturing, operates as a constant inducement to manufacturers to employ female labor, and the labor of children, to the exclusion of men's labor, because they can be had cheaper." "There was," wrote Edith Abbott in her study of women in industry published in 1910, "a general acceptance of the propriety of children's labor in the early days of the factory system." Part of this acceptance came from a false analogy: Children working on family farms learned valuable skills and lessons in diligence and perseverance; therefore it was good for children to work, even in factories. But factory work—even though, like farm work, it might keep the family together—taught nothing but how to live with dullness and exhaustion. It was not like apprenticeship, universally praised earlier as a way to teach a child a trade. As a matter of fact, by this time, local child labor laws prohibited apprenticeship "in all skilled trades" for children under sixteen. Responses by legislators to factory work by children were less humane.

Inventors were praised and rewarded if they devised machines that could be used by children. Carding, roving, and spinning machines were designed to be separate, so that the carding could be done by a girl or woman, with the yarn fed into it by a child, and both the roving and the spinning could be done by a child alone. There were some early efforts to make twelve the minimum age, but this was often ignored or evaded. Need was the mother of mendacity. One boy, when asked how old he was, answered, "I'm ten on the outside but twelve in the mill." Some boys were so small they had to climb on the spinning frame to reach the broken threads and put back the bobbins.

Despite compulsory education laws (starting as early as 1836 in Massachusetts), school was a luxury few could afford, and mothers felt forced to keep their children with them, at work. A mill worker in 1891 lamented, "I am a widow, with three children—two boys and one girl. I am not able to send my children to school. I have to work and have them work. This is a cause of grief to me, as they are bright children and would be smart in books if they had a chance."

When reformers tried to prohibit night work in the factories, working mothers protested. "I am strong and healthy and I am glad to work and take care of my children. Else what will become of them? . . . They might shut down and then [pointing to the little girl] she will have nothing to eat and nothing to wear. I don't want to have to work days, as then my children are alone." Another added, "I want to work nights so I can take care of my children in the day. Why ain't men's pay more so women wouldn't have to work?" The women averaged four and a half hours of sleep a day, in one-hour snatches. Their children learned to keep quiet, or play outdoors.

Mill families sometimes lived in subsidized housing provided by the owners; this was intended to keep them available and docile. Yet they were willing to risk the owners' wrath to keep their children safe. After a smallpox scare at one mill, forty workers refused to go back to work or to allow their children to return. The manager "gave them fifteen minutes to get back into the Mill, and also told the parents that if they didn't send their children in the Mill immediately, that they would have to vacate our houses at once. All came back in time, and I let them all go to work except the one that started the bolt—I discharged him and have made him get out of the company's house."

Certain Unalienable Rights

Such absolute power of one man over another's life and family was uncomfortably close to slavery. After the Civil War the country began to reexamine and reaffirm the basic premises on which this nation had been founded. Since all men were created equal and had certain unalienable rights, social visionaries argued that women, children, immigrants, freed slaves, the mentally ill, prisoners, and other neglected segments of society had to be included in the American dream. A spur to the reformers was the decreasing emphasis on original sin and the optimistic view that man could evolve. Jacob Riis put it this way: "The child is a creature of environment." Change the conditions in which a child grows up, and you change the child.

The revolutionary idea that childhood was a sacred time, and that children had rights, formed the moral basis for a reform movement that gradually reduced the involvement of children in the labor force. In earlier times, parents and masters had had obligations toward their children; now, the children themselves had expectations that they would be treated with consideration. Felix Adler, chairman of the National Child Labor Committee and founder of the Ethical Culture Society, placed the reform movement squarely in the American tradition: "Child labor is intolerable and unjustifiable namely, because it is contradictory to the dominant principle, the fundamental idea of the civilization which is being developed on this continent. That dominant principle is the moral equality of all human beings, the right of each human being to develop freely." Child labor prevented this and stunted "mental and moral growth and that is the unpardonable offense."

Child labor, both by definition and in the reality of long hours and deadening monotony, was an evil to be destroyed as slavery had been. In 1908 the National Child Labor Committee, dedicated to eradicating the evil through federal legislation, published a "Declaration of Independence by the Children of America in Mines and Factories and Work-Shops Assembled":

> *Resolved 1, that childhood is endowed with certain inalienable rights, among which are the right to childhood itself; the right to play and to dream; the right to the normal sleep of childhood, during the night season; and the right to an education that we may have equality of opportunity for developing that there is in us of mind and heart.*

The crusaders had occasional successes and predictable setbacks, but by the 1920s the number of children from ten to fourteen years old in nonagricultural jobs had dropped by two-thirds. Despite the protestations of social reformers that local and state regulations were inadequate and "when an evil is a national evil, it must be cured by a national remedy," it was not until 1938 and the Fair Labor Standards Act, which prohibited products made by children in interstate commerce, that child labor was really outlawed nationwide. Its widespread use had, by then, virtually disappeared, hastened by the changing face of manufacturing and a tendency for children to stay in school longer as well as by the efforts at reform.

Some of the reformers were motivated as much by economic realities as by human kindness. Organized labor in the person of Samuel Gompers argued against child labor as early as the turn of the century, pointing out that working children and women took jobs away from men. The argument was even then an old one. As early as 1836 a report of the Massachusetts Committee on Female Labor pointed out that working women not only took jobs from men, they neglected their children. "The physical organization, the natural responsibilities, and the moral sensibility of women, prove conclusively that her labors should be only of a domestic nature." By the 1930s, when the National Recovery Act under Franklin D. Roosevelt prohibited homework, the sweatshop ended, and the option of working while staying home with the children became more elusive.

The middle-class ideal of the sacred family with the father its sole support became the ideal for all Americans. Not all could achieve it, of course. Many married women who had had to work alongside their children had understandably longed for an easier life, but found it hard to find. Some eventually worked part-time in service jobs. They tried to balance economic reality with the injunction that they should concentrate on family responsibilities. Those who were able to enter the world of nonworking middle-class women—or whose daughters were—paid an unexpected price. They left behind some of the power they had had as economically important contributors to the family. As Mary Simkhovitch of New York's Greenwich House discovered, the immigrant mother had a position of power. She "paid not only the rent, insurance and food, but also bought the family's clothing and gave the husband and children enough for carfare and lunches. This built up a solid family life, where each was dependent on the other."

But this interdependence stunted children who had to work instead of play or go to school. The mothers who worked beside them were often so overburdened that child care deteriorated into simple survival, and even that primary goal was elusive. The one misfortune that was avoided was separation of mother and child, a misfortune that overtook some children of immigrants sent far from their parents to homes in the country in a well-meaning effort by reformers such as Charles Loring Brace to better their lives.

THE SETTLEMENT HOUSE SOLUTION

From the first it seemed understood that we were ready to perform the humblest neighborhood services. We were asked to wash the newborn babies, and to prepare the dead for burial, to nurse the sick, and to "mind the children."

—*JANE ADDAMS OF HULL-HOUSE*

SCIENCE, philanthropy, social conscience, and practicality coalesced in the settlement house—a "settlement" of educated do-gooders in the midst of the slum. Jane Addams was the mother of the movement, "an experimental effort to aid in the solution of the social and industrial problems which are engendered by the modern conditions of life in a great city." When she and her friend Ellen Starr moved into a run-down mansion on Halsted Street in Chicago in 1889 only one other settlement house was operating in this country, and Hull-House soon became the most famous and the most influential. The house itself was one of the few buildings in the area to survive the Great Chicago Fire of 1875, which had begun a few blocks away.

Eighteen nations were represented in the neighborhood. The melting-pot ideal embraced by the settlement house reformers offered hope that they could be blended into one, and appealed to a country only recently recovered from the shattering divisions of the Civil War. Wounds had to be healed. It was clear that all Americans must put aside their differences and merge into one country or the nation could not endure. In 1892, just three years after Hull-House started and four hundred years after Columbus's voyage, the pledge of allegiance to the flag was first published in the popular children's magazine *Youth's Companion*. The words "one nation, indivisible, with liberty and justice for all" ("under God" was added later) reflected the hope that the United States would survive the influx of foreigners as it had the Southern rebellion. Between 1880 and World War I, 17 million immigrants landed on this nation's shores.

They crowded into cities such as Chicago. "Little idea can be given," Addams wrote, "of the numbers of children filling every nook, working and playing in every room, eating and sleeping in every window-sill, pouring in and out of every door, and seeming literally to pave every scrap of yard."

Hull-House seemed the perfect place to bring different peoples together and to put into effect new ideas about children and about poverty. Darwin's theories had put mankind squarely within the spectrum of the animal kingdom: The world was evolving into a better place, and the child was its chief hope; it could be changed by changing its environment. Followers of Auguste Comte, the French philosopher who coined the term "sociology," had earlier rejected metaphysics and embraced modern science as the way to reform society. Poverty was not evidence of Providence's displeasure, but the result of social circumstances—and when society changed these circumstances, most poverty would disappear.

Together, these two streams generated the conviction that human intelligence could change the human condition. The new thinking proposed that children come down, as Walt Whitman put it, "from the showered halo and the moonbeams." They were not only angelic, they were infinitely malleable. Social Darwinism, an early offshoot of Darwinian theory that saw people and society as limited by intrinsic forces and shaped by the survival of the fittest, did not fit the optimism of the day. "The [old] notion of biological heredity and of innate capacity, as a determining factor, would have a paralyzing effect upon the young social worker," the director of one of the newly established schools of social work declared. "Without the hope and courage which the new theories of social causation and social control give, no one would long endure social work."

These new theories cast a long shadow. The belief in the "inherent (or at least potential) goodness of the child, and in the vulnerability of the child to environmental badness (including inept parentage) has pervaded our assumptions about children through the past hundred years. . . . The child is a cultural invention as well as a cultural product," points out Dr. Lloyd J. Borstelmann, who has studied changing attitudes about children from antiquity to the twentieth century.

The cultural climate of optimism at the turn of the century and a new faith in science were beginning to nudge religion to the sidelines. George Bernard Shaw complained, "There is nothing that people will not believe nowadays if only it be presented to them as Science, and nothing they will not disbelieve if it be presented to them as religion." Science would solve the problems of the world, answer all the unanswered questions, and provide unassailable guidelines. Hull-House attempted to reconcile the new with the old. It was to practice "scientific charity" while at the same time embracing the principles of Christian Socialism, the application of Jesus' teachings to the practical world. The settlement workers would do sensible good for rational reasons, and this would lead mankind to the kingdom of heaven.

They certainly tried, eventually mapping the area they served so they would know who lived where, what services were available, and what the needs were. They applied scientific child-rearing principles, recognizing, as Addams said, that they must "follow the development of the child; . . . expect certain traits under certain conditions; . . . adapt methods and matter to his growing mind."

Once these methods were clearly understood all that remained would be to apply them to the child (Addams never had children of her own) and the world would be a better place. The movement toward a scientific attitude about how children grow was given impetus by Bronson Alcott, Louisa May's father. He meticulously recorded her development day by day, convinced that he would thereby understand the metamorphosis from babbling infant to intelligent child and influence her to become perfect. Child-study groups sprang up around the country, and children became the subject of scientific inquiry. As early as 1888 some upper-middle-class New York mothers joined together as the "Society for the Study of Child Nature." By the end of the century, specialized child-study journals were being published by universities and professional organizations. Child rearing was a rational process, the thinking ran, and now that scientific attitudes had revolutionized medicine and technology, they would soon revolutionize human development. In France, Louis Pasteur had recently proved that microorganisms caused disease; in Germany, Robert Koch had demonstrated his test for tuberculosis; and anesthesia was for the first time making surgery less excruciating. With this sweep of progress, life itself seemed on the threshold of yielding to systematic investigation and improvement.

Remarkable Women: Jo's Girls

At Hull-House Jane Addams gathered around her a new generation of new women. They were the first to go to college in significant numbers (in 1870 there were only 1,378 college women; by 1893 the number had tripled; by 1900 women made up 40 percent of those who graduated from institutions of higher learning), the first to stand on the shoulders of women's rights pioneers such as Susan B. Anthony and Elizabeth Cady Stanton, and the first to forge acceptable lives outside the bounds of domesticity. Like almost half of their college-educated contemporaries, most of the women at Hull-House never married. One member of the core group—Florence Kelley—had been married and had three children, but she was divorced and liberated far in advance of her time. She was also financially independent. In 1893 Hull-House had fifteen residents. By 1900 the number had more than doubled. A few men joined the group, but they were always a small minority. The women ran the show. They chose a new, independent way of life, free of the demands of homemaking and children, and made it socially acceptable by, ironically, doing what traditional women did—nurturing the poor, the neglected, the young. They were able to find a niche in American society during a transitional period, when women were poised on the edge of reaching for roles wider than those of hallowed mother and wife. It was a time when, as the historian Christopher Lasch put it, "The discovery of the poor was bound up with the discovery of the self."

They depended on a community of women. Grace Abbott, who campaigned against the exploitation of children as the first director of the child labor division of the U.S. Children's Bureau (established in 1912), remembered it this way: "There was a residents' dining-room where we had dinner together and a residents' breakfast table in the public coffee-shop—where we argued in relays, over the morning newspapers. Although we were a large group of residents, we were a kind of family group together." Mary Jo Deegan, a sociologist who studied Hull-House, called it a "commune." Others have likened it to a college dormitory. The women lived together without having to bother with individual housekeeping or cooking or child care. Like their New England contemporaries, some established "Boston Marriages"—close, continuing, loving relationships that may or may not have been given physical expression. Jane Addams, in a break from her serious duties, wrote lighthearted affectionate poems for the birthdays of Hull-House "sisters." They sustained and supported each other while forging satisfying lives as "spinsters" at a time when most women were still dedicated to being virtuous wives. The settlement women were, in a way, heirs of Jo in Louisa May Alcott's 1869 autobiographical novel *Little Women*, whose tomboyish independence and literary ambitions captivated Jane Addams as they did generations of girls after her. Freed by communal living arrangements and industrial advances that provided such time-savers as ready-made clothing and the telephone, the independent women at Hull-House could concentrate on their careers and their contributions to the larger society.

And what contributions they were! They gathered statistics, wrote articles and books, poked into factories and tenements, and lobbied locally and in Washington for their causes. They transformed the information they collected into action. Julia Lathrop became the first head of the Federal Children's Bureau. Alice Hamilton, a doctor, relentlessly exposed the connection between disease and disability and poverty. Florence Kelley pioneered in the crusade against child labor. Jane Addams fought the Chicago political bosses and helped set up the first public playground and the first juvenile court. She became the charismatic guiding force for a whole social movement dedicated to transforming the lives of the poor.

How did these properly brought up, eminently ladylike women accomplish what amounted to a social revolution in the days before they even had the vote? Historians are divided on the answer. Some say they moved into a vacuum left by men who were busy making money rather than exercising political power to deal with pressing social problems. Others point out that the areas in which they worked—the welfare of children, hygiene, the problems of immigrants—were extensions of women's traditional concerns. They did not so much challenge existing women's activities as expand them from private to more public concerns. No longer "lady bountifuls," they were still ladies, and still in a woman's place, taking care of the children, the poor, the benighted. When Jane Addams was only twenty years old she recognized that women were better at "civic housekeeping" than men, who tend to concentrate on the military or the national income. As long as women stuck to "housekeeping," they were beyond criticism, even when that housekeeping swept away at serious social problems. She saw a way to thrust women's nurturing into the wider arena: "So we have planned to be 'Bread

Givers' throughout our lives," she wrote, "believing that in labor alone is happiness, and that the only true and honorable life is one filled with good works and honest toil, we have planned to idealize our labor, and thus happily fulfill Women's Noblest Mission."

Jane Addams

Born just before the Civil War in Cedarville, Illinois, Jane Addams grappled in her own life with many of the problems that tormented other privileged women of her time. She graduated from Rockford Seminary, started medical school, and then dropped out because she was immobilized by physical and mental breakdowns. Like Alice James, Henry James's talented but unfulfilled sister, she became an invalid and for two years was rudderless, not knowing what she wanted to do or how she should go about doing it. Then she traveled to Europe on trips designed to restore her health and had her first encounter with overwhelming urban poverty in London's dismal Whitechapel district. Toynbee Hall, the pioneering settlement house there, seemed to her "perfectly ideal." It was a community of young college-educated men who lived in the slums "yet in the same style they would live in their own circle. It is so free from 'professional do-ing good,' so unaffectedly sincere and so productive of good results in its classes and libraries" that it offered her a model for her own life.

It was part of a wider movement to change the lives of the poor, not by benevolence from afar, but by living among them. Tolstoy, whom Addams had read and was later to meet, had discarded the trappings of Russian wealth to dress like a peasant and work among them. Influenced by him as well as by Toynbee Hall, she resolved to put her ideals and knowledge into action in the slums of Chicago, and in 1889 established Hull-House with Ellen Starr, who had been one of her traveling companions. They displayed heirloom silver in the dining room to introduce the poor immigrants to the finer things in life. Addams envisioned the settlement as serving two pur-poses: It would help the poor "Germans and Bohemians and Italians and Poles and Russians and Greeks and Arabs in Chicago, vainly try-ing to adjust their peasant habits to the life of a large city," while at the same time giving privileged young women a purpose and a place. She would save not only the downtrodden, but also the "invalid girls" pushed into neurosis, as she had been, because they saw no way to use themselves. "I have seen young girls suffer and grow sensibly lowered in vitality in the first years after they leave school," she wrote. "In our attempt then to give a girl pleasure and freedom from care we succeed, for the most part, in making her pitifully miserable. . . . They [young women] hear constantly of the great social maladjustment, but no way is provided for them to change it." She began her dual crusade as what one Chicago club woman described in wonder as a "frail, sensitive girl," and matured into a matronly agent of reform. Addams and her followers saw that if they were to go beyond the tradition of being lady bountifuls they must learn from the people they served. The lessons began early. Soon after Hull-House opened, they held a Christmas party for neighborhood children. Candy was to be the great treat. To their dismay, many of the children refused it in disgust. They learned that the underage youngsters worked sixteen hours a day in a neighborhood caramel factory to earn pennies to help their families survive. Child labor laws became a vital part of the wider agenda of the Hull-House group.

Another item on their agenda was to move immigrants from their cramped, insular lives into the wider world. In many cases, they succeeded. Hilda Satt Polacheck, one of the neighborhood children, credited Hull-House with introducing her to music and politics and beauty and making a reality of the American dream that all peoples can live together. At another Christmas party, one which this Hungarian Jewish child attended only after a Christian friend assured her she would not be killed there, she discovered that "we were all poor. Some of us were underfed. Some of us had holes in our shoes. But we were not afraid of each other. What greater service can a human being give to her country than to banish fear from the heart of a child? Jane Addams did that for me at that party."

The social ends she embraced made Addams a prime mover in the first "mother's pension" law and other legislation to protect women and children. She did not shy away from controversy and was seen in her long life (she died in 1935) as everything from "Saint Jane" and the *Ladies' Home Journal*'s Foremost Living Woman to "the most dangerous woman in America" as a result of her stand against World War I and her continuing pacifism and support of radical causes. In 1912 she made the seconding speech for the the nomination of Theodore Roosevelt for president by the breakaway Progressive party eight years before women had the vote by constitutional amendment. (Six western states had already taken the forward step, one at a time.) For the Progressives this was the worst of times. They believed that "the majority of our people are more unsatisfied with conditions than at any time in our history since the Revolutionary War. Some are asking for one kind of change and some for another; but all demand change—progress toward conditions under which they can live better and enjoy more fully the fruits of their toil." Roosevelt was, however, unable to capitalize on this discontent, and he lost the election. Soon Jane Addams's reputation was tarnished by her pacifism, but as the reality of World War I receded, she again became respectable. In 1931 she was awarded the Nobel Prize for Peace along with Nicholas Murray Butler. The award, which linked her with the president of Columbia University, a well-known anti-Semite, was seen by some as only grudging recognition of her work in the Women's International League for Peace and Freedom.

Despite the ups and downs of her reputation, more has been written about Jane Addams than any other American woman. Yet relatively few Americans know who she was. The memory of her life has been relegated to the historical dustbin in which this country stores its forgotten past.

Minding the Children

The forgetfulness extends not only to Addams herself, but to the child-care programs she and other settlement house leaders established almost one hundred years ago. Their day nurseries provided care for young children from the time a mother went to work until she came back at night. There was drop-off care for a few hours, care for sick children, and twenty-four-hour care, if necessary. Children were fed nutritious hot meals. Babies as young as two weeks were accepted if there was real need, parents were involved as teaching assistants and in parent education classes, and caretakers made home visits to provide carryover in the child's life. Today, day-care advocates are rediscovering programs such as these as if they were untried and unproven—the national amnesia again. The philanthropic day nurseries of the late nineteenth and early twentieth centuries, supported by private contributions, were criticized as the condescending meddling of well-meaning wealthy women in the lives of the poor. But, as Margaret O'Brien Steinfels reported in her book *Who's Minding the Children?: The History and Politics of Day Care in America,* "In retrospect their creation seems flexible, practical and, above all, genuinely responsive to the needs of working mothers."

Hull-House's day nursery grew accidentally, out of necessity. Shortly after the settlement opened in 1889 Ellen Starr wrote to her parents, "We are getting on well with the 'Neighboring' . . . a woman . . . has requested to leave her baby with us one morning while she moved her household effects. Miss Blaisdell took care of the Creche, as we called baby Marcus. He was very good." Mothers needed not only short-term care for their children, but some place to leave them while they worked twelve-hour days. Many were single parents because of death or desertion, or women who were forced to support their families because of an unemployed, dissolute, or sick husband. Addams was distressed and shocked to hear of children locked in their tenement apartment with a bowl of porridge on the table in case they got hungry while their widowed mother worked. She was told they banged on the door calling "Let me out, let me out" until they were tired enough to crawl onto the bed their mother had made for them. One of the most pitiful cases was that of a little boy who had spent all day for three years locked in a tenement kitchen, tied to the leg of a table to keep him safe. His older brother rushed in at noon from his factory job to release him briefly and give him lunch. The confinement crippled him, Addams was told.

In a reversal of the cold-weather system, children were locked out of the steamy tenement rooms in the summer. Their worried mothers did not dare leave the doors open for fear of thieves, and the children balked at the heat and stuffiness, so they wandered the streets and sometimes slipped into the cool hallway of Hull-House. When they were fed dinner at noon, some of them opened their fists and offered a penny they had kept safe "for something to eat" since their mother had left in the morning. During the day, they were effectively motherless.

Jane Addams was herself a truly motherless child. Her mother died when she was two and a half years old. When she was six, her older sister Martha, who had stepped into the mothering role, was killed by typhoid fever. Judged too young to go to the funeral, Jane stayed home alone. She later told another sister, "My horrible dream every night would be Martha's death and no one to love me." She understood children who were left alone.

It was clear that Hull-House's informal arrangement of having a volunteer watch the children in one bedroom or another had to be replaced by a more systematic approach. Churches and charitable associations, as Jane Addams knew, ran day nurseries for the children of working mothers, and Boston had established one as early as 1828. In New York in 1891 as many as five thousand "babies" were cared for by a single philanthropy. In New England, dame schools had regularly taken very young children. A woman who began school at "Aunt Hannah's" when she was two years old explained, "The mothers of those large families had to resort to some means of keeping their little ones out of mischief, while they attended to their domestic duties. . . . If a baby's head nodded [at school], a little bed was made for it on a soft 'comforter' in the corner, where it had its nap out undisturbed."

A continuing debate raged about whether or not out-of-home care was good for children. Penny-pinching critics also pointed out that poor children could already be cared for in almshouses and orphanages, and said that nurseries would only encourage fathers to desert or default on their financial responsibilities. But Jane Addams knew that mothers who had to work needed a way to keep their little ones out of mischief and safe from harm even more than mothers who stayed home. With her usual inspired simplicity she moved briskly in Hull-House's second year to set up a day nursery in an apartment in the house. It then moved to a six-room frame cottage on a side street, and finally into a building of its own. Most of the costs were borne by one of her wealthy friends.

The nursery was seen as a substitute for institutionalization by making it possible for a family to stay together even if the mother worked. It was an answer to a new need, as old family institutions crumbled under the pressure of immigration and industrialization made it possible for a needy mother to find work outside the home. And mothers had to work, since no public assistance was available to feed or clothe children whose parents could not support them. The irony of this reality was not lost on Addams. "It is curiously inconsistent that with the emphasis which this generation has placed upon the mother and upon the prolongation of infancy, we constantly allow the waste of this most precious material." From what she had seen in the slums of Chicago, she was convinced that it was a "wretched delusion that a woman can both support and nurture her children." For women who were forced by necessity to be breadwinners, the day nursery was a savior—but a temporary one. Her hope was that eventually society would pick up its proper share of the burden and provide financial help for mothers in need so they could stay home.

A mother paid five cents a day to leave her child at the crèche—the French word for day nursery. Mrs. S., whose gambling husband had deserted her, but who kept hoping he would return, brought her "three delicate children every morning to the nursery; she is bent under the double burden of earning the money which supports them and giving them the tender care which keeps them alive." The doors opened at seven in the morning, and the children stayed until they could be picked up—5:00 P.M. or later. The program was in session in all seasons, and every day except Sunday. In summer average attendance was fifty children; in winter there were between thirty and forty. Health was a great concern. The summer of 1896 was "remarkably healthy," a report said, because the children spent one day a week in the parks during July and August. Every Tuesday morning at nine they went off in a bus, had a picnic lunch, napped on the grass, and returned to the settlement house at six o'clock. Fresh air, the new science of hygiene declared, would help the children withstand the onslaughts of disease that decimated youngsters in the crowded, dirty, fetid tenements.

In later years, the nursery became part of the United Charities of Chicago, which screened the participants for health, financial need, and suitability. This entangled Addams in a dilemma that foreshadows today's questions about AIDS and children in school. Because of the screening, a little girl whose mother had syphilis—the sexual plague of the time—was identified. The director of the nursery forbade the teacher to admit any children "where there is known to be syphilis in the family regardless of whether the disease is in an infectious stage or not." No matter that syphilis, like AIDS, is not spread by casual contact. The fear and stigma attached to the parent were passed on to the child. No matter that "many children in many nursery schools may come from homes where there is syphilis but the facts in regard to this are not known and so the children are allowed to attend." Addams was asked to convene a meeting to discuss the matter with a medical expert; the results are not available.

In the nursery, an experienced teacher and two assistants tried to provide an atmosphere that would not only substitute for home, but improve on it. Although most day nurseries were content to provide only custodial care, Hull-House had loftier ideas. One of the missions was to give poor immigrants a glimpse of the world's cultural riches, and this began as early as possible. Pictures of Raphael's Madonnas and reproductions of plaques of the Virgin and Child by

Donatello and Della Robbia were hung low enough on the walls of the nursery for the children to see them easily. "The children talk in a familiar way to the babies on the wall," Jane Addams reported, "and sometimes climb upon the chairs to kiss them. Surely much is gained if one can begin in a very little child to make a truly beautiful thing truly beloved."

No paintings of fathers adorned the walls. Fathers were often seen as the problem, rather than a part of the solution. They gambled away their money (like Mr. S.), or drank too much, or disappeared. They kicked pregnant women in the stomach and caused miscarriages, and children died because they "wouldn't let me send for the doctor, there was no money to pay for the medicine."

Some women stayed with husbands who were clearly unsuitable. One stuck it out while her children were small because she was always proud of her husband's "good looks and educated appearance." Another fooled herself again and again that her hard-drinking husband would be redeemed by taking the pledge before the priest. She continued to support her three children. Jane Addams was impressed by these mistaken, "heroic women." She even had an understanding of the wayward men, based on her belief that environment, not depravity or bad genes, was often the basis for poverty. They were "sorry men who, for one reason or another, had failed in the struggle of life. Sometimes this failure was purely economic." One woman who had been an early nursery mother reported later what had happened to her five children after she "got tired of taking care of him" and left her husband, saying she would support only her children. "All of them except Mary have been arrested at one time or another," she told Addams. Without a father's firm hand, the four boys got into serious trouble. "I tell you," she said, "I ain't so sure that because a woman can make big money that she can be both father and mother to her children."

One of the children in the day nursery came to a tragic end as his mother struggled to care for him and work, too. Every day she wrapped him in her shawl and carried him to Hull-House. The children called him "Goosie" because he was covered with the feathers that clung to him from the shawl his mother wore at work in a brush factory. As she hung out the wash at six o'clock one March morning, he was literally blown off the roof. She called to him to "climb up again . . . so confident do overworked mothers become that their children cannot get hurt." But his neck was broken. After the tragedy, as the mother sat forlornly in the nursery, Addams asked if there was anything she could do to help. The woman wanted only one thing—a day's wages, so she could miss the next day at work. "I would like to stay home all day and hold the baby. Goosie was always asking me to hold him and I never had any time."

The nursery was not just a place where babies could be held and mothers could be helped. It was also the first step on the road to Americanization. Children were to be introduced to good hygiene, good manners, and proper eating habits and helped to shed the foreign, superstitious, unhealthy attitudes of their peasant backgrounds. They were regularly given good scrubbings, since, as the head of the New York Day Nursery Association put it, the child "is someday to be an American citizen, and to this end it ought to be given the trend toward personal cleanliness and order." Obviously, parents (read "mothers") had to be educated, too—and parent education was built in from the beginning. As Addams wrote, "The chief objective of our parent education is to raise the standards of living and especially child care through mediums that are comprehensible to our type of parents."

To accomplish this, each mother was asked to provide a daily report on her child's activities—such things as bedtime and the all-important bowel movements. Consciousness was raised about the need for regularity in both. Weekly mothers' meetings included instruction in making children's clothes, American style, and preparing American foods. For some the meetings were the only respite in a burdened life. "Through this medicine the faces of the mothers have been noticeably softened," Addams reported.

Since few of the mothers spoke much English, it was thought best to begin simply—with instructions for making the children's favorite school dessert, chocolate pudding. The mothers "immediately began telling how their children had asked for it. Now they said, 'I make it.' " They were taught lullabies and encouraged to take advantage of the free health examinations and instruction in the best way to care for children. Instead of hanging bags of salt around their children's necks to ward off the evil eye (and prevent the crippling effects of rickets), they were induced to substitute cod-liver oil, without any direct attempt to discredit the superstition or the belief that disease was the work of Providence. The aim was to help parents recognize problems and get help for them. "We have tried to accomplish this," a report said, "through the Nursery School as an extension of the home and the child as the 'bridge,' so to speak, back to the parent's heart and interest."

Addams saw not only that children were influenced by their parents and caretakers, but that children influenced the adults, and the nursery took advantage of this reality. "The wonderful devotion of the child seems, at times, in the midst of our stupid social and industrial arrangement, all that keeps society human, the touch of nature which unites it, as it was the same devotion which first lifted us out of the swamp of bestiality." The attitudes and manners the children learned in the nursery would help their parents, too, blend in with the New World.

It wasn't long before the nursery school idea spread in Chicago, but it was sometimes distorted to put the emphasis on economic gain rather than children's welfare. Working mothers needed care for their children, and profits could be made by charging a small sum or soliciting money by going door to door for "charitable" contributions. In 1917 the Juvenile Protective Association (started by one of the women of Hull-House) found one hundred commercialized "baby farms" with "deplorable" conditions. A few years later, investigating a dozen new complaints, they found children unclean and crowded into one small room without any playthings, and several nurseries in which the "superintendent" did not even know the last names and addresses of some of the children. The privately run agencies charged with supervision of the nurseries excused their deficiencies as the result of World War I, which made finding adequate staff and space difficult.

Meanwhile, the Hull-House nursery continued to meet the needs of the poor women in its district. But times were changing. Some of the broad social reforms for which Addams and her compatriots had worked so hard were becoming realities. In 1925, the United Charities suggested that its part in the nursery should end because of "the greatly increased amount of money which is being given to families [Mothers' Pensions, for example, given to widows with children, another Hull-House project, amounted to $750,000, although it did not nearly meet the need] and the greater efficiency of all the social agencies dealing with the families around the nursery." The profound change in attitude about the need to keep the mother at home so she could care for her own children owed at least as much to the professionalization of social work as to any philosophical transformation. As schools to train social workers became established, specialization within the field led to the creation of family social work. With professional help available to keep families together, and the establishment of what seemed a benign bureaucracy, the need for a place for children to stay while the mother worked seemed to have diminished. The family—even what today would be called a "dysfunctional family"—was seen as the place for children to grow up. There was, of course, still a need for education and health care, and the report suggested that Hull-House should carry on with these in its own nursery, without the help of United Charities.

The shift in attitude and emphasis from care outside the home to care within it had begun years before the United Charities' move. In 1905 Dr. Lee J. Frankel told the conference of the National Feder-ation of Day Nurseries that "the Day Nursery is only a make-shift. The great issue is the family, and the proper place for development is the home." (Of course, at that time and a decade earlier, children of immigrants were kept at home—but to work, not "develop.") By 1915, Dr. Carolyn Hedger was ready to go even further in criticizing care for very young children. She said, "It takes mother-love, mother arms, mother breast and considerable common sense to grow a hu-man properly for the first nine months, and no institution, no matter how scientific, how philanthropic, can replace these things."

The Children's Garden

After infancy, however, a child might benefit from scientific care out-side a mother's benevolent arms for part of each day. The experts seized on the kindergarten as the best way to improve children so they could improve the world, and by the time settlement houses were firmly established at the end of the nineteenth century, the kindergarten was an accepted fact of life for many poor city children.

Jane Addams needed no prodding to apply the power of the kindergarten to the task of molding the poor, immigrant children of Chicago. Within two weeks of moving into Hull-House, she started one with a trained teacher and enthusiastic support from John Dewey, a University of Chicago professor and member of the first board of directors of Hull-House.

The kindergarten came to this country when Germans fleeing the aftermath of the 1848 revolution brought with them the revolu-tionary ideas of Friedrich Froebel. Froebel believed that young chil-dren learned by doing, and that they learned through play. He saw the function of education as "deliverance." Toys were not frivolous; they were important aids to child development. In a "children's gar-den" (kindergarten) the child would grow to be the best that it could be. His ideas owed something both to Rousseau and to Pestalozzi, who believed in the innate goodness of the unspoiled child.

The practical German idea of the kindergarten fit neatly with the theoretical concepts of the influential, pioneering American psychologist G. Stanley Hall, who invited Freud to make his first visit to this country. Child rearing, Hall believed, was a science, and too difficult to be left to bumbling mothers who operated on intuition rather than scientific principles. Children developed in stages, and each stage had its expectations and requirements. Parents (read "mothers" again) had to be educated to respond appropriately to the child at each stage, or their offspring would fail to fulfill their potential. The idea of the "educated mother" was born. Hall's influence spread into the next generation through his students, who included Lewis Terman, the originator of the American version of the IQ test, and John Dewey, father of progressive education. In the Progressive Era of political and social change, when concerns that had previously been private moved into the public arena, the obligation to help children develop according to scientific principles expanded from being the mother's to being society's as well. The country needed not only educated mothers, but also educated teachers and educated lawmakers. Jacob Riis saw this when he wrote, in 1892, "The problem of the children is the problem of the State. As we mould the children of the toiling masses, in our cities, so we shape the destiny of the State which they will rule in their turn, taking the reins from our hands."

In this country, the kindergarten (run by private, charitable organizations at first, and then picked up by the public schools) was seized on as a way of dealing with a major social problem—how to assimilate the children of immigrants now crowding these shores. By 1862 the word had come into the language, and the number of kindergartens grew along with the number of immigrants: In 1875 there were 75 kindergartens; in 1880, 348; in 1890, 1,311; and by 1900, with the flood of immigrants, there were 5,000. Society had once again approved what it needed to care for its children and embraced the kindergarten. The first president of the New York Kindergarten Association put it this way: "The kindergarten age marks our earliest opportunity to catch the little Russian, the little Italian . . . and begin to make good American citizens of them. The children are brought into a new social order; they are taught to have regard for one another, and they do acquire such regard along with a new and highly valuable respect for law and order."

Black women saw the value of the kindergarten as a way of

breaking down barriers. In 1898, Anna Evans Murray of the Colored Women's League in Washington, D.C., worked successfully to have twelve thousand dollars in federal funds appropriated for kindergartens in the district's public schools. "The real solution of the race problem lies in the children," one of her colleagues asserted, "both so far as we who are oppressed and those who oppress us are concerned." And, as had happened with day nurseries, strategies to improve the lives of the poor trickled up to the rich and middle class. By 1920, about 10 percent of this country's children, poor or not, attended kindergartens.

The kindergarten began, though, as an agent of social reform. Jacob Riis called it a "jail deliverer." Sarah Cooper, a San Franciscan who ran a charity kindergarten, declared, "Society has no right to punish crime at one end if it does nothing to prevent it at the other." In addition to its value as a delinquency deterrent, New York's Ethical Culture Society in 1878 saw kindergarten as a "preventive" that would avert "future unhappiness and misery by educating skillful, intelligent and independent working men." Studies (since criticized as poorly designed) tried to prove that children who went to kindergarten learned to read more quickly, or repeated fewer grades, or moved ahead in school faster (or slower). In three hours (the usual length of the kindergarten day), five- to seven-year-olds from impoverished, often foreign, backgrounds were to be trained to catch up to their more fortunate contemporaries.

Riis called kindergarten the best truant officer, putting older children in school where they belonged: "There are lots of children who are kept at home because someone has to mind the baby while father and mother earn the bread for the little mouths. The kindergarten steps in and releases these little prisoners. If the baby is old enough to hop around with the rest, the kindergarten takes it. If it can only crawl and coo, there is the nursery annex."

Appeals for support from the National Kindergarten Association echoed this optimistic, environmentally based view that the child was redeemable. One Christmas appeal had Ragamuffin Jim saying to Ragamuffin Joe:

I thought I had a place to go
Where I could learn to be
As smart as any other boy
That's better off than me.

Today's Head Start programs as well as other early intervention strategies are descendants of these early attempts to level the playing field of life.

At first, there was little distinction between day nurseries and kindergartens. Later, the nurseries concentrated on custodial care for younger children, and the kindergartens on education. One thing they continued to have in common was the emphasis on cleanliness. Jacob Riis found that in an inventory of supplies for a kindergarten in a tenement loft on New York's Lower East Side, soap was "the moral agent that leads the rest." The list included "several boxes of soap and soap dishes, 200 feet of rope, 10 bean-bags, 24 tops, 200 marbles, a box of chalk, a baseball outfit for indoor use, a supply of tiddlewinks and 'sliced animals' [jigsaw puzzles?] and 20 clay pipes." The pipes were to "smooth the way for a closer acquaintance with the soap by the friendly intervention of the soap bubble."

Although this list did not contain any toys immediately identifiable as teaching tools, Froebel's work suggested such kindergarten materials, and Milton Bradley, an enterprising toymaker, was soon producing them. Bradley published the first manual on the kindergarten and called it *Paradise of Childhood*—a considerable change from the Puritan view that children were inherently evil and pleasure a sin. Bradley had had his first quick success when he produced The Checkered Game of Life, a board game he packaged along with others in a slim pocket kit for Civil War soldiers. The game is still being produced today with a face-lift for the socially conscious nineties that awards points for good deeds. In 1869 Bradley marketed his first Froebel toys, having been influenced by Elizabeth Peabody, who started the first American kindergarten in Boston in 1860. As the movement gained popularity, the Milton Bradley Company prospered. It is now part of Hasbro Industries, the largest toymaker in the world.

Addams was more sensitive than some of her contemporaries who wanted to mold all children in America into their own image. She did not want to wipe out the immigrant past but to give the children an appreciation for their heritage as well as the tools to move into the New World. But this was also the time when the Carlisle School for Indian Children in Carlisle, Pennsylvania, made determined efforts to turn Indian children into what one official called an "imitation of a white man," attempting to "whitewash" them as others were attempting to assimilate immigrants. Just how far assimilation should go is still a question. In a time closer to today than the turn of the century, Eva Hoffman, who came to Canada as a thirteen-year-old from Poland in 1959, expressed the eternal dilemma this way: "But how does one bend toward another culture without falling over, how does one strike an elastic balance between rigidity and self-efface-ment? Every anthropologist understands the difficulty of such a feat; and so does every immigrant."

Sometimes custom and common sense collided. The kinder-garten teacher took back home a little five-year-old girl who had come to school in a "quite horrid state of intoxication" from the wine-soaked bread she had eaten for breakfast. Her southern Italian mother listened politely to a recitation of the dangers of giving alco-hol to children while, at the same time, hospitably setting out her best wines. The teacher refused anything to drink, and the mother, trying to be a good hostess, disappeared and returned with a glass of whisky, saying, "See, I have brought you the true American drink." The teacher reported all this with the rueful statement that "the im-pression I probably made upon her darkened mind was, that it is the American custom to breakfast children on bread soaked in whisky instead of light Italian wine."

The "darkened minds" were to be lightened through home vis-its more succesful than this one, in which the teacher could demon-strate by example. One immigrant mother told a teacher in New York, "I am ashamed of my rough ways when I see how patient you are with the children. I did not know before that you could make children behave if you were gentle with them."

The learning was a two-way street. One little Italian boy re-fused to sit next to Angelina because "we eat our macaroni this way" (pantomiming fork and plate), and "she eat her macaroni this way" (dropping great quantities of imaginary pasta into his mouth). These class differences between gentry and peasant shocked the democratic teacher.

Critics have suggested that Hull-House and places like it tried to impose middle-class values and wipe out the old culture. Settle-ments were certainly pervasive in large urban centers, and their numbers grew to accommodate the surge of immigrants: In 1891 there were six settlements, in 1897 there were seventy-four, and by 1900 there were over one hundred. They have been seen as centers of indoctrination rather than, as they saw themselves, a way of opening a wider and better world to the poor immigrant. In probably the only account of what Hull-House meant to children who went there for parties, after-school programs, or kindergarten, Hilda Satt Polacheck disputes the negative view. To her, "America has not yet awakened to the realization of what it owes to Jane Addams. No one will ever know how many young people were helped by her wise council, how many were kept out of jail, how many were started on careers in the arts, in music, in industry, in science, and above all in instilling in their hearts a true love of country—a love of service."

As Hilda recognized, the settlement house was a home away from home for mothers and their children. It offered a doorway to the American experience for the children and helped the mothers cope with the bewildering demands of a new country and a new culture. For the socially conscious pioneers who settled in the heart of the slums, progress was not only possible but practical. Begin with the children, they believed, and the world would become a better place for everyone.

THE EXTENDED FAMILY: JEWS, ITALIANS, BLACKS

It's up to me . . . to take care of the kids and I'd no more go back on them than I would on my own children.

—*RUSSIAN-JEWISH IMMIGRANT*

JANE ADDAMS SAW THE STRENGTHS as well as the heartrending problems of the immigrant family, uprooted from all it had known and struggling to survive on strange shores. The strengths lay in strong kinship ties that held together the remnants that had made it to the new land. She applauded the power of the extended family in the man who told her in his crowded apartment, "These are the five children of my brother. He and his wife, my father and mother, were all done for in the bad time at Kishinef [where Jews were massacred]."

The feeling that it was up to relatives to "take care of the kids" existed with striking unanimity among the immigrants and migrants crowding into the squalid cities in the period between 1880 and World War I. Whether they were southern Italians, eastern European Jews, or Southern blacks (the groups to be considered here), they turned first to whatever fragments of "family" had made the same perilous journey. And the safety net for children was usually (although not always) made up of the knotted cord of female relatives on the mother's side—her mother, sisters, aunts, and in the black community, women who played these roles with or without blood relationship. In all these groups neighbors, too, stepped into the breach when kin and pseudokin could not. In a Lower East Side tenement, one woman remembered that "if someone got sick, the neighbor took care of them. My mother went for an operation and the neighbor took the younger children." In the Italian community called "East Urban," the buildings were set up with two families to a floor and a shared toilet. With such close living, each family provided a child-care network for the other.

The realities of slum living, with each group banding together partly in reaction to the prejudice of the larger society and partly for the comfort gained by being with their own kind, made shared child care possible. In Providence, Rhode Island, half the Italians and a third of the Jews lived close to their relatives early in the great wave of immigration that started in 1880. In Rochester, New York, a Sicilian immigrant reported, "Most of my relatives lived within one neighborhood, not more than five or six blocks from each other. That was as far apart as they could live without feeling that America was a desolate and lonely place. If it could have been managed, they probably would have lived under one roof."

It is tempting to see the extended family at the turn of the century as the chief rescuer of children whose single mothers faced what has since been called "the feminization of poverty." But researchers looking at what they call "subfamilies"—those that contained family members from outside the nuclear family of father, mother, and children—found that only a small proportion of both black and white children from single-parent families lived in such an arrangement. They concluded, "These figures suggest that, for blacks as for whites, the romantic view that prevailed for many decades of a past golden age of extended-family households was mainly a myth. The majority of households were neither prosperous enough nor large enough to take in subfamilies."

These recent studies, which dispute the importance of the extended family, concentrate on the search for two or three generations living in one household. What they tend to neglect is the pattern of same-generation shared living quarters (sisters, for example) and the tendency of family members to live next door or a few blocks away (as those in Rochester did), expanding the concept of "home" to include a neighborhood. These patterns existed in the black population as well as among immigrants.

The closeness of the extended family group compensated, in part, for the loss of those who had been left behind, but poverty and crowding limited the kind and amount of help available. Italians sometimes were able to manage living "under one roof," since, in cities such as Pittsburgh, they were more likely than Jews or blacks to live in private houses (which they rented or owned) with room to take in another child or family. Close family members sometimes shared a multiple-family home, making communal child care easier. As Marie Rotunno and Monica McGoldrick, specialists in ethnicity and family therapy, explain it, having come from a world in which successive waves of conquerors, from Saracens to French, had displaced them from their homes, renting an apartment seemed too precarious.

The Jewish Extended Family

Most immigrant families came to this country in bits and pieces: first the young men, then their parents and wives and children in a haltingly constructed chain. The Jews were most likely to come together as nuclear families, although they, too, often took years to transplant their kin. They were most likely, too, to come with no thought of returning to the killings, poverty, and persecution of the old country. Once here, they were here to stay. They headed for urban centers to be with their landsmen (those who had come from their home area), whose familiarity might soften the shock of the leap from the Old World to the New. Many thousands moved no farther than the streets of New York, whose Jewish population soared to more than a million by 1910. But between 1880 and 1900 an estimated fifty thousand went as far as Chicago, and some then moved on to the cities of the Midwest and South.

Hannah came to New York from London (a way station on the road from Russia), with her husband and four children. One morning, as she was shoveling coal into the small stove in the tenement in which they lived, her long, flowing skirt caught fire. Frightened that her three-year-old son, who was at her side, would be hurt, she rushed onto the fire escape and became a human torch. In one of those chilling coincidences that are more likely when family members live a few crowded buildings away, her sister was in the street and saw the flames. She frantically asked a man with a horse and cart for his horse blanket so she could beat out the fire, but he refused. "First, how much will you pay me?" he asked. Hannah died, leaving her children, the eldest of whom was eleven, to be parceled out among family members. The eleven-year-old went to live with the aunt who had helplessly watched the tragedy. Another slept "wherever there was a bed." A third, the youngest girl, stayed with her mother's uncle and his extended family (two daughters, their husbands, and eventually, their children) in a brownstone in Brooklyn. There, she found herself working hard, treated like a maid rather than a relative—she was not allowed to go to high school because she was needed at home, and her great-uncle, the head of the family, reminded her again and again that it was her duty to be grateful. The small boy who had watched the fire engulf his mother stayed with his father, who soon remarried. Though these children were brought up in different homes, they remained close to the end of their lives under the protective (although not always ideal) umbrella of the family. Extended families such as this one offered care without the legal safeguards of the earlier apprenticeship system or the social oversight of what was later called foster care.

In one of these less-than-ideal families, a seven-year-old boy from Poland was taken in by a childless uncle and aunt when his mother died. When this boy was ninety years old he returned again and again to the painful memories of never having enough food and being kept home from school because he had to work, although he loved to study. When his father remarried, he did not take him back. His poignant refrain was "I was never loved." Society's assumption that children cared for by family members will always be treated more kindly than those taken in by strangers does not necessarily fit reality.

The definition of family among eastern European immigrant Jews included not only the nuclear family but all those who shared some blood connection. The little girl whose mother was consumed by fire went from home to home and spent time with an aunt and also with her mother's first cousin. They were all kin, and all shared the injunction—both religious and cultural—to care for the less fortunate.

Despite the stereotypical closeness of the Jewish family (and

stereotypes have a kernel of truth), many children struggled in single-parent families without close kin nearby and with no father to
provide for them. Their mothers were faced with caring for them
alone when the father died or deserted—either out of desperation
because he could not earn a decent living in the new land, or as the
first step toward a religiously sanctioned divorce, which required a
period of separation, or because he wanted to distance himself from a
wife and children he no longer felt close to. Sometimes the father,
who had come first, was more "Americanized" than his wife, and
found her an embarrassing burden. Whatever the reasons, enough
Jewish men deserted their wives for the Educational Alliance, a New
York settlement house, to establish a Desertion Bureau "for aiding
and advising the families of deserters and seek[ing], whenever possible, to reunite husband and wife." In 1911 this led to a National Desertion Bureau: 561 men were identified in that single year. The
Jewish Daily Forward regularly printed "A Gallery of Missing Husbands" to help in finding the deserters and to encourage them to get
in touch with their families. The *Forward* also carried in its advice
column letters from desperate women. In 1910 it printed this appeal:

> *Worthy Editor,*
> *My husband [here the name was given], deserted me and our three chil-*
> *dren, leaving us in desperate need. I was left without a bit of bread for the*
> *children, with debts in the grocery store and the butcher's, and last month's*
> *rent unpaid. . . .*
> *It breaks my heart but I have come to the conclusion that in order to save*
> *my innocent children from hunger and cold I have to give them away.*
> *I will sell my beautiful children to people who will give them a home.*

The editor, first appealing to the husband to come home, then
turned to his readers to "take an interest in this unfortunate woman
and to help her so that she herself can be a mother to her children."
Evidently there was no extended family to open its arms to them—or
whatever family existed had no way to stretch its meager resources to
care for another child.

The Italians

In the New World the Italians, too, had to broaden their understanding of family, and of who was available to care for those who could
not care for themselves. In city slums, close living provided a helping

network that had not existed in the old country. In the small villages of southern Italy, according to some writers, the family had been the nuclear family, insulated from neighbors and even other relatives because of suspicion, jealousy, and the fear that others would curse their good luck with the evil eye. Even when they were in trouble, they clung to the tight security of the immediate family and did not ask for help from the outside. In Avigliano, a small town in Sicily, Leonard Covello remembered that when there was no food in the house, they bolted the door and rattled pots and pans so the neighbors and relatives would think they were cooking as usual. "The intimate things of family life remained sealed within the family," he wrote, "and we created for ourselves a reserve both as individuals and as a group." A southern Italian proverb warns, "If you want a happy life, stay away from your relatives." Yet, inevitably, there is another view. Donna Gabaccia insists that far from being insulated and isolated in a tight family, Sicilians "desired and valued ties to people outside their nuclear families."

In America, the attempt to re-create Sicilian village life in enclaves that became known as Little Italies forced the extension of the concept of family to include not only close relatives but also those who had come from the same town and spoke the same dialect. Unlike the experience of other immigrants who had an extended family pattern in the old country that fragmented when they emigrated, southern Italian immigration encouraged a pattern that had rarely existed before. A close, supportive extended family may have been an ideal, but one that could rarely be risked in the pervasive poverty and social isolation in which most people lived in Italy. The idea that a cohesive, extended family was the norm was largely a myth that grew up in the minds of second-generation Italian-Americans who had never suffered the suspicious, constricted past of their European-born parents, according to Humbert S. Nelli in his book *From Immigrants to Ethnics: The Italian Americans.*

Between 1880 and World War I, 17 million Italians (mostly southern peasants) left their isolated villages to journey to America to work. By 1910, half of those who had come since the turn of the century had returned. This back-and-forth pattern gradually changed as women and children as well as men made the trip. Families were established, and they stayed.

Mass migration owed its success not only to the enterprise and determination of the immigrants, but to a revolution in shipbuilding—the development of the coal-fired iron steamship liner. The triumph of steam over sail at the end of the nineteenth century made it possible to keep to regular schedules, and cut the time of the journey across the Atlantic from a month or more to a mere ten days or two weeks. With steam, ships did not have to leave from northern Europe and the edge of the Atlantic, but could pick up passengers in the Mediterranean. Leaving from Naples, closer to home, made the trip seem less daunting and the two to three weeks crowded into steerage more endurable than the longer passage under sail.

Although in Italy the nuclear family provided the only trustworthy refuge, it was recognized that *la famiglia* extended through the father's line to distant cousins and aunts and uncles. Wives traditionally moved to their husband's parents' homes or villages, and the father was revered and feared as a patriarch. This male bloodline network was enlarged by the custom of having godfathers who entered into a parentlike position. The old family lost some of its male dominance in the New World despite retaining an appearance of patriarchy. One reason may have been that mothers and daughters now lived close together in crowded enclaves. No longer did a daughter become a member of her husband's parents' household, perhaps in another village. But some things, such as the ambiguous nature of the Italian woman's role, did not change in the New World. Although descent was calculated through the male line, it was the female line that most often provided the help and support needed when children were involved, as it had in strictly patriarchal Italy. As an immigrant woman in Providence, Rhode Island, told the historian Judith E. Smith: "I cannot tell why it [this apparent contradiction] was so, but when a mother died [in Italy] the family usually fell apart. The small children were taken over to the mother's relatives, and the older ones felt that they could not live at home anymore. So they moved—one to an uncle, one to an aunt, where they would help in all kinds of work and thus earned their keep."

In America this helping tradition was intensified and expanded. As Arlene Mancuso of Fordham University found when she studied two generations of women of what she called Old Town in the 1970s, "One can trace a close-knit domestic network of exchange of goods and services. This set of ties performs a crucial economic function in the distribution of scarce resources, a function different from middle-class networks, which serve primarily for social and emotional support." The web of female kin provided "economic, social, and emotional support for its members," in the immigrant generation and the one that followed. It is strikingly like the helping network of black women that has also persisted through several generations.

Similarities also connected Italian and Jewish immigrants. Italian mothers, like Jewish mothers, are legendary. Both are assumed to equate love with food, both are inordinately attached to their children—particularly their sons—and both continue this attachment throughout life. But there are differences. For the Italian mother, the love is utterly unconditional. No matter what the child does, there is no threat of the withdrawal of love, no playing on guilt. It is this warm certainty that Colleen A. L. Johnson, who looked at the role of the mother in Italian and Italian-American families in Syracuse, New York, credits with ameliorating the effects of the rigid, harsh discipline meted out by traditional immigrant Italian fathers. The mother's role as the wellspring of unconditional love balanced the father's role as authoritarian guardian of honor and correct behavior. The father got respect; the mother, love. Traditional sayings include, "One can have a hundred fathers but only one mother," and, "One can have another wife and children but never another mother."

Despite open expressions of affection and concern, the family was not child-centered but family-centered, and a child was expected to put aside his or her needs and aspirations to further the larger goals of *la famiglia*, according to Johnson. In this hierarchical system the father was at the top, and he ruled by fear.

Discipline could often be swift, harsh, and physical, a practice that continued in second-generation Italian-Americans. Although the children of immigrants had not forgotten the near-cruelty with which they had been punished, they saw this as linked to love and the proper parental role. Parents who let their children run wild were not doing their job. Yogi Berra, brought up by Italian immigrant parents in St. Louis, said, "Like my dad, I have been very strict with my kids. We are very close."

Immigrant enclaves of all kinds were insulated from the child-rearing ideas of the larger society by their economic, geographical, and linguistic isolation. Although settlement houses such as Hull-House tried to educate poor women to treat their children with understanding and kindness, as middle-class American norms now suggested, they reached only a small fraction. And even this fragment often paid lip service to the new ideas while carrying on with what they themselves had known and their society approved. A second-generation Italian-American mother, asked if she and her friends had adopted the modern, permissive ideas of the post–World War II era, said they had generally been rejected as unworkable and alien. "Dr. Spock didn't have an Italian mother," she explained. In her generation as well as earlier ones, "the back of the hand" was preferred to long explanations based on psychological understanding.

Immigrant women rarely had their own mothers to turn to for help with child care—they had often been left behind in the old country. Their daughters had the advantage of a neighborhood family network to care for children when they needed a few hours off, or when they worked to supplement their husbands' incomes. Although southern Italian culture frowned on wives working outside the home, and fewer of them worked than did blacks, necessity sent some into the workplace. The work was often intermittent. In Providence textile mills, one woman returned to the job she had had before she was married while her mother or mother-in-law took care of the babies. Another paid her mother while she worked at a box factory, and demanded more for her work (she earned about twelve dollars a week) so she could cover child-care expenses. She told an interviewer for the Federal Women's Bureau that she got up at 5:00 A.M. to make her husband's breakfast and clean the house, then cooked supper and put the baby to bed after work. "She cried during the interview," the investigator reported, "and was obviously unstrung from her week's effort."

In an unusually enlightened situation in Endicott, New York, where Italian women worked in the shoe factory, the employers realized that the mothers of young children needed special consideration. Most of them left their children with extended family members or neighbors during the day, but if a child was sick, the mother could take unpaid time off. Some remembered staying home for as long as a week. And school-age children were permitted to come to the factory after school and wait nearby until their mothers had finished working. Despite the strong cultural prohibitions against married women working outside the home, these rules evidently could be bent if economic necessity was great enough, if the workplace was populated by relatives and friends, and if the factory was close enough to the Italian part of town to make it feel like an extension of the safe, familiar home. New York, where most Italians settled, did not have industries that fit these requirements, so women worked at home or took in boarders to make money. But in Providence and

Tampa, Florida, for example, they also worked in factories. In the to-bacco factories of Tampa they earned more than their husbands did as laborers.

Orphans were parceled out among relatives. This was assumed to be a kinder way of treating them than sending them to institu-tions. It also fit in with the cultural attitude that outsiders—the gov-ernment, social agencies, even the church, which was seen as the tool of the upper classes—could not be trusted. In southern Italy a shadow government developed based on bloodlines, not laws, and this attitude survived the sea change. But care by relatives was not necessarily kinder than that given by strangers. Only one thing was certain: The child would be more likely to be exposed to the same values and attitudes his own parents had held.

An orphan girl of the immigrant generation was brought up in the home of a childless aunt, who kept her working hard at house-work and refused to send her to school. (The traditional attitude was that children should contribute to the family and schooling was a waste of time, wrenching them from their duties and teaching them to disdain their background.) This reluctance to permit children to be educated was strongest among Italian groups. Both blacks, denied literacy during slavery, and Jews, who saw learning as their only portable asset, embraced education as the way to freedom. "Every morning at two o'clock," reported Jerome Krase, who studied immi-grant Italian women and their college student daughters in Brook-lyn, one orphan who lived with her uncle's family "got up to go outside to wash the clothes for the boarders as well as for the family. She scrubbed, cooked, mended and polished to her aunt's satisfac-tion. However, she wanted to learn how to write—at least enough to sign her own name. With the excuse that she had to make the beds, she would go upstairs with a letter her aunt had received and pa-tiently copy it over again until she could write her own name."

Another first-generation Italian woman came with her husband to a mining town near Pittsburgh. Children followed, one after an-other, and the husband, desperate in his poverty, took two of the six and gave them to his sister, who had no children of her own. He did not even discuss his plan with his wife. When these children came to visit their parents with the aunt who was rearing them, their mother never touched them or kissed them. She just stood back, tears welling from her eyes. One of the girls learned only as an adult that they had been taken away without their mother's consent, and that she had mourned them ever since. "But," she asked an interviewer, "how do you make up for the hurt of so many years?"

The Blacks

Scholars have tried to account for the particular structure of the black family—its extension of the definition of family to include kin and nonkin, the centrality of the mother-child relationship, the widespread sharing in the care of children. Some, such as the pioneering anthropologist Melville Herskovits, have pointed to West Africa, from which many of the slaves came, as the source. Others have found in the brutality of slavery itself, which often separated women and children from their fathers and gave women who worked along with men a measure of equality, the deciding factor. In her study of ten extended black families in Chicago, Joyce Aschenbrenner, another anthropologist, concluded that "the American Black family was fashioned in the crucible of slavery; whatever its antecedents were, they were not as compelling as conditions in the New World." Still others point to urbanization as the force that tore apart the black nuclear family that had survived slavery—as it had broken some immigrant families. Statistical data confirm this suggestion. The researchers do not minimize the effect of slavery, but conclude, "Once we recognize that the matrifocal black family is a product of economic discrimination, poverty, and disease we cease to blame the distant past for problems that have their origins in more recent times. It was, and still is, much easier to lament the sins of one's forefathers than to confront the injustices of more contemporary socioeconomic systems."

Despite this sound of certainty, it is well to remember that all attempts to understand the black family, slave and free, are based on fragmentary evidence, gathered on one plantation or another, or in a few cities, or from a small sample. And manuscript census information, which seems to provide the comforting solidity of national numbers, is itself suspect. It is based on few interviews, hard-to-find respondents, and the possibility that the census takers, mostly white, did not get accurate information from blacks. More research is needed to put together what is and is not known, delineate what cannot be known, pinpoint the questions that matter, and come up with a more comprehensive picture.

A persistent puzzle is the question of why powerful mothers are seen as the strength of one group (among immigrants) and as a problem in another (among blacks). One thing that is known is that the expectation that a mother would fulfill all the obligations of motherhood as defined in the larger world was never a part of the realities of slave living; motherhood was, of necessity and perhaps by African tradition, shared. This does not mean that the mother-child bond was not a strong one. Slave mothers yearned to be with their children, masters recognized that mothers and young children should be kept together, if possible, and the law gave a child the status of its mother, making her bloodline and not the father's the one through which descent was traced. This may have been a way of acknowledging the prevalence of rape and the impossibility of proving fatherhood, but it also had economic causes. A child born of a slave mother, no matter who its father, was legally a slave. (In English common law, on the other hand, a child's status was determined by its father's. In contrast, Jewish law, designed for a people who were also subjected to rape and oppression, also traces bloodline through the mother.)

In this country during and after slavery, as in Africa, a woman gained in stature by being a mother, and her maternal role stretched to include children who needed her whether she had borne them or not. As a result, children in the black community in the years after slavery and before World War I (roughly the period considered here) were more likely than other children to be cared for by an extended family network. But even widespread use of this kind of child care did not do the whole job for women who were more likely than white women to work (this was true until the 1990s) and to be unmarried mothers. Addressing the unmet need, black women social reformers near the turn of the century established kindergartens and day nurseries in Chicago, Cleveland, Atlanta, and other cities to take care of the children of working mothers. The historian Linda Gordon argues that proportionately more of these child-care facilities existed in the black urban community than in the white despite the pioneering efforts of settlement houses such as Hull-House. Black women were so concerned about their children that they turned to taking in laundry they could wash at home rather than living-in as domestics. In that way they could be there to care for their own children and those of their relatives, neighbors, and friends if necessary.

The black extended family as a safety net for children extended far beyond blood relatives. Although most children were cared for by their own parents in their own homes, others often stepped into parental roles. They could be grandmothers, aunts, uncles, cousins, or fictive kin who were neighbors or close female friends of the mother or people who had come into the family constellation so far back that no one remembered when or why. Like the caretakers of black children on the plantation, they were often called "aunt" and "uncle." They could also be complete strangers, like the woman who took in Otis Moss. His mother died when her three children were small. A few years later, his father perished in a car crash. As the boy stood on the sidewalk watching the wreckage a woman came up to him, comforted him, and said, "Come home with me." He grew up in her family and went to high school, the army, and college.

Shared child care lasted for a few hours, a week, or the rest of the child's life, depending on need. Strong links with close adult females—usually the mother's relatives and friends—made this system workable.

Ida B. Wells, the crusading newspaper reporter and editor, was born into slavery in 1862 in Holly Springs, Mississippi. She stepped into the role of mother for her younger brothers and sisters when she was just sixteen years old, to save them from being distributed among neighbors and friends after the yellow fever epidemic of 1878 wiped out her mother, father, and baby brother. She had been in the country visiting her grandmother when the plague struck. On the freight train ride back home in the black-draped caboose, the conductor pointed out she was risking her life by going into an infected area. When she asked why he was running the train and exposing himself to pestilence, he said someone had to do it. "That's exactly why I am going home, " she said. "I am the oldest of seven living children. There's nobody but me to look after them now. Don't you think I should do my duty, too?"

She lengthened her dresses to make her look older and got a job at a country school six miles out of town to support the children. The pay was twenty-five dollars a month. Every weekend she rode home on the back of a mule. At first, her grandmother cared for the children during the week. Then the grandmother became ill, and the network of female helpers expanded to include a woman who was an old friend of her mother's. When Wells moved to Memphis for a better teaching job, the older boys stayed behind and went to work on the farm of their aunt Belle, her mother's sister, who also took a handicapped sister who had barely escaped being shunted off to the poorhouse when the first plans were made for the care of the children. In Memphis, the two younger girls were cared for by another member of the extended family, Aunt Fannie, her father's sister. The helping network for Wells, as it did for many, included women on both her mother's and her father's side, although in general a mother's relatives were most likely to help with child care.

This pattern survived in the immediate postslavery period and persisted through the stress of urbanization even when a mother was alive. Anthropologist Carol B. Stack found in her study of a Chicago black community in the 1960s, as others had noticed a century before, that "close female kinsmen . . . do not expect a single person, the natural mother, to carry out by herself all of the behavior patterns which 'motherhood' entails." Women wove their lives together to provide a fabric of support.

A folk system determined who could and who could not be part of this domestic network, which required trust and demanded reciprocal obligations. Children were sometimes circulated from one family to another, or informally adopted for long-term stays. Households had elastic boundaries and could not be defined by architectural criteria. Members of a "household" did not all necessarily live in the same house or apartment, but might sleep in one place, eat in another, and call "Mama" the woman who reared them rather than the one to whom they had been born. The household shifted shape as the "family" composition changed. When family therapists Paulette Moore Hines and Nancy Boyd-Franklin examined the history and current shape of the black family, they found a simple question could sort out the extent of the kinship and fictive kin network: "Who can you depend on for help when needed?" Stack found that a mother's intention often determined if the help was to be temporary or permanent. If the mother planned to take full charge of her children in the near future, the temporary arrangement did not affect her rights to determine what happened to them. If, however, a grandmother, relative, or friend took the children for the long term with no plan to return them to their mother, the substitute parent assumed the rights and privileges of parenthood. The rights of the children were not mentioned in her study, nor was it clear how schooling was handled when children were shifted from one home and neighborhood to another. They always knew who their real mother was, though, even as they were taken into the kinship network of the "mama" who cared for them.

When slavery ended, bands of freed slaves tramped the roads

looking for relatives who had been sold. Others stayed on their plantations, in the hope that family members would find them there. Slavery may have separated families but it did not destroy the idea or even the reality of family. As late as the turn of the century, almost fifty years after slavery, relatives were still searching for their lost kin. The *Planet*, a black newspaper published in Richmond, Virginia, the center of a flourishing slave market, ran a regular column titled, "Do You Know Them?" dedicated to finding family members who had disappeared—not because of desertion, but as the result of bondage. In 1900 George Williams of Alexandria, Virginia, wrote, "I am hunting my relations. My mother was named Lucy and her two daughters were Agnes and Lucinda, and my brothers were named William, Aaron, James and Peter. All were sold in 1844. Their master's name was Gen. Wm. F. Gordon from Edgeworth, Albemarle County, Va. The man that bought them was named Poindexter. He carried them down Mississippi. I am the oldest son of my mother who is making inquiry." The dreadful litany of names and places was repeated in letter after letter.

Despite this poignant evidence of shattered families and the determined efforts to reunite them, when the historian Herbert Gutman examined records from fourteen Southern cities and counties, he found that between 1865 and 1880, 70 to 90 percent of black families had two parents. In Boston, too, another study found that in 1870 black family structure was very much like that of their immigrant Irish neighbors, with most children living with both parents.

Although the vast majority of black families were nuclear and were headed by a man, the black experience also produced another system characterized by single-parent families and extended-kin networks. Black children were more likely than Irish, for example, to be taken in by relatives or friends. An informal adoption and fostering system ensured that all children would be cared for no matter what their parents' marital or financial condition. No one questioned whether they were "deserving" or "undeserving." Blacks had few institutional alternatives, since they were systematically excluded from the orphanages set up for and by whites, and almost as carefully denied the meager philanthropic help available to the poor. Even when widows' pensions began in Illinois in 1911, proportionately few poor black women were deemed worthy of such aid. The community had to care for its own.

Most blacks lived in rural areas until the great migration north at about the time of World War I. In 1900, a look at these areas found that although the proportion of children living with a single parent was low in both the black and white populations, black children were about twice as likely as whites to live with one parent, usually a mother. In the cities, the percentage more than doubled. It was in the cities, too, that black children were more likely to live with relatives other than their parents. In both rural and urban areas, the proportion of children who lived with mothers who had never married was about five times higher than in the white population. It is hard to take numbers and turn them into actuality; it is possible that out-of-wedlock children were underreported in the white population and freely reported in the black. Marriages, on the other hand, may have been underreported in a black population unaccustomed to registering them officially. And an important factor in figures for both whites and blacks is that most children living with a single parent lived with one who was widowed.

The relatively large proportion of never-married women with children has been attributed to several possible factors. Those who see African survivals in the New World point out that pregnancy before a union was formalized was encouraged among certain groups, since it provided proof of a young woman's fertility. On her dead father's Sea Island, Georgia, plantation after the Civil War, the English actress Fanny Kemble's daughter found that "the negroes had their own ideas of morality, and they held to them very strictly; they did not consider it wrong for a girl to have a child before she married, but afterwards were very strict upon anything like infidelity on her part." Herbert Gutman sees a possible close connection "between the relatively early age of slave women at the birth of a first child, prenuptial intercourse, slave attachments to a family of origin and to enlarged slave kin networks, and the economic needs of slaveowners." The more babies, the more slaves. The more slaves, the more wealth. After freedom, this pattern of having children continued. But it was not a direct legacy of slavery, researchers who studied the census records of Philadelphia insist. "To the extent that the female-headed family appeared during this period," right after the Civil War, they write, "it emerged, not as a legacy of slavery, but as a result of the destructive conditions of Northern urban life." Most former slaves lived in two-parent families, so, they reason, slavery itself cannot be blamed for the female-headed family. "The data provide no evidence," they conclude, "for believing that Philadelphia's blacks valued anything distinct from what poverty and death often denied them: to raise their children in stable and continuous families." Susan P. Randall's situation in Hartford, Connecticut, in 1858 illustrates the problems of a woman caught in what she called an "unfortunate condition" that her culture did not support. She asked for help from Wendell Phillips, a leading white abolitionist from Massachusetts, since the child's father had rejected her and "I must not go home to my Mother." It is likely that the same shame persisted after the war, although it is possible that the earlier freedmen who had bought or been given their freedom before the Civil War adopted the standards of the white community and poor blacks later did not.

Separate but Similar

Despite widely different experiences and backgrounds, these turn-of-the-century ethnic and migrant groups had striking similarities: a concern for children, although this concern did not take precedence over the basic need of survival; the expectation that relatives (and among blacks, fictive kin) would be willing to share the burden of child care; discipline aimed at producing proper behavior; and large numbers of female-headed households because of the ravages of death and desertion as well as unmarried motherhood.

Immigrant and migrant women both depended on a community of other women to help them deal with the overwhelming burdens they faced in caring for their children. Men, too, left with children they could not tend, turned to substitute mothers within the family constellation. The extended family patterns that developed or persisted from the past made survival possible.

There were other similarities between black and Italian families at the turn of the century. Both were seen as troubled and "marked by considerable confusion, conflict and disorganization." This statement was made about Italians, but repeated in almost the same words by E. Franklin Frazier about blacks.

Frazier's view of "disorganization" caused by slavery has been challenged by Herbert Gutman, who found that the vast majority of blacks soon after Emancipation and closest to the slave experience lived in intact, two-parent families. As for Italians, a 1911 observer saw the "disorganization" among the Italians as part of "an undeclared state of war between two ways of life," when "the children press down upon the first-generation family an American way of life."

New research techniques stressing statistics rather than what seem like commonsense assumptions are documenting these unexpected similarities and strengths among diverse populations such as immigrant Italians and Jews and migrant blacks. The new findings are still preliminary, but they open the door to a fresh look at old conclusions. They also suggest that whatever the forces acting to pull the family apart, the vast majority of children during this period lived with their own two parents, whether they were European immigrants or migrant blacks.

As Peter C. Holloran found when he studied Boston, "Black family structure did not differ significantly in 1870 from that of white neighbors. Approximately 18 percent of the migrant Black families and 22 percent of the immigrant Irish families in Boston in 1870 were female-headed because of the death or desertion of a spouse." A 1900 manuscript census of seven major cities showed 8.5 percent of children living in single-parent families (mostly female-headed)—a proportion approximately the same as in 1960. The researchers Linda Gordon and Sara McLanahan pointed out in their preliminary study of turn-of-the-century families that "contrary to our expectations, we found no significant difference in the prevalence of single-parent children among immigrants, migrants, and nonmigrants." Clearly, single motherhood has a long history that does not depend for its existence on the evils of slavery or the stresses of immigration. And even in harsh times, the vast majority of children lived with their own parents. This does not diminish the reality of the one-parent family or the burdens it placed on women as they sank deeper into poverty. Yet Judith Stacey, author of the book *Brave New Families*, points out, "The view that two-parent families are better . . . is a widely shared prejudice whose validity cannot be confirmed by . . . studies. Research on the effects on children of different family structures yields contradictory findings, and few comparative studies take adequate account of profound differences among families in economic and social resources, support networks, quality of child-care options or kin relationships." The extended family—probably the earliest mechanism for child placement in human history—has served early and late to cushion the blows of single parenthood, death, illness, and desertion.

THE IDEAL INSTITUTION

*I think to be an orphan means to survive. You tell yourself, "you
made it this far and you're going to make it the rest of the way."*

—*RESIDENT OF TWO ORPHANAGES*

BEFORE THERE WERE ORPHANAGES there were almshouses, and before almshouses there was child abandonment. And accompanying
abandonment was infanticide, the ultimate remedy. At times all these
methods coexisted, desperate attempts to deal with children who
were impoverished or unwanted or unable, for whatever reasons, to
live in homes society deemed suitable. In the early years of the nineteenth century, poor orphaned children could avoid the institutional
scrap heap of the almshouse in two ways that often seem even more
cruel. They could be auctioned off at a vendue (sale) to the lowest
bidder—someone who would charge the community the least
amount of money to feed and clothe them. Or they could be kept at
home with a paltry sum paid by the local government in "outdoor relief" for their inadequate care. In addition, desperate women, following age-old practice, sometimes deserted infants they could not rear
themselves.

It is hard for us to accept the idea that children might be sold or
given away or deposited on doorsteps, but abandonment is a custom
that goes back to the mists of antiquity. Moses was the most famous
foundling. Abandoned by his mother to save him from death, he was
rescued by royalty, raised with great kindness, and became a central
figure in Western religious history. His own mother was hired to be
his wet nurse. Her secret act, for the good of her child, is seen again
and again in real life and in literature—the myth of the secretly caring mother transmuted into fact. Far from being a cruel act, as John
Boswell points out in *The Kindness of Strangers*, abandonment was often the expression of a desperate hope that the child would be found
and cared for, not that it would die of exposure. It is not that life was
cheap, but that it was hard.

In 1601 the English poor laws first provided for public responsibility for the care of destitute children. The laws stated, among other
more or less humane propositions, that if they were young enough
poor children could be auctioned off to the lowest bidder who would
agree to care for them in his home. These laws, which also covered

apprenticeships, the workhouse, and the poorhouse, were the model for the United States for three hundred years, until the passage of the Social Security Act in 1935.

In the early years of this nation (before large-scale orphanages), parents (and single parents) gave their children away or left them on doorsteps as a way to give them a better chance in life or reduce financial pressures on the family. The assumption has been that most abandoned children were illegitimate, that the mother wanted to conceal her shame. But recent careful studies of New York State records hint that poverty may have been at least as important. Of course it is possible that a woman would pose as married to protect herself and her child, but it is also possible that these desperate women took the most humane course open to them when they were left without husbands. In 1820 Bridget Malone, whose husband deserted her before her baby was born, and who had three other children, left an infant on the stoop of the Catholic bishop's house. Brought to court for abandonment, she said, "I have no house or home nor any of earning to live by and I trust my poor forsaken infant to the kind mercy of god and your goodness." The court ruled she had broken no law since it was her intention that the child be cared for. She said she was going to the country to recover her health, and on her return would reclaim the little girl. Like many mothers, she saw the arrangement as a temporary expedient to get her through a dreadful time.

Other parents, in less dire circumstances, gave their children to people they knew or to relatives—some of them childless. If there was an inheritance that would go begging because there was no male heir, a boy might be given to his aunt and uncle to give him a better chance in life and keep the money in the family. Boys were also placed because their families were too poor to care for them. But on Southern plantations only girls were put out to other families—boys were too important as future managers and workers, and girls were only dowry liabilities.

Sometimes the giving away accomplished its purpose of a better life for the child and gave it an admirable substitute family. Virginia Wilcox was brought up in her doctor uncle's house after her parents died. She went west in the Gold Rush in the 1850s, became deathly ill on the journey after the birth of a child, and was saved by her uncle, who chased after the wagon train. She called him and his wife "my more than father and mother."

The straightforward giving away of children continued as late as the start of this century (and undoubtedly still goes on, despite the modern recognition that children are not puppies to be handed out or sold at will). The existence of large-scale institutions in the nineteenth century may have lessened the need for this kind of care, but it did not abolish it. Mary Alice Hughes was given by her mother to a couple she met when she and her two girls were in Boston for an exposition. The childless couple were from southern Illinois, seemed nice, and were very taken with eleven-year-old Mary Alice. They took her home then and there, and her mother was free to take a job as a housekeeper in a wealthy home in New Hampshire. In later years, in a curious turnabout that psychologists recognize as a way of giving yourself (through someone else) what you never had as a child, Mary Alice took her aged mother in and cared for her with diligent devotion until she died. She would never tell her children what life had been like in Illinois: "It was so bad I never talk of it" was all she would say. But she warned her own daughters that "if anything happens to me go to an orphanage because that way you won't have to be grateful to anyone the rest of your lives."

Questions, approval, and criticism dogged all these institutional and noninstitutional arrangements. Public-spirited citizens were concerned that help would encourage the poor to remain dependent. Of children in almshouses a report of the Massachusetts General Court said in 1858, "Lastly, and the greatest evil of all [it] creates and perpetuates *paupers*, by accustoming all the children in them to an easy, happy life in an almshouse, where they are well fed, clothed and instructed, so that the inducement for them to labor for their own support—and that of their parents—is completely lost sight of."

Despite the dangers of dependency, well-meaning, frugal reformers saw institutional care of the poor as the best of all systems. In the minds of people like Mary Alice's mother, it would also spare the children a great burden—the need to be grateful. Almshouses in community after community dumped old and young, sick and well, degenerate and worthy in one building and often in one room. Most were dreadful places for children, who were exposed to the underside of life at close quarters. Drunkenness and despair led to fights and murders, and the insane muttered and shrieked without hope of help. Many infants, underfed and neglected, died in their cribs.

As the century progressed, some communities, mindful of the physical and emotional torment the children suffered, began to separate them from the rest of the almshouse discards. No stranger to the workhouse himself, Charles Dickens approved of what he saw in Boston in 1842: "The orphans and young children are in an adjoining building; separate from this but part of the same institution." He was struck by stairs built for small legs and chairs "of lilliputian measurement. . . . And after observing that the teachers were of a class and a character well suited to the spirit of the place, I took leave of the infants with a lighter heart than ever I have taken leave of pauper infants yet."

Despite Dickens's enthusiasm, the limitations of most almshouse care had by then become apparent to American philanthropists. More harm than good resulted from the indiscriminate crowding of men, women, and children in filthy quarters from which they had little hope of escaping, except by death. A report on the care of children in almshouses by a New York State Senate committee in 1857 pointed out that "an association with their destitute parents, and their necessary poor house companions, is not only a deprivation of the attention and comforts which they ought to enjoy during their tender years, but it is a fatal exposure to examples of most evil tendency. Their chance to become virtuous and exemplary citizens is the most desperate of all human chances." Clearly, some other mass method had to be found that would avoid the cynical profit-taking and human misery engendered by the poorhouse.

The answer seemed to be the orphanage—an "asylum" (originally "a sanctuary, a refuge," and extended to mean "a benevolent institution") designed solely to nurture children until they could be apprenticed to make their own way in the world. Orphanages were established for the best of reasons to handle children in the worst of times. The idea that children were the hope of the future, not just small creatures marking time until adulthood, had finally filtered from the larger community to the slow-to-change, insulated world of the institution. It was important to help them, not just house them. Industrialization and immigration were changing the face of America, pressing people together in urban areas and closing them off from the supports for the family and children that had existed in a more rural time. Epidemic disease and later the carnage of the Civil War burdened the system, and it became urgent to find a new way to care for children set adrift by these changes. The orphanage was honestly believed to provide the best of all possible worlds. It probably did. Orphanages gave children comparatively safe places to live, with enough food to sustain life, if not health (disease was a daily threat), some moral training, and even rudimentary schooling. From society's point of view, law and order were also served. The two institutions examined here—Girard College for Orphans in Philadelphia and the Colored Orphan Asylum in New York—assured supporters that their children would not "people our alms houses and prisons, or swell the mass of vice and misery which accumulates in our large cities." It was also cheaper to institutionalize children than to provide public funds to parents or guardians to keep them at home. So, morally, financially, and in the interests of civic order, the orphanage was admirable. There was, writes Arthur E. Fink in his standard text, *The Field of Social Work*, "sincere conviction at the time that institutional care was the best method of providing service to children."

The first orphanage in this country owed its existence to seven Ursuline nuns in New Orleans in 1798, but only fifteen other privately supported orphanages were founded between 1800 and 1830. Then public and private organizations, dissatisfied with the almshouse solution, launched an optimistic orphanage boom. By 1850 New York State alone had twenty-seven asylums. "State institutions were probably far more effective . . . than they have ever been since. Private agencies enjoyed their greatest confidence and success about the same time," asserts Peter Holloran, a historian who has studied the progress and decline of the child welfare system and disputes official claims of its increasing effectiveness. Although it is hard to believe today, in the mid-nineteenth century, orphanages were widely hailed as ideal institutions.

Girard College

The most unlikely of these establishments (a private one) was Philadelphia's Girard College for Orphans, which opened the imposing wooden doors of its Founder's Hall to one hundred "poor male white orphan children" on January 1, 1848. It is unusual because it still exists in the same place in which it started; it is typical because its history reflects the changes in the past century and a half in the ways institutions have cared for the youngsters in their charge. It was (and remains today) completely funded by income from the estate of Stephen Girard, reputedly the richest man in America. When he died in 1831 he left the vast sum of five million dollars to establish an institution that would place orphan boys "above the many temptations to which, through poverty and ignorance, they are exposed." In addition to protecting a boy from worldly hazards, Girard's plan recognized an ancient wisdom later endorsed by the followers of Freud. Boys were to be admitted when they were young, between the ages of six and nine, because "we must begin with the child. . . . We must watch it in the tender germ of infancy, remove the weeds which would choke or poison it, and so water and invigorate it as it rises to catch the air and the sun, that like a healthy and useful plant it may bring forth fruit, as well as leaves and flowers." The boys were to be fed, clothed, and educated until they were between fourteen and eighteen and then apprenticed in the community, well on their way to becoming solid citizens.

Mrs. Elizabeth Hamilton was one of the Pennsylvania mothers who turned to the college for help in the late 1800s. "Dear Sir," she wrote, "I write to you in regard to my two boys being admitted to Girard College. Their ages are seven and nine years. I am left a widow without means and seven children to care for. It would be a great favor done them as well as me if I should get them placed in that institute." The letter, one of many stored haphazardly today in a room on the top floor of Founder's Hall, gives no hint of whether the boys were admitted.

A contemporary of Thomas Jefferson who shared Jefferson's mastery of architecture, Girard left detailed instructions—including the height of the stair risers—for his "college." (He used the word in its French sense of a secondary school.) The cornerstone was laid July 4, 1833, and after years of controversy about both the will and the design of the building it was finally completed in 1847 according to the plans of Thomas U. Walter, architect for the graceful dome of the U.S. Capitol. In a paroxysm of elegance he added thirty-four Corinthian columns to Girard's original four-square plan. Even today, according to one architectural historian, Founder's Hall is "unsurpassed as an example of Greek Revival architecture," although a contemporary critic complained about "the building of a Palace instead of a school for orphans."

It looks like the Parthenon incongruously set down on forty-three acres in what is now a decayed, inner-city area of North Philadelphia. The columns skyrocketed expenses several hundred thousand dollars above original estimates and delayed completion of the building because, among other things, craftsmen skilled in working with marble were hard to find in the young country. Charles

Dickens was struck by the building and the delay. In his *American Notes* he wrote, "Near the city is a most splendid unfinished marble structure for the Girard College, founded by a deceased gentleman of that name, and of enormous wealth, which, if completed according to the original design, will be perhaps the richest edifice of modern times. But the bequest is involved in legal disputes, and pending them work has stopped; so that, like many other great undertakings in America, even this is rather going to be done one of these days, than doing now."

Stephen Girard, the man who founded the largest orphanage of its time, was a curious paradox. He could be mean-spirited and hard-hearted with people he knew; generous and self-sacrificing with a mass of anonymous strangers—a not uncommon philanthropic pattern. An immigrant from Bordeaux, France, he lost his mother when he was twelve and shipped out as a cabin boy at fourteen. In 1776 he detoured his ship to Philadelphia to evade the British blockade and settled in to become the new country's preeminent merchant and banker. As a disciple of the French Enlightenment, he rejected the idea that children were inherently evil and saw them as innocent creatures corrupted by their environment. As an educator, he was a follower of the Swiss Pestalozzi, who said, "When I am a man I shall take the side of the poor."

Even by the tolerant standards of his day he was eccentric, stuffing his receipts and bills in his hat, wearing a different pair of shoes each day of the month, and expressing a profound dislike of doctors. Those who worked for him had better be prompt, proficient, and honest. He had no patience for laziness or for late payment of debts and rapidly developed a reputation for miserliness. Yet this seemingly hard-hearted man left a fortune in his will for poor orphans he would never see.

Perhaps he hoped to ease their lives as his had not been eased. The orphans were not allowed to ignore his pain as a boy, handicapped in early childhood by a severe injury to his eye, bereft of his mother, and separated from his father by hard labor on the high seas. They were reminded that "Stephen Girard knew what it was to be lonely, to be friendless, and it may be in the quiet hours of the night shed honest tears in the memory of his boyhood, and being childless, he yearned to gather to his empty heart and fireside the fatherless boys of his adopted city." They were exhorted to feel "deeply grateful . . . to the Founder of this College! You truly may call him father, for you are his children. Most bountifully has he provided for you out of his store, and you will be faithless and ungrateful if you do not honor him by making a suitable return in earnest and honest lives."

The generous will was bedeviled from the very first by challenges from Girard's French relatives, who complained they had been slighted in favor of misguided philanthropy. For their final appeal they hired that thunderous orator Daniel Webster to carry a unique argument to the U.S. Supreme Court. The will was invalid, he argued, because it was un-Christian. Girard, a free thinker although born a Catholic, had decreed that "no . . . minister of any sect whatsoever . . . ever be admitted [to the grounds of Girard College] for any purpose, or as a visitor, within the premises." Posing as an orphanage, the college was really designed to spread atheism, Webster declared, and if it became a reality Pennsylvania would be a "reproach and odium to the whole clergy." Despite Webster's "impassioned appeal to emotion and to prejudice," Justice Joseph Story ruled that it was possible for an institution to be nonsectarian but wholesomely Christian and refused to break the will. In 1967 it was finally broken when the National Association for the Advancement of Colored People successfully challenged the "whites only" provision. The school is now about half black and half white, and one-third of the students are girls, who began to be admitted in 1984.

The will presented still another problem. What did Stephen Girard mean by "orphan"? This conundrum went to former president John Quincy Adams, who said in a letter of May 8, 1833, that he thought at first "orphan" meant what immediately comes to mind: a child without either parent. But he reconsidered and suggested that an orphan was a child who had lost either a mother or a father. Men whose wives had died were likely to marry again quickly and reconstitute the family, but throughout the nineteenth century about 10 percent of American families were headed by women, and even in the early twentieth century the percentage was distressingly high.

It was the woman-headed family that won out in the definition debate. The Supreme Court of Pennsylvania decreed that Girard meant an orphan to be a boy who had lost his father—one from a female-headed or no-parent family. The court was in line with English common law and current practice. It was a father, not a mother, who had chief rights to custody and the right to appoint a guardian for the child after his death. If the father was not around, the child was essentially parentless. Mothers had no legal rights. Custody was often determined by the ability to support the child, and since many widows were hard-pressed, guardianship often passed to the state as fatherless children sank into poverty.

Early feminists fastened on the inequities of this traditional paternalism as one of their major themes. In an 1854 speech to the New York legislature one of them complained, "By your laws, the child is the absolute property of the father, wholly at his disposal in life and at death." By the end of the century, however, many courts recognized that mothers had special rights, and children special needs. Only a mother, said the courts, was uniquely equipped to nurture a young child. The legislatures followed later, and reluctantly.

Boys found their way to Girard if their relatives could not care for them or wished to give them an opportunity for a better life, or if they were bereft of all family. In its early years, most of the youngsters were of American stock, with children of Irish, German, and English immigrants making up the next-largest group. In this Girard was unlike other urban institutions, whose halls were filled with the children of immigrants washed up on their shores.

Women whose sons went to Girard College for Orphans (the "for orphans" was dropped in 1906) were required to indenture their boys to the city of Philadelphia and "relinquish all further control over the said orphan until he arrives at the age of twenty-one years . . . to prevent relatives or others from interfering with, or withdrawing such orphan from the Institution or his master." In other words, a mother (or "next friend" or relative) legally surrendered a fatherless boy during the whole of his childhood. Only after his apprenticeship was he expected to return home. Financial need was, in this patriarchal time, to be attested to by "two respectable male citizens, who can vouch for the time and place of the birth of the boy."

In accord with the policy of Christ's Hospital in England, after which Girard was modeled, this provision meant that no bastards could attend, and poor families not living moral lives had little chance of placing a boy. The "undeserving poor," as Shaw's Mr. Doolittle called them, went to almshouses, which could not pick and choose.

Some of the children who eventually reached Girard had been abandoned. Historians of childhood argue that abandonment in earlier times did not carry with it the stigma that it now does, since children had not yet acquired an aura of infinite value. Yet as far back as 1556 a woman named Norton whose child was taken to Christ's Hospital was pilloried and a sign put on her head "wherein was written in great letters Whipped at Bridewell for leaving and forsaking her child in the streets and from thence carried into Southwark and banished for her offense out of the city." Perhaps this is evidence not of society's attachment to children, but of its fear of having to bring up paupers at public expense. Nevertheless, it calls into question the view that children could be discarded at will. Institutions, from the ancient Christ's Hospital to the more modern Girard College, cared for the castoffs who were often left in the streets even in ancient times in the hope that they would be rescued.

Once the imposing iron gates at the entrance to Girard closed behind him, a boy was engulfed by unfamiliarity. Theodore L. DeBow, a member of the first class, told the boys of fifty years later how he had been overwhelmed. "No one can know without its experience the loneliness of a boy bereft of his father; none but the Infinite eye witnessed the tears shed on many a narrow bed as the boy, separated from all he loved, entered upon his life in Girard College."

Remembering later his own first-day experience as a nine-year-old in 1884, Ernest Cunningham pictured the admissions scene in the director's room where "one of the boys was bitterly opposed to being left at Girard, and . . . went around the room kicking the chairs and causing his mother much concern." After Ernest, who was a good boy, stoically left his mother behind, "I was then taken into the class-room and given a vacant desk and seat at the rear of the room. I was given a slate and pencil and set some easy problems in arithmetic, but as I worked on the problem I thought of the fact that this was the first time I had been away from home, that my mother had gone, that I wouldn't see her again for a month [it was felt best to keep visits to a minimum] and as I thought about it tears came into my eyes and fell on the slate. I have never forgotten that homesick feeling."

Ernest's first breakfast was "ground up meat with potatoes mixed in and well seasoned. The boys called it ground up hash." Each got an equal helping. With growing boys of different sizes and appetites, this must have left many of them with half-empty stomachs. At other meals, too, the scene was Dickensian. Each boy took his plate to the end of the room where his portion was dished out. Officially, seconds were available as long as the food lasted, and bread was not rationed, but the boys were often hungry. Dinner—served in the middle of the day—was meat ("the toughest and cheapest available"), potato, and vegetable. Supper was bread, butter, and tea, and once in a while an apple or a pear. On Stephen Girard's birthday there was a special treat—an orange. A more regular luxury was the Hum Mud, a large, flat dark ginger cookie made in the early days with molasses from Girard's plantation and served each Friday at lunch. It is still on the menu.

From the very beginning, the boys grumbled about the food. The president wrote the board of directors in 1850: "The complaints of the boys about their table fare are not entirely without foundation and I beg leave to suggest a revision of the bill of fare, with a view to having more variety in the food." The complaints went unheeded then and later. Expenses had to be kept low, since income from Girard's estate fluctuated with the country's financial state. To keep one boy for a year cost three hundred dollars in the nineteenth century, when men often made five dollars a week; during the first ten years of the twentieth century it cost four hundred dollars; today, it takes about twenty-four thousand dollars.

Early mealtimes were not only meager but silent. Before the college opened, the plan was to make time for both conversation and silence. "But," reported a historian of the college, "the practice of silence at meals grew, and ultimately all conversation was under the ban." Forcing hundreds of boys to sit silently on stools as they spooned up their dinners was unnatural. In 1915 the board of directors found this "an unwholesome and undesirable arrangement" and allowed the boys to act like boys rather than monks and chatter to each other while they ate. "Although such conversation resulted in a good deal of noise it did not create any real disorder, and the practice once tried was continued."

Disorder was to be feared, not only in the orphanage but on the streets and in society as a whole. As immigrants with their strange ways and strange ideas flooded into the country, fears multiplied that the fabric of America would unravel unless they—and their offspring and all the poor—were held tightly in check. The greatest praise one could give an institution came from a visitor to Girard in 1849, the year after it opened: "No spectacle can be more pleasing and beautiful than to see the order and propriety of the infant scholars at their evening meal, under the eye of their matron; and at their evening devotions, under the solemn ministrations of their president." (Although Girard had put his college off-limits to all ministers of the gospel, this did not keep laymen from leading the boys in meditation and prayer of a nondenominational, Christian sort.) The great age of the orphanage coincided with Girard's establishment in 1848, and it became a model for many that came afterward. By 1850 New York State alone had twenty-seven asylums. With the Civil War, the existing institutions could not keep up with the surge of children left fatherless by the slaughter, and in the 1860s the number of orphanages doubled in a vain attempt to meet the need. At Girard, strict geographical entrance requirements were dropped to provide for the needy children of war widows. Not surprisingly, the changing needs of a society faced with the consequences of a human cataclysm had led to changes in the way needy children were cared for. Orphanages were no longer seen as substitutes for almshouses or grudging charity, but as institutions in their own right, a place where children could best be nurtured, taught skills and moral values, and prepared to rejoin the outside world.

Institutional meals have always been the target of complaints, but the loneliness and shock of being shut in with hundreds of strangers were what proved too much for some of the boys. By the terms of the will, the students were chiefly from Philadelphia and nearby Pennsylvania, and it was no hard job for agile boys to scale the ten-foot wall, "at least 14 inches thick, and ten feet high, capped with marble and guarded with irons on the top," and head for home. In a special report in 1850 the president bemoaned the "discontent and truancy then rife."

The problem was at its worst in September, after the boys had visited home during the summer. When the runaways returned, they were humiliated by being exhibited as examples. "One of the strange sights of the dining room," a man who was at Girard in the 1880s remembered, "was a group of about thirty boys dressed in the most outlandish costume, marching to some vacant tables in the center of the room separated from the regular sections. In addition to white socks and knee breeches, a disgrace in those days, they wore fantastic colored coats. They were served bread and water [for two weeks!] and marched back under guard and locked up."

Boys were kept from close contact with their pasts in part because "it was found that the frequency of visits to the college disturbed the order of the institution and arrangements have been made by which every mother (or next friend) may visit the College once a quarter and every boy visit his mother and friend once in the same term." Despite this forced separation the directors felt the boys "have retained all the filial and domestic affections with which they entered the school." Incongruous as it seems, they may have been right. Like other children who were abruptly disconnected from their previous lives, the Girard boys tended to go back home once they were out of the institution. As we shall see, even when children were sent hundreds or even thousands of miles away, many of them managed to return to the streets from which they had been rescued.

The substitute mother in the orphanage was the matron, who was in charge of day-to-day living with the help of "governesses"—at first chiefly women who had already reared their own families. As the first entrants moved toward their teens their guidance was turned over to men who were also their instructors.

Miss Jane Mitchell, who started as principal teacher and became matron when the first one resigned in the school's first year, was remembered by one of her boys as "stern in appearance and word, but conscientious in matters of duty, compelling obedience from all, superintending our comforts by day, and watching by the beds of the sick at night. She was childless [unlike some others on the staff] yet the mother of hundreds. And when the boys went from here to make a start in the world she packed each trunk with her own hands, into which she put a copy of the Scriptures and a prayer." This is a picture not very different from one that could be drawn of a good mother of this period, who was expected to be strict for the child's own good. The school administration recognized, though, that life at Girard was different from life at home, and it was the duty of the governess (child monitor) to help a boy cope with "the bigness and the strangeness of the place and the overpowering effect of numbers and the necessary methods" as well as separation from his family. A contemporary observer recognized the impossible conditions under which matrons and monitors labored: "Take the best mother that ever lived," he wrote, "and set her to bring up her family in obedience to the dictates of a dozen self-important aunts and uncles [committee of overseers] who visit frequently and are free to criticize and alter what they please, and tell her to keep her house open for an hour or two every week that the public may go through and write letters to the newspapers—how do you think it would work?"

The boys at Girard lived a mass childhood. In the early days, one hundred to three hundred boys shared one "mother" (although the "governesses" took hour-by-hour responsibility)—with a hundred sleeping in each vast dormitory. The children were even deprived of the comfort of kinship: Only one child per family was allowed entrance, to spread the benefits of the institution as widely as possible. Each day the boys rolled off their beds at dawn (any time between 6:00 A.M. and 7:00 A.M., depending on the season) and spent their strictly scheduled time in studying both vocational and academic subjects, doing chores and playing games. To keep order in the halls they marched everyplace two abreast. They brushed their teeth together, studied together, played together, ate together. They lived regimented lives hermetically sealed from the outside world. Half an hour was allotted to each meal, and two periods a day were set aside for nondenominational prayer and Bible reading. At a time when poor children as young as six toiled twelve hours a day in factories and fields, this was a privileged existence.

It was clearly privileged in the education it offered. Five years before the first *McGuffey Reader* was published in Pennsylvania, Girard envisioned and provided for a system of education and training for poor boys that was the equivalent of all but the best of the private academies. Like most sectarian orphanages of the mid-nineteenth century that had their own schools, it offered a better education than could be found, in general, outside its walls. Primarily a trade school, it also offered instruction in astronomy, experimental philosophy, French, and Spanish—although not Latin and Greek, which the founder did not recommend. When Stephen Girard wrote his will, there was no system of free elementary education in Pennsylvania. Over half the children between the ages of five and fifteen did not go to school at all, and only children whose families had money could count on an education. Certainly, the aim of the educators at Girard was enlightened. But soon after it was founded, complaints surfaced that the boys were used to help in the construction of sorely needed additional buildings, and their training was neglected in favor of their labor. The directors urged the staff to be more mindful of the children's needs.

On paper, discipline by parent surrogates at Girard was enlightened for its time, too. But, as the dining-room scene shows, reality and rhetoric did not necessarily coincide. One early rule stated, "The discipline of the institution shall be mild and paternal. . . . It shall consist chiefly of the deprivation of indulgences; seclusion, either wholly or in part; change of the ordinary diet; admonition; and in extreme cases that do not yield to mild means, corporal punishment shall be inflicted, but that shall be permitted only after a resort to the ordinary means of reformation have been tried and failed." As for children in their own homes, the best-selling equivalent of Dr. Spock's manual of child rearing in those days, *The Mother at Home: or, The Principles of Maternal Duty Familiarly Illustrated*, published in 1833, counseled parents to punish swiftly and severely enough to cause "real pain" if their commands were not obeyed promptly. "After the child's resistance is shattered, there is then occasion to speak to him of repentance." How closely parents adhered to expert advice cannot be known with certainty, any more than there is a way of getting a realistic picture of discipline at Girard. Child-rearing manuals—and rules for institutional behavior—are evidence only of what the people who wrote them thought should be done, nothing more.

At Girard the thinking, at least, gradually changed. The 1860 annual report sounds more like a manual for today's behavior modification techniques than the earlier "spare the rod, spoil the child" attitude. "With the majority of our pupils," it declared, "rewards for good conduct and industry are stronger incentives than penalties for disobedience and idleness and that as rewards are multiplied and made attainable by reasonable effort, in nearly the same ration will the necessity for punishment diminish." Deserving pupils earned visits to the outside, trips to museums, and extra food.

In later years, boys looking back at Girard felt that "the boys inside have, on the whole, a very much better time than the boys on the outside," and, "A studious Girard College boy has a better outlook for earning his living and battling for a successful career than a very large percentage of rich men's sons." When the board of directors of City Trusts (who administered the institution) surveyed the graduates in 1898, fifty years after its beginning, they found many had become carpenters, painters, factory hands, and farmers. One was a fresco painter, one a commissioner of immigration, one a deputy collector of customs, one a deputy recorder of deeds, and one a tipstaff (or constable). Recent graduates had gone on to further training, and some had become doctors, lawyers, and druggists. Certainly, they had moved farther in life than most other poor boys of their time.

Life at Girard influenced not only learning, but personality. No one has left a record of what its early graduates were like, but Paul Beers, who graduated in 1948, wrote a quick sketch that, given the striking persistence of institutional practices, probably applies to earlier students as well: "The typical Girard product tended to be self-reliant, somewhat quiet but sociable, polite, a diligent worker, even-tempered and gentle, and often a bit shy." In other words, he would be someone who could fit in, who did not rock the boat, who had succeeded in meeting the requirements of institutional living. The current president of the school, who is also a graduate, says the boys share one other attribute: "I don't know of an alumnus who has not been a good father, and that's the most important thing." Like many other parents, they have tried to give their children what was missing in their own lives.

As orphanages became routine and sank into some of the same abuses of neglect and overcrowding that had plagued the earlier almshouses, Girard participated in innovations that began sweeping over the "ideal institutions" orphanages had once been considered. Ten years after it began—earlier than most others—Girard's president suggested, "Whatever shall make the college more like a family will be a progressive step towards real reform." Dormitories became smaller and dining rooms were distributed among several buildings. These changes reflected a recognition that attitudes about what children need, and what society can do about it, were changing. Some of the changes were purely semantic. During the Civil War, Girard had become known as "the Hum"—short for "The Home"—but as institutions searched for a new, more acceptable identity, they were characterized as "schools."

As time went on, Girard continued to change to accommodate the realities of life outside and within its walls. Brothers were occasionally admitted. The apprenticeship system faltered and disappeared as craftsmen became obsolete in the industrial age. New buildings were added, less elegant and more suited to an increasing population. (In 1933, during the Great Depression, the school's population reached its peak—1,735.) In the 1940s fewer and fewer children climbed the imposing marble stairs to Girard. Social Security, which began under Franklin D. Roosevelt, gave mothers money to keep their children with them. Companies paid widows' pensions, and the American social climate, which had never approved of sending young middle-class boys away from home, began to be uncomfortable about uprooting poor children.

The Colored Orphan Asylum

The idea for an orphanage for colored children grew out of a chance encounter on a spring day in 1834 when Anna H. Shotwell and her niece Mary Murray noticed two ragged, dirty Negro children playing in front of a two-story brick building on Cherry Street on New York's

Lower East Side—then home to the city's black population. Leaning out the window was a woman who said she was keeping an eye on the boys until they could go to the poorhouse. The two concerned Quaker ladies gave her some money to buy clothes for them and went on their way. A few days later they returned and to their amazement saw six children, all neatly dressed, playing in front of the same house. The caretaker explained that the money had been enough for four extra youngsters—just a few of the children who had no place to go. On the spot the women decided to work toward establishing an institution to take care of destitute children such as these.

Two years later, with the help of sixteen other Quaker women and five men in "advisory" positions, the organization that established the Colored Orphan Asylum began its work. The men were "advisory" because the women were determined to keep power in their own hands. Well aware that married women could have no property of their own, they made it clear in their constitution that the men were required to be accountable for "any money [received] from his wife belonging to said corporation." It could not just disappear into the family assets, which he alone controlled.

No one would rent a house for "Negro occupancy," an early example of the "not in my backyard" phenomenon coupled with racial discrimination that even today plagues the placement of group homes and institutions, so the women bought a two-story white cottage on West Twelfth Street near Sixth Avenue in what is now Greenwich Village.

Eleven children were the first occupants. They had been held in the cellar of the almshouse in the care of a "half deranged man." No coach would carry them from there to the asylum because of their color, so the indomitable women picked up the younger ones and led the way, like mother ducks, halfway across town through the New York streets to their new home.

By April 1847, eighty-one boys and sixty-two girls lived in the larger quarters that replaced the original cottage. In a leather-bound volume in spidery handwriting the secretary of the association recorded, "Whereas the Alms-House for many years made no suitable provision for Colored Children, who were found by the Managers of the Colored Orphan Asylum interspersed with the adults in the crowded apartments of Belview, surrounded by vicious influences and destitute of schooling, with no incentive to industry or any effort apparent to instill into these susceptible minds principles of morality or religion. These friendless and neglected little outcasts, claiming their sympathy and attention were elected among the first inmates of the institution." Between 1837 (when it started) and 1863, 1,257 children lived in the Colored Orphan Asylum (COA).

"Child savers" were, for the most part, concerned with saving their own or leading others into their fold. Catholic, Protestant, and Jewish philanthropists and organizations established orphanages during the nineteenth century to serve the poor and abandoned of their faiths and keep them from the disaster of conversion. They did not usually admit outsiders.

Most clearly outside the sectarian and even the public fold were black children, who were firmly excluded even when there was no place for them except the jails or the poorhouse. Even in forward-looking Philadelphia, when reformers mounted a campaign in 1891 to break Stephen Girard's will and allow "colored boys" to enter his institution, the city solicitor upheld the provision of for "white orphan boys" only, and segregation triumphed.

Before the Civil War, "colored" boys and girls in the North— children of freedmen, or manumitted by their owners or Northern philanthropists, or purchased by free relatives—faced many of the same problems as other poor children whose families were either nonexistent or unable to care for them. Lives were disrupted by death, illness, or desertion, and poverty made hunger the constant companion of childhood. But the similarities masked vital differences. At the base of many of the situations faced by black children lay the peculiar problems of black people in the North. Families faced increasing discrimination in the decades before the Civil War, as rising abolitionist sentiment led to riots. The panic of 1837 and the immigration of large numbers of poor Irish also pressed the already hard-pressed freedmen further into the pits of poverty. With the Emancipation Proclamation in September 1862, hundreds of thousands of blacks poured northward, increasing the competition for scarce work. In New York, many of them settled on the Lower East Side, which later became the home of successive waves of newcomers to the city.

Because they were at the bottom of the economic heap, black families struggling to maintain themselves were beset by a host of special difficulties. Black women were more likely than white women to work, and most of them were live-in domestics. What could they do with their children if their employer wanted only the woman, and the extensive kin and pseudokin network that sheltered black children on and off the plantation was torn by the elusive benefits of freedom? Black men, too, were having a harder time than the rest of the population. Long involved in working as carpenters and craftsmen, they had also made a niche for themselves as stevedores. By the 1850s even this work was denied them as the Irish moved onto the docks. Many of the men, deprived of other avenues of work, went to sea, and left their families behind. Voyages could last as long as three years. Although some fathers were diligent and protective, many others were "intemperate" or deserted their families on shore, leaving the women to deal with the children. James Gulliefield set off for Liverpool and cut his ties with his family. Fourteen months later his wife placed eight-year-old Henry Augustus at the COA, unable to struggle to keep him any longer. As Michael Sappol, who studied the asylum's records, reports, "Of the 2,000 black seamen shipping out of New York in 1846 . . . only a hundred lived with their families." Women, too, sometimes worked on ships. Anna Maria Piner took a job on a steamboat after the death of her husband, who had been a waiter on a boat. The sole support of five children, she had no choice but to put them in the asylum. Black women were often the sole support of their children, despite desperate efforts to keep families together. In New York it was unusual to find black parents and children living in the same household, and 40 percent of the asylum children were the children of single mothers; 19 percent had just fathers.

In addition to being separated by the sea, families were also separated when men took agricultural jobs and left wives and children in the cities. The work could be an echo of slavery. George Jemison "died of exhaustion in the harvest time" while his wife and son lived on Broome Street in Lower Manhattan. When she could no longer care for the boy, he was sent to the asylum. We don't know if the founders of the Colored Orphan Asylum were aware of Stephen Girard's will, which caused a flurry of excitement when it was revealed in 1831, six years before the COA received its first children. Nor is it clear if there was a philanthropic network that exchanged information and ideas. But it is likely that the Quakers in New York discussed with their Philadelphia counterparts the most enlightened methods for caring for poor children. We do know that Stephen Girard, who began as a Catholic and ended as a freethinker, was profoundly influenced by his Quaker neighbors.

The Quakers who started the COA were, like their coreligionists elsewhere, ardent abolitionists and felt that they had a special mission beyond just caring for poor children. They were determined to help these children improve the status of their race and were completely committed to saving them from the shadow of slavery. In June 1855 they were involved in a dramatic footnote to history. A French ship foundered off the coast of Long Island with "several native Africans aboard." Two of them were boys who were taken by a concerned neighbor to the COA to wait out the two months the captain estimated would be needed for repairs before he could sail again. Although the United States had outlawed the slave trade in 1807, the 1850s saw an upsurge in illicit smuggling as the price of slaves skyrocketed, and there was the possibility that this ship was running contraband. "Fears were subsequently entertained," the records of the COA report, "that if taken away by the captain the boys were liable to be sold as slaves, and much effort was used to induce him to leave them under our care." The effort was successful, but Kilo, the younger, died suddenly of measles four months after he had been admitted. Donga, the elder, survived. He learned to read and write within two months, and, the report continued, "The ladies want to put Donga in a school so he might get a religious and liberal education and return to Africa as a missionary."

On another occasion, the directors had the bitter duty of accepting a child placed in their care as the result of a law they fervently opposed and could not circumvent. Jacob Beckett's father was a slave who had fled his master's plantation in Virginia and made his hazardous way to New York. His master found him, and with the aid of the fugitive slave law, which provided the help of federal marshals to capture runaway slaves even when they had reached free territory, the father was returned to the South. Soon afterward, Jacob's mother died of consumption and he was shifted to the care of one of her friends. But the friend could not keep him and placed him in the safety of the COA.

The directors of the COA began by admitting only children like Jacob, who had no parents, but soon after opening accepted those with only one parent, and it made no difference if the survivor was a mother or a father. In 1879, as at Girard more than a century later, "worthy" needy children with two living parents who were unable to provide adequate care could also be taken in.

Children were placed at these and other institutions for similar reasons and received similar treatment. They came because of death or desertion of one or both parents, because of a family crisis, or because life inside seemed to offer educational and moral advantages. Some had been unceremoniously abandoned. Ten-year-old Francis Martin was one of these. After his parents died, he was "under the care of a vicious sister, who turned him out of doors. He had been sleeping in the streets." There were other striking similarities. Children were to be placed in supervised apprenticeships once they were old enough—at the COA at the age of twelve, at Girard at fourteen. Meals were dependable but kept to a frugal minimum. And a similar treat—a gingerbread cake—was served once a week. Although a matron received permission to use the rod in 1839, discipline (as at Girard) was to be benign and such use was "discouraged." The children at both institutions went out into the world armored by a gift Bible to guide and protect them.

When the COA first started, children were sometimes spirited away from caretakers who were mistreating them. One little six-year-old orphan boy "lived with a degraded family of Coloured people who employed him in begging. He was literally taken from the street, and without consulting the people who had charge of him brought to the asylum." Mary Ann Lyons was only nine years old when she was sent by her widowed mother to be a servant to a Mr. Roberts. She, too, was whisked away to the asylum by a concerned neighbor, after she had been threatened with a knife by Roberts, who abused her and kept her "half naked through the piercing winter."

Despite the best efforts of its founders to provide a loving atmosphere for the hundreds of children in their charge (brothers and sisters could be admitted together, for instance), loneliness was as endemic at the COA as elsewhere. So were disease and death. John Tomata, eight years old, was manumitted by his owner and brought to New York's Committee of Vigilance of the Anti-Slavery Society, which placed him in the COA. He had been brought up in Havana, lost his parents, and was "suffering from disease of the spine." The uprooted, sick boy soon died, moaning, "In mournful tones, 'no father, no mother.' " In or out of institutions, children died at dreadful rates from everything from cholera to measles to diphtheria. In the COA's first year, the directors reported that "of the six children taken from the Alms-House last summer, three have died." In 1847, "Ill health at the orphanage, superinduced by the condition of the children before they were admitted, reached its peak and out of one hundred and ninety children there were sixty cases of measles and twenty-four deaths." Nursing the sick sometimes took up so much time that the ordinary, everyday running of the institution suffered.

Although the children were black, the staff was usually white, and as at other institutions, often hard to find and to keep. In 1837 a woman was hired on a trial of one month for eight dollars and fifty cents (she lived at the institution). She got an additional two dollars "to supply herself with extra provisions which the moderate but wholesome fare of the Asylum does not afford." If she proved satisfactory, she was to get one hundred dollars a year—and, of course, the two dollars a month.

Still, according to Michael Sappol, "Conditions in the asylum (at least up until the 1870s) were superior to [those in] equivalent institutions for white orphans—a fact which occasioned resentment against the asylum among the white lower classes." This resentment erupted during the catastrophic Civil War draft riots in New York that began on July 12, 1863. "Toward the end of the day," reported *Harper's Weekly*, "the rage of the mob was exclusively directed against colored people, who had no more to do with enforcing the Conscription Act than the Pope of Rome." But they had been used as strikebreakers a month earlier when Irish longshoremen walked off the docks, and they served as highly visible targets for the resentment of Irishmen who heard their names called first to serve in a war that was not theirs. The bloodiest riots in American history, with estimates of the dead ranging from a hundred to more than a thousand, were quelled only after the federal government diverted twenty thousand troops to regain the city, block by block, and keep it quiet.

In its march from east to west on Forty-third Street, the mob set fire to the asylum, which was at Fifth Avenue and Forty-third, and it was gutted in a roar of flames. One brave eight-year-old girl ran back into the inferno and carried with her to safety the Bible that was regularly read to the children. It was the only object to survive and is now in The New-York Historical Society. All the children were rescued and transferred to the almshouse on Blackwell's Island until they could be moved four years later to a new building accommodating forty boys and girls.

The COA shared in the generally favorable view of all orphanages and "for a short time, both the black community and the white philanthropic elite saw [it] as an exemplary institution, one of the very few respectable places where young black children could be boarded." *Harper's Weekly* called it "a noble monument to charity." A few of the children even went on to higher education, with two girls requesting "the concurrence and assistance of some of the ladies" so they could attend Oberlin College. By 1913, however, when the institution had moved to Riverdale on the Hudson River and times had changed, W. E. B. Du Bois, the black editor, criticized the asylum for both its white and black staffs. The white staff, he wrote, "do not as a rule love or sympathize with their poor little black charges." The black staff was made up of "the kind of Negro who smiles and cringes and does his work in a slipshod manner" because he has been chosen for his submissiveness to white leadership.

Some children stayed days, others years. The average stay has been estimated to be two years—hardly the cradle-to-maturity time span assumed by popular thinking. Children as young as eighteen months of age were surrendered by the signing of an indenture agreement—again as at Girard—giving up all rights. But in 1843 the COA recognized that some children might be able to return to their parents instead of being assigned to a master, and if the parents were "decent and respectable" and had paid the fifty cents a week that was technically required for room and board (although it could be reduced or waived in cases of need), the child was returned home. What is significant here is that institutionalization was recognized as a way to preserve—not erase—family ties. And yet, the ties sometimes remained so strong that some parents could not tolerate long separations and were accused of "enticing" their children away from the orphanage. As at Girard, summer vacations often revived old attachments and renewed separation proved too painful for both parent and child to face. Josephine Satters was four years old in March 1844 when her mother, "a very respectable woman," put her in the asylum. In August two years later she was allowed to go home for a two-week vacation visit—and just stayed.

Orphanages and the problems they dealt with seem very much alike. However, unlike the residents of other asylums, some children in the COA were not destitute, just the children of servants and working men who had no other place to turn. The parents used the asylum as a kind of paid boarding school, for temporary care, and reclaimed their children when they were again able to care for them. The children's chances of having at least the rudiments of an education, a clean bed, playthings, moral guidance, and training in the habits of industry were better than they might have been in the outside world.

By all accounts the earliest orphanage for black children in this country, the COA is evidence that institutional care of black children has a long and often successful history. Many of the children it saved went on to live productive lives. The philanthropists who helped them were dedicated not only to the usual social aims of "child savers" everywhere, but to the proposition that slavery and its after-effects had to be eradicated.

PLACING OUT: THE ORPHAN TRAINS

For bringing the child into normal, healthy and practical relations with the world, there is no asylum equal to the farmer's home.

—*CHILDREN'S AID SOCIETY, 1910 REPORT*

IN A MASS DISPLACEMENT rivaled only by the Children's Crusade of the thirteenth century, more than two hundred thousand orphaned, neglected, and abandoned children were transported from the crowded, filthy streets of New York and the eastern cities to the salubrious air of the midwestern countryside in the seventy-five years between 1854 and 1929. Most of them were in the care of New York's Children's Aid Society, which characterized itself as the first organization in this country dedicated to improving the living conditions of children. Under its wide umbrella, a variety of child services was established. It claims to have been the first to provide lodging houses for working boys, the prototype of probation officers for juveniles, and classes for crippled children who had, until then, been hidden away in their homes by fearful parents. The earliest of these services to be established was the "placing out" of city slum children in what came to be known as the Orphan Train movement. Charles Loring Brace, an innovative, idealistic minister turned social worker who was a founder of the society in 1853 and its first secretary, was convinced that institutional life (and the only other alternative, life on the squalid streets) turned poor children into adults who were likely to be either a danger or a burden to society. The first task of the society, he decided, was to find another way to care for these youngsters. Borrowing the idea from the Boston Children's Mission, which was the first to use placing out, Brace popularized this method of rescuing "uncared for waifs before evil environment has done its deadly work." He was ahead of his time in recognizing the evils of institutionalization (which was then almost universally praised) and the need of children for a close relationship with caring adults, and his ideas attracted the attention of forward-looking philanthropists such as Theodore Roosevelt's father, who served on the society's board of directors.

In 1863 it was estimated that as many as thirty thousand homeless, vagrant boys and girls lived in squalor on the wretched streets of New York. The girls were often crossing-walk sweepers, cleaning up after horses, the chief means of transportation; the boys begged, stole, or sold newspapers on street corners. They were likely to be the children of German and Irish immigrants, who in 1852 alone flooded into New York at a rate of about a thousand a day, six days a week. "Part of this immigration has been good," wrote Brace, "but another portion was composed of the offscouring from the poorest, most degraded districts of the Old World. Naturally the most ignorant and shiftless had settled in New York, their first shelter, and stagnated here." These children of "genetically inferior," impoverished immigrant parents were often abandoned, mistreated, or separated from their relatives by the confusion of coming to a new country. They had to be taken out of the hellhole of the city and exposed to a healthier way of life. To this end, street workers of the society combed alleys, theaters, taverns, and gutters for children who were neglected, deserted, or "in such a state of poverty as to be improved by being taken to good homes in the country."

They looked on their charges—as did the other child savers of their time—with benign condescension. The organizations had names such as the Olivet Helping Hand Society and the Home for Little Wanderers. They had no doubt that erasing the immigrant past would make good, nonhyphenated Americans out of these "poor benighted children."

The society's workers were told to use the chance at a better life as the lure to persuade parents or guardians to give up the children. "To the parents of these poor children, representations should be made of the great advantages which a good Western home offers over the poverty and ignorance, and temptation, to which they are exposed in the city." Some critics have seen this as enticement and claim that middle-class standards equated poverty with abandonment. Yet it is unlikely that the children would have been better off left to spend their time hungry, in crowded tenements, or on the streets at a time without compulsory education or financial help to keep a family together. Conditions at that time in one New York slum, the Five Points area, have been characterized by Columbia University's Professor James Shenton as "making Calcutta look like Paradise." The society was convinced the children would have sunk into delinquency and degeneracy and peopled the prisons of the future. The children themselves were told "that a real home, was the nicest possible thing they could have, and so they were happy about going."

Environment was crucial. Brace believed it could change the "gemmules," which each cell in the body gave off continually and which influenced the reproductive cells and determined inheritance. He and other optimistic social reformers borrowed the gemmule idea from his friend Charles Darwin, who insisted on publishing this egregious scientific error over the objections of Thomas Henry Huxley, his great interpreter. The expectation was that children of "bad" parents could become parents of good children themselves if they were removed from noxious influences early in life. The environmental impact on their "degenerate" cells would change them and they would pass on the goodness in their bloodlines. It was too tempting a concept for nonscientists to turn their backs on, particularly at a time when society saw itself in an inexorable march to perfection.

Instead of orphanages, Brace proposed "the family as God's Reformatory" and sent the children first to nearby farms in New Jersey and New York and then west on trains that were then making the wide-open spaces accessible. The children were gathered from orphanages and other institutions as well as the streets, and some were delivered to the society's doorstep by distraught parents who could not care for them.

Embracing the farmer as the epitome of excellence was part of the tenor of the times. Horace Greeley exhorted young men to "go West," and the frontier was America's answer to any major problem. Then, too, there was (and remains) a sentimental nostalgia for the virtues inculcated by the plain living of American country life. Even presidents have paid their respects to what historian Richard Wohl has called the Myth of the Country Boy. Abe Lincoln started life in a log cabin, Harry Truman was a farmer in Missouri, and even Ronald

Reagan made sure he was photographed on a horse as a California rancher.

The rise of the railroads made it possible for the Children's Aid Society and a few other child-saving organizations to gather up children and ship them to the transforming countryside. The first group of children steamed from New York on a boat, with forty-six boys and girls from seven to fifteen years old bound for Detroit, in 1854. For the children the ride was a great adventure. From the steamer they got their first look at apple orchards and stretched their arms toward them "all screaming, 'Oh, Oh! just look at 'em. Mister, be they any sich in Michigan? Then I'm for that place; three cheers for Michigan.' " At Albany, they switched from steerage on the boat to a windowless railroad car crammed tight with westward-bound immigrants. Haphazardly, one boy was added to the roster when he begged to come along after two others had been taken home by passengers on the steamboat. After this crowded journey, the society focused its travel plans on regular railroad cars, and the children were not again subjected to the terrible conditions of steerage.

The first regular passenger railroad run from the East to Chicago was on October 25, 1848. Six years later, the first Orphan Train (really part of one railroad car) carried the first children west. In the 1880s, seventy thousand route miles were laid, opening wide the plains and prairies to whoever could buy a ticket, and as the iron horse snorted its way across the country it carried with it thousands of poor children. Their passage was arranged at special rates by socially minded tycoons reaping a double benefit: More people meant more business, and migration was a safety valve for the problems of the cities. The movement did as much to transform the countryside as it did to transform the children. The offspring and descendants of these children helped to people large stretches of the Midwest.

The train trips were planned to coincide with good weather and were usually uneventful, but in 1863 a larger-than-average shipment of sixty children got snowed in, missed three railroad connections, and as a final indignity, came down with the measles. The children were particularly vulnerable to disease. Whether from the streets or from orphanages and almshouses, they were generally undernourished and undersized.

By today's standards, the readiness with which parents turned their children over to strangers seems callous and somehow unnatural. Yet in the climate of the nineteenth century, children were just beginning to be seen as precious beings in their own right. And among the poor, children often lived away from their parents. But as the urban middle class developed the concept of "psychological parenting," it began to look down on any parents who did not live up to its standards of continuous, loving care. Poor, immigrant parents were, therefore, almost by definition, neglectful and abandoning, although they may just have been making the best of their limited resources by sending the children out to work, or to live with others. The rich, of course, had always sent their children away from home or left them at home when the parents went away. In medieval times children of noble parents served as apprentices or pages in other aristocratic families; later they went to boarding schools, or stayed behind when their parents traveled. Family separations were the norm. The Victorian middle class, however, began to deify parenthood and the attachment of the child to its mother. Continuity of care became the standard by which families were judged. This is a modern notion that, in the nineteenth century, was a luxury only the middle class embraced. Superiority over the poor was made even more evident by contrasting the seemingly casual attachment of the lower class with middle-class filial devotion.

Another factor in addition to cultural attitudes influenced the ease with which children were turned over. Those who went west were most often the children of immigrants uprooted from their European homes in search of the Promised Land. And it was the chance for a better life for their children that drove many poor parents to give them up. They loved them no less than middle-class parents loved their sons and daughters, despite the Children's Aid Society's convenient illusion that their distress at parting was more show than depth of feeling.

This discrepancy between what the society assumed and what the children and parents experienced is highlighted by the story of Maggie Dickenson. Maggie was a toddler when she was sent with her two sisters to Iowa. In a report the society said, "These three children lost their mother, and when an agent of the Children's Aid Society found them, their father was drunk. Their poor bodies were covered with filth and their hair had to be closely cut [because of lice]." Maggie's memory of the scene when she and her sisters were taken away was quite different. "My father was holding our little sister on his lap and crying. . . . I guess he knew he would never see us again." Interviewed shortly before her death, Maggie appreciated with adult compassion her father's having relinquished his children: "For years I resented him sending us away, but now I look back after reading about living conditions of that time and realize he did what he felt he had to do."

Eliza Clements's mother, too, did what she had to do. Word of the Orphan Trains and of the opportunity children could have across the ocean reached even to England. Eliza was only four years old when she and her brother were sent to New York from Bristol, England, in the care of a man who placed orphan children in the United States. The children were slowly starving, and this seemed their only hope. Their father, a drunken seaman, had shipped out and disappeared. Eliza's mother, far from being casual about giving up her children, flung herself down on the "dirty rough wharf to shut out the sight" of them boarding ship. They eventually came to the society and were sent west.

As puzzling by today's standards as why parents surrendered their children with such unseemly alacrity is the question of how people could take in and sometimes adopt children about whom they knew nothing. (The society's children were minimally screened. Some were recommended by the institutions in which they were living, some chosen by the society's own workers. But this was more for appearance and "goodness" than for the suitability for placement.) Clara Comstock, who traveled west with groups of children from 1911 to 1928, put it this way: "On my first trip with a party of children to West Point, Nebraska, I thought it the most incredible thing imaginable to expect people to take children they had never seen and to give them a home, but we placed them and never failed to accomplish it. The home is always there, it is for the worker to find it."

The procedure for placing children was established early and continued with very little change for seventy-five years until the Orphan Trains slowed to a stop in 1929. Committees of leading citizens in local communities scouted for likely families, notices were posted in churches and other public places, and the children lined up to be picked once they had had a chance to clean up after their trip. They dressed in the best clothes the society could supply so that they would look at least as desirable as local children. Sometimes the committees did a good job; other times, afraid to offend friends or customers, they approved unsuitable placements. Occasionally more than one try had to be made to place all the candidates. A week or two after placement, the children were visited to see if things were going well.

The posters to herald the coming of the children took different forms. One began, "Children without Homes—A Number of CHIL-DREN brought from NEW YORK are still without homes. Friends from the country please Call and see Them." Another read: "Wanted, Homes for Children, a company of homeless children from the East will arrive at Troy, Mo. on Friday, Feb. 25th, 1910. . . . Come and see the children. . . . Distribution will take place at the Opera House." The children ranged from toddlers to sixteen-year-olds, but an agent who traveled with them reported that "the babies always called forth the most interest and this interest helped to place the older children, so that we tried to take a baby with each party."

Seventy-five years later, one of the "babies" could still sing the song she had sung at the kind of "show-and-tell" performance the children put on to melt the hearts of the onlookers:

If I only had a Home Sweet Home, someone to care for me,
Like all the other boys and girls, how happy I would be!

For older children, the lineup in the church or opera house was more like a slave market than show-and-tell. Farmers were looking for strong boys who could do their share of the haying and plowing. Noah Lawyer recalled in an interview with a writer for *Smithsonian* magazine that when he arrived in northwestern Missouri in 1907 he was expected to work, although he was only seven years old. "My brothers were all picked the first day, but I wasn't taken till the second. People came up and felt our arms and legs, and mine were kind of spindly."

Brothers and sisters were supposed to be placed together or, at least, close enough to visit one another. When she was eight years old, Sara Hunt, her sister Margaret, and her baby brother, Robert, arrived in Sidney, Iowa. They had been abandoned when their father was out of work and put in the Five Points House of Industry in New York, which soon transferred them to the society. The sadness Sara felt when they were sent to separate homes in the Midwest haunted her for the rest of her life. "The parting I felt keenly as sister Margaret and Robbie were the only persons I knew in the world. Mother Hutchison, as I now called the lady who took me, had purchased a little band ring for my finger and given me a bag of candy but while we were waiting for her horse and buggy to go home, I pondered the situation. I told her she could have these but I wanted Margaret. I thought my sister was being traded for these things. I would be taken now and then to Thurman to see Margaret so I didn't feel so lost and alone."

Not surprisingly, many of the children—even those who were well treated—felt lost and alone. The secretary of the society asked that each child keep in touch twice a year. Some youngsters wrote on the backs of the secretary's form letter, telling him how they were getting on. Through many there runs a trail of barely suppressed tears. Giuseppe, like other immigrants, was cut off from his culture as well as his friends and asked, "Did you ever hear from that Italian Boy that come out here with me?" Another boy, sent to Indiana, wrote in anguish, "I have a good Horse and Buggy and have all the money I need, but still Mr. Macy I am not happy. I feel lonely in the world without a Father or Mother. . . . Please tell me straight of my parents fate and also where my brother was taken."

Turning street Arabs into Tom Sawyers and Becky Thatchers was harder than Brace had expected. His faith and optimism never wavered, but he eventually conceded that the older, teenage boys had a tougher time adjusting than the younger children, some of whom were adopted. The unremittingly hard work and isolation plus the cruelty of some farmers led many of the boys to run away.

At other times, it was the farmers who were dissatisfied. An Iowa farmer complained in 1863, "If you cannot have the boy taken away, I will put him in the House of Correction. He stole my wife's wedding ring." (The society did not officially apprentice children, as other organizations did. Children could be moved at will, and the families who took them had no legal power over them.) On the other hand, a boy wrote in purple ink on lined paper, "You said that you heard from Mr. ——— and that he said I was running all over the country I am going to tell you what the reason is [he] would lick me and kick me so I ran away from him."

There were other rumbles of discontent. In 1878 an agent of the society in Cherokee, Iowa, reported that of "most of the 30 boys who were sent out . . . but five remain in the county." He adds that some have kept in touch and "several chums worked hard and have their earnings deposited in BK [bank] others have not done as well, and a few are of a natural roving disposition, shifting from place to place till the realities of life and their experiences will induce them to settle down in earnest." He ended with the credo of the whole project: "I have no doubt that *all* have benefited by their migration as the surrounding influence of Western life will naturally tend to make men out of them."

In a 1910 look back, the society claimed that 87 percent of the children had flourished and recorded its notable successes. John G. Brady was one of the stars. Sent west after his mother died and his drunken longshoreman father deserted him, he was taken home by Judge John Green of Tipton, Indiana, who had gone down to meet the train. (In the early days of train travel each arrival was a celebration, breaking the monotony of small-town life with a whiff of the city.) The judge later recalled that the twenty-seven children from the Randall's Island orphanage were "the most motley crew I ever did see. I decided to take John Brady home with me because I considered him the homeliest, toughest, most unpromising boy in the whole lot. I had a curious desire to see what could be made of such a specimen of humanity." The "specimen" grew up to be appointed governor of Alaska by William McKinley and was reappointed by Theodore Roosevelt.

On the same train was Andrew H. Burke, another half orphan. Years later he recalled, "The long railway ride on the Erie route, the tearful eyes, the saddened hearts, the arrival at Noblesville [Indiana] on that clear, sunshiny day; the dread I experienced on awaiting to be selected by one of those who had assembled in the Christian church, at that place; and how my heart was gladdened when taken by Mr. D. W. Butler—for his appearance indicated gentleness." Burke became a drummer during the Civil War and was elected governor of North Dakota in 1890. In a letter to the society the next year he exhorted the boys who were in the position he had faced thirty-three years earlier to "struggle for a respectable recognition amongst their fellow men. In this country family name cuts but little figure. It is the character of the man that wins recognition"—a clear statement of the American Dream. Another boy listed in the roster of outstanding successes became a justice of a state supreme court. As for most of the others, "The younger children placed out by the Society always show a very large average of success. The great proportion have grown up respectable men and women, creditable members of society. . . . The majority have become successful farmers or farmers' wives, mechanics and businessmen." Critics of the placing-out system have pointed out that the youngsters who didn't make it dropped out of sight and, therefore, out of the statistics. The failures were never recorded.

Why did some boys succeed when so many others never recovered from the blows of their early childhood? The psychoanalyst Leonard Shengold supports conventional wisdom when he writes in

Soul Murder, his book about child abuse and abandonment, "Human events are immensely complicated and we know relatively little about the resiliency of some individuals in the face of terrible and tragic events." Yet today's research on children with troubled pasts who unexpectedly live satisfying lives may offer some clues. Investigators have come up with evidence that a person, often someone outside the family, to whom the child becomes attached, can make the difference. In John Brady's case it was Judge Tipton, who saw him as a challenge. In Andrew Burke's it was the kindly Mr. Butler, whose face he focused on as an infant focuses on its mother's face. Some experts would say that even these committed, well-meaning adults could not have healed the emotional scars and set the boys on the road to outstanding achievement unless there had been someone even earlier to lay the groundwork. Although Brady had been beaten and abandoned by his drunken father, for a time his mother had been alive, and her early influence might have made the difference. Burke, too, was listed as a half orphan.

Constitutional factors—those built into the brain and the body—also play a role in determining how a child withstands dreadful events. When one Orphan Train rider was asked how he explained his successful life he said of his unknown birth parents, "They must have had good genes." He may have been right. Dr. E. James Anthony, a child psychiatrist with a special interest in what has come to be called "the invulnerable child," has often told the story of the three dolls: "[They] are made of glass, plastic, and steel and exposed to the equal blow of a hammer. This results in a complete breakdown in the first doll, permanent scarring in the second, and apparent invulnerability in the third." He is quick to point out that human beings are not as simple as dolls, and that many factors play a part in who makes it and who doesn't, but a piece of the answer may lie in inheritance rather than environment. This view, which gained popularity in the 1970s, reflects a swing of the pendulum again from an emphasis on early childhood experience (Brace's "environment") to the genetic capabilities a child is born with.

Despite protestations from the society that parents were encouraged to keep in touch with their children and vice versa, Helen Steinman, who is now in charge of postadoption services at the society, believes that once the children were placed, further contact and the chance to be reunited were discouraged. Still, some children persisted in the search. Saying this was his fourth unanswered request, a

Minnesota boy wrote, "please try and I know God will reward you. Please write as soon as possible and let me know for I will never be content until I search for them. I know they are alive that I am sure of."

The Children's Aid Society fiction (which may also have been true in some cases) was that the children soon forgot their past lives and the people who had placed them. Certainly they were encouraged by their new parents to repress the past so they might have a future. Clara Comstock reported, "They rarely showed any desire to return to New York and soon forgot they ever lived there. I do not remember but one boy who wished to return, he was a boy of 12 and wanted to become a fireman in New York."

In contrast to this view, the society's records show that in the early days, 70 percent of the children who lived with one or another parent when they were surrendered eventually returned to New York. (How many later headed back to the country is not known.) And even when they had no parents in the city, 42 percent returned.

Like parents who used orphanage placement as a temporary expedient, these parents never gave up hope. One little girl was surrendered to the society by her mother after her father, a streetcar driver, abandoned the family. The mother went to work as a domestic but in 1898 "the mother begged for the return of her child and we therefore brought her back to the city." Other children were reunited with their families elsewhere. One father who "owing to great poverty and illness had been compelled to give up his children . . . succeeded in re-establishing himself in St. Louis and the family [including a girl who had been in "a happy placement" for eight years] was re-united." Another girl was taken back by her mother, who traveled to the Midwest to be near her, took in washing to support herself, and finally reestablished her home.

Lorraine's Story

Some of the children were foundlings, abandoned in earliest infancy, and had no parents to go back to. Lorraine Williams was one of these. She is one of a small band of venerable Orphan Train riders who remember what it was like to go west at the end of the placing-out movement in the 1920s. Surprisingly, her story could be exchanged for that of someone who had made the journey fifty years earlier—nothing essential had changed.

About the orphanages she has no doubt, although she was only four years old when she left. Her early memories are like flashbulb pictures, each significant moment lit up and imprinted with vivid clarity. Lorraine remembers that the Geneva, New York, orphanage she entered at five weeks in 1919 and in which she spent her first three years had a big tin roof, and "when it rained it was the worst noise you ever heard." She can still picture the concrete backyard and the wire fence with a hole in it large enough for her to stuff her tiny fist through. The woman who lived opposite the fence would send her little cross-eyed boy out to play holding soda crackers—and Lorraine would grab the crackers because she never had enough to eat. ("How do I know he was cross-eyed?—I don't know, but I just do," she insists.)

When that home closed, she was sent to the Goodhue Home on Staten Island, a short-term facility maintained by the society to house children until they could be sent west. "It was not like the pictures of white tablecloths and children dressed in frilly aprons," she says. Those pictures were staged for public view, to counter criticism of orphanages as harsh and depriving and to encourage charitable contributions. In reality, the children sat at long tables and used tin plates for bowls. When her food was ladled out she gulped it down and held the pan up immediately for more—but there was no more, just as there had been no more for Oliver Twist half a century before. She remembers sleeping four to an ordinary bed and "being the smallest they told me, 'you can sleep in the center and if you pee the bed, you'll have to sleep on the outside." Most vividly of all, she can see the matron giving out toys discarded by more fortunate children. "She would start pulling them out of a box and I would push forward as well as I could. I was always one of the last. Once I got a broken doll—it had only one arm, but *it was mine.*" Her story recalls one Anna Freud told of a three-year-old boy rescued from a Nazi concentration camp where his whole family had perished and brought to safety in England. He followed each nurse around asking, *"Bist du Mein?"* Do you belong to me? Is there something in this world that is mine alone? Is there a person who cares only about me? Are you the one I lost?

Not long ago Lorraine went on a pilgrimage to uncover her past and time flashed backward. She found the fence and the concrete and the man next door said, "Yes, there used to be an orphan asylum here, and a woman would send her son out to play." "I was triumphant," Lorraine says. She really did have a recognizable past.

Her Orphan Train past began with the enormous wheels of the train that are her image of the start of the trip that ended in Kirksville, Missouri. She was one of fourteen children, with the babies taken care of by the older girls. For the two days it took to get there in the heat of July 1924, "All I had was a little white dress—like a Mexican one, with embroidery—and a brown sandwich bag with a piece of bread with jelly on it and a change of underwear," she says. In addition to her personal bread and jelly, provisions for the journey also included hampers of sandwich makings, fruit, and canned milk for the little ones. The emergency bag held bibs, cough medicine, and that indispensable accompaniment of children, larkspur ointment, "in case any vermin should escape the vigilant eye at the different homes from which the children had come." The remedy, made from ground-up seeds of a relative of the delphinium plant, was rubbed into heads to rid them of lice. It has since been found to be toxic to animals and humans as well as bugs and has disappeared from the medicine chest.

Before Lorraine's train was to arrive, the minister from nearby Sedalia, Missouri, announced in church that at 2:00 P.M. the next Sunday the children would be sitting in the front row and the public could come and choose the ones they liked. The childless college professor who became Lorraine's adoptive father asked his wife if she would like to have a child.

The next Sunday they watched as four-year-old Lorraine was first picked up by a man who wanted her as a dishwasher. "He had a prickly beard, and I whimpered," she recalls. The chaperone who had come with the children said the man could not have her because children could only go if they were willing. At that, her father-to-be rushed out and came back with a strawberry ice-cream cone. "My greedy little paws reached for it," she says, "and he said, 'if you want it, you have to sit on my lap. If you come home with me, you can have one every day.'" So, of course, that's where she went.

Her attachment at first was only to him. When he left for work in the morning she sat on a brick in the summer sun in the front yard and waited. When he came home at noon she went inside, then followed him out again to resume her vigil. He was the first person to whom she had ever belonged. Finally her "mother" said, "If you don't make up with me, we'll have to send you back," and that was enough to make her extend her loyalty.

The fear of being sent back was a real one. After a week the society's representative made home visits to make sure the children and their new parents were both content with the arrangement. At the sound of his knock, Lorraine dove under the bed. "For a year," she says, "if anyone knocked on the door, I would make a dive under the bed. I would listen for a familiar voice, and if I didn't hear one, I would stay there. Mother said there were no dust balls under that bed."

Her parents told her they were her father and mother, but she remembered a time before she knew them. One night she stayed with her grandmother and asked the question that had been haunting her: "You won't lie to me, will you, Grandma? This isn't my real father and mother, is it?" The grandmother said, "I won't lie to you. Yes, you are right," and Lorraine never mentioned it again.

In first grade her teacher made sure Lorraine knew she was not like the other respectable children. When the teacher passed out paper for Valentines, the other children got red, Lorraine got blue "because you're an orphan" and, presumably, marked by the stigma of illegitimacy. When she was fourteen she was officially adopted. The reason for the delay is unclear. Her parents said it was because of the rules of the agency, but it is also possible there was difficulty in getting a release from what is now called her birth mother. Today, Lorraine is the prosperous wife of a retired Air Force pilot and the mother of two daughters.

Harold Williams (no relation) is an Orphan Train veteran who had a much harder time. He went to Chicago under the auspices of the New York Foundling Hospital, a Catholic institution that, to protect its coreligionists from falling into the hands of Protestants, started its own westward movement.

He remembers that he was about three years old and held a teddy bear on his lap as the train puffed its way from New York to Chicago in 1916. Unlike the Children's Aid Society, the Foundling Hospital bound its children to previously selected families by standard, formal indentures. In his letter to the hospital asking, like so many other Orphan Train children and their descendants, for information about his beginnings, he summed up his experience as an indentured child in Chicago with, "That's not a form of adoption. It's a form of slavery."

Harold was first given to two Polish spinsters and then a year or two later was walked to another placement (he doesn't know why) in a family of a mother, four daughters, and the eight children of one of the daughters. There was no adult male on the scene. The mother was a tyrant. "The woman loved no one. I don't think she loved her-

self. She would beat me with a rubber whip for the smallest infrac-
tion. Also, if I became ill I would be beaten. According to her, if you
became ill you must have done something wrong."

Every year Mrs. Stafford, a regal-looking woman from the hospital, would come and ask him, "How is everything?" He would look
up at this grown-up and say automatically, "Fine," following the two
cardinal rules for orphans: "Be better than other children. Never
complain." When he was about sixteen he finally worked up the
nerve to tell her about his awful situation, and she said, "Harold, I
have to take you out of there." He has never stopped wondering
"How come a grown-up believed me?" (Children who have been
abused or neglected, therapists say, have lifelong trouble learning to
trust adults.) Back in New York he ran away, lived on the streets, and
became an alcoholic. At eighteen he was sleeping on the subways. Finally, the Catholic Youth Service found him a job in the butter-and-
egg business and he "straightened out." He fought in the steamy
China-Burma-India theater during World War II, married, and became a succesful businessman. But he never had children. "I don't
know who I am. I don't know what would come out," he says.

From its beginning, the Orphan Train movement was considered cruel and underhanded by some—tearing children from their
families, converting Catholics to Protestants, and contaminating the
countryside with New York's young criminals—and brilliant and humane by others, a precursor of today's foster care. The Children's Aid
Society's placing out was finally, in 1899, given the approval of New
York's Committee on the Care of Destitute and Neglected Children
and lingered on for another thirty years as one part of a program that
also included neighborhood training schools and housing for neglected children. Harold and Lorraine were among the last to be uprooted. The society had shown that institutions were not necessarily
the best way to care for dependent children and had survived rumors
and criticism, including one that the children's names were changed
and therefore a brother might even marry a sister later without
knowing it.

By the time the placing-out system ended, attitudes about separating children from their families—even dysfunctional ones—had
changed. The family was seen as a haven from the pressures and turmoil of the outside world, and mothers—even tarnished ones—were
enshrined on pedestals. According to the new thinking, every effort
should be made to give all children the benefits that middle-class
children derived automatically from being brought up in their own

homes. The Orphan Trains were criticized on these new grounds. In 1930 Henry W. Thurston, in his book *The Dependent Child*, insisted, "It does not seem fair to relatives that they be compelled to surrender a child permanently in order to get whatever care he may need temporarily." And a later social critic complained, "Social Workers carried out the program with little conflict or guilt in the face of mass auctioneering of children to unknown foster parents. The rescuing of unknown children from their unknown parents for placement with unknown foster parents was unquestioned."

These critics chose to look at the placing-out system from the perspective of their own time. They ignored the dismal realities of the previous century's crowded tenements, children roaming the streets, and the absence of widespread social programs to deal with overwhelming numbers of immigrants. By contrast, the contemporary *New York Sun* in 1860 compared placing out favorably with what had gone before and reflected the nineteenth century's lingering attachment to orphanages: "We mean no condemnation of the asylum system itself. As compared with the abandonment of children, it is an immense good. No one can deny it. But a new system, we claim, has been discovered, which is nearly as much in advance upon the asylum system as that is in advance of nothing at all."

Even as the Orphan Train children were changing their lives, society was changing the way it thought about the needs of children and the mechanisms that could be created to address them. This newly emerging idealization of the family, bolstered by Freud and confirmed by later studies of institutionalized infants, colors our thinking today. William Goldfarb, in the 1940s a psychologist with the Jewish Board of Guardians in New York and now a child psychiatrist, studied three-year-olds who had been placed in institutions and compared them with toddlers in foster care. He found that early institutionalization was "profoundly detrimental to their psychological growth," and that foster care (Brace's "Family as Reformatory" again) was clearly superior. Behind his thinking was what he summarized in the *American Journal of Psychiatry* in 1945 as "the typical family experience of the baby":

1. There is warm, loving contact between specific parent and child.
2. This contact is continuous in terms of life span and also in terms of detailed daily routine. The child is in the company of the mother for many hours during the day and for many months.

He added that the earlier the child is placed in an institution, the greater the damage.

Many of the children in orphanages and placing-out systems in the nineteenth and early twentieth centuries had spent their early years with one or both parents. Perhaps this protected them from the devastated lives they might have been expected to live. On the other hand, many children taken from foundling homes and almshouses where they had been since birth and then transferred to orphanages when they were three or older did well by society's standards, too, although they had never had "the typical family experience of the baby." Today's psychoanalytically oriented experts would probably say that they bore deep scars despite their apparent contentment. Since they lived in an age when the popularity of introspection was yet to come, we will probably never know. But there are echoes of Goldfarb's findings in some of the earlier accounts of growing up outside one's own family. In general he found that the children who went from institutions to foster homes at the age of three "all indiscriminately demanded affection and attention." One little boy, while still taking bites out of one apple, would go to the refrigerator to get another. He could never be sure there would be enough love, or enough food. Among Orphan Train children there was the girl who asked her foster mother during the early part of her stay, "And do we really get to eat again today?"

That children need families, not institutions, became the prevailing wisdom early in the twentieth century, and has continued so today. President Theodore Roosevelt, whose father was among the first trustees of the Children's Aid Society, called for a conference on the Care of Dependent Children in 1909 and declared, "Personally I very earnestly believe that the best way in which to care for dependent children is in the family home. In Massachusetts many orphan asylums have been discontinued and thousands of the children who formerly have gone to orphan asylums are now kept in private homes, either on board, with payment from public or private treasuries or in adopted homes, provided by the generosity of foster parents." As David Rothman observed in *Conscience and Convenience: The Asylum and Its Alternatives in Progressive America*, "The pride of one generation had become the shame of another." And this pattern has been repeated again and again as orphanages, first praised, then damned, gave way to sending children from the evil city to the transforming countryside, and that practice bowed to criticism and re-

vised thinking and was followed by foster care as without question
the answer to the problem. Jacob Riis, the journalist and reformer,
summed up the view at the turn of the century with, "Every baby is
entitled to one pair of mother's arms." Today, of course, foster care
has become the shame of this generation as what New York senator
Daniel Patrick Moynihan calls the "no-parent family" of drug
abusers has strained the system to the breaking point. With each
wave of social change, society has moved to devise ways of dealing
with the children who are left stranded.

The question discussed by the experts in 1909 is one that has
repeatedly recurred: "Should children of parents of worthy character, but suffering from temporary misfortune, and the children of
widows of worthy character and reasonable efficiency, be kept with
their parents—aid being given to parents to enable them to maintain
suitable homes for the rearing of children? Should the breaking of a
home be permitted for reasons of poverty, or only for reasons of in-
efficiency or immorality?" As the pendulum swung once more away
from institutionalization and back to "outdoor relief," children were
no longer seen as just smaller and weaker adults, marking time until
they could enter the workforce. They had privileges and rights.
Modern childhood had been discovered.

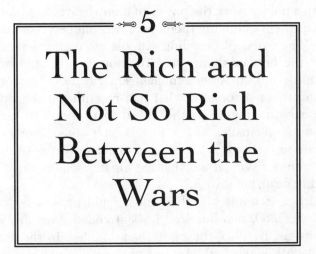

The Rich and Not So Rich Between the Wars

BOARDING SCHOOLS, CONVENTS, AND OTHER LIVE-IN ARRANGEMENTS

There is nothing natural about sending children away to school.

PETER W. COOKSON AND CAROLINE HODGES PERSELL, Preparing for Power: America's Elite Boarding Schools

BY THE START OF World War I the major elite boarding schools for boys—Groton, Exeter, Andover, Lawrenceville, and a dozen others—were well established. These were the schools that really mattered to the inner circle of the socially correct. About seventy more were in the next rung, scattered throughout New England, the South, and the West. Some had started as Colonial academies; others had been set up near the turn of the century to meet the needs of an expanding country with expanding educational expectations. Although the schools saw themselves as superior in every way, they had not always been seen that way by early observers. In 1902 George C. Edwards wrote in the *Educational Review*, "The boarding school is an attachment to the family of those who have wealth, and it tends to turn from a nobler work the power of men's hearts and brains by the simple expedient of buying them, here with money, there with social prestige. The worst of boarding schools are ineffectual reformatories, and the best of them are scrupulously cultivated hotbeds of snobbishness and un-American class superiority." He continued by comparing these schools to what had recently metamorphosed in professional thinking from the "ideal institution" to a necessary blight—the orphanage: "This fact is that these costly boarding schools are in reality but a species of orphan asylum—only without the claim on our sympathies that legitimate asylums have. The parents are not dead, but selfish."

Boarding schools saw their most rapid growth between 1880 and 1930. In 1880, two hundred boys attended venerable Exeter in Massachusetts. By 1905, the figure had doubled. In the decade that straddled 1901, when J. P. Morgan founded United States Steel, at least six elite boys' boarding schools were established on the New England model. They rose on a flood of new money from railroads, steel, and the machine gun, a new weapon Americans sold to warring Europe, and carried the old New England schools along with them into a sanctuary of snobbery. The new schools were Episcopalian (the fashionable religion) or nominally nondenominational. Groton, for example, founded in 1898, was to produce "Christian gentlemen," denomination not specified.

The schools were costly enough to keep out all but those on the top rung of the financial ladder, although a few scholarships did permit proper but comparatively poor boys to attend. In the late nineteenth century Lawrenceville and St. Paul's charged five hundred dollars for room and board, which was higher than most. By contrast, in 1900 the average wage for an unskilled worker in the north was four hundred and sixty dollars a year. In 1934–35 the fees had jumped to fourteen hundred dollars for St. Paul's and one thousand and fifty dollars for Exeter. In the 1930s the average family income was a little more than a thousand dollars a year.

In the 1880s, as immigrants crowded into the cities and the public schools, the newly rich and the old patricians fled to the suburbs, exclusive summer resorts, and the recently popular country clubs. In effect, they were withdrawing into safe houses and building fences around them, cutting themselves off from outsiders who had neither the right amount of money nor the right blood. As part of this trend, they sent their sons away to boarding schools to escape the contamination of heterogeneous public schools and the decline in educational standards that followed the Civil War.

That war marked a switch from a rural economy to an urban one. In 1860, the number of cities with a population of more than fifty thousand was sixteen; in 1910 it was 109. Farming and small business enterprises were overshadowed by huge corporate giants, with a resulting inequality of wealth. Strident anti-Semitism appeared for the first time on the American scene. It, too, was part of the surge toward status and the need to differentiate "real" Americans from foreign upstarts. The same impetus lay behind the Sons of the Revolution (1883) and the Daughters of the American Revolution (1890). Egalitarianism as an American dream faded in the face of the threat posed by bomb-throwing foreign-born anarchists, the armed battle of the Homestead Strike against Carnegie Steel with the attempted assassination of its head, Henry Clay Frick, and the ragged protests of Coxey's Army marching on Washington for jobs.

Although the new industrialists welcomed immigration as a pool of cheap labor, the old-stock Protestants deplored it as pollution. They tried to distance themselves from new money and new men. When the *Social Register* appeared in 1887, it provided printed evidence of who was socially respectable and who was not, and headmasters often consulted it before deciding to accept a boy. But money soon displaced ancestry as the mark of distinction, and both groups found common ground in setting themselves apart from the hungry hordes. *Forum* magazine estimated that in 1891, 120 men had fortunes worth more than ten million dollars. By 1910 more millionaires sat in the U.S. Senate than had existed in the whole country before the Civil War. The newly wealthy needed a seal of legitimacy and looked to England for coats of arms, real or imaginary. They adopted boarding schools and nannies as their own, and distorted the upper-class English accent into a nasal approximation of the real thing.

Boarding schools were a meeting place where the sons of patricians could join the sons of new industrial millionaires. They were, as Peter W. Cookson, Jr., and Caroline Hodges Persell point out in their book *Preparing for Power: America's Elite Boarding Schools*, barracks rather than family surrogates, dedicated to turning out soldiers in the Darwinian battle to survive at the top of the heap.

But even if families recognized this purpose as part of the reason they sent their sons away, they continued to see the schools as extensions of themselves, providing genteel family living in a home away from home. They developed the tradition of sending their sons, generation after generation, to the same school. The Vanderbilts were devoted to St. Paul's in Concord, New Hampshire, the Tafts, of course, to Taft (founded by the president's brother), and the Mellons to Choate, which they had helped finance. An upper-class boy was expected to leave home by the eighth or ninth grade. But, as one Groton father assured his apprehensive son, "It won't be like going away from home. Groton is a *part* of home."

Leaving home for the family school wasn't a matter of choice but of predestination, just as it was in England, from which all correctness flowed. In 1891 an upper-class English mother who criticized Eton for undermining the morals of its charges with its sadistic hazing and homosexual liaisons nevertheless sent her boys there. When asked why by an American visitor she replied, "How can we help it?" In the same vein, a New Englander whose father had gone to Milton Academy in Massachusetts went there, too, because "it was expected." A few days after his own son was born, he enrolled the boy, securing him a future place.

The nineteenth-century schools usually took boys from sixth or seventh grade through high school. Later they became strictly secondary schools, starting with the first year of high school. Junior schools with boarding students as young as nine or ten years of age took care of the younger boys until they could go on to elite prep schools. Some parents, as Edwards surmised in his *Educational Review* article, needed to have their children taken care of away from home so that they could continue their busy lives. Too old for nannies or governesses, the boys required a different surrogate. For other boys the schools were a respite from conflict at home or frequent moves that disrupted education, or from parental illness or neglect. But they could also be simply an opportunity to learn in a community of peers, and one more way of carrying out the culture patterns of their particular group. For all the boys, they were a way of wrenching them away from their mothers (or mother substitutes) so they could become real men, taught by men (not by women, as in the public school system) with properly manly interests and skills.

Roger Duncan, now a writer and editor specializing in the Maine seacoast, went to Exeter in 1932. His father and grandfathers on both sides of the family "way back" had gone to Harvard, and "it was expected" that he would go there, too. But he was an indifferent student in the suburban high school he attended, and his chances of following the family pattern seemed slim. His father before him had gone to boarding school; Exeter looked like the answer. "It never occurred to me," he says, "that going to Exeter would cost a lot of money. I don't know what would have happened to me if I hadn't gone. It kind of got me going."

A diminutive pixie of a man, he was the smallest boy in his high school class and was "trampled on." At Exeter, he found his place as coxswain of the rowing crew. And he studied. "People always did their homework," he explained. All his teachers were men, and with classes limited to sixteen boys, they sat around a table and discussed their assignments. "There was no way you could hide. The teacher was right there. There was nobody between him and me." In his case, peer pressure worked as a positive force to encourage him to do his best rather than, as in high school, as a negative pressure to goof off.

He got into Harvard, as did many of his classmates. They had studied the required two years of Latin, as well as the usual English, history, science, and math. Getting into Harvard wasn't too hard, he says: "If you could pay the tuition and had a coat and tie you could get in." And, of course, having a long family history of Harvard attendance plus his time at Exeter did not hurt.

Life at the Top

Elite, mainstream boarding schools for boys were modeled on the eighteenth-century English system. The English sent their boys away at the age of seven to learn to be leaders of their nation. They were subjected to harsh discipline, cold showers, uncomfortable living quarters, and indifferent food to teach them to conquer life and the colonials with a stiff upper lip and an equally stiff class system. In this country, schools for the sons of the old and new rich produced men dedicated to success, not service—captains of industry, lawyers, and doctors rather than prime ministers and admirals. Franklin D. Roosevelt, who went to Groton, the fashionable school founded in 1898, was the first president with a boarding-school background, a sharp break with the American log-cabin tradition for politicians. American schools, like the English, tried by an austere regimen to instill character along with a superior education. This attempt was, according to a critical survey by *Fortune* magazine in 1936 of the twelve "best" boarding schools, a failure: "The point to be made against the American schools is that, having imitated a model, they have imitated the superficial appearance and not the substantial merit."

The Colonial academies from which early elite schools grew (particularly in New England) were designed to provide secondary education in a land bereft of it. They took both day students and those who lived in distant towns and cities and stayed with reputable families nearby during the school term. By the end of the Civil War, schools in which students boarded on campus had superseded the old boarding-in-town system, and by the turn of the century the family boarding school (so called because it, like other institutions of the time such as insane asylums and reformatories, was designed to mimic the virtues of family living) had spread from New England to the western states. Gradually the academic focus of the schools changed with changing times and they became primarily preparatory schools for those heading toward Ivy League colleges.

The men in charge of the schools shared the standards and hopes of the parents who sent their boys to them. A recent ad for a dean of the faculty for the Lawrenceville School, founded in 1810, reconstituted in 1883, and now coed, might have appeared at any time in the school's history. In addition to the usual educational and administrative abilities, it required that the dean have "high intellect, great heart, generosity of spirit, and impeccable integrity." For writer John Hersey, his headmaster at the Hotchkiss School in Lakeville, Connecticut, in the 1920s epitomized these qualities and more, and hoped his students would follow his example: "He wanted a man not just to be learned, but rather to be wise, decent, humane, generous, forgiving and light of heart in heavy days." He was also in a veiled conspiracy with the boys against their parents. On the day before graduation, Hersey's headmaster subjected visiting parents—"not his most beloved category of humankind"—to a reading of a short story mocking the solemnity of school graduations. "Was his notorious treatment of parents mere rudeness for its own sake?" Hersey asked in his book *Life Sketches*. "I am certain it was not. I think it was a combination of a deep, deep shyness he had, along with a shrewd sense of alliance with the secret souls of the boys in his school, who were condemned by nature in their formative years to a helpless war with the very idea of parenthood." The headmaster was not only an ally, he was a role model who "gave us the great gift of his example." In this, he and other teachers and headmasters resembled the earlier masters of apprentices who also lived with young boys and instructed them as much by what they were as by what they did.

The Schools

Boarding schools trimmed and trained their graduates to be, like carefully clipped bushes, immediately identifiable and able to fit in to upper-class society. What the historian Richard Bushman termed "gentility" served as a class marker in the turbulent times of the early and mid-nineteenth century when cities were growing at three times the rate of the rest of the country. As the century came to a close in the anonymous urban centers, how was one to tell the right people from the wrong? By manners, of course, and habits of speech, and dress. Going to the right school was one way of learning the rules of the ruling class. The schools inculcated these rules in an atmosphere of total living, a setting in which these markers became unquestioned accoutrements of daily life. A 1932 graduate of Andover recognized that the requirement that "neckties will be worn at all meals" was equivalent to an initiation ceremony. Wearing a necktie became a sign of belonging.

These symbols were important as more and more Americans acquired secondary education. In the 1870s and 1880s, 73 percent of all secondary school students went to private schools. By the 1900s, only 0.1 percent did. This figure is misleading, however. By the turn of the century, more students than ever before were going to public high schools. Education beyond grade school ceased to be a mark of privilege and a monopoly of the private schools. It was now open to all, socially acceptable and unacceptable. As high schools became commonplace, the percentage of those who attended boarding schools shrank, although the actual numbers increased. One of the selling points to parents considering sending their sons away in 1903 was that in certain places boys in the upper grades were "from their nationality, objectionable personal habits, or what not, undesirable." Unwritten quotas kept the "undesirables"—Catholics, Jews, Negroes—for the most part out of the sacred precincts.

Despite their commitment to the manners and mores of their class, the schools each had individual characters and distinctive ways of dealing with the boys. Some were more demanding intellectually than others, some more spartan. At Kent in Connecticut, founded in 1902, boys made their own beds and and waited on tables. At traditional Andover and Exeter, founded as academies in the eighteenth century, they were groomed for Harvard.

The traditional schools, usually small and homogeneous, were designed to foster group cohesiveness. Living together for four or six years, isolated from the rest of society, the boys formed a community whose links were expected to extend into adulthood. These links were one step on an escalator to success, smoothing the way into the power-wielding establishment.

Along with a commitment to perpetuating the attitudes, values, and social networks of the dominant Anglo-Saxon Protestant establishment came a commitment to its prejudices. At Lawrenceville, *Fortune* magazine reported in 1936, they played a softball game called "Nigger Baby": "From such games as this Lawrenceville derives its flavor," the magazine declared. Groton celebrated May Day with a dance around the maypole, one of the boys in a wig playing Queen of the May—mocking both ethereal young women and homosexuals. In fairness, it is necessary to remember that these attitudes were widespread and hardly even worthy of editorial comment at the time.

Early in the schools' history theirs was an exclusive community, and in large part they remained insular and bigoted. But as the country expanded and wealth spread even to the sons of immigrants, they began to broaden their reach and take in a few "outsiders"—even a few Catholics and Jews. Bo Goldman, the Academy Award–winning screenwriter, was sent to Exeter by his businessman father—the son of immigrants—who "desperately wanted to plug into the dead center." He couldn't do it himself, so he sent his son. Goldman recalls, "The people I grew up with . . . ran the banks and hospitals and the law firms. . . . All I wanted was acceptance. And it almost corrupted me." He found what his father may have understood but never spoke about; once "plugged" into the elite, he was "unplugged" from his family forever. As Calvin Trillin wrote of his own experience, his Jewish father saw that Yale's purpose (like that of the prep schools) was "to turn the likes of us into the likes of them." But "the likes of them" were not always accepting of the outsiders. A 1925 graduate of Andover remembered that there was "a strong undercurrent of anti-Semitism which at least once a year would break out in really vicious incidents."

Even the boys who were "the right kind" to begin with did not always fit comfortably into what seemed an inevitable progression from the right prep school to the right Ivy League college to the right job, the socially correct wife, and children who inevitably repeated the whole lockstep process. As Cookson and Persell show, the students learned in this process that "the price of privilege is the loss of autonomy and individuality."

A 1922 Andover graduate granted that in later years the school placed some emphasis on individuality, although, "We were in the sink or swim days. The swimmers among us report on the success of such a method. The sinkers are silent."

A member of the class of 1925 who became vice president of Time, Inc., was even more specific. He admitted to having hated the school while he was there, but "the years cast a golden glow." The glow did not completely obliterate the shadows. "Boys were no longer birched, it is true," he wrote, "but it was known as a tough school. And it was. It was not a good school for the 'poorly adjusted boy,' or even the conspicuously gifted boy. But for a normal competitive youngster who could take it, who could cope with its college-like size [it was one of the largest, with 562 students in 1916], its utterly impersonal attitude, its rigid rules and standards, for that boy Andover could provide a remarkable education."

A remarkable education was what many parents expected of the elite boarding schools. They offered rigorous training in the classics, as did the British schools, and subjected their students to mental gymnastics, requiring them to memorize long passages to exercise their minds. Young minds were seen as chaotic, needing firm guidance toward the fountainhead of knowledge, and that fountainhead was the classical world. It was not until late in the nineteenth century that "soft" subjects such as English, history, and math were added to the curriculum. As in England, sports were important as builders of character and stamina. They also released tension and, followed by cold showers, kept the boys from dwelling on sex. Although the schools gave lip service to the idea of cooperation, they imbued their students with a fierce competitive spirit on the athletic fields and in the classrooms.

Public high schools at the turn of the century adapted to their new role as educator of the masses by offering a two-track program. One focused on English, the other on Latin. Otherwise the curriculum was the same. Upper-class, conservative parents who wanted their children educated with their own kind, in their own way, chose to send them away from the dangers of democracy to the familiar homogeneity of the boarding schools. They provided not only a special education but a place for a boy to grapple with a special time—adolescence.

The Discovery of Adolescence

Adolescence and elite family boarding schools were both born in the nineteenth century, as James McLachlan has pointed out in his book *American Boarding Schools.* Of course, adolescence—or youth—was recognized as a definable stage by the Greeks and Romans and by Comenius and Rousseau as well. And Samuel Phillips, Jr., founder in 1778 of Phillips Academy at Andover, Massachusetts, which evolved into one of this country's most prestigious boarding schools, was true to his Puritan ancestors when he warned against "the first dawnings of depraved nature"—sexuality—as young men grew toward manhood. Youth was seen by Rousseau as a time of developmental crisis when a moratorium from life's demands would allow a boy to mature into a man. This "time out" effectively stretched the years of irresponsibility that used to extend only until the early teens, when a boy was expected to earn his own way and could even marry without parental consent. But it was G. Stanley Hall, this country's original scientific psychologist, who first enumerated adolescence's characteristics and warned of its dangers in a book published in 1905. He called his treatise *Adolescence: Its Psychology and Its Relations to Physiology, Anthropology, Sociology, Sex, Crime, Religion, and Education.* Although many of his ideas have now fallen into disfavor, his views had a profound effect on the way teenagers were seen and treated. His assumption that human development proceeds by distinct stages—mimicking the stages of man's evolution—set child behavior clearly apart from that of adults. Children were not just miniature grown-ups but creatures proceeding along their own developmental course.

He considered adolescence "a new birth, for the higher and more completely human traits are now born," but along with the first emergence of this ethical sense he warned that "development is less gradual and more saltatory [proceeding by leaps], suggestive of some ancient period of storm and stress when old moorings were broken and a higher level attained." This stormy time led to "not only arrest, but perversion, at every stage, and hoodlumism, juvenile crime and secret vice."

Adolescence identified as a dangerous time for both society and youth fit the social concerns of the new century. Close to a million young immigrants threatened the status quo; Americans were moving off the farms and into cities as industrialization expanded. New York's population jumped from a million in 1880 to a million and a half in a decade. Juvenile delinquency was recognized as a major problem and the first juvenile court, established with Jane Addams's help in 1899, aimed at providing more humane treatment for youngsters. They did not commit "crimes" as adults did—they committed "delinquencies." Yet the Juvenile Court Act "to Regulate the Treatment and Control of Dependent, Neglected, and Delinquent Children" also marked adolescence as a threatening phase. If they needed a special legal system, they must be a danger to the social fabric. Popular magazines in the twenties and thirties featured such articles as "Parents Wake Up" and "Why Adolescents Go Wrong."

Hall warned of the temptations of urban life and the breakdown of old standards and values that was setting young people adrift. He declared, "At its best, metropolitan life is hard on childhood and especially so on pubescents, and children who can not pass these years in the country are robbed of a right of childhood that should be inalienable." The "Myth of the Country Boy"—the idea that cities are corrupting and rural living ennobling—now applied particularly to that marked creature, the adolescent. Elite boarding schools set up in small towns or in the countryside provided the wholesome atmosphere championed by Hall and desired by parents willing to pay for the best for their children.

The country as the preferred place for adolescents had also been advocated by Rousseau in the eighteenth century. In *Emile*, his "novel" propounding his views on education, he suggested that if a young man were to have the best chance in life, he should be sent away from his parents and the evils of the city into the country with a devoted tutor. In this same vein, boarding schools put a group of students together with a group of tutors and protected the youngsters from the dangers of the world while exposing them to the right kind of care. Roger Duncan sees Exeter's community of boys as having distracted him from adolescence: "There was no reason to get in trouble, there weren't any girls around anyway." One of the heirs of Rousseau's thinking, Emmanuel Von Fellenberg, declared in the early nineteenth century that "the great art of educating consists of knowing how to occupy every moment of life in well-directed and useful activity of the youthful powers, in order that, so far as possible, nothing evil may find room to develop itself." Von Fellenberg's school in Switzerland greatly influenced American boarding-school philosophy. Woodrow Wilson, speaking at the centennial celebration of the Lawrenceville School in 1910, said it and others like it succeeded because "it organizes life from morning to night." Dangerous impulses had to be contained by the straitjacket of a rigid schedule.

Separating vulnerable adolescents from both younger and older children and worldly vice (and, particularly for boys, overconcerned mothers) seemed like a good idea. The proliferation of boarding schools as the twentieth century approached mirrored the somewhat earlier proliferation of other institutions that segregated particular groups for their own and society's good, usually in country settings out of sight—the insane, the blind, the deaf, the emotionally disturbed, the feebleminded, the delinquent. These people were somehow different and somehow dangerous, either to themselves or others, as adolescents were assumed to be.

Boarding schools of one sort or another based on the family as a model were the preferred way to deal with problem populations. The Office of Indian Affairs, established in 1834, set them up for children who, "for their own good," needed to be separated from their parents and culture in order to be converted into "real" Americans, indistinguishable from those of European descent. One commissioner of Indian affairs saw that teaching young Indians the three Rs would not be enough: "If they do not learn to build and live in houses; to sleep on beds; to eat at regular intervals; to plow, and sow, and reap; to rear and use domestic animals; to understand and practice the mechanical arts; and to enjoy, to their gratification and improvement, all the means of profit and rational pleasure that are so profusely spread around civilized life . . . what is learned in the schoolroom proper will be completely valueless." The objective was to "kill the Indian and save the man." Like other "total environments," the Indian boarding schools were designed to pass on the attitudes and standards of a culture.

The Helpmates

Socially exclusive girls' schools, most founded between 1880 and 1920, dedicated themselves to producing good wives who could create the proper setting for their successful husbands. Manners were supremely important; book learning was not. As a matter of fact, some doctors thought that too much studying could be harmful to a young woman's delicate constitution.

The woman founders of these schools were usually unmarried, with impeccable social pedigrees. They were determined to sequester their students as safely as the nuns did in Catholic convent schools, which served as models, even though they were reluctant to admit Catholics as students. Girls were to be kept pure and taught only enough to be cultivated helpmates for the men they would inevitably marry. But a trend toward unmarried females that had begun at the time of the Civil War eventually forced the schools to train women to be more than ornamental. By 1860 eight eastern states had more marriageable women than men. In New York State alone young women exceeded young men by almost thirty-nine thousand. If they lost their right to marriage, they must be made fit to fill a role that might not include the ultimate goal—motherhood. For upper-middle-class and middle-class girls this could hardly mean working in a factory or even an office: The boarding schools must prepare them for more training, rather than acting as an end point for the production of idle "ladies." They could be productive "ladies," if necessary, helping the poor like Jane Addams and her unmarried colleagues, or teaching the next generation.

Around the time of World War I, most of the schools, rather than a few, accepted reality and emphasized college preparation. More women were going on to higher learning (between 1900 and 1913 the number of women college graduates doubled) and needed better scholastic training.

Emma Willard's Troy Female Seminary, founded in 1814, anticipated this trend toward educated women and is usually credited with laying the groundwork for "normal schools" that trained women to be teachers. A few years later, Catherine Beecher's Hartford Seminary opened and enlarged the options for further education available to young women. Beecher envisioned a wide network of seminaries, since "it is to *mothers* and to *teachers* that the world is to look for the character which is to be enstamped on each succeeding generation, for it is to them that the great business of education is almost exclusively committed."

Women gradually replaced men as teachers in the public schools. (In private schools for boys, however, men continued to hold sway.) By 1900 more than 70 percent of teachers were female. By 1925, the figure had grown to 83 percent. They were, on the philosophical level, deemed more fitted to nurture the young. On the practical level, their pay was one-half to one-third that of men.

Some schools, such as the Shipley School, founded by Quakers in 1929, were designed specifically to give girls the groundwork necessary for them to go on to college. Others, like Miss Porter's, founded in Farmington, Connecticut, in 1843, maintained their reputation as "finishing" schools long after other schools had begun to put more emphasis on academics. Miss Porter's mission, according to *Fortune*'s 1936 survey, was to prepare a girl for her "destiny as a wife." In a tradition that became emblematic of elite girls' schools, the girls went into the fields before graduation to gather daisies, which were then woven into a chain by a commercial florist and carried by the girls in their procession. True to their expectations for the future, they were spared the manual labor (of making the chain), for which they could hire someone else.

Families often sent both boys and girls away to school, but the major stated reasons were often different: The girls were to be polished, the boys educated. A woman who sent both her daughter and her son to boarding schools told the readers of *Harper's Monthly* in 1926 that "I believe that home has done its best for a boy by the time he is fifteen and that after that it often does its worst." Her son went to a large school with boys from all over the country who got "no pampering, no coddling, no nonsense." In public school in the small midwestern city in which they lived, he had been neglecting his studies. Away from home, he worked hard. She lamented the lack of discipline in a home with few children and parents who were too attentive. "The parent today," she wrote, "knows his child, sympathizes with him, understands him, becomes his chum and playmate."

The girl went to boarding school at fourteen when mother and daughter were tangled in the usual adolescent tussles about boys and dating and following family rules. The school was not a fashionable one but emphasized scholarship and "breeding," and "going away to school gave her back her home and her mother, not as workroom and mentor, but as haven and confidant." Her children, she insisted, see their home as "playground and haven, instead of the combination dormitory and penal institution which the home of many young people is today," and they see their parents as "best friends" rather than "despots." In essence this woman sidestepped her children's adolescence, turning over to teachers and monitors the thankless task of taming the turbulence that leads, eventually, to maturity.

These parental evils, of course, came about through the new psychology as well as the realities of small families. In the 1880s, the average family had three children; by the 1920s, only two and one-third. The reasons for this drop in the birthrate are obscure. Perhaps increased infant survival because of medical advances made it unnecessary for parents to produce excess children as insurance against family extinction; perhaps birth control played a part. Whatever the reason for the decline, fewer children meant more parental attention per child. Up-to-date parents who read the advice in popular magazines knew that children should be treated as individuals, even as friends. The strictness of the past, with a feared but loved father meting out swift corporal punishment, was replaced, at least in the advice columns, with the parent as understanding companion.

When parents are friends, this mother went on, "It is rather difficult to interrupt this relationship suddenly in order to become judge, jury and executioner as in the old days." Boarding school, "*in loco parentis*," seemed the best way.

The Moravians

Throughout this country's history boarding schools of minority religious groups provided parents with a way not only of avoiding adolescence but of providing for younger children as well. These schools were frankly child-care as well as educational institutions, since they took in young children as well as teenagers. Often they accepted preschoolers as well as high school students.

The first of these schools was started by Moravians, a small, breakaway religious group with a tradition of caring for its community's children. The earliest boarding school for girls in this country's first colonies, it was established not to polish them into ladies but to give them a superior education to fit them for superior motherhood. Countess Benigna Zinzendorf of Saxony founded the school in 1742 in Germantown, Pennsylvania, when she was only sixteen years old. Its long history recapitulates the evolution of the whole boarding-school movement.

The young countess had been reared in the philosophy of John Amos Comenius, the John Dewey of the seventeenth century, who thought that women were at least as capable as men and deserved excellent educations to prepare them for their future role—not as wives, but as mothers charged with educating the next generation. Comenius advocated universal, free, compulsory education without regard to sex or station in life (prefiguring later public schooling)—so the Moravians educated girls and Indians and blacks as well as white boys. As their doctrine put it, "Wherever a church is built in heathen lands, beside it stands a school."

Countess Zinzendorf had come with her father, the count, to

the New World to visit the peace-loving Moravians whom he had saved on his estate in Saxony after they had been banished from their native Moravia and Bohemia by the Germans after the Thirty Years' War. In 1740 a small band had settled near the banks of the Lehigh River in Pennsylvania, determined to carry out what they saw as their destiny as thanks for having been rescued from extinction: missionary work and education. Two years later, when the count and countess arrived, they were industriously involved in bringing the word of God to the Indians. Within a month the tiny school the countess started in what was then the far western frontier of the American colonies moved with its sixteen students and four teachers from Germantown ten miles away to Bethlehem, where, after a few early dislocations, it persisted. In 1785 the first non-Moravians were admitted, and gradually it was transformed by financial and cultural pressure to resemble other girls' boarding schools and finally merged with its male counterpart to form a modern, coeducational institution—The Moravian Academy. During its first century, the girls' school provided a home and education for about seven thousand pupils. In 1929, only 103 girls were in attendance.

The Moravians, like other groups that established boarding schools, wanted to accomplish what education of the young has traditionally set out to do: pass on the values, standards, and customs of a particular group while preparing the child to enter the world. The experience of small, sectarian schools such as the Moravian Seminary may seem marginal, but it set the stage for women's education in women's colleges along with Emma Willard's and Catherine Beecher's seminaries.

The girls were taught in small classes, isolated for the most part from other youngsters and adults who did not share their religious views or cultural background, and subjected to strict supervision to shepherd them through the turbulence of growing up. Unlike students at elite girls' schools, where attendance was a mark of privilege, many of these girls came from a less rarefied social atmosphere, true to Comenius's conviction that children of various backgrounds should be educated together. Nevertheless, they were clearly separate, socially and financially, from their more plebeian stay-at-home contemporaries.

Anticipating Piaget (who edited his works in 1957), Comenius, the Moravian bishop and educator, divided growing up into stages and declared that education should be tailored to fit the capacities

and needs of the child at each level. For the first six years children
were to be instructed by their mothers in the rudiments of such subjects as arithmetic, physics, geometry, optics, history, and, of course,
piety and religion. Mothers had to be prepared to handle this daunting task. Then, with teaching conducted in the vernacular (which, for
these Moravians of central European background, was German),
children were to be introduced to academic subjects, music instruction, and vocational training. At the age of twelve, the traditional
classical curriculum including Latin and Greek was to begin.

Comenius was remarkable in that he anticipated later psychological and educational theory by about three hundred years, insisting (like Maria Montessori in the twentieth century) that children
learn by doing—by using their senses—not just by rote, and that education of the whole person, for his or her maximum individual development, should be the aim. He suggested that pictures, models,
and real objects enhanced the learning process and made it enjoyable
rather than the grim torment he had experienced. In his lifetime he
was hailed as an educational reformer—not the first, but one of the
most influential. Tradition has it that he was invited by John
Winthrop, Jr., to become the president of Harvard in the 1600s but
declined. As time went on, his extraordinary views, now considered
commonplace, were neglected except by his devoted coreligionists.

The Moravians were revolutionaries in religion as well as education. They consider themselves the first Protestants. Their
founder, Jan Hus, was burned at the stake in 1415 for defying
Catholic dogma—a century before Martin Luther posted his theses.

When they settled at Bethlehem, Pennsylvania (so named at
Christmastime because the first rough dwellings housed animals as
well as men, as the manger had done), they were forced by circumstances to ignore Comenius's writing, which insisted on the mother
as first instructor. Faced with the need for women to work in the
fields and as missionaries, the Moravians set up communal child
care—resembling the kind the Oneida community established a hundred years later. Children from eighteen months to five or six years
were cared for together in a nursery by "sisters"—unmarried women
who lived together in one of the houses. (Under the Moravian system,
single men, single women, children, and married couples lived in separate quarters.) After that, the children were placed in the boarding
school, where they completed their education. Girls went to one
school in Bethlehem, boys to another in nearby Nazareth. The girls'

education, it is generally agreed, was better, since they stayed in school steadily while the boys were likely to be pulled out of classes or even out of school entirely to work in the fields.

Although the communal nursery ended with the dissolution of communal living in 1762, the boarding schools continued to care for children from the age of about five to eighteen. In 1913 the name was changed to the Moravian Seminary and College for Women, since, as the principal of the school had said in the 1890s, "The whole tendency of the times among girls and young women seems to be to go to college." The Moravians, long experienced in the intelligent education of girls, eventually expanded their school to accommodate college students. This pattern of having young children and twenty-one-year-olds under the same roofs continued through the 1920s and 1930s.

At first, Moravian girls were taught in German to preserve the language; by 1789 they were taught in German every day except Wednesdays, when the whole school spoke English. This early experiment in bilingual education was also followed in the church, where a sermon in English was preached once a month. By 1817, all instruction was in English.

This and other changes at the seminary to accommodate to changing times reflect the changes taking place in child care and education in the larger world. In the mid-nineteenth century, with Mother at the center of a child's world, the school began to emphasize the loving care it provided to substitute for maternal warmth. The seminary also kept up with modern educational thinking. Courses in typing and home economics were added, and girls were even prepared to be teachers, the socially acceptable profession. When higher education for women first became popular, girls who graduated had the required credits to go on to college if they wanted to. But the school continued to do what families traditionally do: provide a haven for the growth of the young in a setting that passes on the received wisdom of the particular group.

The need to provide for children what they might have had in their own homes colored Moravian education with a strong substitute family tone. Since necessity is often the mother of psychology, parents who sent their children away for whatever reason were reassured that "the family idea is at the very basis of all its government and instruction, and affectionate personal supervision the chief peculiarity of its method." Little girls were cared for "as if by a tender mother's love." The satisfied mother of a graduate testified that "under such a theory the School becomes simply an enlarged home, where authority is that invisible influence of personal sympathy and fellowship and interest that constitutes the order and government of the family. Whatever weakens this homogeneity is denied; all that inspires it is encouraged." This kindness was based on Moravian precepts. Comenius had declared that the learning process—at home or away from it—should be humane, "for a rational creature should be led not by shouts, imprisonment and blows, but by reason. Any other method is an insult to God, in whose image all men are made."

Living arrangements in the old rough stone buildings that formed the school persisted, with adjustments of course for indoor plumbing, heating, and electricity, with surprising consistency through the centuries. The girls were divided into "room companies"—four or five who shared a sitting room/dressing room and study and were supervised by two "tutoresses." Most of them slept in dormitories, with a few seniors privileged to have more private quarters. In 1891 a girl wrote to a friend: "You know we sleep in dormitories . . . [in alcoves] curtained off by white curtains with red borders. . . . The first night I slept there I thought of horses in their stalls. . . . We are not supposed to talk in the dormitories." A 1921 photograph shows similar red-bordered curtains.

Supervision was complete and inescapable—as if each girl had an all-seeing and ever-present mother. An 1817 student wrote, "The girls were never left alone, one teacher was always with them, whether studying, walking, or at play." Even in the next century, the close supervision was continued. A catalogue reassured parents that the school would be a better parent than they could be—the hope of all parents who send their children away to school: "If the protection of human character, in its moulding period, against private and insidious vice that saps its roots and sows decay, and the preservation of the native purity and vigor of fresh young life, are not the all-momentous, imperative duty to youth and nation, what is? And duty none the less because too rarely called to the thought of parent and guardian, and in tones too soft. . . . [The school] keeps open its eyes to physical dangers to the young and protects them against themselves by systematic forethought and direction. All study goes on in the study-parlor, in the presence of a teacher. The games in its seven acres of park . . . the dances in the gymnasium, the weekly mending hour, the letter-writing hour, work or recreation, all are alike shared by the 'duty teacher.' " With privacy only behind the curtains of their beds, the girls were constantly available for correction, guidance, and observation, with little chance to develop the individuality Comenius had commended. As a later graduate lamented, "There was no provision for the expansion of personality."

The curriculum was, however, aimed at the expansion of the mind. In the early days, when the school was, according to one newspaper, "the most fashionable school in the United States" (non-Moravians were admitted as early as 1785), the girls studied history, geography, logic, rhetoric, botany, astronomy "with celestial globes," philosophy, chemistry, and grammar. In addition there were music lessons twice a week, practice every day, drawing and painting, "worsted work," and the usual three Rs. As the years went by the school had to compete with other boarding schools for young women and bowed to the demands of the larger world with courses in home economics, access to classes in shorthand and typing at a business school in Bethlehem, and training in "expression." It never succumbed to the temptation to become just a finishing school, maintaining the simplicity and educational rigor with which it had begun. For a time in the 1920s and 1930s the school housed girls from first grade through four years of college.

Music was always an important part of the curriculum and Moravian life. Moravians are credited with introducing church music into the colonies and establishing the first symphony orchestra in 1748.

Music had wider uses, too. Legend has it that Bethlehem, on the fringe of the western frontier, was saved from a raid by hostile Indians during the French and Indian Wars by the trombone choir playing such celestial sounds at sunset that the Indians, convinced the Great Spirit was their guardian, crept away in reverential fear. The trombone, an ancient instrument whose sound has been described as closest of any instrument to the human voice, was traditionally played by the Moravians in Europe from the cupolas of their churches. At Bethlehem, trombones were traditionally sounded from the school roof on festive occasions or to announce the death of a member of the community. Today, a trombone choir still plays every Christmas from the catwalk of the cupola of the church that stands across the street from the stone buildings the boarding school occupied between the two world wars.

In the days of its early glory, the school had such illustrious students as George Washington's grandniece, the daughters of John Jay, the first justice of the U.S. Supreme Court, and the three nieces of Stephen Girard, whose will set up Girard College as an orphanage for white boys in Philadelphia. Later, most of its students were the daughters of merchants or of missionaries, and included Phoebe Vanderbilt, the daughter of Commodore Cornelius. Like most boarding schools, what had come to be known familiarly as Fem Sem took in girls whose parents were busy with their professional or social lives, those who had only one parent, and those who lived or traveled extensively abroad. It continued to take girls from the Caribbean islands, where Moravian missionaries had been active in the early days, and girls who, one way or another, had some personal connection to the church or the school. Tuition in 1925 for the junior school, including room, board, and laundry, was seven hundred dollars. For the seminary (high school) it was seven hundred and twenty-five. (In 1817, "bedding included," it had been a hundred.) Day students who came from the surrounding towns paid about half that amount. (As a comparison figure, in 1916 seven elite boarding schools for boys charged an average of nine hundred and fifty dollars a year.)

Supervision was unbending and pervasive. In 1925 girls who did not live at the school were required to report for chapel at 8:45 and stay on campus until 3:15 unless they went home for an hour's lunch at noon.

As one of the few Protestant boarding schools to accept young children as well as teenagers, Fem Sem continued to emphasize its role as a home away from home, offering "a safe and happy solution of the care of the child." Separate space was set aside for the youngsters "in the very heart of the Seminary," with a teacher quartered in the dormitory to see "that children do not become timid at night and at the same time keep off temptations which might arise if the young people were without this loving, motherly supervision." The first teachers were Moravian sisters—unmarried women who felt called to teach the young as their way of serving the church. Later teachers continued in the tradition of viewing their role as a "calling," although they made some demands that they be treated like instructors in other schools. In 1939 the first full-time housemother was finally hired, relieving teachers of some supervision outside the classroom.

Older girls were assigned a younger to look after as a special friend, providing a semblance of sibling care as well as parental concern. For children whose parents could not have them at home even at holidays or over the summer, the school made arrangements to place them with families in the village.

For the girls in the seminary (grades seven through twelve) the school offered better than parental training, allowing mothers, for example, to sidestep the need to deal with adolescent sloppiness. The *Handbook* for 1939–40 informed boarders, "Neatness is a habit to be cultivated in youth. Rooms will be inspected daily, and a weekly inspection of drawers, cupboards and closets will be held." The neatest room at the end of the semester earned a prize. Like so many other attitudes and regulations, these inspections were a holdover from earlier days. In 1817 Harriet Gould Drake Tinkam described the "sitting room" in which each girl had a drawer in a table assigned to her. "In this drawer we kept our ink, writing book, goose quill pens, and pencils. . . . These drawers were carefully inspected by the room keepers."

To make group life bearable in a setting in which curtained rows of girls filled the dormitory, the 1939 *Handbook* warned that "early rising before seven is forbidden. In fairness to other girls, early risers should not use alarm clocks." Girls were chaperoned at concerts and games and had to get written permission for "gentlemen callers" to come to the recreation room on Saturday. On Sunday, all students (Moravians or not) were required to attend church services in the elegantly simple church across the street.

Aware that girls would need more than the three meals a day offered in the dining room, the *Handbook* listed pretzels, crackers, shelled nuts, fresh fruit, "and a limited amount of confectionary" as the foods girls might bring into their rooms. Lights out was at 8:30 for the younger girls, 9:30 for the high school students, and despite the close supervision, it is clear that the girls managed to stave off hunger after they were in bed. In 1938 two eleven-year-olds wrote poems about the results: "Oh, the crunching and the scrunching of the crumbs, somewhere underneath your shoulder on the sheet Where they calmly keep you from your sleep," wrote one. The other replied, "It's your fault for breaking laws With never a thought of a pause. Even crumbs must have a cause!" Following Comenius's philosophy, practical matters were not neglected. The girls made their own beds and dusted and swept their rooms. Every Saturday morning they had "mending hour," sitting with a teacher who supervised their repair of their own clothes. That tradition, like the conviction that women deserve an education at least as good as that of men, continued through the centuries and survives today.

During its long history, the school has adapted to new ways while continuing many of its hallowed customs. Its blend of old and

new, and its evolution through precarious economic times to continue to attract girls in a shrinking boarding-school market, reflect
the struggles of other girls' schools to find a way to produce educated, yet genteel, young women.

Young Children, Hard Choices

Some children went away to school, not to learn to be genteel, but to
survive. Life has a way of making a painful choice seem the only way
of caring for a young child. This was true in medieval times when babies were left on the doorsteps of churches, and much later when
children were sent away to boarding schools. Necessity often forced
those who were not affluent to send their children away. The family
was not so poor that the almshouse or orphanage was an option, nor
so rich that they could afford live-in help. Parents who could not care
for their children themselves had to find a place that could play surrogate parent. The placement, they hoped, was temporary. Often,
the children were much younger than the usual boarding-school
population.

Letty Cottin Pogrebin, a founder of *Ms.* magazine, was shocked
when she discovered that her mother had deposited an earlier daughter named Betty in a boarding school at the age of three. The mother
(who subsequently married Pogrebin's father) was divorced and
working to support herself and her child. She could have left Betty
with her immigrant mother but was afraid the child would become a
"second-generation greenhorn," doomed to second-class status. Instead, she placed her in an upstate New York boarding school in 1928
and visited on Sundays. To the men she dated, she presented herself
as single and unencumbered. In her autobiography, *Deborah, Golda
and Me*, Pogrebin confessed, "I have trouble understanding how the
fiercely maternal, overprotective woman who was my mother was the
same woman who could leave Betty in a boarding school at the age of
three." When Pogrebin's own daughters were three she tried to
imagine "depositing those angelic little toddlers in some school dormitory." Finally she was able to understand that "what now looks like
cold-hearted rejection must have been to her way of thinking an act
of loving sacrifice."

"An act of loving sacrifice" was what three-year-old Marion's
parents felt they performed by putting her in a boarding school. Her
brother, four years older, was there, too. The Depression had forced

the parents to move to a single hotel room and try to work together to make enough money to live. They scrimped and saved to pay for the children's keep. But for Marion it seemed that "they used their money to put my brother and me away. It left me feeling I was not a good person, otherwise why would they do this to me?" They lived with fifty children in what would now probably be called a group home in Brooklyn, since the older children went outside to public school. At that time, however, it characterized itself as a "boarding school." It charged tuition and took full responsibility for the children in its care.

She was the youngest—pretty and bouncy, with black curls, and the center of attention. On Sundays (when parents were allowed to visit) she was paraded into the living room to entertain. She remembers singing "Memories" and reciting, "I am a little girl three years old, My mommy makes me dresses out of silver and gold, A pen in my pocket, a dolly in my hand—Ain't I cute?"

Like any little girl, she resisted having her parents leave. "People there would trick me and send me into the other room, or I would have to go to the bathroom and when I came back they would be gone." They probably thought they were saving her from being upset, but "I remember looking out the window and seeing them walking to the subway. I was crying and yelling. It was a very sad time for me."

She rarely saw her brother, since he went to school and lived with the older boys. In the summers, they both went to a camp run by the school. When she was five, they came back home with Miss Nolan, a "governess" who had been with them in the boarding school. "She was stern and strict and would spank with a hairbrush. My only choice," Marion recalls, "was back or bristles." It was this "governess" who sent her to school a year early, to get her out of the house. When asked how old she was, she would reply, "I'm six in school but five at home."

Despite her separation from her parents, Marion always "felt they loved me." In later years she talked to her mother about that painful time. Her mother explained that they had done the best they could.

Faced with the death of his wife, Eileen Simpson's father did the best he could, too, and put her and her sister (aged three and four) with relatives, then in a "preventorium," and finally in a convent "with the nuns." The "preventoriums" and TB sanatoriums housed many children who, it was feared, would die of the dread disease.

They were boarding facilities—if not boarding schools. Eileen and Marie were sent to Farmingdale, Long Island, to sleep in the open air and avoid the dreaded fate of their twenty-seven-year-old mother. Eileen remembered her first night: "My original plan, to spend the night in Marie's bed, had been thwarted by the matron, who, making a bed check and finding us huddled together, led me back to where I belonged. I lay on my cot, crouched under a mound of heavy blankets, every muscle flexed. . . . Surely this was a new form of punishment, rather than a treatment to make us well."

Separation from a loved parent was always a punishment, whatever the parents' intentions. The fear of tuberculosis was so pervasive (it was a major killer of young people) and its course so mysterious that the recommended treatment for adults as well as children was years-long confinement in a sanatorium. These dotted the countryside, located where the air was "good" and patients could strengthen their weak lungs by rest. Eileen Simpson's father was following expert advice, considering her mother's early death from "the white plague," when he tried to strengthen his daughters to fight the disease to which they had been long exposed. But the preventorium was only a temporary solution to his problem of child care.

Trying to find a more permanent and benign answer, Eileen's father sent them to the Ursulines at Tarrytown where his sisters had been educated and then, more appropriately, to the Villa Maria in Dobbs Ferry, New York, which was accustomed to young children. There they stayed for five years, and when their father died when Eileen was seven, she was sent to live with relatives. She dedicated her book, *Orphans, Real and Imaginary*, to her sister—"Marie, my companion in the wilderness."

The Nuns

Sending children to the nuns to be cared for has been a time-honored way of solving both a child-care and an educational problem since the fifteenth century. Even well into the twentieth century, convent schools were equipped to house toddlers as well as elementary and high school–age girls.

The author Mary McCarthy was eleven—hardly adolescent yet—and in the seventh grade when her grandparents put her in the Forest Ridge convent in Seattle, one in a worldwide family of schools of the Sacred Heart. Her grandmother was Jewish, her grandfather Protestant, but her father's family, and Mary herself, were Catholic.

Both parents had perished within a day of each other in the World War I influenza pandemic that wiped out more than half a million people in this country alone.

The Seattle Sacred Heart school was an elite Catholic boarding school, more sophisticated and more educationally demanding than many others, with a few day students. Founded in France in 1800, the order took with it around the world French intellectual standards and a curriculum that emphasized philosophy and rhetoric and had hardly changed since it was promulgated in 1805. Rose Kennedy had gone to a Sacred Heart school in Europe; she sent her daughter Kathleen to one in this country when she was twelve because she was "irritated by her . . . popularity with boys. [She] was on the phone with them for hours at a time." Mrs. Kennedy, too, was sidestepping her child's adolescence.

The girls called the nuns Madame, followed by their real last names rather than religious names (as was customary at other Catholic schools), or just *Mère* or Mother for short. They played *cache-cache* (hide-and-seek) and had *goûter* rather than a snack. The nuns, Mary declared in her *Memories of a Catholic Girlhood*, were "intellectual women," and although she spent only two years at the school, she devoted three chapters of her short book to that experience.

It was not the austere, emotionally constricted life one might imagine. "We ate, studied, and slept in that atmosphere of intrigue, rivalry, scandal, favoritism, tyranny, and revolt that is common to all girls' boarding schools and that makes 'real' life afterward seem a long and improbable armistice," she wrote. Emotions were heightened by an undercurrent of religious mystery and fervor.

During one three-day retreat in which the girls were forbidden to speak, the priest lectured on unchastity. Mary was overwhelmed by guilt. She later joined the line of girls waiting to confess. She told the priest she had "committed a sin of impurity" with herself and with other girls, but not with a boy. Then she revealed her transgression. She had been looking up words such as "breast" in the big dictionary at home, and discussing them with her friends at school. She was eleven years old.

Modesty was a vital ingredient in everyday life. The girls slept in curtained beds (as did the Moravians) and took weekly Saturday night baths with an embarrassed nun sitting in a curtained corner, discreetly supervising, unseen but very much there.

The students were the daughters of lawyers, grocers, dentists, and realtors, plus "heiresses of the Chevrolet agency and of Riley and

Finn, contractors." These Irish Catholics had hardly made it into the corridors of power. Mary was a five-day boarder who went home on weekends, and she found herself outside the charmed inner circle who stayed on grounds all week, condemned to the company of others on the fringe. Then she concocted a plan to make herself the center of attention. She announced she had lost her faith. The nuns and the priest confronted her in dismay and tried to dissuade her. But she found, almost to her surprise, that her loss was a real one. She continued to attend mass and go through the motions, but she was now a celebrity and enjoyed the rest of her time at school. In 1925, she transferred to a local public high school because she felt deprived of the presence of boys. After one year, she again was sent to boarding school—a Protestant one, this time.

Though students at all-girl schools groused about the lack of boys and complained of the strictness with which their behavior was monitored, many later sent their own daughters to the schools they themselves had attended.

Jane Trahey did not follow that tradition. In her book *The Trouble with Angels*, she wrote, "The only difference between the school Mama picked out for me and The Girls' Reformatory was tuition. Mama paid for me instead of having me committed. Other than that, the rules, the hours, and the food were just the same." Jane was a rebellious twelve-year-old when she went to the nuns; her mother hoped she would come home a well-mannered, charming, polite, and educated young lady. Despite her griping about the discipline, she—like many of her schoolmates—looked back in later years and found her convent experience good. "If I could live it over again, I wouldn't change a minute of it," she wrote.

Although they were all strict, each of the orders of nuns had a different history, and different schools. Cornelia Connelly, who founded the Sisters of the Holy Child Jesus and their schools, was an unusual nun. With her black hair stylishly pulled back in a loose bun and her large dark eyes, she looked like a serene young mother—which she was. Married in 1831 to an Episcopal rector, she entered the Catholic church only after he decided it was his mission in life to become a Catholic priest. She was pregnant with their fifth child before they both took vows of perpetual chastity to increase his chances of ordination. By the time her husband became a priest and she became a nun only three of her five children still survived. One had died at the age of six weeks, another a year later when he was only two and a half and fell into a vat of boiling cane sugar syrup. These tragedies marked her with a great sadness and a concern for all children. The plan she devised, with the help of a sympathetic Jesuit priest, was to start a school in England for the education of Catholic girls. That way, she might keep the two younger children at her side.

After only one uncomfortable year as a priest, Cornelia's restless husband left Catholicism and returned to the Episcopal church, expecting that his wife—or former wife—would rejoin him and reestablish their family. When she declined, having found what she regarded as her true calling, he kidnapped their children and refused to allow her to see them. According to the laws of England, the children were the property of their father, and she was powerless.

Cornelia Connelly's experiences marked the convents established on her principles, just as the lives of Ann Lee, who founded the Shakers, and John Humphrey Noyes, of the Oneida community, left their imprint on the child care of their followers. The schools of her order (the Sisters of the Holy Child Jesus) founded first in England, then in the United States, were staffed by nuns who were called Mother. The idea was (once again) to provide children away from home with a substitute family—the kind of home she had been unable to give her own sons and daughter.

In Suffern, New York, a village in the Ramapo Mountains not far from New York City, nuns of her order set up the School of the Holy Child in 1912. Mrs. Thomas Fortune Ryan, the wife of a financier, donated a huge white stucco house and forty acres. Despite its imposing appearance, the house was in disrepair and its accoutrements consisted of "twenty beds, one billiard table, five goldfish and one cow."

When Ilka Chase, the actress and wit, was sent there at the age of seven shortly after it opened, the upstairs rooms had become dormitories, but the downstairs was still equipped for the pleasure of its previous owner. "There was a pool room," Ilka recalled, "and in the room, a pool table; and the dear Sisters had seen no reason for removing it. We all played continually, and it was a pretty sight to see Mother Mary Agnes, who shot a mean ball, leaning backward over the table, her veil slightly askew, while with her cue tucked under her arm she aimed swift and true for the corner pocket."

About sixty-five to seventy boarding students, almost all of them in grades seven through twelve (later nine through twelve), were cared for by twelve to fourteen nuns. (Ilka seems to have been one of the youngest exceptions.) There were also a few day students. The nuns were strict but kind. "We loved them, and they knew we loved them," one explained. "They were our children." As with the Shakers and the Moravians, women who would never have children themselves took on the emotions of motherhood.

The girls could go home weekends with permission, but many stayed on campus except for vacations such as Thanksgiving, Christmas, and Easter. "They didn't have to go home. They *were at home*," one nun who taught at the school for more than a decade insisted.

The usual system was for five girls to share a room, make their own beds, and keep their belongings tidy. The great crime was to sneak off into the village without permission—but, since the girls all wore uniforms, they were immediately identifiable and retrievable. They came from all parts of the country and from Latin America and even Hawaii. Two Hawaiian princesses were among the early students. Most of them were daughters of upper-middle-class professionals. Sometimes both parents worked (like Ilka Chase's) or traveled a lot and needed a haven for their children. Sometimes there was only one parent, or a succession of parents with multiple divorces and marriages, and the school provided stability. Sometimes the school offered better educational advantages than the small town in which the families lived.

Ilka's Protestant mother had sent her to the convent because she felt Ilka would get love as well as training. There was another reason, too. Edna Woolman Chase was an early career woman, the editor of *Vogue*, and needed some way to work and be a mother at the same time—or, at least, to be a mother from time to time. She departed from the pattern of her social class, which was to have nannies and governesses so that women could fulfill their fashionable and benevolent duties. In her set very young children were cared for at home. She departed in other ways, too. When Ilka was nine her mother talked about her conflicts as a working mother to a reporter from the *New York Herald Tribune* and acknowledged that she and her daughter both suffered from the separation. "I'm like a man," Mrs. Chase said. "When I am here [at the office] I plunge into my work and forget everything else. But when I go home at night—ah, then I want Ilka to go home, too. And that's just what I can't have, because I don't dare trust her to the people I would have to employ. And so I compromise on a convent. The child is well taken care of there, but she longs to be with me."

Ilka had started out in the care of nurses—her mother went back to work when she was one month old. Despite Mrs. Chase's comment to the reporter about problems finding adequate help, and Ilka's own confirming account of why she was sent away, it seems clear that Mrs. Chase could not keep Ilka at home because she could not bear to compete with another caretaker. "Ilka didn't long to be with me then," she commented of this very early period. "She screamed bloody murder when I took her up; her nurse was her mother."

As this country's chief arbiter of fashion, Mrs. Chase had to spend months in Europe in the summer looking at the new collections, so she could rarely have Ilka with her then. And Easter and Christmas vacations were hard, too, because, "those are my busiest times . . . with a Christmas number to get out and the child coming; how shall I manage?" Yet, this, too, is a disingenuous explanation, since magazines are fully prepared months before they appear and she would long since have finished with the Christmas and Easter issues.

Clearly, it was important to her to present a certain picture to the public—that of the devoted mother and devoted editor, struggling to blend both her lives. "The mother who must work like a man and be away from her child isn't happy," she said. "And yet . . . I couldn't be happy without my work. What's a woman to do?"

Ilka was sent first, at the age of five, to the Convent of the Holy Child Jesus on Riverside Drive in New York, and then, after two unhappy years, to Suffern. In her autobiography, *Past Imperfect*, she reported that she was, in general, happy at Suffern, except for one thing—homesickness: "Homesickness seems to me one of the most terrible maladies, and one which you do not necessarily outgrow with age. It lies in wait like a recurrent illness, and sometimes, quite unexpectedly, the old familiar pain will surge over you. The desperate longing for home and the people you know will so engulf you that nothing on earth matters but the urgency of your need."

This need surges out of the letters she sent home. When she was eleven years old (she stayed at Suffern for five years) she wrote, "Mother dear, I implore you [stick drawing of a praying figure] please do something in the way of letting me know in some way if POSSITIVELY I am going home on Thursday so I can tell sister. Please do Mother darling you can't imagine the suspention I'm in. You see I want *so much* to go home."

Although she spent very little time at home, separation only seemed to attach her more firmly to her mother. Ilka tried to be a dutiful daughter. Acutely aware of her mother's sensitivity to fashion, she asked hesitantly for permission to dress like the other girls. "You know mother," she wrote, "all the girls have socks and I have not. . . . Would you please send me some if you will let me ware them." And in December, she offered a gift to gladden the heart of a mother who was also editor of *Vogue*: "P.S. I have invented lots of new dresses and am going to draw them when I come home."

But the influence of the school was powerful, too. She had come so young she had adopted its ways as her own. The program at the school emphasized proper behavior as well as religion and a modest amount of book learning. The nuns' training sometimes made life at home difficult. Ilka would start her lectures to her parents with "Sister says," and follow it with dictums against blowing your nose in public or slamming a door. "What are you supposed to do?" her mother asked about the first, "let it run?" As for religion, Ilka held dawn services for her dolls when she was at home on Sundays, pinning towels over her shoulders so she would look like a priest in vestments and muttering nonsense syllables for the Latin. Worried that she might be tempted to convert, her parents took her out of the convent and sent her to a Protestant boarding school in Rye, New York, when she was thirteen years old.

When she was away at the convent, her mother cleaned out her closet and gave her cherished teddy bear to "some poor little children." Ilka was devastated. Her mother protested that she hadn't known Ilka was so attached to the animal—she had so many other toys. "You should have known, you should have known," the child sobbed in the universal complaint of children who feel betrayed.

Elizabeth Macksoud was another student at Suffern. She had come because the one-room schoolhouse in Upper Ridgewood, New Jersey (only about twenty miles from Suffern), that she had attended was too small, and her mother decided she needed a better education and better manners. "I fought with the boys and my mother didn't think that was the right way to raise a child," she explains. Like Ilka Chase, she enjoyed the school and the dramatics and went on to act and direct, but the golden glow of memory has not erased some of the less enticing aspects of boarding school. The food, for instance. "We called it DVOT," she says. "Dog vomit on toast. It was probably nourishing. And in the spring we always said they gave us lots of things to keep us girls from being interested in boys. The rumor was they put saltpeter in the mashed potatoes." (Saltpeter is potassium nitrate, universally used, or so it was said, wherever frisky young people were separated from the opposite sex, whether at school or on a ship at sea.)

Another girl, who went to a Catholic boarding school in the Midwest, says that the girls, free of the supposed saltpeter, went wild on vacation. When they were finally able to be with boys without the strict chaperonage of the nuns at occasional dances, they tried to make up for lost time.

Despite the advantages of all-girls' schools, Sister Frances Heron, who spent more than a decade teaching at the School of the Holy Child in Suffern, says, "The age of the [Catholic] girls' boarding school is over. It had its time. There are no longer the nuns to staff them, since fewer women are taking vows, and those that do prefer service in inner cities or third-world countries." Without dedicated, unsalaried religious, the old system cannot operate. (The same is true of Catholic boys' boarding schools.) The Suffern school closed in 1972.

The schools, religious or not, were affected by the emphasis, particularly after World War II, on the vital importance to the child's psychological and emotional well-being of being cared for by his or her mother. During the war Anna Freud had found that young children who stayed with their mothers during the nightly terror of the London Blitz were better off than those evacuated to the safe countryside, and Bowlby and Spitz a few years later warned of the dangers of institutionalized child care. Child-rearing advice became more firmly anchored in psychoanalytic thinking than ever. In response, schools dropped care for very young children, since parents hesitated to put them in residential care and schools hesitated to accept them. Even missionaries such as those whose children had helped fill Moravian schools were encouraged to keep their youngsters with them on overseas assignments. The opinion of the experts was that a child (particularly one not yet in its teens) was best kept with its parents.

But between the world wars, economic necessity (during the Depression, for instance, when both parents had to work) and the lack of other satisfactory child-care arrangements made paying for a child to live away from home seem a necessary but painful choice. And among the social elite and certain religious groups (Catholics, for example) long custom and community approval supported the continuing existence of such schools.

The need to produce a continuing stream of homogeneous, educated leaders ensured the survival of the upper-middle- and upper-class schools that proliferated at the end the nineteenth century. So did the need for a sanctuary in which children could ride out the storms of adolescence apart from their concerned parents. As it did in regard to nannies, the latest psychological thinking applied only to the poor and the middle class. Somehow, the wealthy were immune to the growing emphasis on motherly care as the best care and family life as the best life. For them, tradition was more important than any new theory.

Children sent away to school between the two world wars, whether they were rich or not so rich, had separation from their families as a common thread. They also shared segregation of the sexes as a way to minimize temptation and maximize the opportunity to concentrate on education. As with all child-care systems, this one was good for some, bad for others. Religiously based schools—such as those run by the Catholics, the Moravians, and the Quakers— tended to inculcate their philosophies along with the usual academic subjects, even though they were open to students of other faiths. The elite boarding schools for boys and girls, most of them Episcopalian, imbued their young charges with the standards and attitudes of their class rather than their religion, although chapel was often built into everyday life. Whatever their orientation, these schools flourished before so much focus was lavished on the psyche of the child. Many of them struggled to maintain their student body and their financial soundness as psychological thinking changed, and in order to survive, some metamorphosed into coed schools that mimicked those that served students living at home. As for the Catholic boarding schools, there are no longer Schools of the Holy Child to care for and educate girls, and residential boys' schools have fallen on hard times. Sending children away—unless they need the discipline of a military atmosphere or special care of some kind—is a custom that survives chiefly in families for which the socially acceptable road to success is paved with attendance at an elite boarding school.

NANNIES

We not only had two parents of whom we were extremely fond, but also that strange English institution, a perfect nanny.

RUTH PLANT, Nanny and I

WOMEN HAVE ALWAYS HELPED other women carry the burdens of child care. For the very rich and those who were scrambling to climb the social ladder before and after World War I, there was the nanny, preferably English, bringing with her an overlay of aristocracy on top of her own working-class origin. Some nannies were horrors, others lifesavers. In some families they completely replaced parents, who made only brief state appearances. In others, parents and nannies worked as a team.

The classic nanny evolved in England from the lowly nurse-maids and rockers (whose only job was to keep the baby clean and soothed) who had existed for centuries. By the mid-1800s these bottom-rung servants had been supplemented or replaced by the accomplished nanny (the word is a diminutive of Ann or Anna, presumably the name of an early paragon). Her rise coincided with the wider distribution of wealth precipitated by the Industrial Revolution and an explosion in the size of the average family to six or seven children in 1830. The upper middle class and middle class clearly needed and could afford a child-care specialist—the nanny.

At a time when children were seen as soaked in sin, someone had to prod them into shape and set them on the right path. Jonathan Gathorne-Hardy, who wrote *The Unnatural History of the Nanny,* says that the character of the nanny developed early, "compounded of love and discipline, of control exercised down to the smallest, minute detail, that complete absorption in the world of the nursery." Before World War II middle-class and upper-class children in England had nannies just as surely as they had treacle pudding and custard—two nannyish treats that survive on the menus of men's clubs today as a tribute to the close relationship between food and love.

Nannies came across the ocean in the late 1800s with the wave of adulation of all things European that brought with it pseudo-Versailles palaces as country "cottages" and solid city mansions ornately decorated with gilt and marble. At Newport, the favorite summer resort of the very rich, William K. Vanderbilt made his wife a gift of the elegant forty-room Marble House. The house had a nursery and nanny quarters but the three children were clearly unimportant to the elegant social life lived there. The presence of a proper nanny, like the extravagant importation of French wallpaper, raised snobbery to its highest level. She could keep the children in their place—away from public view—and act as one more ornament to a lavish way of life.

Nanny Says

One of the remarkable things about nannies is that they preserved and passed on the wisdom and petty nonsense of the medieval world.

In 1475 a book of rules for children admonished them sternly not to put their elbows on the table or drink with their mouths full or speak until they were spoken to. In the twentieth century nannies said the same things without the slightest idea that they were doing anything except repeating current rules of common courtesy. Like the child-caretakers of France, who came from the peasantry and were the repositories of what Charles Perrault published as *Mother Goose Tales* in 1697, these women acted as conduits from the collective memory of the lower classes to the children of their social betters.

Their sayings and attitudes, emphasizing self-denial, order, good manners, and respect for authority, have been credited with sustaining the British Empire. In this country, they were the basis for the culture of the socially elite—those whom F. Scott Fitzgerald called "the princely classes." Families who hoped their newfound wealth in oil or railroads or the stock market would pry open the carefully guarded doors of the vieux riche hired nannies to care for their children in imitation of those who had long lived with wealth and eminent lineage.

Imported nannies brought a whiff of the old English to these descendants of the new who continued to look to the "scepter'd isle" as the home of correctness, good manners, and aristocratic standards. Some nannies were recruited on trips abroad—in England nanny agencies were well established by the 1860s. Others already in this country were passed from wealthy family to family as children grew up. And word-of-mouth recommendations as well as ads and local agencies provided other nannies with jobs. Among wealthy families in this country having a nanny was commonplace and as necessary to maintaining one's position in society as visiting cards. "I didn't know anyone who didn't have a nanny. I thought that's the way it was for all children," a woman whose family moved in New York's social circles remembers.

Nanny-reared children were subjected to surprisingly similar attitudes and methods, no matter where they lived. "Kindness but firmness, my dear," said Nanny Huggins when asked her method of child rearing. She brought up three girls in the American Midwest. "You can't just drag them up and let them do as they please. That is not bringing them up. That is dragging them up and they'll come to no good in the end." Although the Evanston, Illinois, in which she was employed was far from the London from which she had come, her standards had not suffered a sea change. "Children should never sit at table with their parents until they can pare an apple perfectly," she believed. When a child fell and skinned a knee or came to her in the throes of a difficult problem or conflict she was likely to remind her cheerfully that things weren't so bad: "Worse at sea, my dear, worse at sea." England, as a seafaring nation, knew that life on land was a breeze compared to the storms on the ocean.

Robert Louis Stevenson, who dedicated his *A Child's Garden of Verses* to his nanny, Alison Cunningham, "the angel of my infant life," summed up her teachings with,

> *A child should always say what's true*
> *And speak when he is spoken to,*
> *And behave mannerly at table;*
> *At least as far as he is able.*

Manners were important, and so was consideration for others. "Save your breath to cool your porridge," Nanny was likely to say if a child talked too much. This pithy phrase has an eminent lineage: Jane Austen used it in *Pride and Prejudice.*

Some nannyisms were left over from Queen Victoria's time. "Chest, not breast" is what one should say. And as for sex, Nanny, like many Victorians, was of two minds. For herself, it was nonexistent. But in her young charges, it was an accepted part of life. Not masturbation, of course. But when children got older, if Nanny was still part of the household, she was likely to be accepting of dating and the inevitable fascination with the opposite sex. When she had grown up one woman remembered her nanny as "quaintly Victorian but surprisingly modern in her romantic concepts. If I were out with a young man she would look the other way and possibly even wink."

When this proper but spirited nanny came to visit her now-adult "child" in New York shortly after World War II, they attended a ballet performance of *Romeo and Juliet* by the shockingly modern Ballet Russe de Monte Carlo. There, onstage, was a bed. And at one point Romeo and Juliet lay down on it together. The "child" cringed and wondered if she would ever be forgiven for exposing Nanny to such inappropriate entertainment. Nanny was unperturbed. "Isn't that kind of them to have a bed right there so they can rest? They must be terribly tired after all that dancing," she said sweetly.

Although Peter the Great of Russia was taken down the aisle of the church for his christening in a cradle with wheels in the late seventeenth century, the baby carriage as we know it was not invented until 1848, in New York. It transformed the lives of nannies. Its inventor soon moved to England and established a niche in society when Queen Victoria, the mother of nine, ordered one of his revolutionary contraptions. Begun as a kind of wooden stroller—a "baby buggy" miniature of a horse buggy—with two high, spoked wheels and a long rod in front for pulling, it evolved into the elegant perambulator (from the Latin for "walking about"), allowing the baby to sit or lie down. With this vehicle (criticized, as the early automobile was criticized, because it had a tendency to mow down pedestrians), the nanny was free to leave the house. Nanny society flourished, with well-known gathering places for them in parks to sit and gossip— usually about their employers. In today's terminology, these park benches provided space for support groups for women who had been largely cut off from regular contact with their own kind before the perambulator made its appearance and liberated them from the lonely confines of the nursery and the garden.

In London, one gathering place was Hyde Park. Joyce Grenfell, the English actress, reminisces that "when I was a child, Hyde Park nannies were very grand indeed. Their standards of the outward and visible were high; their values seem less reliable, but then, they took colour from those who employed them. There was much competition about the social position and possessions of their Bosses; over the glossiness of their prams—some bore coats of arms—and about their charges' clothes."

New York's Hyde Park equivalent was Central Park at about Seventy-second Street, on both the East Side and the West Side of the city. The great mansions were within easy walking distance, and so were the newly popular apartment houses. The apartments were as close as their architects could come to spacious town houses piled one on top of another. The first luxury apartment house, the Dakota, at Central Park West and Seventy-second Street, opened in 1884. Across Central Park, 635 Fifth Avenue, built in 1912, had one apartment of thirteen rooms and four baths on each floor, carefully divided, as the mansions were, into private, public, and servants' quarters. The ceilings soared, the floors were parquet, and massive fireplaces added atmosphere to the central heating. Each apartment had four bedrooms, four servants' rooms, and a servants' hall where they could gather for meals and relaxation. Nannies in these buildings took their charges down ten or twenty floors in safety elevators, pioneered by Elisha Graves Otis in 1852. Elegantly uniformed doormen held the heavy doors to the street open for them and even watched the children, acting as substitute nannies as the youngsters played in the lobby or on the sidewalk for brief periods.

Nannies were as snobbish as their employers, and the employers, particularly if they were reaching for a handhold into the upper class, were snobbish about their nannies. Nanny Huggins's appearance in Evanston, a suburb of Chicago, certified the family who employed her as wealthy and correct. She had been hired because she would add luster to the mansion and the gold-plated plumbing and teach the children proper manners.

New York was even more enamored of nannies. Zelda Fitzgerald described the scene in a 1928 article in *Harper's Bazaar:* "In the bright gusty mornings, Park Avenue is animated with sets of children, slim and fashionable, each set identically dressed and chaperoned by white and starched English nurses or blue-flowing French nurses or black and white maids. They clutch, in gloved hands, the things that children carry only in illustrations and in the Bois de Boulogne and in Park Avenue: hoops and Russian dolls and tiny Pomeranians."

Caretakers who were not English nannies, but the almost-as-elegant mademoiselles and fräuleins and American nursemaids, brought with them their own petty rules. Miss Werner, who was German and went back home and joined the Nazi party in the 1930s, subjected "her" two little New York girls to a regimen they later called "cleanliness über alles." If one of them brushed against her towel in the bathroom they shared, "she got furious. If you picked your nose you felt that you were really dirty. It was terribly guilt-producing. The message was don't do anything except be clean." They cleaned their teeth and washed their hands again and again during the day. Miss Werner also made them keep their bedroom door closed tight at night—a scary rule for two little girls who felt trapped even though they knew that she was reacting to the kidnapping of the golden-haired Lindbergh baby, who had recently been spirited out of his bedroom. No matter that his kidnapper had come in through the window. The safety measure Miss Werner insisted on fed their terror. The pervasive fear that other rich children might be the targets of kidnappers kept many youngsters and their caretakers on edge.

The Classic Nanny

The classic nanny was hired to care for the children, not to help the mother. She ruled over a tiny kingdom of tiny people—the nursery—an area set off from the rest of the house with its own hours, its own commandments, its own needs. English is one of the few languages in the world that uses the same word for a place in which children or young plants are tended and trained. The plant/child similarity is also embodied in the venerable proverb, "As the twig is bent, so the tree will grow."

The nanny was in charge of bending the twig—teaching manners and morality—and the everyday life that included changing diapers for infants, instituting toilet training for toddlers, and acting as constant companion. When her children were ill with colds Nanny Huggins appeared with endless bowls of bread and milk sweetened with honey, and the custard she made herself. She cooked nothing else—that was the province of the cook—but she was responsible for cleaning up after herself and the children unless there was also a nursemaid to handle the chore. Nanny bought the children's clothes, kept them clean, and mended them. She took her charges to the doctor and the dentist (unless there was a crisis) and outdoors for airings or for play.

When Daniel E. Sutherland studied servants in the United States from 1800 to 1920 he found a surprising consistency in what was required in child care throughout that long period: "A good nursemaid [read "nanny," though not necessarily the starched and stiff English variety] was indispensable in a household with children. . . . A nurse had to be a perfect blend of intelligence, cleanliness and morality. It was important that she be an early riser and light sleeper, and she ought not to be overly fond of night life. . . . She should have no speech impediment, and it was desirable that she be pretty and fair complexioned. Hers was a full-time job; she was to the children what the lady's maid was to their mother. She attended the children at all hours of the day, dressing them, playing with them, and sleeping near them. Indeed, many upper-class children saw more of their nurse than of their parents." But there remained an ineluctable difference between nannies and parents; no matter how much power the nanny had, or how much time she spent with the children, it was the parents who were ultimately responsible for what happened to them.

In England before 1914, nannies came to their positions by a kind of apprenticeship. Joyce Grenfell's nanny "had no formal training but had learned by doing, first at home . . . then at fourteen as a nursery maid under an established nanny. Finally, when she was twenty-one, she left to take on her first baby 'from the month' [after its birth] and we loved each other from the day we met until the day she [nanny] died, fifty-three years later." How important it was to a child's later life to have nanny take over immediately or soon after its birth is impossible to assess. Certainly, in many families, the nanny replaced the mother as the loved figure. Yet, as the British psychologist H. R. Schaffer points out, "Whether a child's first relationship is in any way the prototype of all future relationships we do not as yet know. The clinical material bearing on this point is hardly convincing."

After the war, nanny schools became popular and existed alongside the older apprenticeship system. Nanny Huggins was trained in a London school and came to this country especially qualified to provide care and increase the social standing of her employer. Unlike the vieux riche who had had nannies themselves and were firmly established in the social hierarchy, the family that hired Nanny Huggins was nouveau riche, struggling to spend its money properly.

Who's in Charge?

Differences between caretakers and mothers were inevitable. Nannies and others came with their own experiences and ideas on how to rear children, and mothers, who were often educated and wealthy, had other views. Yet, if the child was in the charge of the nanny from morning to night, and the mother was only peripherally involved, the old ways usually persisted and triumphed. Miss Werner, the compulsively clean fräulein, had methods that were in sharp contrast to her employer's avant-garde attitudes about child rearing. The mother was an advocate of John Dewey's progressive ideas and had been in psychoanalysis with A. A. Brill, one of Freud's disciples. She never knew what went on under Miss Werner's tyranny. Like many other "advanced" parents, she was totally unaware that her children were being brought up in an age she had determinedly discarded. "If she had really looked at Miss Werner she would have been upset. But we were scared to report what she was doing," one of her daughters says. They were never questioned directly, either. "Today, maybe parents ask kids, but they probably aren't really interested. They're like the waitress who asks, as she's walking by your table, 'how is everything?' They'd rather not know." (Parents of younger children who could not tell them what was going on even if they wanted to had to become detectives. Was Johnny sitting quietly in his stroller because he was sick? Because he was being mistreated? Because he was frightened? The parent may never have known.)

Some mothers were glad to have someone else in charge. "My mother was relieved to have Nanny there when we were growing up in the late twenties and thirties," one woman explained, "but I think she was jealous because we kids preferred Nanny and perhaps loved her more." Nanny, on the other hand, understood that the mother was "incapable of motherhood. She wanted to be somebody's child, not somebody's mother. Bless her heart, she just didn't have the capacity."

Some women were committed to maintaining their position as mother-in-chief, even when there was full-time care for their children, and a kind of partnership might seem to be the logical result. Various strategies accomplished this end. Hiring young caretakers was one way of avoiding competition; another was limiting the time a nanny could stay, so that the children never became thoroughly attached to her. The mother in this way asserted her sovereignty and was never in danger of being replaced.

Mothers such as these may have been overly concerned about sharing their children's attachment. As Jerome Kagan of Harvard and others have shown, children can have close, loving attachments to several caretakers at the same time. Multiple mothering is neither new nor necessarily harmful. In some cases, it provides a way for a child to avoid disaster. If a mother or nanny is not good, the child can turn to the other. As Jonathan Gathorne-Hardy concluded after interviewing dozens of nannies and their "children," children "can get sufficient love and security in a vast variety of ways. It is this variety, these different routes, which are interesting; not the search for the single perfect one."

Mothers who were less than perfect turned to others to provide their children with the care they were unable or unwilling to provide themselves. The immediate post–World War I world was a time when the morals, maxims, and methods of comfortable, smug turn-of-the-century America were blown up as the young soldiers had been blown up in the trenches. At least for the citified, up-to-date flappers and men about town who had caught the excitement of "eat, drink, and be merry, for tomorrow we die," it was difficult if not impossible to settle down to be good parents. F. Scott Fitzgerald said, "My contemporaries have found their own lack of religious and moral convictions makes them incompetent to train their children," so they hired someone else if they could afford to.

Scottie, Zelda and Scott Fitzgerald's daughter, was always dependent on the kindness of a succession of strangers—nurses, nannies, governesses—who appeared and disappeared at Zelda's whim.

"Becoming a mother did not have a noticeably quieting effect on Zelda," her biographer, Nancy Milford, commented, detailing the continuing outrageous, hazardous escapades of the couple who came to epitomize "the roaring twenties." Scottie was left chiefly in charge of whatever woman they could hire wherever they went, from Minnesota to London to the Riviera, but Zelda was frequently dissatisfied with whoever tried to fill the role about which she was painfully uncertain.

Scottie was born in St. Paul, Minnesota, on October 26, 1921, after a long and difficult labor. She was then left with her grandparents while Scott and Zelda went to New York to look for a house. While Zelda went to pick up the child, Scott stayed behind and later met them at the train station with a nursemaid ready to take the baby in her arms immediately and relieve the mother of her burden. Zelda soon fired her. She fired her replacement, too, because the nursemaid refused to eat at the same table with the other servants. Evidently, Zelda did not know that in the hierarchy of the Downstairs world, nannies ate with the family, not the servants.

In Paris, when Scottie was three years old, Zelda hired an English nanny, Lillian Maddock, who—spit, spat, as Mary Poppins said—transformed chaos into order. Like nannies the world over, this one could turn any foreign space into a cozy English nursery. She briskly issued orders to lesser souls—hotel staffs, shipboard stewards—until she got what she wanted. And if Zelda interfered with her care of Scottie, she did not hesitate to complain to Scott.

On the Riviera, the Fitzgeralds and the legendary Murphys and the Archibald MacLeishes stayed up late, drank hard, and played even harder. Mrs. MacLeish remembered that Zelda rarely appeared during the day. "Sometimes we swam together, but I rarely saw her with Scottie at the plage [beach]. You'd see Scottie with her nanny."

When the Fitzgeralds returned to the United States to live in a rambling house in Wilmington, Delaware, Nanny was replaced by Mademoiselle, a French governess. Zelda disliked her, too. She seems never to have been able to turn her child over to someone else without feeling that person was a rival. Yet she was aware that Scottie suffered because of her ambivalence. After Zelda had been hospitalized for a mental breakdown and was putting her life with Scott together again in the outside world, she wrote an autobiographical sketch (in 1932) that obliquely recognized what was happening to her child: "And there was the lone and lovely child knocking a croquet ball through the arches of summer . . . and singing alone in her bed at night. She was a beautiful child who loved her mother. At first there had been Nanny but Nanny and I quarrelled and we sent her back to France and the baby had only its mother after that, and a series of people who straightened its shoes. I worried. The child was unhappy."

When she was twelve years old Scottie herself told a reporter for *The New York Times* that her parents' generation "don't seem to think a lot about their children." The children, she said, respect their parents, "I guess. It's just that they don't know them so well."

Children of other famous parents, too, had only a series of people who straightened their shoes. Pia Lindstrom, the daughter of Ingrid Bergman, remembered that shortly before her mother left her father in Hollywood to run off with Roberto Rossellini, "There were people in the house, and I remember there was a woman who looked after me. But by and large I was alone."

"She Was My Mother"

Mothers living their own lives and turning over almost total care of their children to others were not unusual in upper-class circles in the time between the two world wars. Women did not have careers, but they had social obligations that kept them perpetually busy. When Gloria Vanderbilt the elder was appealing the decision to award guardianship of her daughter to the girl's aunt, Gertrude Whitney, she said, "They've permitted Gertrude Whitney to keep Gloria because I was away from her too much. Now if that be sound reasoning, then no mother on Park Avenue has any right to have her children. . . . Anybody who knows anything about these things knows mothers and fathers in this position in life see very little of their children. When the babies are young they are taken care of by nurses and governesses. Mothers are busy with the duties that their social lives entail. You will usually find them out to lunch and then on to cocktails somewhere. They rush home to dress for dinner and away they go again. . . . When the children are old enough they are sent to private schools—often out of town. During the summer holidays they are off at camp. Now that is the life of ninety-nine children out of 100 whose parents are in the *Social Register*."

One of those children lived with her brother and her nursemaid on the third floor of her parents' East Seventy-second Street mansion in New York. "It was like being in a separate world," she says. "You eat with your nurse. It wasn't until I was thirteen that I was allowed to have dinner with my parents except on special occasions like Christmas. In the late afternoon I would see my parents in the library as they had a drink and a smoke." Another woman reported, "My parents were given a schedule of when they could see us. I honestly don't remember seeing mummy and daddy until we were bathed and ready for bed. They would be in the living room having a cocktail." Paradoxically, it was Prohibition that made the cocktail hour an inevitable part of daily life for fashionable Americans. For the first time, men and women drank together in public in speakeasies, and this togetherness continued in their homes. A new pattern was established, and it continued even after Prohibition ended in 1933. A generation of scrubbed children equated time spent with their parents with time spent with alcohol. Children were briefly presented at their shiny best to parents who were at their relaxed best.

Little Gloria's life, spread before the American public with her custody trial in 1934, titillated and horrified newspaper readers who saw mothers as more than ornamental. For Gloria, her nanny, Emma Sullivan Kieslich, hired at her birth by her grandmother for $125 a month, was her real mother. Years later she wrote, "To me, family was my Grandmother Morgan . . . and my nurse . . . Dodo. No father anywhere reachable [he had died when she was very young] and Mother who was always coming in and then going out—mostly going out."

In Paris, Gloria lived with her mother's identical twin sister in addition to her mother and grandmother. The Morgan sisters were famous for their beauty, their glamour, and their astonishing resemblance. Gloria saw so little of her mother that when the twins were together, she could not tell which was which. She tried desperately to memorize all her mother's clothes so that she could be sure to recognize her.

This inability to distinguish her mother is remarkable. Although identical twins are often mistaken for each other by acquaintances, family members usually have no trouble knowing who is who. Babies and young children recognize their mothers by smell, by touch, and by voice; young Gloria's confusion is a testament to how little she saw of her mother, how seldom she was picked up and held by her, and the reality that Dodo (with the grandmother's help) was in total charge.

But even though Gloria could not tell her mother from her

twin sister, she could recognize that Dodo, somehow, was not enough. She saw herself as, in a sense, an orphan. "I don't care how rich or poor, a child without a parent is forever an orphan. The guilt—'I was so bad they left me or each other, or they died'—never really goes away." In adulthood, she collected Little Orphan Annie dolls and doodads, recognizing that she and the red-haired castoff had something in common. They had both learned to overcome formidable odds to triumph in the end. She also identified, like Jane Addams before her, with Jo in *Little Women* and found models of independent women to fill the empty spaces in her own life.

Dodo's total devotion to Gloria was supposedly based on her own past. She was said to have married when she was quite young, had a son, and deserted both son and husband in unhappy desperation. The baby, left with her husband's sisters, died. Whether the story is true, or is one that Dodo concocted to tell Gloria later in life, it is psychologically plausible. Dodo may have been trying to give Gloria what she had not been able to give her own child, even her imaginary one.

Separation

It is the fate of nannies, as hired help, to leave. Sometimes the leaving is gentle, after the child has grown enough to be independent, and sometimes the connection is never really severed because there continues to be visiting back and forth. But too often there are what Gathorne-Hardy called "brutal and incomprehensible partings."

One girl who got a whiff of the unspoken decision to send her beloved nanny away mobilized her sisters and brother to prevent the dreadful deed. "We can't let this happen," she told them. "We're going to keep her in the bottom of the linen closet [where there was a large space] and you have to promise to bring her food from all of your meals." The nanny was whisked away so fast they never got to tell her about the plot. But the tie was never really broken because this nanny wrote to them and saw them regularly after she retired.

Another child was not so lucky. When she was was one year old Alice settled into her life. "She was warm and wonderful. I remember sitting on her lap. She taught me about love. She taught me my prayers. And then she disappeared." The child was three years old and never learned why Alice was fired. Another woman, still puzzling over the abrupt disappearance of her beloved nanny, remembers thinking, "But you can't fire a mother!"

The effects of losing the nursemaid she called "Weedie" have been lifelong for a woman who grew up in the family of a New York stockbroker. She, too, has never found out why Weedie left. Probably parents did not bother to talk about the leaving with young children for fear of upsetting them and making the parting worse, or because they felt they could not understand. But this attempt at protection left a haunting mystery in the lives of the children. Just as children whose parent dies wonder if they were responsible—if the parent vanished because they had done something wrong—so these children wonder if their behavior drove the beloved caretaker away.

When Weedie left after five years, "It was a major, major loss for me. She just went and we never saw her again. I felt bleak and I mourned, but I never protested or inquired," she recalls. Weedie, to her, was "magically beautiful." She had soft brown eyes and a bun out of which stuck tortoiseshell hairpins. They spent three months alone together in an apartment in Florida when the little girl was thought to have tuberculosis (a major killer of children at that time and the feared disease Gloria Vanderbilt was thought to have, too), and this interlude made them even closer. How could she disappear? "This is one of the dangers of transferring a child to another parent figure. For me, the damage was irreparable. I never became attached to another nurse. Later, I was able to transfer my love and affection to my mother." But she was always wary of attaching herself completely to another adult, even in marriage. "The first lesson I learned," she says, "was that you can't depend on anyone because they might disappear." Repeated disappearances deepened the earlier wound. Her parents were often away traveling, and her mother died at the early age of forty.

Current psychological theory illuminates this woman's experience. The thinking, based on modifications of Freudian theory, suggests that a child subjected to the abrupt departure of an early love object will be permanently affected by the painful rupture. The earlier the parting, and the more often it is reinforced by other disappearances, the deeper the damage. Gathorne-Hardy speculates that the British upper and middle classes may owe their reputation for emotional coldness to the fact that they were so often cared for by nannies and nurses who came and went at whim. The average stay, he says, was about five years. In the absence of any careful studies, no one can prove or disprove this proposition. But it seems to fit in with the stories of men and women whose caretakers left them abruptly.

This Indenture Witnesseth,

That *Thomas Keelin who was under Indenture to James Rosey now cancell'd in consideration of fourteen Pounds paid by Jona. Meredith.*

Hath put *Himself* and by these Presents, doth Voluntarily, and of *his* own free Will and Accord, put *Himself* Apprentice to *Jonathan Meredith of the City of Philad. Currier* to learn *his* Art, Trade, and Myſtery, and after the Manner of an Apprentice to ſerve *Him & his Aſsigns* from the Day of the Date hereof, for and during and unto the full End and Term of *Eight Years from Nineteenth Day of October 1774* — — — — next enſuing. During all which Term, the ſaid Apprentice *his* ſaid *Maſter* faithfully ſhall ſerve, *his* Secrets keep, *his* lawful Commands every where readily obey, *He* ſhall do no Damage to *his* ſaid *Maſter* nor ſee it to be done by others, without letting or giving Notice thereof to *his* ſaid *Maſt. he* ſhall not waſte *his* ſaid *Maſters* Goods, nor lend them unlawfully to any, *He* ſhall not commit Fornication nor contract Matrimony within the ſaid Term. At Cards, Dice, or any other unlawful Game, *He* ſhall not play whereby *his* ſaid *Maſts* may have Damage. With *his* own Goods, nor the Goods of others, without Licence from *his* ſaid *Maſt. He* ſhall neither buy nor ſell, *He* ſhall not abſent *himself* Day nor Night from *his* ſaid *Maſters* Service, without *his* Leave: Nor, haunt Ale-Houſes, Taverns, or Play-Houſes; but in all Things behave *himself* as a faithful Apprentice ought to do, during the ſaid Term. And the *Maſt. ſ*hall uſe the utmoſt of *his* Endeavour, to teach, or cauſe to be taught or inſtructed, the ſaid Apprentice in the Trade or Myſtery of *a Currier* and procure and provide for *Him* ſufficient Meat, Drink, *Apparel* — Lodging and Waſhing fitting for an Apprentice, during the ſaid Term of *Eight Years, to have five Quarters*

Schooling, & at the expiration of the Term to have ten compleat Suits of Apparel, one whereof to be new

AND for the Performance of all and ſingular the Covenants and Agreements aforeſaid, the ſaid Parties bind themſelves each unto the other firmly by theſe Preſents. IN WITNESS whereof, the ſaid Parties have interchangeably ſet their Hands and Seals hereunto. Dated the *Tenth* Day of *February* in the *Fifteenth* Year of the Reign of our Sovereign, Lord *George the third* King of *Great-Britain*, &c. Annoque Domini, One Thouſand Seven Hundred and Seventy-*five*

Philad.

Sealed and Delivered in
Presence of us

Bound before

Jo. Meredith

Sam. Rhoads Mayr.

The indenture document, written in duplicate and torn or cut (indented) irregularly into two parts, set out the duties of master as father and apprentice as son. The two parts, fitted together, proved who was apprenticed to whom.

THE MAMMY.

Plantation mammies such as this one in Kentucky not only looked after the children of their white masters but often also managed their households. The mammies' own children were usually cared for in the slave quarters by men or women too old to work in the fields.

3   The celibate Shakers, with their villages divided into artificially organized Families, took in orphans and other children as their hope for the future. The Church Family members of Hancock Village, Massachusetts, posed here about 1870.

4

John Humphrey Noyes, the charismatic founder of the utopian Oneida Community, stands, hands clasped, surrounded by his followers. The children, born under a system called "complex marriage," which was seen by the outside world as "free love," belonged to the whole community rather than to their parents. Noyes was the spiritual father of them all.

Children of the Oneida Community danced and sang in the evenings in the upper sitting room of the Mansion House, where they and the adults all lived. They spent some time at the end of each day with their mothers, but did not share their quarters.

5

Children in institutions grew up en masse, as this 1898 photograph of a dining room at Girard College, an early Philadelphia orphanage, demonstrates.

A teacher addresses a room of uniformed students at New York's Colored Orphan Asylum in 1861. An angry mob destroyed the building during the Civil War Draft Riots.

More than two hundred thousand orphaned or abandoned children were shipped west to find new families and a better chance in life under the auspices of the New York Foundling Hospital and the Children's Aid Society, among others. The Atchison, Topeka and Santa Fe carried these youngsters to the farms of the Midwest in 1900 in a precursor of today's foster care system.

Dressed in their best finery to attract prospective families, Orphan Train children posed with their chaperones in Lebanon, Missouri, in 1909. All twelve of these children found homes.

10

Day care for the children of working mothers in the building in which they live has a long history. Here, in a tenement at 48 Mulberry Street in New York in 1898, toddlers play in a nursery set up by the charitable wife of a doctor. The charge for ten to twelve hours of care was five cents a day.

11

To provide for "the total child in the total situation" Hull-House, the settlement house founded by Jane Addams, supplied health care and along with it disease-preventing baths in basement tubs.

FRANK LESLIE'S
ILLUSTRATED
NEWSPAPER

No. 1,380.—Vol. LIV. NEW YORK—FOR THE WEEK ENDING MARCH 4, 1882. [Price 10 Cents.

NEW YORK CITY.—TIMELY INTERVENTION OF AN OFFICER OF THE SOCIETY FOR THE PREVENTION OF CRUELTY TO CHILDREN. FROM A SKETCH BY A STAFF ARTIST.—SEE PAGE 23.

Overburdened families crowded into dingy rooms sometimes treated their children with shocking brutality. The Society for the Prevention of Cruelty to Children, founded in 1875 and modeled on the SPCA, stepped in with court backing to rescue them.

Poor children, black and white, worked in the cotton fields alongside their parents, who needed what the children could earn and had no safe place to leave them. Although slavery had ended, its legacy remained.

14

Children worked hard in the textile mills, often next to other family members, who supervised them. Addie Laird, a spinner in a Vermont cotton mill, was only ten years old, although she claimed to be twelve— the official working age.

15

This immigrant mother and her children picked nuts while she nursed the baby. One broken nut disqualified a whole batch. All together they made a dollar-fifty to two dollars a week.

The controversy over who shall mind the children has erupted, been ignored, and then appeared again since shortly after the Civil War.

Upper-class parents at the turn of the century turned their children over to nannies, fräuleins, and mademoiselles, who took their elegantly dressed charges to Central Park, summer and winter.

Black "mammies" continued to take care of Southern white children outside the constraints of slavery. Here, in 1908, "Mrs. Chapman" cares for her charges near Davidsonville, Maryland.

Far from home in the 1920s, two Hawaiian princesses (daughters of the last queen) pose in their First Communion dresses with the daughter of Thomas Fortune Ryan, the industrialist whose wife's mansion was the site of the School of the Holy Child in Suffern, New York.

19

Girls kneel in prayer at bedtime at the Phoenix Indian School in 1900. The boarding schools of the Indian Service, like other full-time child-care institutions, tried to pass on the attitudes and standards of a community— in this case, the white community, dedicated to an effort to "kill the Indian but save the man."

20

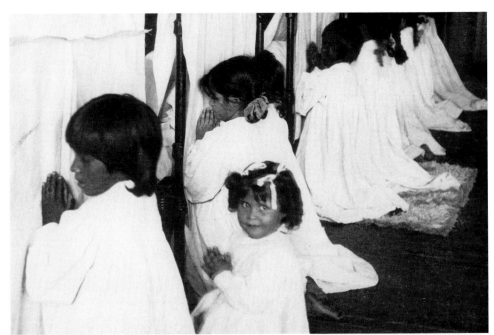

The Moravians, a small religious group, founded this country's first boarding school for girls in 1742. The dormitory of the Moravian Seminary in 1912, with its curtained cubicles, looked much as it had a century before, when a student compared the cubicles to horse stalls. The school still exists, although, like many others of its kind, it has joined with its brother school to become coeducational.

21

22

With the decline of the orphanage, the family home again became the preferred place for neglected, orphaned, or abandoned children to grow up in. This "typical" foster mother and child of 1940 illustrate the ideal sought after by social agencies: a family of the same race and religion as the child, in a suburban neighborhood where the mother stayed home.

23

Before- and after-school care were routine elements in World War II child care, since women working to further the war effort needed a place for their children for eight to twelve hours a day. This comprehensive, federally funded system established under the Lanham Act has been almost forgotten in the usual American amnesia for the past.

Women were so desperately needed for farm work during the war that Lanham Act Centers for the children of migrant workers were set up in tents near the fields. Children squint in the bright sunlight in California's Imperial Valley.

24

Even the fear that a nanny would leave could be devastating. Gloria Vanderbilt, faced with the news that Dodo's mother was dying, thought that if her nurse left to go to the sick woman's bedside she might not be allowed to return. Gloria was so frightened she would lose the only mother she had known that she grabbed her nurse's legs and begged her to stay. She did. This was not a situation in which there was multiple mothering; there was only one "mother," and she was Dodo.

On the other hand, the behaviorist psychological theory of Dr. John B. Watson, popular between the two world wars, supported the idea that a succession of caretakers was good. The parents of children like Gloria Vanderbilt might have known about his view and used it to support their method of arbitrary hiring and firing. "I sometimes wish that we could live in a community of homes where each home is supplied with a well-trained nurse so that we could have the babies fed and bathed each week by a different nurse," Watson declared. He told the story of one child, cared for by an "over sympathetic and tender nurse," who cried for three hours when the replacement nurse arrived. This one left at the end of a month, and he cried for only half an hour when faced with a new caretaker. She stayed only two weeks, and "as often happens in well regulated homes," the third nurse came and "the child went to her without a murmur. Somehow I can't help wishing that it were possible to rotate mothers, too."

One woman under Watson's spell deliberately avoided putting her children in the care of any one person for any length of time. She hired only eighteen-year-olds and made it clear that their job would last only one year. Then she would hire someone else. At all costs she wanted to keep them from becoming deeply attached, and from threatening her authority.

She may not have avoided attachment entirely, even with that short stay, if the testimony of another nanny is to be believed. Ruth Lindstrom, who came to this country in 1913 and worked for both wealthy and middle-class families, said, "Sometimes it's really hard to leave 'em, I tell you. I took care of two little girls. . . . Their father was all alone. The little girl was one year old and the older one was four. I stayed with them for two years. That little girl she stood there by the door and she pulled my skirt and she said, 'Mommy, don't leave me.' Oh, how that affects you! I have letters from them yet. Oh yes, you get very attached. They cry and they reach out their hands to you. You want to stay. That's the worst, to leave them. That's really hard."

Today, theoretical descendants of Watson provide an alternative way of looking at the revolving door through which caretakers come and go. Instead of seeing this as a problem, the vice president of the International Nanny Association, an organization protecting the interests of nannies, suggests, "It's important for them [the children] to know that wonderful people move in and out of their lives. Above all, they are friends."

Nannies in the old-line aristocratic homes were not only friends and surrogate parents, they were often institutions. Instead of moving in and out of the lives of their charges, they stayed. Some cared for a succession of children, and then took on other duties or retired to the nursery, which then became their private domain. When Sebastian Flyte, in Evelyn Waugh's *Brideshead Revisited*, brings his friend home from the university, he takes him to see only one person—his aged nanny, settled securely in her cozy parlor.

Some nannies moved away but stayed close emotionally. Ruth Plant said of her English nanny, whom she memorialized in her book *Nanny and I*, that "although she had to leave us when I was not very old we never lost her as a devoted friend." She constantly went to stay with her, and Nanny's house—"the only place I would go without my mother"—was always open as a refuge in a family crisis.

Nanny Huggins stayed with her family in Evanston for seventeen years, through three children, and then, when the family lost its money, stayed on out of kindness to care for the aging grandfather who had first hired her. Finally, she went to New York and a job with the Luigi Rothschild family. Her youngest Chicago "child" was left adrift at the age of fifteen when her parents divorced. "Without Nanny and without anyone to support me, there was no safety net," she remembers. She would pour out her heart in letters, and invariably, along with the reply would be a twenty-dollar bill. Rothschild "put Nanny in the way of some stock," so she had a small income for the rest of her long life, but she spent nine months of every year with her youngest "child" ("She was much more my mother than my mother") and the rest of the time with her own sister in Florida. She died when she was ninety.

She Was All Loving, All Benign/She Was the Bad Witch

Good nannies are remembered as all good, bad ones as evil forces. Attitudes about them vary as widely as the children they took care of and the parents who hired them. The writer A. J. Liebling compared his caretakers to evil Roman emperors.

Nanny Huggins was one of the "perfect" ones. She not only cared for her charges with love, kindness, and the baked custards she made herself, she was "that little tender rock on which all the shaky boats of the family were moored." Nanny was tiny, energetic, and unfailingly cheerful. She smelled of lavender sachet. The family, on the other hand, was wildly eccentric and creative, with Grandfather a flute player, Father a writer, and Mother a pianist. They were, says their youngest daughter, "a kind of 'You Can't Take It with You' gone wrong." In this chaotic household, Nanny was a stabilizing influence. "I wonder if the three of us wouldn't have gone in drastically different directions without her abiding love and dauntless devotion. I have the feeling that my sisters and I might have been set emotionally adrift in a hostile world. She was our anchor." She softened the effects of hair-pulling sibling rivalry, protected them from parental battles that finally ended in divorce, and was "incredibly caring."

In another chaotic family with a mother who drank too much, a young Scotswoman acted as the buffer in the family. "She saved me," says the "child" she cared for. "She was round," she remembers, "a cushiony sort of shape. That explains my shape. I want to be like her, not stylish and chic and fashionable like my mother." In psychological terms, this woman identified thoroughly with her mother substitute, even to the extent of becoming physically more like her than like her biological parent. This recalls the ancient belief that a child acquired characteristics from its mother's or its wet nurse's milk—that development continued after birth as it had in the womb. Mothers were cautioned to choose wet nurses carefully: A red-haired one might give a child a bad temper, a misshapen one a bad body. Although nannies seem to have descended from "dry nurses" rather than from those whose milk fed the baby, there is a lingering, irrational feeling that their influence might affect not only the child's personality but its physical makeup. Perhaps this happened through the basic psychological process of identification in which a child actually "takes in" an important figure in its early life and becomes like that person—even in eating habits.

The importance of nannies was underscored in a 1990 death notice in *The New York Times* that reads, "To my beloved Nanny. May you rest in peace now, 101 years after freely giving love and devotion, patience and guidance, and for teaching me and all your other babies how to live our lives with integrity, dignity and concern for humanity. You have my eternal love and gratitude for the wisdom you shared, the gifts you have generously given and will be remembered forever as the best friend a very lucky child could have hoped for."

In this country, Mary Poppins is seen as the quintessential nanny, the one any child would be lucky to have and any parent lucky to find. But Humphrey Carter, an English writer, points out that she was created by an Australian, P. L. Travers, who only came to England when she was seventeen years old, and who imagined, rather than experienced, Mary Poppins. "She has not got the details quite right," he insists. "Mary Poppins's snappish bad temper, her constant put-downs of the children and her invariable habit of saying no to all their requests are the behavior not of a typical nanny but of an over-strained domestic servant—a cook or parlormaid. A true nanny would certainly have had bouts of bad temper, but she also would have been very indulgent toward her charges."

The perfect nanny, like the perfect mother, is rare and devoutly to be wished. Is one interchangeable with the other? Is the ideal nanny as good as the ideal mother, or vice versa? The notion that the mother is always preferable presupposes an exemplary standard of motherhood. And nannies are human, too. In this less-than-perfect world they have acted as buffers, saviors, and protectors, another pair of knees to run to when parents are absent or inept, but they have also, like some mothers, been the agents of harm and the objects of fear.

Nannies did have one big advantage over mothers, as Joyce Grenfell, the English actress, pointed out: "Unlike most mothers today nannies only led one life at a time and that life was fully dedicated to the nursery. . . . There was no maternal 'smother-love' loving in our kind of nursery; common sense and kindness prevailed."

"Smother-love," the sentimental overprotection of the devoted Victorian mother, became the pitfall to be avoided by the modern woman as the twentieth century progressed. This attitude supported mothers whose tradition and needs made the nanny a necessary part of life. Distance was good; closeness, bad. A survey of magazine articles aimed at mothers between 1910 and 1935 found that the writers considered the greatest threat to the child to be "too much love." In Dr. John B. Watson's scientific bible of child care, *The Psychological Care of Infant and Child*, published in 1925, he warned of the "danger lurking in the mother's kiss." "Spoiling" was as much to be avoided as one of the infectious diseases—poliomyelitis, for instance—that might cripple a child for life. Watson warned that "once a child's character has been spoiled by bad handling which can be done in a few days, who can say that the damage is ever repaired?"

His book built on the writings of L. Emmett Holt, Jr., a pediatrician whose *Care and Feeding of Children*, first published in 1894 and in use as late as the 1940s, was a reaction against what he saw as the Victorian tyranny of the child. Holt was the Dr. Spock of his day, consulted by mothers who wanted to be sure to do the right thing. His influence was enormous. By 1940 his book had sold a whopping one million copies. It was a standard part of the library of the concerned parent, and a special favorite of the upper classes. Holt and his family went to the Fifth Avenue Baptist Church along with the Rockefellers, and his advice was funneled from his wealthy friends to the nannies and mademoiselles who cared for their children.

Holt dismissed parenting by instinct and proposed that child rearing was a profession that had to be learned, as a foreign language was learned. In question-and-answer format, his book provided rules (he called it "a catechism") for "mothers and children's nurses." "Babies under six months old should never be played with," he declared firmly, because "they are made more nervous and irritable, sleep badly, and suffer from indigestion and cease to gain weight." (This is in stark contrast to the findings of John Bowlby, the English psychologist who first focused on infant-mother attachment in the 1950s and concluded that infants who are not handled and enjoyed waste away.)

For Holt, regularity in everything—including feeding and toileting—was of utmost importance. Babies were treated like mechanical toys that could be programmed to dance or be quiet at specified intervals. "Training in regularity of feeding begins in the first week of life," he wrote. Demand feeding—even when the mother breastfed—was not good for the child. Toilet training could be accomplished "usually by the third or fourth month if training is begun early enough." From today's perspective, his advice to hold the child on a potty at frequent, regular intervals sounds as if the mother or nanny, not the infant, was trained. He prohibited rocking and pacifiers and warned against the expression of affection, although the feeling of affection itself does not seem to have been banned. "The less kissing, the better," he wrote. Most important of all, he declared that a crying child should not be picked up or the bad habit would triumph. The way to avoid this was by "never giving a child what he cries for."

Eleanor Roosevelt followed his ideas when she put her infant daughter Anna Eleanor in a box with wire sides and bottom perched outside the windowsill for her fresh-air naps and left her there even after her persistent howling prompted a neighbor to consider calling the American Society for the Prevention of Cruelty to Children.

Mrs. Roosevelt was the quintessential uncertain parent. She had been orphaned young and felt she did not know how to be a mother. It would be best for her children, she believed, to turn their care over to professional nannies who knew how to do the difficult job. Watson and Holt would have agreed with her. Watson in particular was gloomily pessimistic about the way children were being brought up, and dedicated his treatise to "the first mother who brings up a happy child." "The oldest profession of the race today is facing failure," he declared. "This profession is parenthood." He proposed a "sensible way of treating children. Treat them as though they were young adults. . . . Never hug and kiss them, never let them sit on your lap. . . . If you must, kiss them once on the forehead when they say goodnight."

So bad were his day's child-rearing practices, in his view, that he proposed a moratorium on births for twenty years, except for the few children who would be needed as the subjects of scientific experiments. "No one today knows enough to raise a child," he declared flatly. "Parenthood, instead of being an instinctive art, is a science, the details of which must be worked out by patient laboratory methods." Only when this had been done could child rearing be left to mothers and fathers. (Observation of the child in the laboratory was to become one of the major methods of understanding child development. The other method—observation of the child in its own milieu—owes its beginnings to nineteenth-century Bronson Alcott, who carefully recorded the day-by-day growth of his daughters.)

Watson felt that until the science of parenting had been perfected, "It is a serious question in my mind whether there should be individual homes for children—or even whether children should know their own parents." A nanny who kept the child as far as possible from its parents seemed the best and most humane child-care situation anyone could devise until the experts came up with their final solution. If parents were so inept and, in fact, dangerous, it was better for a child to be brought up by someone trained to do the job who would not mess it up with that unscientific, unmeasurable quality— mother love. Watson's ideas sound like a throwback to the Oneida community's communal child rearing and their attitude that no child should be especially attached to its own parent.

Nannies as mother-surrogates protected their charges from too much parental love and also from parental disputes and whisked them out of the way if inappropriate behavior threatened the smooth course of their days. Sometimes this was a kindness; other times it made life more difficult. Pia Lindstrom says she was completely surprised when her mother, Ingrid Bergman, left her father for Roberto Rossellini in Italy. "I had no idea about anything. I never saw any arguments. I was completely cut off from my parents. I had no idea what might have been going on." She secretly believed that her mother would come back and was completely devastated when her father told her that would never happen. "I don't remember the sequence of events after that very much. I remember I had a governess who left at exactly the same time, I had the feeling everybody was leaving." She was about ten years old.

Some nannies have been not only insensitive but downright mean and harmful. Eleanor Roosevelt regretted, in her later years, that she had left her children in the care of "trained English nurses who ordered me around quite as much as they ordered the children." It never occurred to her that she should care for her own babies; in her class, no one did. She even felt she had to support the nurse's discipline without question and "as a result, my children were frequently unjustly punished." Had she only gotten along without servants, "My children would have had far happier childhoods," she lamented. One particularly pernicious caretaker was finally fired when liquor bottles were found in her room.

From the child's point of view, bad nannies, fräuleins, and other caretakers were, as the writer A. J. Liebling saw his own, "immemorial enemies, interposed between my parents and me, like wicked bailiffs between kind barons and their serfs. They were the bad doorkeepers of a benign sultan. Without their officious intervention I was sure, I could have been with my parents twenty-four hours a day, and they would have been charmed to have me." He described his bad nurse, Martha, as "one of the worst." She took him to see the Iron Maiden, a legendary torture device that was said to "squash and blind simultaneously." Then the bodies were thrown down a well. Martha told him solemnly that "it happens to naughty children, too."

Children usually suffered silently until things got so bad they could not be ignored. A wealthy New York family hired a woman they called a governess to take care of their three-year-old. "I think of her as dressed in black," the "child" says. "She's the bad witch. Nothing I did was right. When I think of her I get the feeling of being pinched all over." The little girl stopped eating after the "monster" threatened to kill her. Like all small children, she took literally what may have been exasperation rather than a death threat. "My throat closed up. I could feel her hands around it. I would put food in my mouth and hold it. I wouldn't swallow. I also threw up."

She got so thin her parents were afraid she would die. Dutiful and wealthy, they got the best medical advice and put her on a diet of dry toast and dry salad to eliminate the vomiting. Finally, they took her to the same sensible doctor who had taken care of Gloria Vanderbilt when she had stomach pains. Dr. Schloss, a white-bearded Austrian, said, "Give her back all the food she loves and get a kind woman to take care of her." They did, and she recovered. Looking back now, she thinks her mother hired the "monster" because she wanted her to be "beaten into shape." Children needed more than to be directed or led, her mother believed, and her father, who had been trained at West Point, expected his children to follow orders and show no emotion.

This woman now says, along with many others of her class and time, "Most of us grew up swearing we would never have anyone else take care of our children because so many things went on that the mother didn't know about." They had baby-sitters and housekeepers who helped with child care, but not full-time, full-control nannies or governesses.

MAIDS AND OTHER HELPERS

She became the weather in which my childhood was lived.

—HOWELL RAINES, OF GRADY, HIS FAMILY'S MAID

NANNIES AND THEIR FRENCH and German counterparts were largely a Northern phenomenon, the ornaments of wealthy homes with other servants and parents who had themselves been cared for by someone other than their mothers. For families in the South between the wars—and even in many cities in the North—child care was more often in the hands of a black woman who also acted as maid. Her job was not to care for the children full-time, but to act as a mother's helper in all areas of the household. Often, child care was an incidental duty, particularly since most women did not work away from home, had few social obligations, and were on hand to deal with their children much of the time.

The classic nanny, on the other hand, had a clearly defined place. She took care of the children and their needs, nothing more (although some nannies did "help out" when staffs shrank after World War I). She was not a domestic servant, but she was not a member of the family, either. Her social position was a special one, a half-step above the other staff and several steps below her employer. She was of the same race as her employers and, ideally, stayed in the same family as long as there were children to be reared. The maid, on the other hand, was clearly a servant with household as well as child-care duties. She was often of a different race, and there was little ex-pectation, except in some Southern families that had experienced the pre–Civil War mammy, that she would stay long. She often lived away from the child's family and had children of her own (unlike the nanny, who was likely to be unmarried), and just as often she was the only servant.

Mothers who employed maids rarely worked, although there was no typical mother of the time. They were wealthy or not-so-wealthy, old-line Americans or immigrants. Unlike the families that hired nannies, these families did not necessarily have a tradition of servants. In Savannah, Daisy came to work for a family of Greek im-migrants when she was seventeen years old. She stayed for fifteen years, helping to rear three children, doing the ironing, the cleaning, and the washing. Daisy came into Mark's life—he was the eldest, and the only son—when he was five and a half years old, and was still there when he came home from college. He remembers her as the "buffer." His mother would hit the children on the back of the legs if they misbehaved, and they would run to Daisy for hugs and consola-tion. A "demon for cleanliness," the mother would punish the chil-dren if they came in muddy and also if they broke a glass or a plate. "It was an accident," Daisy would say in their defense. The mother would counter with "This way he'll remember and won't do it again." What he remembered was Daisy's support.

Like classic nannies, Daisy also protected the children from family conflict. "Once," Mark says, "my mother found lipstick on my father's handkerchief. She was sure he was playing around with a woman he worked with at the fish market. The man who owned the fish market lived upstairs, and she called him down and screamed and cursed. Daisy shepherded us outside."

Discipline was the gray area. The Daisys of the world had authority—but they didn't. Clearly the mothers had the last word. Yet the maids were with the child day after day. They often worked out their own ways of dealing with this reality. One of the twenty-six black domestics who had worked in the 1940s and 1950s in Philadelphia and New York interviewed by sociologist Bonnie Thornton Dill told her she handled tantrums this way: "If he kicked me on the shins, I'd kick him back."

Behind the conflict about discipline lay a difference in attitude about child-rearing methods. Maids and other helpers often treated the children in their charge as they, themselves, had been treated. Familiarity rather than expert advice guided their actions. Mothers, on the other hand, were offered a smorgasbord of advice, some of it contradictory, which allowed them to choose among competing theories—or be thoroughly confused by them. Do they want to believe that a child will develop according to an inborn timetable whether the parent does much or not? Choose Arnold Gesell of Yale. Do they want to believe that a child is malleable and can be trained to be what the parent chooses—that it is made, not born—then opt for John B. Watson. Do they want to believe that the mother has sole (or almost sole) responsibility for what happens ? Choose Watson or L. Emmett Holt, Jr. Or that freedom from Victorian constraints will lead to flowering? Side with Freud and his revisionists. That one expert contradicted another did not necessarily lead to motherly paralysis: The same mother could follow now one, now the other, and pass these conflicting ideas on to the caretaker of her children. Mothers who read women's magazines as well as the latest writings of Watson and the avant-garde interpretations of Freud were not without some comfort as they were buffeted to and fro. A *Parents' Magazine* article in the 1930s reassured them with "Don't let Watson and Freud frighten you. It's perfectly safe to love your children if you want to."

Common sense did not disappear even among the professionals. In 1931 the bulletin of the Child Welfare League of America (an umbrella social work organization bringing together agencies from around the country) printed this satiric look at the rule of the experts by Dorothy Ashby Pownall:

IN THE MODERN MANNER

Go to sleep, darling, sweet peace to your soul!
Mother will pray for your motor control.
Check up statistics on mental hygiene;

Look at your brain through an X-ray machine;
Hushaby, darling, it's mother's ambition
To get your reflexes into condition.
Mother is wise to the new sociology,
Psychoanalysis, endocrinology,
She'd like to sing to you, but the psychologists,
Preschool authorities, learned biologists,
Ban lullabies for the kids of the nation
Lest you develop the mother-fixation.
Make your good night scientific and formal—
Experts say kissing will make you subnormal!
Angels are watching o'er each nerve and gland—
Hushaby, lullaby—ain't science grand?

Mildred, Alice Childress's fictionalized child-care worker in her book *Like One of the Family: Conversations from a Domestic's Life*, told her friend that her employer, who looked to the experts, kept insisting she didn't "understand the modern methods of teachin' children." Children should never be denied something they want, or disciplined without an explanation. Mildred struck back. "I know that half the time you're givin' in to that boy because you don't want to be bothered with him. . . . I'm *tellin'* you that you get sick of him a whole lot of times and then he does somethin' naughty to make you give him things and try to prove that you love him! . . . You never tell him what's on your mind, but you will always be on hand just in time to shove a piece of candy in his mouth and start talkin' about love." Rejecting the mother's modern ideas that children should not be inhibited, Mildred continued, "In spite of what you tell him, it is not his *right* to walk over everybody, to be rude and sassy, to hold me up from doin' my work, to make everybody sick 'cause he feels like playin' in their food."

The Effect on Children

Domestics, unlike the classic nanny, might be expected to have had less influence on their charges, since mothers were more likely to be in the picture, and the maids' time was fragmented by the need to do housework. Their influence might also have been diluted by their differences from their charges; they were usually of a different race, social class, and cultural background. Parents have sometimes hoped that their children would gain greater understanding of another group, or develop cultural awareness, or grow up to be bilingual. But the University of Southern California's Madeline Stoner, an assistant professor of social welfare, says, "There is no empirical evidence anywhere in history that any kind of cultural transmission in fact takes place in these situations."

Yet some adults today, reflecting on the past, paint a picture of the way their "maid" profoundly affected their values and their lives. Although he grew up in the 1950s, just after World War II rather than before it, Howell Raines's story might have been told about an earlier time and place. He was seven years old when Grady came to his family in the Deep South. He was fourteen when she left. In his moving Pulitzer Prize–winning memoir in *The New York Times* he credited her with giving him "the most precious gift that could be received by a pampered white boy growing up in that time and place. It was the gift of a free and unhateful heart."

As she did her chores, she talked to him about the way things were for herself and other people like her, and his affection for her cut through the wall of prejudice to help him understand what segregation really meant.

Mark, too, the son of Greek immigrants in Savannah, developed a sensitivity to the realities of life for Daisy, his family's maid in the thirties and forties. She did not talk to him about it, particularly, but he knew from knowing her that the stereotypes he heard repeated were not necessarily so. When his mother, in Greek, complained that Daisy "stank," he spoke up: "How do you expect her to keep clean and put food on her table when you pay her only $4 a week [a good wage at the time]? You would stink too. Where does she start? Toothpaste? Bread?" Daisy died in her thirties of a burst appendix before the ambulance could get to her distant mill area on the outskirts of town. "That was part of the tragedy of being black in Savannah," Mark says. "They were far from medical help. They weren't considered terribly vital."

The other side of the meeting of two races or two cultures is that scorn, rather than understanding, may be the result. In Los Angeles, where Latino and Anglo culture met most often in the care of children, many parents hoped their youngsters would learn Spanish, or a respect for different cultural values. But this was not the way it usually happened. And even today the old attitudes persist. One mother told the *Los Angeles Times* she doesn't think her son will grow up "thinking of Spanish as a second language, but meaning second class." Another boy talks to his baby-sitter as if she were mentally re-tarded and hard of hearing. "Me want juice," he says loudly, then ex-plains, "I have to talk patchy or she won't understand."

Sometimes there is a deep and abiding individual connection, but it does not extend to the whole group. A man wet-nursed by a black mammy who worked for his family in the Deep South ex-pressed his love for her and saw to it that she was cared for later in life. But he kept up his invectives about "damn niggers" for so long that his adult daughter, caught up in the civil rights movement, walked out of his house.

The pressures of the segregated South made many children re-ject their own personal attachments: They succumbed to the dictates of their society and accepted its prejudices. But this conformity came at great cost. Lillian Smith, the writer whose novel *Strange Fruit* broke the silence about black-white sexual relations, was deeply af-fected by her own mammy: "I knew, but never believed it," she wrote, "that the deep respect I felt for her, the tenderness, the love, was a childish thing which every normal child outgrows. . . . I learned the bitterest thing a child can learn: that the human relations I valued most were held cheap by the world I lived in."

A South Carolina man whose family's black maid was fired be-cause she spent more time with him than on her housework, ac-knowledged that he was fond of her but knew he had to keep his emotional distance. He did not allow himself to feel what Lillian Smith had felt. "She was an older person who could have possibly taken the place of a surrogate mother but never quite did," he said. She "never quite did" because even as a child he recognized that be-ing a maid had a certain stigma attached to it, and so did the fact that she was of a different race. His response fits the results of those stud-ies that found no real attachment (in the sense of deep, lifelong bonding) between caretaker and child, in contrast to the attachment of mother and child. And yet, other studies have hinted that such an attachment is possible. The reality is that reactions are individual and generalizations dangerous. Children, like adults, mask and dis-tort their true feelings in response to the injunctions of the outside world.

Mothers worry that their children will pick up values and ways of seeing the world they would rather they didn't from caretakers of different races or cultural backgrounds. One Texas woman was dis-turbed to find her son being encouraged in "macho" behavior by their Mexican maid. The little boy padded into the kitchen in his blue-footed pajamas and said in Spanish he wanted something to eat. Eggs. Two of them. "Pronto, Maria," he ordered in his loudest voice. Maria was delighted. The mother was not. Parents such as this woman comfort themselves with the view that it is the parents' attitudes that will prevail, no matter how much time a caretaker spends with the children. They may be right. Doris Silverman, a psychologist at New York University who has examined the research on infants and bonding, found that "women's propensity for entrainment with infants—that is, their intense, deeply ingrained reactive responsiveness—leads to powerful, immediate connections so that a little of mother may go a long way."

How much a mother has to be with her children to "go a long way" is a touchy area for many parents. They understand that coverage—arranging for someone to be there—is not parenting, but they are at a loss about how to maintain their influence when someone else is with their children from morning to night. They are also often uncertain how adequate their mothering can be. One woman recognized her limitations and told her daughter, "Well, I can't help you nurse your children. I don't know how. I never nursed you at all." Instead, a black woman did the job and taught her to respect her own children. "Respect is the greatest power I know," she said, and "I learned that from the colored."

Treadmill Life

For some caretakers in the 1930s and 1940s the job seemed a repetition of the conditions under which their predecessors had labored during slavery: "I not only have to nurse a little white child, now eleven months old, but I have to act as playmate . . . to three other children in the home, the eldest of whom is only nine years of age. . . . I am not permitted to rest. It's 'Mammy, do this' or 'Mammy, do the other' from my mistress all the time. . . . Not only so, but I have to put the other three children to bed each night and I have to wash them and dress them each morning, I don't know what it is to go to church; I don't know what it is to go to a lecture or entertainment or anything of the kind. I live a treadmill life."

Along with the treadmill life these helpers faced some of the same tensions faced on the antebellum plantation by mistress and nurse or mammy—rivalry for the child's affection, worry about her own children, resentment at being always at the beck and call of someone else. But time had taught them one thing: If they lived out, not in, they were better able to maintain some semblance of independence and family life and avoid being on call twenty-four hours a day. This discovery came with freedom and was one way of marking a difference from slavery.

Of course, this was not always possible. The woman who lived the treadmill life lived in and called it "lifetime bondage." She was able to see her own children only when she was out with the children she cared for, or when they came to the yard of the house in which she worked. But this happened seldom, and briefly, because "my white folks don't like to see their servants' children hanging around the premises."

Other women lived out so they could at least give some care to their own children. One rushed home to nurse her eight-month-old baby and finally weaned him because as long as she nursed him he fussed at being offered the bottle when she was at work. Most said they had to work to support their children. One walked to work on a day that was so cold the buses weren't running. Halfway there she stopped and was tempted to go back, but "my children was small then, and I knew I had to take care of them. I thought of my little children, and I went on to work."

Her young children were placed in the care of a somewhat older sister or brother, a relative, or a neighbor, or just left to fend for themselves until she came home. Some women were able to snatch a few minutes during the day to check, if they worked close to home, but many youngsters went hungry and untended. White employers hardly thought about what happened to the children of their domestics. If they did, they were likely to believe that they were well taken care of by the legendary extended family of the black servant—kin and fictive kin (not necessarily blood relatives)—that even in slavery had provided a safety net. One employer said her maid's three-month-old baby was well cared for because she was left with a blind grandmother who was helped by one nine- or ten-year-old or another—never questioning why the ten-year-olds were not in school.

Susan Tucker, who reported this story in her book *Telling Memories Among Southern Women*, feels that white women, declared to be weak and helpless by their own cultural mores, needed to find other role models. "Thus, it is not difficult to see how white women wanted to continue to believe in the strength of black women. If black women could be seen as strong, then perhaps it was possible for all women to attain strength," she speculates with feminist hindsight.

Black women exhibited their strength early. Melissa Howe was twelve years old in 1924 when she worked baby-sitting "for a lady . . . she paid me fifty cents a week to sit with her baby. Stay at the house, me and the baby, wash dishes and clothes." The woman was just one step up the economic ladder—she worked shelling crabs, but "these white people, soon as they got able, they used to get a colored person to do for them." For the colored women, domestic service or doing laundry were the only jobs open. After Melissa married, she worked for two and a half dollars a week to take care of her children, "because the men wasn't making hardly anything." A European woman who lived in and hoped to save enough money to go back home and give her children a better life sums up the feelings of women who have to leave their children and take care of someone else's: "It hurt in the heart, taking care of somebody else's happy children. I love them but oh, I miss my girls."

For the families who hired them, status certainly was attached to having a domestic servant, although it was not nearly as much as the status gained by having a real nanny. Odette Harris said she thought her employer preferred a black domestic to a white one because "If somebody comes to the house and sees a black girl, they know she's a maid."

Between 1900 and 1930 two million black people had migrated north—mostly to urban areas. After World War I, black servants were replacing white—usually Irish—who had supplied domestic labor in the late nineteenth and early twentieth centuries. Blocked from sales and clerical jobs, the women searched for factory work that did not have the stigma of domestic service, but despite their efforts and qualifications, they made up an ever-increasing proportion of those working in laundries and as maids.

For white workers, the distinguishing mark was not skin color but a uniform. A young Philadelphia woman balked at this identifying costume: "What I minded, though . . . was being made to put on livery. I went as a nurse, because my health had broken down in teaching, and I loved the children dearly and they me. But when I asked not to put on the cap and apron, Mrs. L. got very red and said, 'You must remember that if you take a servant's place you have to accept the limitations of a servant.' 'If you have no other thought of what I am to the children than that,' I said, 'I had better go,' and go I did."

Status was only one of the auxiliary functions of a child-care worker; for many women, the servant offered companionship as well as household help. One woman whose husband traveled a lot admitted, "I hired her partly to help me take care of the baby and partly because I didn't like being alone so much."

Employers need to feel that the caretaker is "part of the family." This conflicts with the need to give her orders, to pay her, to supervise her activities. Yet the "part of the family" fiction goes way back, and it is impossible to generalize about the reactions of either the parents or the caretakers. Right after the Civil War, Annie, who had been a slave, came with her mistress when she married, and even went out to work to help the destitute family. She is buried in the family cemetery lot, and her gravestone lists her name and the dates of her birth and death—just like all the other headstones. She may even have considered herself part of the family. But others have made clear that though they are part of the household, they are not kin. Alice Childress's outspoken fictional Mildred corrected her employer with "I am *not* just like one of the family at all! . . . when you say, 'We don't know *what* we'd do without her' this is a polite lie . . . because I know that if I dropped dead or had a stroke, you would get somebody to replace me."

This reality produces confusion. Women have often assumed that those who care for their children should behave as they themselves would behave, doing whatever has to be done, no matter how long it takes. They should act not like workers who have eight-hour days but more like—well, members of the family. But, of course, the workers are quite clear in their minds that they keep their jobs at the pleasure of the women who hire them, and they often leave at the end of the day to go home to their own families.

Even though there are expressions of fondness, there are also evidences of unawareness. Mildred complained that her mistress talked about her to her friends as if she weren't there. Women often gossiped about their maids while the maid was going in and out of the room, as if she could not understand English. A peculiar twist on this "invisibility" occurred in the life of Daisy, the black maid in a Greek immigrant family. The women who came to the house for their monthly "coffees" would do the usual complaining in Greek— unaware that Daisy, from the kitchen, could understand every word they were saying because she had picked up the language from her employers.

Black domestics not only suffered indignities, they also avoided some because child care offered a way to circumvent the laws and customs restricting their activities. As servants, they could move in and out of places forbidden to them as individuals. One child nurse remembered that, if she had white children with her, she was not confined to the infamous "back of the bus." "So long as I was in charge of the children I could sit anywhere I desired, front or back," she said.

When Southern black women, nannies, fräuleins, au pairs, and other helpers made it possible for other women to be mothers, they also served unintended psychological purposes. A. J. Liebling was convinced that the fräuleins under whom he suffered were "a remarkably effective device for siphoning off from the parents the hostility that analysts assure us is the parents' due. . . . To the child who began conscious life under the rule of a fräulein, even the least bearable mother appeared an angel."

On the other hand, he felt that kind English nannies "siphon off not the hostility, but the affection, leaving the protagonists incapable of liking anybody for the rest of their lives."

Shared motherhood—whether it was the upper-class nanny or the mundane maid who took over all or part of the mother's job—served practical as well as psychological purposes. Full-time confinement with an infant or a young child is one of the most demanding and time-consuming jobs in the world, and women have found ways, since perfect motherhood became the goal in the mid-nineteenth century, of easing the burden imposed by the assumption that only a mother can care for her children. For the upper class, nannies provided substitute care and socially acceptable distance between mother and child and made possible busy lives outside the home. For the less wealthy, the maids and child-care helpers commonplace in their own circles diluted the intensity of the mother-child tie, permitted a modicum of freedom, and cut down on the work. The experts supported both closeness and distance, full-time maternal care and substitute mothers. A mother, made to feel inadequate by all the professional advice, could take her choice or be buffeted from one conviction to another, never free of the feeling that she might, in some way, be neglecting her job and harming her children.

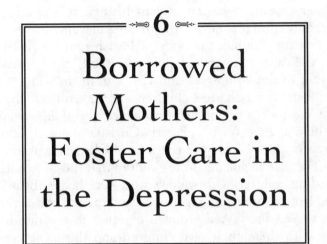

6

Borrowed Mothers: Foster Care in the Depression

Man is a social being. He springs from the soil of family life, from it he draws sustenance, to it he is bound by innumerable fibers. When for any reason he is uprooted, his well-being demands that he be transplanted and nurtured with the same tender solicitude for conditions of atmosphere, soil, and sun that the careful gardener displays toward his seedlings.

—*U.S. Children's Bureau, 1936,* The ABC of Foster-Family Care for Children

LIFE FOR ELEANOR EMPSON was so hard after the death of her husband that she gave two heifers to a family that agreed to the "nursing, keeping and relieving" of her young daughter, Mary, for two years. If Mary died during that time, they were still to keep the cows. The year was 1661. The place was Maryland.

This early American example of foster family care, in which a mother was "constrained to dispose of the said child above specified for the present relief, otherwise it might have perished in the condition [she was] left in," prefigures the foster family system that replaced apprenticeship as a way of caring for destitute children and existed in tandem with orphanages centuries later. When the extended family could not take a child in, other systems had to do the job.

Foster care itself has an ancient history. It is (along with extended family care) the oldest form of child placement. The Old Testament and the Talmud, the body of Jewish oral law, both contain rules for the care of dependent children. "God," the Psalms declare, is "a Father of the fatherless," and He "setteth the solitary in families." Orphaned or fatherless children were taken in by the families of relatives or, when no kin were available, by childless couples who reared them as their own. The early Christian church followed the same precepts. But Nero's persecutions of Christians produced such a flood of orphaned and destitute children that the church had to begin boarding children with widows who were helped by a small fee collected from church congregations. By about the end of the second century, these widows had grouped together in separate buildings, bringing with them their own children and those the church was supporting, and the first child-care institutions were born.

Foster family care as the ideal in place of the orphanage, once considered the ideal institution, was enshrined as early as 1909 in the first White House Conference on Children, which concluded, "The carefully selected foster home is for the normal child the best substitute for the natural home." (Children were expected to earn their keep as they had under the apprenticeship system.) Like most innovations, this philosophy was only slowly incorporated into practice. The question of whether foster care or institutional care was better for children raged for about one hundred years. In 1875 New York State's "Children's Law" forbade putting young children (between three and sixteen) "of proper intelligence" in almshouses along with adults, stating that they should instead be cared for "in families, asylums and other appropriate institutions." Societies for the Prevention of Cruelty to Children (based on the Society for the Prevention of Cruelty to Animals and sometimes combined with it) pioneered in investigating child abuse and removing children from unsuitable homes starting in 1874. Their policies may have contributed to the number of children taken from their parents and were the precursors of today's public child-welfare agencies. But the societies had to struggle against the pervading philosophy that outsiders should not interfere in parent-child relationships. On a federal level, the Children's Bureau, established in 1912 to look after the welfare of children, was specifically prohibited from entering any home "over the objection of the head of the family" to assess the fate of the children.

Institutions were most familiar and most popular as a way of caring for children who could not stay home, but a gradual drift to foster care began along with a growing awareness that institutions might not be best for all children. Placing a baby in an institution in the early twentieth century was the equivalent of a death sentence. In many of them, 100 percent of the infants died within the first year. The New York Foundling Hospital, in 1916, was able to cut this devastation in half by placing some of the healthier infants with wet nurses in their own homes.

In the 1920s, faced with this grim reality and the new professional hesitancy about taking children from their parents, the Societies for the Prevention of Cruelty to Children began to focus on preserving the family rather than removing the child. But this attitude was not universal. Not all families could or should be saved, and some alternative had to be available. A study in 1920 finally compared children in institutions with those in foster care and concluded that "both types of care are doing good work and are needed . . . all claims that boarding-out is generally better for the average dependent child than institutional care rest upon unwarranted assumptions . . . to abolish institutions for the care of normal dependent children, as advocated and urged by boarding-out extremists, would result not in a gain but a distinct and irreparable loss both to the child and the community." It was not until the 1950s with John Bowlby's and Rene Spitz's demonstration that infants did not survive the emotional and physical neglect of institutions that the instinctive feeling that home care was better—at least for the very young—received scientific validation. Even when foster care was chosen over an institution, children were often sent far away from their parents, making it almost impossible for them to reestablish emotional or physical contact.

Charles Loring Brace and his Orphan Trains, which sent "homeless" children from the evil streets of New York to more desirable homes in the rural Midwest, were the most visible reminder of the ancient custom of placing children in families other than their own. Started in 1853 under Brace's guidance, the Children's Aid Society—one of the largest, most innovative and long-lasting private philanthropies in the country devoted to the welfare of children—reflects in its history the pendulum swings in attitudes about what it called "the best interests of children." By the 1920s the emphasis had shifted from preserving the child by taking him out of a "bad" home to preserving the family so the child could be kept in the home or returned to it after a brief respite. In 1923, in response to "a growth both in our conception of our duty towards children and our method of accomplishing it," the Society started a boarding-home project "so that children could be placed in the metropolitan area and keep in close touch with their families." Nevertheless, Orphan Trains continued to ship children to the Midwest until 1929.

To preserve families and avoid placing children elsewhere, even if it was close by, the society, in cooperation with New York's Junior League, began a pioneering homemaker service that put experienced women into homes to care for children temporarily when the mother was ill, or away, or just unable to look after them properly. Widows' pensions established by many state legislatures already provided money to women for child care when the family breadwinner had died. But despite the laws and the sentiments, by 1934 only half the counties authorized to provide these funds were actually making them available. The child placement rate increased rather than decreased between 1910 and 1933, one more indication that wisdom and practice do not necessarily agree. Juvenile courts, established around the turn of the century, may have contributed to this trend. They were charged with attending to the needs of neglected children as well as delinquents and often took children from unfit parents and shifted responsibility for their care to public or private philanthropies, which then placed them away from home. The Depression and its economic pressures put more children at risk of being separated from their families.

Hard Times

The children suffered most. Grace Abbott, head of the federal Children's Bureau, told the White House Conference on Children in 1930 how bad things were for youngsters who could never regain what they lost during these hard times: "You can't feed children skimmed milk this year and make up by feeding them cream next year. What they didn't get this year you can never make up to them, and there are great numbers of children all over the country that aren't getting even skimmed milk this year, for whom the milk ration was long ago stopped." In Chicago a social worker discovered that at the same time budgets were cut for the provision of milk to children, large dogs at the animal shelter were allotted more money for meals than a man on relief.

In early 1933, twelve million men and women were out of work. As the Depression lengthened and deepened, whatever slender resources they may have had disappeared, and multitudes of middle-class working families slid into the trough of poverty. President Franklin D. Roosevelt said one-third of the nation was "ill-housed, ill clad and ill fed." In July 1933 New York's Society for the Improvement of the Condition of the Poor estimated that one in five children was "under par" in health and nutrition. (Newspapers printed advice on what to feed youngsters on a limited budget. One expert suggested concentrating on milk and bread as both filling and nutritious.) Thousands of homeless older boys between sixteen and twenty years of age roamed the streets of cities such as New York without hope of jobs or a better future. Parents, faced with harsh economic realities, flinched from bringing more children into such a cruel world. The 1930s were the first decade in this country's history when the number of children under ten declined. The birthrate stayed extraordinarily low until 1942, when, after the start of World War II, the Depression was finally over.

Traditional methods of philanthropy seemed to be enough to respond to what was almost universally perceived as a short-term problem. One wealthy woman, getting ready for just one more gala benefit to raise funds, said cheerfully that the social whirl during the economic downturn was going to be just as exciting as it had been during the Great War of 1918. Even professional social workers were misled. The Church Home Society of Boston, painfully out of touch with what was happening, allowed its foster-care facilities to be used for a "Gold Spoon" child, the son of a board member. The board decided that Tom should be placed in a foster home for a month so his mother and older brother and sister could visit relatives, and his nurse could have "a much needed vacation." His father visited him, just as if he had been "born with a tin rather than a gold spoon in his mouth." The nurse was the only one who seemed disturbed by the baby's being taken from her and put with other less fortunate foster children. "She was distinctly relieved and, it would appear, a bit surprised when the reasons for his acceptance having been fulfilled, he was returned to her care none the worse for his adventure."

Hoover's secretary of the interior, Ray Lyman Wilbur, always the optimist, suggested that the Depression might be good for children because they would avoid "the neglect of prosperity" by being cared for by their parents rather than servants. His comments elicited a caustic reaction from Homer Folks, director of New York's State Charities Aid Society. He said 10 to 20 percent of the nation's children were suffering dreadfully, with more joining them every day. "These children have never known the neglect of prosperity . . . they are not now getting the care of adversity," he said. "They are getting the neglects, hardships and hunger of adversity." Folks, one of a handful of remarkable men like the "remarkable women" around Jane Addams, was for more than fifty years an outspoken advocate for children. Like many of his philanthropic contemporaries, he combined Christian goodwill with political know-how. His long life (he died in 1963 at the age of ninety-six) spanned in time and attitude the movement from the idealism of the Progressives at the turn of the century to the realities of the New Deal.

The children he was now concerned about were often the children of the new poor, normally self-sufficient and hard-working, not the "shiftless dregs" who had previously been the burden of private and public philanthropy. In seven months between 1931 and 1932, *The New York Times* reported that fourteen hundred homeless women came to New York social agencies asking for help. They were a "new type—young, intelligent, often cultured, well trained and eager to work." Grace Abbott pointed out that "this kind of dependency is the result not of personal difficulties or character complications, or any of the things that make dependency in normal times, but is simply due to the absence of the wage earner's wages."

Unemployed men scoured the country for some way to make a living and left their wives and children behind. In 1934 an anguished mother wrote to the president from California, "I am a mother of seven children, and utterly heart broken, in that they are hungry, have only 65¢ in money, The father is in L.A. trying to find something to do,—provisions all gone—at this writing—no meat, milk—sugar—in fact, about enought [sic] flour for bread two meals—and that's all." In that same year, the Children's Aid Society of New York set "unemployment" at the top of a list that included illness, death, and desertion as reasons for children being placed in foster care.

Children were also placed because of their own disruptive behavior. "Each one of these children may be reckoned a potential delinquent," the society declared in 1930. Boys were more likely than girls to be hard to handle. The 1933 *Annual Report* of the State Charities Aid Society of New York, another foster placement agency, confirmed this finding, reporting that during the previous year they had

had requests for 9,093 girls and only 4,417 boys as foster children. The agencies felt that giving troubled children the benefits of a stable family life would help not only them but society at large. Like the earlier kindergartens, this care would change the child by changing the child's environment. At the same time that many children were to be helped by being removed from their unsuitable homes, the Children's Aid Society's Foster Home Department, established in 1925, was charged with "assist[ing] in keeping families together" by providing temporary care until conditions improved enough for the children to be returned to their own parent or parents, or the child's behavior changed for the better.

By 1933, even this well-established society was having trouble meeting the needs of all those asking for "fostering." Like those of many other private philanthropies, its funds had dried up, and parents were able to contribute only about 10 percent of the cost of boarding a child. Between 1929 and 1930, one-third of the hard-pressed private agencies went under, unable to raise the money they needed. As Hastings Hart, a pioneering child-welfare leader, pointed out, it was time for government to step in with far more than it had ever done to deal with this unprecedented crisis. In September 1931, with Governor Franklin D. Roosevelt leading the way, the New York State Legislature finally passed the first law giving relief to the unemployed. By the end of December 1933, what was called Home Relief had started all over New York City. This was the beginning of the change from the dominance of private philanthropy to the dominance of public welfare, and the recognition that citizens had a right to expect to be taken care of.

But getting help wasn't made easy or pleasant. William Matthews, head of the Emergency Work Bureau in New York City, protested, "The whole damn theory of the thing is to make relief giving so unpleasant, so disagreeable, in fact so insulting to decent people that they stay away from the places where it is given."

As William Bremer detailed in his book *Depression Winters*, recipients of private and public charity were subject to scrutiny, told what they could and could not buy, and even accompanied by "voluntary shoppers" who supervised their purchases. Buying cigarettes, beer, candy, pies, and cakes was forbidden. And no cash changed hands. Recipients were given bags of coal and clothing, food tickets, and rent vouchers, and storekeepers were forbidden to give them change in cash. Early in the Depression, desperate recipients accepted these restrictions. Their homes were visited, their closets inspected to be sure they deserved help. Later, as more and more people were forced "on the dole" and some of the stigma lessened, relief recipients complained of being treated like children. The red tape, *The New York Times* asserted, "hanged" people. "A hungry man is hungry, and the discovery that he is 'undeserving' by some professional social service test cannot make him less so."

Even to themselves, the poor who could not support their families in this time of desperate trouble were "undeserving." In their eyes, they had failed to live up to what the sociologist Kenneth Keniston called the myth of the self-sufficient family. This all-American standard had its roots in the pioneer spirit that assumed unlimited opportunity and the life-giving virtues of independence. It didn't matter that industrialism had changed the ground rules. As Keniston put it, "If a family proves less than independent, if it is visibly needy, if its members ask for help, then it is by definition not an 'adequate' family."

The stigma attached to "inadequacy" kept many people from accepting help. One woman, the mother of three with another baby on the way, wrote to Eleanor Roosevelt enclosing a list of the baby clothes she would need and asking if the First Lady could send them. The woman had refused the suggestion that she go to a relief agency: "Somehow we must manage—but without charity," she wrote. In her letter she sent two rings, one that her husband had given her and one that had belonged to her mother—and asked Mrs. Roosevelt to keep them as collateral until she could pay for the layette.

An Oregon mother was even more destitute. It was painful, she wrote, for "a mother to hear her hungry babe whimpering in the night and growing children tossing in their sleep because of knawing plain HUNGER." In the fall of 1931 it was estimated that more than six hundred thousand homeless and dependent children would need help from welfare agencies during the coming winter. Despite the family aid stressed by relief programs, J. Prentice Murphy told the annual conference of the Child Welfare League that "the number of children from broken homes who will need assistance from social agencies this Winter is increasing steadily." Yet in the face of this increase in need and numbers, relief budgets were cut because of inadequate funds. The assistant director of the Chicago Housing Authority in the 1930s told Studs Terkel, the oral historian, that "a mother of nine children was receiving two quarts of milk. Because of a bud-

getary crisis, she was cut down to one quart. She raised hell at the relief station. She became vituperative. The case worker wrote her up as
a psychotic. And sent her to a psychiatrist. Fortunately, he responded
as few did at the time. He said: When this woman stops reacting the
way she does, let me know. Then she would be abnormal."

Some women, faced with the chilling choice of watching their
children starve or giving them away in the hope that they could at
least be fed, chose to give them up. They were too proud to ask for
what they saw as handouts. So widespread was this problem that the
federal government felt it had to warn social workers, "The mother
who hesitates to accept relief to enable her to keep her home together must be educated to see that it is far more self-respecting to
do so than to be willing to part with her children."

Between 1925 and 1935 the number of children in foster homes
more than doubled. Of course, this was not only because of the Depression. In a critical look at the child-welfare system in America,
Leroy H. Pelton suggests that it was the need to keep the professional staffs of social agencies busy that increased the number of children in foster care. "At least since the beginning of the twentieth
century up until the mid-1970's," he argues, "whenever child welfare
agencies expanded and staff size increased, then the foster care population increased."

Whatever the complex reasons, social agencies grappled with
an increasing need for foster care. In Philadelphia in 1932, "In spite
of the efforts of social agencies to keep families together," the Children's Aid Society faced an ever-increasing caseload. In two days in
January, it had to find homes for nineteen children. "In many of
these cases," its report continued, "unemployment has been a factor
in the family breakdown, even though it is not the direct cause." The
Depression propelled more children into boarding-home foster care
(under private or public auspices, with payment at least partly from
public funds) than ever before. The economic crisis also changed the
face of the care itself: "In this continued need, to keep children for
increasingly long periods of care, the Department's original goal,
short-time care, has necessarily been modified. Yet the need for
short-time care continues," the *Eighty-second Annual Report* of the
Children's Aid Society declared.

Some children were put in foster boarding homes because they
themselves had physical or mental problems, but most became foster
children because their families could not care for them. A 1927 study

of ten agencies by the U.S. Children's Bureau showed that marital discord, divorce, or desertion accounted for 19 percent of the placements; 16.3 percent were placed by unwed mothers (these were most likely to be available for adoption); about 10 percent had mothers who were ill. There is no reason to believe the figures were much different a few years later, although by then poverty had added to the basic problem.

The dismal trends continued even though well-meaning professionals stressed—as they had since 1909—that "under all circumstances a dependent child should be maintained in his own home when poverty is the principal factor that calls for his care away from home." During the Depression an Adopt-A-Family program was organized to raise money to pay for temporary homemakers instead of moving children out of their homes. A newspaper article about this supposedly superior system sparked a letter from Ella Cara Deloria, a Plains Indian, detailing the way her own American culture dealt with such problems. "There were no charity cases in our primitive society," she wrote. Instead, children were taken into families not their own in the name of someone who had died. "No impersonal, hired machinery for administering love by remote control was this; instead, smoothly and effectually the practice of 'likening some one to another' went on and on."

The "impersonal, hired machinery" troubled the larger society, too, as it groped for ways to care for children whose parents were unable to do the job because they just didn't have the money. The trouble was that welfare relief was often inadequate to provide even minimal care. Institutions and foster homes offered children a better chance at an adequate diet and a warm bed. Torn between providing material comfort and maintaining emotional ties, the Child Welfare League of America suggested that "children suffering a certain measure of destitution (short of actual deprivation of food and clothing, such as it is) should remain home even when foster organizations are able to guarantee certain additional comforts of which the children would be deprived at home. If possible, the money available for board away from home should be used for relief in the children's own homes." Under normal circumstances, it went on, it costs twice as much to keep a child in a foster home as it does to maintain the child in its own home.

As early as 1930, Grace Abbott of the Children's Bureau had suggested that the mother's pensions (paid to widows for the care of their children) be extended to include all children who needed help during unemployment in the family—even if the father was alive. Her proposal was unacceptably radical, but it signaled the start of the movement that led, finally, to Aid to Dependent Children (later Aid to Families with Dependent Children) under the Social Security Act of 1935. In 1931, without a federal law, 82 percent of the mothers receiving pensions were widows. Proportionately few of them were black. In Chicago in 1917, six years after the state initiated these pensions, blacks formed only 2.7 percent of those receiving aid, although the black population had been swollen by post–World War I immigration. Black women were less likely than whites to be seen as "deserving" of this aid. Under Social Security, more and more blacks were included, and eligibility was widened in some places to include not only widows but unmarried mothers as well.

The widow's pensions laws on which this act was based reflected the recognition that poverty had social origins. The recipients, assumed to be "worthy," could be trusted with cash rather than vouchers or bags of food. As Kansas City juvenile court judge E. E. Porterfield testified in favor of Missouri passing such legislation, "If the poverty of the mother forces her to neglect her child the poverty should be removed and not the child." In 1911 the first such laws were passed; by 1935 all but two states had followed the lead of Illinois and Missouri.

The decision that money should be provided to meet the needs of children—rather than the needs of a parent—recognized a change in the status of children that had been gathering momentum since the second half of the nineteenth century. Children were no longer seen as chattels of their parents but as individuals in their own right, who needed certain conditions to reach their full potential. Darwin had shown that mankind was malleable. Freud had emphasized the importance of the early years in determining a person's future development. G. Stanley Hall and the child-care experts who followed his lead demonstrated that child rearing was a science and a profession worthy of the attention of serious adults. Therefore, attention must be paid to the child, not just the parents who were expected to supply food, clothing, and shelter. The Depression provided the impetus for propelling this view firmly into the world of legislation. It also made Americans less willing to "go it alone," and for the first time led them to expand the role of government as protector of the underdog. The New Deal was the start of the Welfare State, and children were among its first beneficiaries.

Under Social Security matching funds were funneled to the

states, which then distributed them to mothers. But the aid was minuscule and hedged by requirements. The average grant per family was only eight to ten dollars a month, and varied widely state by state. It amounted to only pennies a day. Some states were reluctant to embrace the new focus on the needs of the child and denied help if the mother was "not the kind of woman that deserves this kind of assistance," as one investigator put it. Even in what had become a family-centered society, some families were more worthy than others.

In practice, if not in theory, the new law, like the old mother's aid state legislation, ignored the children of widowers or unemployed men whose wives could not care for their children. The 1927 U.S. Children's Bureau study of ten agencies affiliated with the Child Welfare League of America showed that the single largest group of children placed away from their homes by ten different social agencies—22.3 percent—were the children of widowers; only 8.4 percent were the children of widows.

In addition to poverty and death of a parent, disease was a major stress on families. Tuberculosis killed women of childbearing age at a dreadful rate; it was the leading cause of death of women aged fifteen to forty-four, surpassing the complications of childbirth. Even when it didn't kill, tuberculosis took a sick mother away from home for long periods of time. So did mental illness, another scourge of young women.

The pressure on men left with young children was crushing. One young father came into the offices of the Children's Aid Society in New York carrying a three-month-old baby and holding his two-year-old son by the hand. He told the caseworker, "I don't want to give up my children," as the boy clung to his leg, "but they must have food. They have had nothing but tea and bread for three days. I've been to the Relief Agency but they say to come to you." His wife had suffered a "nervous breakdown" after the birth of the baby, and he was struggling to hold the family together. He had been trying for months to find work, without any success. Now his only choice was to put the children "with a kind family until their mother's better and can take care of them." That would give him "new heart" and freedom in his job hunt and, he promised, "I'll work my hands off to pay you back."

Although the older, informal placing of children in the homes of relatives persisted alongside the professionalized foster-care system, this man had no family member to turn to. In another case, one in which the family was able to step in, one man learned only when he was six years old that the older boy who had always lived with him and his parents in three cramped rooms in New York during the 1930s was not his real brother but a cousin. Told by another child at school that his "cousin" would pick him up, he insisted Aaron was his brother. Only then did he discover that when Aaron's parents died within a few years of each other, the three children were distributed among family members. It was not that the fostering was a secret; it just was not spoken about. Now the younger boy, who grew up to be a social worker, identifies himself as "an only son with a brother." In the formal foster-care system, relatives were not usually paid to take in children. They were assumed to provide free homes and were usually free of supervision as well. Only in the mid-1980s did it become general policy (and often the law) for an agency to pay board to keep a child in what was considered a preferred placement because of blood ties and the fact that he would be in a familiar setting with familiar people, thus minimizing his turmoil.

In addition to the effects of the Depression, families were reacting to the long-term effects of World War I. Charlie Bertram lived with weak lungs as the result of repeated gas attacks during trench warfare. Despite his disability, he married and had a child, at which time his wife quit her office job. The need for extra income forced Charlie to overwork, and his old breathing problem flared up. When the doctor prescribed "irony for the poor, complete rest and freedom from worry," his desperate wife came to the Children's Aid Society in New York. "She could not leave the baby to careless hands," the society reported, "yet her husband must have care and nursing. Would we place the child in a foster home where she could see it often, then she could go to work with an easy mind and bear the full burden of support until her husband was better?"

Beyond the specifics of illness, death, desertion, and unemployment, the society said children needed foster care: "Because each child needs a home; Because babies need to be cuddled and rocked and sung to and loved . . . Because the school child needs somebody he loves to come home to, somebody who wants to hear his stories of what happened today . . . Because a dad is a big help when a fellow is in a jam—and sometimes only dad will do . . . Because we have faith in American family life." The American family, according to tradition and reality, consisted of a mother, father, and one or more children. Any deviation from this was a deviation from normality. Foster family care, the Child Welfare League of America argued, "is particularly adapted to meet the child's normal developmental needs in a family-centered society." The league cited the growing body of scientific knowledge that placed great emphasis on the importance of serving the emotional and social as well as the physical needs of children. Yet, this faith in foster care as indisputably the best way is questioned by Anthony N. Maluccio, an expert on foster care, who, in the 1970s, looked back at the history of child-welfare services and concluded, "The choice of one type of substitute care over another has typically been determined by prevailing values and biases more than by validated theories and empirical knowledge."

In the nineteenth century, most Americans thought the institution best served the needs of children and society. For one thing, it was cheaper than paying for individual foster care. For another, it could deal efficiently with large groups of children, particularly immigrant children, who were threatening American values. And children had not yet been recognized as individuals with the right to have their emotional, as well as physical, needs attended to. As the century came to a close, the family's divine origins were embraced with added fervor, since the "creator has ordained that human beings shall receive, through it, greater and more lasting social and moral influence than through any sphere of life." By the twentieth century, the family home that had been enshrined earlier for middle-class families as a haven and savior was recognized as necessary for poor children, too. "The recognition that any reasonably good mother is the best and most economical caretaker of her children marks an immense advance over the orphanage," the Children's Bureau declared in 1936. The "reasonably good mother" could be a foster mother as well as a natural mother. Placing children in situations that reproduced, as closely as possible, the "self-evident" benefits of family life came to be seen as the best way. An effort was mounted to choose foster care over institutional placement, and orphanages began to close. Institutional populations also declined because young men and women lived longer and were less likely to die and leave behind young children. Another reason, according to Hastings Hart, was Prohibition, which began in 1919 and lasted until 1933, protecting at least some children, he said, from the devastating effects of living in an alcoholic's home. Alcoholism was a major reason for removing a child.

The shift from the orphanage was less likely to affect black children. As late as 1915, a social worker suggested that institutions that charged nominal board would meet the needs of black children in the North "admirably" and be preferable to day nurseries or foster care. Putting a child in a private family, he feared, would risk the possibility that the child would be abandoned altogether, because the parent would see that it was receiving advantages that he or she could not possibly provide and would decide to leave the child where it was better off. Despite this concern, the Children's Aid Society found in 1939 that it had no trouble finding good foster homes for the black children it was just beginning to serve although child-welfare experts agreed that black children had a harder time during the Depression than their white counterparts.

Proxy Parents

Would-be foster parents flooded social agencies with applications during the Depression because they needed the meager boarding payments to stretch their skimpy incomes. Women without marketable skills were looking for ways to contribute to family resources while still staying home to care for their own children. In 1932, the Children's Aid Society of Pennsylvania had three to four times more applicants than ever before. The society allowed four dollars a week for boarding children under two, and three to three-fifty a week for those over two. The maximum they offered was four to five dollars a week for one foster family. This stipend covered room and board, since the agency took care of medical costs and clothing and parents were asked to contribute what they could. Many applicants were quite frank that they needed the board money, but this presented social agencies with a dilemma: They were hunting for homes, yet the conventional wisdom declared that a child should not be placed in a family that saw the placement as a way of getting extra income. The society warned that "foster home finders must continue to place the needs of the children first in accepting homes among people affected by the depression, and generally foster children should not be boarded in family homes where the board money is needed for relief. . . . An adult under great economic strain may be likened to one under excessive emotional strain. We should avoid using either as foster parents." Nevertheless, foster parents who were paid to keep children often considered this a job and were diligent about doing it well.

The author of a study of successful and unsuccessful foster

homes in Massachusetts in 1932 saw potential foster families under economic pressure this way: "Experience . . . seems to show," the researcher wrote, "that under such circumstances a child may be as cordially welcomed and frequently much more wisely handled than in a foster family where there is little economic pressure."

Yet the caution about placing children with people who needed the money was also based on reality. Three North Carolina girls whose mother died were placed by a social agency in an orphanage, then on a hardscrabble farm. The impoverished foster family was paid fifteen dollars a month for all three, but there was not enough money to buy food and the girls were always hungry and, eventually, exhausted because of their inadequate diet. The agency that placed them found they were anemic and moved them to a "therapeutic home" where they could be fattened up.

Agencies were faced not only with the dilemma of widespread poverty in homes looking for children, but also with the devastating effect of the Depression on well-established foster homes. If, as the 1909 White House Conference on Children had declared in what had since become dogma, "Except in unusual circumstances, the home should not be broken up for reasons of poverty," should a child be moved from a foster home because of financial difficulties? The Child Welfare League of America's conference in 1932 concluded, "None of us feels that we ought to crawl out from under the home that is still good for the child. If the home has broken down we must take the child out, but if the home is still good for the child, the child should stay there and we should try to finance it." The financing was minimal, even in a time when a family of five could live adequately on fifteen hundred to eighteen hundred dollars a year.

Children were placed in boarding homes, in free homes (where no board was paid, as had been the system during the Orphan Train period), and in wage homes where adolescents who helped out at home, on the farm, or in the family business might be paid a small sum. Older girls were easier to place than older boys; they could be handy around the house and were less likely to have behavioral problems. In 1930 in Pennsylvania 80 percent more wage homes were approved for girls than for boys. The children stayed weeks, months, or years.

Ideally, foster parents took children because they loved them, not because they needed the small income the children brought in to help pay the bills. Henry Hildabolt , a foster father in a small town in Ohio, said his wife had at first spent her time "mothering" him, but they soon realized her "maternal instinct might well fulfill a larger purpose and bring happiness to some motherless child." They took in Joe, age four. "We took the boy because we wanted him. This cannot always be said of own parents," Mr. Hildabolt pointed out. He and his wife did not hide from Joe "the facts about his heritage, including the unfortunate ones," since "if you begin by deceiving a child you have to keep on deceiving him." They did not try to adopt the boy, deciding they would wait until he was sixteen and then discuss it with him. Other children like Joe also moved from the status of temporary foster child to permanent adopted child, although this progression may not have been part of the plan when they were first placed.

Foster children were sometimes mis-placed—put in homes where they did not do well. A basic tenet of placing was that brothers and sisters should, if possible, stay together. Ten-year-old, awkward Mary and her pretty baby sister were taken in by a well-meaning spinster. (It was unusual for an unmarried woman to be given a child.) The baby was admired and cuddled, but Mary's rough manners shocked the woman. Soon Mary began to lie and even stole some trinkets from her foster mother's room. Scolding and pleading did no good, and it soon became clear that Mary needed a different substitute mother. Like so many foster children, before and since, she was moved from one home to another. This time a motherly woman with experience in rearing children was able to love Mary and understand her troubles. Her "faults vanished as if by magic," the social worker reported.

Some foster parents had already reared their own children and, as New York's Children's Aid Society put it, they "want[ed] to continue being good parents." (The study of successful parents in Massachusetts found that most mothers were forty or over and had grown or nearly grown children.) Some who still had youngsters at home thought they would enjoy a larger family. And, of course, there was often the financial consideration, sometimes freely acknowledged, sometimes hidden. The society recognized that "motives for taking children fall generally into two or three classes: love of children, a desire for companionship for their own children, or a natural gift in handling children which they enjoy exercising. These motives are frequently accompanied by the wish to add to the family income." In some places by custom, in others by statute, children were placed in families of the same religion and same race. Despite the acceptance of the idea that uniformity of this kind would make life easier for the child (and serve racial and religious community interests), some children were placed in homes that did not fit these criteria. For example, Malcolm X, who was then called Malcolm Little, stayed with white foster parents in Mason, Michigan, near his hometown of Lansing. He had first been placed in their group home as a way station on the road to the reformatory; he continued to live with them after the other boys in his group had left. They encouraged him to do well in the local almost all-white junior high school, although, in spite of their good intentions, they did not hesitate to talk about "niggers" in front of him. He said they were "good people." In 1919, about twenty years before Malcolm was placed, the Reverend William A. Creditt detailed the special problems of "colored youth" in the North and advocated putting them in institutions rather than foster homes unless the child was an orphan or his parents were utterly unfit to care for him. The foster home, he warned, is likely to be better than his own home, and, "He is then often raised in an environment totally unlike that to which he was born, and often, unfortunately for all concerned, looks down with contempt upon his parents and relatives." Although this may have been the reaction for some children, Malcolm continued to long for the time when his family had been together.

The Children's Aid Society required that parents be Protestants between twenty-five and sixty-five years of age, and that they be able to provide a separate bedroom for the child. Soon this was modified to the more realistic separate bed. The foster mother had to be under sixty when she applied, she could not work outside the home, and transient roomers were forbidden. Private agencies such as this one took children of their religious persuasion and placed them in homes that shared their religious beliefs—Jewish, Protestant, Catholic—so that there would be as little disturbance as possible in the children's lives. Public agencies were nonsectarian, but they, too, as far as possible put children in homes of the same race and religion as their own families. Public agencies sometimes turned the children in their charge over to private sectarian agencies for placement and paid for their upkeep.

Foster parents were recruited from "the same social plane as the child's own home." The fathers were carpenters and cabinetmakers, firemen, farmers, policemen, and chauffeurs. Until the depths of the Depression made it difficult for even these skilled men to hang on to steady jobs, the foster family was required to have a regular, predictable income.

Some of the most successful placements were made in families recommended by other foster parents, but agencies also had active home-finding programs. This poignant appeal appeared in a Philadelphia newspaper in 1932: "THREE little children, 4, 7 and 9 years of age want to borrow a mother while their own mother goes to the hospital for an operation. Must be Protestant; good neighborhood. Board $7 a week. References exchanged." The ad brought 360 replies. Only 15 percent of them were deemed "promising material" by the agency, which carefully checked the prospective foster families. Applicants were assessed for their suitability and, ideally, matched to a child who would fit successfully into that particular family. Hastings Hart, a distinguished child-welfare advocate, had set the tone for the growing profession of social work when he said, "The fine art of the placing out method is the adjustment of the child to the home. You may have a good child and a good home and the two good things may not have any adaptation for each other." In a further attempt to make home finding and child placing a science, rather than the haphazard rescue operation it had been, a "visitor" or social worker kept an eye on the child and the foster family and wrote detailed reports. If things were not going well, the child was moved to another, more suitable home.

Instead of finding homes for children near where they lived, New York's Children's Aid Society placed them in temporary homes in the suburbs. "A comfortable, unpretentious middle-class detached house with a yard or garden where the children may play" was presented as the ideal. This reflected the latest expert thinking. In May of 1928 Jay Nash, professor of physical education at New York University, cautioned parents at a conference organized by Macy's, the great department store, that "play developed the personality of the child" and did it best away from city streets, in a well-equipped backyard. The necessary swings, slides, and sandbox could, of course, be bought at Macy's. This was a time when the idea that children had their own needs, separate from those of the adults with whom they lived, was gaining wide acceptance. These child-centered needs could be met by supporting the consumer economy that had belatedly discovered children as a lucrative market and advertised toys and play as vital to a child's intellectual and emotional development, as the historian William Leach has pointed out. If foster children were to have the chance to live like any other children, they, too, the social agencies reasoned, deserved a backyard so that they could develop their full potential. They also deserved an allowance. In families under the supervision of the Children's Aid Society, six-year-olds got ten cents, seven-year-olds twenty cents, eight-year-olds a quarter, and those fifteen and over one dollar a week. The idea was to teach them the value of money (make them educated consumers, in other words) and help them feel more like their schoolmates.

Some foster children during the Depression were different from their schoolmates because their clothes came by what one foster mother called "The Big Brown Bag" method rather than from the store. "When those bundles came I could not hurt Jack by showing them to him, so I just put things aside and gave him a little here and a little there, as though I had been buying like I buy for my own boys," she said. Agencies were reluctant to provide cash for dressing the children, but the Jewish Children's Society of Baltimore finally decided to put an end to the brown bags. Foster mothers took the children shopping instead, and this brought them closer together. It also helped the children feel more like other children and was "the best way to instill thrift, neatness and care of clothing."

Policy dictated that the foster home in the suburbs could not be so far away that parents could not afford the carfare for a weekly visit, but it should not be so close to the old neighborhood that the sometimes unsavory reputation of the child's own family would haunt it day after day. When New York's State Charities Aid Association looked in the mid-1920s at what happened in the long run to one hundred children, mostly from one county, who had been placed in the years since 1898, it found that "the children who were completely out of touch with the neighborhood in which their families lived and in which their reputation was known, made a much better adaptation personally and socially and gained by a complete detachment from their original neighborhood. Those who remained in foster homes in their own locality, showed a tendency to fall back to the low standards of their own families whose bad reputations were remembered unfavorably in connection with the children." When they were grown (some were forty years old by then) the "children" in this study were more interested in learning about their brothers and sisters than their parents, "for whom many of them could feel little respect or affection." Children whose parents continued to visit them retained the closest ties with their natural families.

The hope was that the foster home would be only temporary, and that with adequate help the child's family could be reconstructed. Foster parents were to provide safety, love, and understanding until the real parent or parents could take over again, not to rescue good children from bad or inadequate parents. This notion was a departure from that championed by Charles Loring Brace: The Orphan Train children, sent far from home to the Midwest, were, essentially, placed for adoption—formal or informal. Although there was lip service to the idea that they might eventually be reunited with their parents, the system made it difficult physically as well as psychologically to maintain family ties. Brace believed that the infinitely malleable children would have a better chance to grow up as contributing Americans if they were torn out of their evil environment and sent to the country. By the 1930s, the question, according to a Pennsylvania child-placing agency, had become, "How do you help your boarding child to retain the precious ties of his home, yet grow up to be a better man than his father?"

Retaining these ties was important because, as one expert recognized forty years later in an example of how these attitudes have persisted, "for almost every child natural parents are always the 'psychological parents.' " In other words, a child's question, "Who am I?" is most often answered by referring to its biological parents.

Even if he or she is not the psychological parent, the foster parent is faced with the day-to-day care and discipline of the child. One foster father, a retired mailman with five children of his own, saw the problem this way: "It's easier to handle your own children. You can pop 'em if you think they need it. With foster children you have to be careful. Spank 'em slightly and the neighbors will say you used a crowbar." This doesn't mean he was a cruel foster father. Spanking was still the culturally accepted way to discipline one's own children. But using this method on someone else's children might be interpreted as abuse. This father also said, "We believe in caring for the children of other people as if they were our own. It's a tragic world, when you think about it."

Foster parents walked a fine line when they tried to do this. They were, after all, only partial parents, lacking a long-term investment in the children and having very little to say about what would happen to them in the future. There was always the reality that many of the children had biological parents who hoped to reclaim them, and the fact that the children had come into the family from the outside. In a roundtable discussion in 1931, experts from around the country warned that several factors could contribute to difficulties for foster children. First, the experts thought that the tendency of foster parents to be more critical of the foster children than of their own undermined self-confidence. Then there was the almost inevitable requirement that the child be grateful—and express gratitude. This led to unreasonable demands. And there was the propensity of foster parents to blame the child's difficulties in their home on the heritage of the home he or she had come from. Despite the twentieth-century recognition that poverty and other problems were often caused by defects in the social structure rather than personal failings, the idea that genetics—a "bad seed"—marked children for life was still a powerful force.

Foster Mother's Clubs grew up around the country as a way to ease the adjustment of both the child and the foster family. In Canton, Ohio, the mothers discussed such topics as Truth and Falsehood, To Spank or Not to Spank, and What to Tell Children about Sex. These topics reflected, of course, the concerns of any parents. But these mothers also considered What Is Malnutrition? (children sometimes came into care in poor physical health) and Adoptions. Just as child-study groups for ordinary mothers aimed at providing them with the latest expert information on child development, these clubs, sponsored by social agencies, hoped to turn foster mothers into "professionals" who depended on scientific guidance rather than intuition in rearing other people's children. "Sometimes parents must wonder whether parenthood just naturally disqualifies them for knowing anything about children or what to do with them, since there are so many arm-chair specialists waiting to tell how they would do the job if they had to," a psychologist told foster mothers in sympathetic understanding. But she pointed out that the experts combined personal interest with detachment and knew a great deal about raising youngsters.

Although they were performing a necessary social service, foster parents who boarded children found themselves stigmatized because they were being paid by an agency that helped the poor. The stigma attached to the children and their parents rubbed off on the foster parents, who were often seen as accepting "welfare," too. On the other hand, social agencies that used foster mothers tried to provide recognition for a hard job well done. One paean went like this:

> She is an artist greater than she knows, for her motherhood has room enough for other people's children and her patience can wait long enough to understand someone's else child. . . . Her courage is more than courage, for it is unsung. Her spirit is more than good will; to the child it is an open door, a new friend and security; to the society, its long arm of service. . . . Her activity begins with the sun and only ends when needs end. For her we speak, though we do not need to—she is her own reward.

Divided Motherhood

In earlier times, family members took in the children of relatives who needed temporary or even permanent care. But in the Depression, the old extended family networks stretched to the breaking point. Relatives, hard-pressed themselves financially, often could not take on the burden of other children, even temporarily. Families dumped on the streets because of nonpayment of rent had no way to help out another family member. And apartments were often so crowded with doubled-up families there was not even space for another bed. The situation was described in this way at a White House Conference on Children in 1930: "First, the payments on the home began to be stopped, and then the home went, and the furniture went, and then the credit was exhausted at the grocery store, and then the family moved in with another family, and they shared as they could, and circumstances were such as to produce almost nothing at all to share." The best plan for many children seemed to be to put them in foster care under the supervision of a social agency.

For families, turning their children over to other people represented an admission of defeat. In earlier times, this shifting of children had been accepted as customary (during apprenticeship) or was seen as a way of bettering their lives (as during the Orphan Train period). Now, having children snatched away by an all-encompassing agency was vivid evidence that the parents had failed. To assuage this terrible guilt, the Jewish Children's Society of Baltimore decided to involve parents in the choice of the family to which their children would be sent, even arranging for preplacement visits. In this way, parents would feel less devastated and helpless, and children would feel a link between the home they were leaving and the one they were going to. Both parent and child, the agency hoped, would be less torn in their loyalties, and the parent would be less likely to sabotage the placement because "the healthiness of the parent's reaction to the entire placement situation is dependent upon his ability to salvage from his charred parenthood a satisfying concept of himself as a person." The foster parent would be chosen, at least in part, by the biological parent rather than being forced on the parent by an impersonal agency.

Parents were encouraged to visit their children in their foster homes when they were able, but this was not always as simple as it sounds. For the mother who was recovering from mental illness (a major factor in the placement of children) or who had been deemed unfit, for one reason or another, the visits could be painful reminders of her inadequacy. Although she told her story forty years after the Depression, Phyllis T. McAdams reflected the experience of natural mothers through the years. "Sometimes a failure to visit frequently on the part of the natural parent," she said, "is not an indication that they don't care, but that they care too much.

"You see your child in a home situation where everything is apparently orderly and calm, and quite often materially superior to anything you are going to be able to offer them, and wonder why the hell you are bothering to rock the boat . . . maybe it would be better to leave your child there, it would be a lot less upsetting for everyone involved if you would just drop out of the picture."

Parents who dropped out of the picture often left their children a fantasy legacy. The unknown, unseen parent became idealized, the foster parent became the bad one, no matter how difficult living had been at home before the breakup. Even parents who were abusive were not always abusive, and children clung to the hope that the good times, not the bad, were what they would find if they went back. They waited and hoped—for a feeling, more than a person, the feeling that represented security and warmth and love. Living in confusion and turmoil, they might insist that their parent was coming to visit despite repeated disappointments. They might not understand why an agency, trying to keep upsets to a minimum during the early days of placement, might discourage visits. Anne Hall Whitt and her sisters spent a short time in a Catholic orphanage on their way to a series of foster homes. While at the orphanage they caught a glimpse of their father from the playground. They ran toward him, but a nun held them back and told him to leave. The two younger girls sat at the top of the slide after that and waited for him to come back until "our legs became numb from the cold steel slide, but we did not give up our vigil." Their father visited once or twice when Anne was in what eventually became her permanent foster family, but, Anne said, "Our conversations were strained, and for days after each visit I was tortured by feelings of guilt. Then as abruptly as his visits began, they ended."

To keep alive a tenuous tie and calm the fears of parents who did not have the time, money, or emotional stamina to visit regularly and see for themselves that the foster home was a good one, the Detroit Children's Aid Society developed a system of photographing the children, the foster parents, and the home at regular intervals. With the pictures, a parent could keep track of his or her child's growth and development, and at least feel somewhat familiar with the substitute parents and the room where the child slept or played or ate. Any contact seemed better than no contact, particularly since the assumption for most children was that they would go back home within a short time.

Competition between natural parent and foster parent was built into the situation. The foster parent had day-to-day care of the child, and the natural parent, a social worker said, "does not dare admit to himself that another person has succeeded with his child where he has failed." When the natural parents took the child out for a short visit, the foster parent was likely to provide instructions: "Be sure he wears his sweater, he's just getting over a cold," or, "Don't be late bringing him back," reinforcing the natural parents' feelings of inferiority.

The mother who was mentally ill faced special problems. Phyllis McAdams stayed in the hospital for a year because she was deeply depressed. When she got out, she was not yet ready to be reunited with her six children, yet she visited them as often as she could and found herself making unrealistic promises. "My kids were able to extract tentative promises of when we would all be reunited, because my pride was killing me and I didn't have the heart to say that I had no home, no money, and no definite time when I would have sufficient emotional and financial resources for getting these things." Her children came home gradually, over a few years. She worried that their foster parents had been critical of her and her situation, and that the children would find her modest home embarrassingly inadequate. She suggested that foster parents could be helpful if they avoided moral judgments about the child's natural parents and let it know that "it is a fact that certain people live differently, but that home condition has no real bearing on the child's worth as a person."

Some children whose homes were dangerously chaotic did not go home for the brief visits that were often part of the plan to return children to their own parents after a brief stay. And some children whose parents were disruptive when they visited the foster home saw their parents only at the offices of the social agency that had placed them. The social worker acted as a buffer and helped the child sort out the confusion involved in having two sets of parents. One social worker recognized that a "child cannot be completely loyal to both mothers." Competition and comparisons were inevitable, yet one set was not necessarily good, the other bad. One foster mother told her foster daughter, who was doubtful about attending the funeral of the father she had rarely seen, "He is your father, Anne, and you must love and respect him for that if nothing more."

The Home Wreckers

Children wrenched from their homes—even for their own good— found it hard to see the social workers or "visitors" or "investigators" as angels of mercy. Instead, many saw them, as did Malcolm X, as "home wreckers." His mother and eleven children were on welfare, his father had died, and his mother was sinking deeper and deeper into psychosis. Yet, although he recognized what was happening— "We were having a hard time, and I wasn't helping"—he believed "we could have made it. We could have stayed together. As bad as I was, as much trouble and worry as I caused my mother, I loved her."

The agencies recognized the turmoil and pain of children such as Malcolm, torn out of their own families and placed in others. In Pennsylvania, one agency regularly sent its foster mothers a letter to help them deal with the child's inevitable sense of loss and betrayal. "It is hard to explain to a child why he is taken away from his own home and parents, and made to live with strangers." one letter said. "He is so young and inexperienced to understand the reasons that we grown-ups see, and sometimes he feels so dreadfully hurt he cannot listen to what we say. Perhaps what we say to him about his own parents will make or mar his whole life—make him rebellious, or bitter, or hard, or self-pitying. Perhaps it won't even be what we say. It may be how we act when he mentions his parents, or when they come to see him."

One young woman remembered that her strategy as a child was "If you don't get involved you can't get hurt. And that was my revenge on the world." Children who have been rejected by their own parents reject new parents, as this one did, before they can be rejected again. This gives the children the illusion that they have some control over their lives.

Life for children shifted from foster home to foster home is even more psychologically complicated. Faced with what another foster child characterized as "constant rejection and abuse," she was left feeling "less than human." In 1991 a look at studies of children like these found that, as in the 1930s, they are often unwilling to attach to any adult, anticipating another painful loss. Then, too, when a child is moved from one foster home to another because of his or her behavior, the move reinforces the message that the child and, implicitly, the child's parents, are failures. The foster parent, who may have started out being seen as "good," becomes another rejecting adult, repeating the earlier pattern.

Therapists who work with such foster children have found that misbehaving before anyone can call you "bad" is another way of trying to be in charge, but this, too, backfires. These transplanted children have special problems of identity. Shifted from one home to another, they worry, as a woman who had been moved nine times in nine years as a child put it, "Who am I? Whose kid am I? Is this my mother? Is that my mother? They're not my parents. But she's not either because she never comes." Some are confused about who should be called "Mommy" and struggle with multiple loyalties as well as multiple identities. As early as 1919, W. H. Slingerland of the Department of Child-Helping at the Russell Sage Foundation warned, "Frequent transplanting of trees will stunt their growth. Frequent changes of homes, schools, discipline, companionship and religious influences are bad for sprouts of humanity."

Like all children, children in foster homes wondered where they came from. One five-year-old, happily placed in a foster home, visited her foster mother's sister. Her two children were being "naughty," and the foster child asked her with great concern, "Where did you get your children, Aunt Mary?" She told her, in one of the favorite euphemisms of the time, that the children had come from the hospital. "Why didn't you get them from the Children's Aid Society? They have good children there," the little foster child shot back. Another girl, placed in a family with one child of its own, asked, "Where did Jackie come from?" "God brought Jackie," the foster mother said, bracing for the inevitable follow-up. "Where did I come from, Mother?" "God brought you, too, Nancy." "Is Miss Smith [the social worker] God?" she asked.

The major difference between a real parent and a foster parent is that the foster parent can get rid of the child if the going gets too rough. The agency—in the person of all the Miss Smiths—stands by to take him or her back. This reality, in some foster families, becomes a club with which to keep the child in line. When Betty, a three-year-old, persisted in playing in mud puddles, her foster mother, pushed to the limits of her patience, went to the phone and threatened that she would call Miss A., the "visitor," and have Betty taken away. The child broke into wild sobs and was finally calmed when the mother assured her she was loved and would not really be sent away. But Betty lived with the fear that if she did not do everything she should do, she would be rejected. She assumed the same was true of everyone else. The night after her outburst, her weary foster father didn't respond to her questions as she sat on his lap while he read the newspaper after work. "Daddy," she said severely, "if you won't talk to me, I'll call Miss A. and have her take you away."

"If you weren't good, you couldn't stay" was the message. Yet Jessie Taft, of the Foster Home Department of the Children's Aid Society of Pennsylvania, warned foster mothers that "it is dangerous to want a child to be all good. Life is never one-sided, it is always good and evil, positive and negative. The negative side has to be put somewhere. It can't be destroyed. It is better to admit it frankly in feeling than to have it coming out in unrecognized, uncontrolled behavior. I do not wish to imply that a child is free to do as he likes, but he should be free to feel what he actually does feel." This official acceptance of children's feelings is an indication that Freud's views were filtering into the child-welfare field as well as into educated, middle-class homes. By the 1920s social workers trained in psychoanalytic theory had shifted their emphasis from an almost exclusive focus on the environment to one that concentrated on the individual. It was no longer enough to make sure a child was fed and warm and kept as healthy as possible; emotional health needed attention, too. Feelings should not be ironed out, but aired. Even parents had to acknowledge their negative reactions, Dr. Taft suggested: "You, too, as a parent, sometimes hate your child when he interferes with your life. To admit hate is not to deny the reality of love. The child has all the emotions which we adults experience and he has a right to them. We should learn to respect his feelings and admit our own more freely."

Since the children were assumed to be staying only temporarily, foster parents were warned not to get too attached to them. As early as the White House Conference on Children in 1909, an "uncle and aunt" relationship was suggested as the preferred distance. It was easier to bring up a foster child than one's own child, one expert pointed out, because "we do not care so much, are not so personally involved, and neither is the child." When one five-year-old asked her foster mother, "Mommy, do you love me?" she was told, "Of course I like you." Even at that early age, she said later, "I knew the difference." In a perversion of what was intended to be kindness, reminiscent of earlier prohibitions against "stickiness," foster children were even moved from homes in which they were deemed to be too loved. Three foster children were removed from a home in New York State, because, the report indicated, the foster parents were "indulging the children with too much love."

What happened to foster children later in life? A study done in 1922 looked at all the children placed in foster homes by New York's State Charities Aid Association since 1898. Some were by then forty years old. It found that 77.2 percent were "living in accordance with good community standards, maintaining themselves adequately, and showing ordinary common-sense in affairs of life." Another 11.1 percent, while not measuring up to community standards, were "harmless." Only 11.7 percent violated accepted standards of "order or morality." A preliminary summary of the study concluded, "The children who develop into capable, competent, citizens, come in almost equal proportions from bad, good and mixed family backgrounds." Homer Folks, head of the agency, warned that it had been impossible to find an "ordinary" population for comparison, and these results sounded almost too good to be true, although he understood the attempt to accentuate the positive. Closer to today, David Fanshel of Columbia University's School of Social Work looked at the later lives of foster children who had been placed in a series of foster homes and whose problems included drugs and violence as well as the older problems of broken homes and dire poverty. He, too, found a surprising "success" rate of 60 percent "who adequately address their income and housing needs, build families, and enjoy relative well-being and good health, and obtain satisfaction out of their lives. . . . This speaks to the resiliency of children. Despite the children's hard lives and even after many unsuccessful placements in foster care, if social workers are persistent, the effects of trauma are not irreversible and children can overcome deprivation." Dr. Warner Bridger, a New York psychiatrist, agrees. When he examined the research on the effects of childhood experience on adult life he found "only a weak relationship." He believes that "early emotional deprivation is significant for adult personality only insofar as it reflects problems (hereditary or environmental) that are likely to persist." In a debate in print on this subject, Jules R. Bemporad, another psychiatrist, confirmed that conclusion: "The results depend on the nature of the stress, the child's inherent powers of adaptation, and the reactions of others as well as changes resulting from the event itself. With sufficient compensatory experience, normal development may be restored." Human lives are too complex, he wrote, to be a simple matter of linear causation, the view of early psychoanalysts, who saw in early childhood trauma the seeds of all adult malfunctions.

And yet, what seems like "normal development" when judged by competence in later life may mask emotional pain. Mrs. Donna Strong, a foster child in Detroit who grew up to marry and take in foster children of her own, was in approximately nineteen different placements. She told a congressional subcommittee on children and youth, "It may seem that my achievement up to now in spite of my experience in foster care can be considered to be successful. This is not true. I grew up as a very angry and resentful adolescent. . . . . I was very lonely. I felt like I was different. . . .

"I have learned to forgive and to forget. I have good relationships with my father and stepmother and the foster families I have lived with. My ultimate dream, therefore, is that foster homes will not be necessary."

That dream seemed a long way off during the 1930s. Children came into foster care for all the traditional reasons that had existed before the stock market crash—and for special reasons related to the economic emergency. The 1927 Children's Bureau study of ten child-placing agencies found that their children were chiefly from broken homes. (The single-parent family, far from being a modern problem, existed at close to today's level for much of this country's history—because of accidents, illness, and high mortality rates, rather than divorce. In 1930, there were more than three million female-headed households.)

Harry lived in one of these single-parent homes with his mother and older brother and sister in New York as the Depression started. When he was born, his father walked out. His mother, devastated by the desertion and the strain of trying to keep her family together, became mentally ill and was hospitalized. For a short time, her sister took Harry and his sister (their teenage brother was on his own), but during the Depression they were too poor to keep the children, and the youngsters were separated. Harry went to a chicken farm in upstate New York when he was about four years old; he didn't last long. For one thing, his foster parents were harsh; for another, he commited the cardinal sin—breaking an egg while he was gathering them. (Faced with a broken egg, chickens learn to eat their own product.) Harry was moved again, and when he was seven years old he was placed in the home of the local shoemaker in a small town a few hours from New York.

"Two more marvelous people you couldn't meet," he recalled sixty years later. "They gave me more warmth and love than most kids get. It was a nice feeling." They had three grown children, one of whom still lived at home and helped support the family, and they took in Harry as one of their own.

Twice a year he went into New York to get his spring and fall clothes. All the clothes were laid out on tables and "you picked three pairs of socks and two pairs of pants or whatever you were allowed to choose. It was very exciting."

For spending money, Harry worked helping to deliver milk or newspapers and even cleaning the house of a woman who paid him ten cents an hour. She paid the same rate when he and a friend painted her house.

Harry never saw his mother again, but he did finally see his father ("I didn't even know what he looked like") when he went to California to go to college. His father was living under an assumed name for some unknown reason, and his older brother urged Harry to meet him. He did, and stayed about two weeks, writing home every day to his foster parents. One time his father came upon him working on his letter and said, "Why do you keep writing every day? They're not your parents." Harry picked up the letter and on his way out of the room made his feelings clear: "It doesn't take a piece of paper like a birth certificate to tell you who your parents were. The people who give you love and warmth are your parents." He soon left and never saw his father again.

He has seen his sister four or five times through the years but "she will say 'I'll see you tomorrow' and then disappear for ten years." Nevertheless, he says, "The amazing thing is that through it all I feel as close to my sister as a Siamese twin." She, too, was in foster homes but "got the dirty end of the stick, and was abused."

He now says he thinks of his foster parents every day and feels grateful: "I never felt I belonged anywhere except with the two people who raised me." With his cousins in New York, whom he saw through the years, he did not feel really a part of the family; and he was resented by his foster parents' own adult children, who were jealous of their parents' affection for him. "I was always an outsider" he remembers, "and I've told my own children, 'You don't know how lucky you are to have a family.' "

According to the U.S. Children's Bureau study in 1927, half the parents of children in foster care with ten social agencies retained parental rights and ultimate control of their children, as Harry's father did. The others surrendered these rights to the agency, voluntarily or involuntarily. These were the children who might be available for adoption. (For much of this period, the term "foster child" was used both for an adopted child and for one who was living temporarily in another family's home.) In earlier times, the custodial rights of children were like commercial and property rights, subject to legal questions of transfer and sale and property rights. Even when the child's interests became paramount, conflict existed between parents' rights and children's needs. Courts often decided that the biological ties were clearly paramount, taking children out of foster homes and returning them to their parents, whom they might not have seen for years.

The idea was that foster care was to be time-limited, with the emphasis on repairing whatever tear in the family fabric had made it necessary for the child to be placed. But by the 1970s Albert Solnit, director of Yale University's Child Study Center, was lamenting that foster care, "originally intended to preserve and support (i.e., foster) the continuity of family ties . . . has increasingly become an irreversible step that separates children from their families." More and more, children came from what were effectively "parentless" families, broken by drugs and demoralization, even though both mother and father might be in the home. Children faced with chaos became chaotic and destructive themselves, complicating their placement in suitable substitute homes.

There was never a clear-cut ending of orphanages in favor of foster care. Both systems continued to be used in the 1930s—sometimes an institution would house children temporarily until they were placed, or a child who could not adjust in a home setting would be sent to a "treatment center." Many children experienced both types of care, particularly if what had seemed to be at first a temporary situation became a permanent one, and they had no real home to which to return. In 1933, more children were still being served in institutions than were receiving foster care, although orphanage populations were declining. Despite repeated statements by the experts that family preservation is the aim of child protection, this goal remains maddeningly elusive.

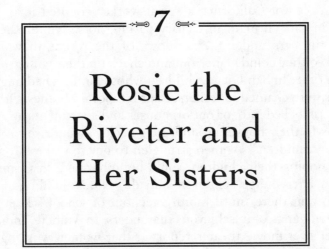

Rosie the Riveter and Her Sisters

Twice we have done something about day care, but never in terms of what the children need. In the depression years centers were maintained with Federal assistance in order to provide employment for adults. In the war years they were maintained in order to get women on the job. It is time now that the whole problem be considered in terms of the welfare of children.

—KATHARINE LENROOT, CHIEF, U.S. CHILDREN'S BUREAU, 1946

IN WHAT IS TODAY a nearly forgotten social experiment, the federal government subsidized nationwide child care for working mothers of young children during World War II. It was the first time in the nation's history that day care for children who were not poor was supported by public funds. The need for womanpower coupled with horror stories of neglected and abused children prodded Washington to recognize that local governments could not possibly handle the stampede of families to war production areas. One and a half million women with children under ten years of age surged into the workforce, enticed by appeals to patriotism and the lure of good wages. Children left alone or with caretakers too old or too young to do a good job were injured or killed in accidents. In the San Fernando Valley of California, a social worker counted forty-five left locked in cars all night in factory parking lots. The mothers positioned the cars under the windows of the rooms in which they worked so they could glance out and check on their youngsters from time to time: In San Diego, children whose families had migrated to get jobs were chained to trailers, their temporary homes. Other children were locked into, or out of, houses and apartments. Many wore the keys to their houses around their necks, giving rise to the term "latchkey children." Women struggled to devise makeshift arrangements, hoping their children would be unharmed. In Connecticut, mothers left younger children outside school buildings and told them to wait there "until Johnny gets out of school." They formed pint-sized gangs of mischievous marauders. In Muncie, Indiana, the manager of a movie theater reported that women working on the night shift parked their children in the theater and "I've had as many as 50 to 60 children left here and sometimes when I leave the closed theater they are still waiting out on the streets for their family." An eight-year-old boy, in the time-honored role of baby-sitter for a younger sibling, picked up his three-year-old sister at nursery school, fed her lunch that he had prepared, then left her alone until he came back home in the afternoon. There were estimates that as many as 2 million youngsters needed some kind of care other than their mothers', with no organized plan to care for many of them. Abuse and neglect were not universal, but they dramatized the problem. The war was a national emergency, these stories cried out; child care was a national responsibility.

Eight months after Pearl Harbor, federal funds were made available to maintain all-day care, before and after school, and vacation care for the children of women working in the war effort. The children ranged in age from two to sixteen. The Lanham Act Centers, as they were called, received 50 percent of their support from the federal government, with states, localities, and parents matching that amount. (Fritz Lanham, the representative from Texas whose bill funded sewers, hospitals, and other necessary services in overcrowded areas, protested that this use distorted his purpose, but he was ignored.) Administration of the centers stayed incongruously within the Federal Works Agency, established originally to deal with structures, not children. During the two and a half years of their existence, the centers received 52 million dollars of federal aid to help run 3,102 centers nationwide. They reflected the social realities of the country. In Southern states whose laws required separation of the races, 259 segregated centers served 12,335 Negro children in 1943.

In the Beginning

The Lanham Act wartime child-care centers rose like a phoenix from the ashes of the WPA day nurseries. Authorized by the Works Progress Administration in 1933, the depth of the Depression, these nurseries were meant to give jobs to out-of-work teachers, nutritionists, nurses, and custodians, among others. The program was a landmark, the first comprehensive support and funding of child care by the federal government, but it was in the old tradition of "for the poor only," serving young children whose families had inadequate incomes or were on welfare. When those make-work day-care centers were discontinued on March 1, 1943, most of them had qualified to become Lanham Act Centers for the children of mothers working in vitally important war-related industries.

The WPA centers in the thirties and early forties had served as many as forty thousand poor preschoolers in a given month in fifteen hundred centers spread across the country. No more than thirty children were in each class, with two teachers or one head teacher and an assistant and often an aide as well. Poor children paid nothing; those whose mothers were working paid a nominal fee.

Since their primary purpose was creating jobs, 90 percent of the center staffs had to be from the relief rolls, which were clogged with unemployed teachers who became the first trained specialists to work in day care. They received an additional three months' instruction to prepare them to deal with children from two and a half to five years of age. "Maybe I'm biased by having lived so long, but the quality of training was outstanding in these centers," Millie Almy, professor emerita at the University of California at Berkeley, says. "They were an opportunity to demonstrate what nursery schools were and what they could be." (The only other demonstration that touched children from all parts of the country had existed sixty years earlier at the 1893 Chicago World's Fair, where a model day nursery handled ten thousand children parked there by sightseeing parents.)

The schools were designed to help parents as well as children. Parents were involved in parent-education classes as students and as teachers and sometimes acted as helpers in the classroom. The parent-education component of the program has recently been criticized by what Dr. Almy calls "reconstructionist historians." "They say it was Big Brother trying to influence parents to adopt middle-class standards," she says, "but I don't think the parents felt that way. All of us were trying to bring those parents into the main stream. I don't think it was intended as a put down, but the revisionists make the point that when you're trying to pull somebody up what you're saying is where you came from was no good." The same concern was expressed about settlement house programs in the 1890s aimed at immigrants and their children. It reflects a vexing American dilemma that runs like a thread through this country's history: How can children of varying backgrounds be helped to succeed in the outside world without destroying or denigrating their traditional customs and attitudes? Are we to be a melting pot or a kind of stew of still-recognizable chunks? Nineteenth-century immigrants were clear that their hope for their children was that they would become "American," and many of them jettisoned their language and customs and embraced the child-care advice given by the experts.

By the 1930s, when immigration had waned and immigrant children were no longer a focus of concern, day care and child-rearing advice were offered to the poor in an effort to lift them out of poverty and provide their children with the opportunity to move into the mainstream. How much it helped and how much it hurt is debatable, but the WPA centers provided the first long-term, large-scale demonstration of how group child care coupled with parent education could improve the lives of children and smoothed the way for what came later.

Threatened with extinction as unemployment decreased and mobilization for war began, the nurseries were supported by groups seeing them primarily as serving the needs of children rather than unemployed teachers. The National Council of Negro Women pointed out that as black women left their homes or jobs as domestics to work in war-related industry and agriculture, their need for child care increased, and the WPA supplied 90 percent of the nurseries for the children of working Negro mothers. At the last minute funds were allotted by President Roosevelt to tide the WPA facilities over, until some other system could be established. In 1943 the earlier centers officially ended. For a short time, the old and new systems coexisted. When WPA funds ended, most of those centers qualified to continue operating under the Lanham Act umbrella.

As noted earlier, the new system differed from the WPA program in one essential respect: These centers were for all children, not just for those whose parents were on welfare. Some Lanham Act Centers kept the educational component of the earlier WPA nursery schools. Others were criticized as providing just custodial care, rather than preparation for kindergarten and grade school. Parental involvement decreased, since these mothers were, by definition, employed and had little free time.

Like all large-scale programs, both the WPA and Lanham Act Centers varied in quality and in the content of their daily routine. Some had only piles of broken toys for the children to play with; others had the blocks, paints, and clay designed to foster learning. But even this was no guarantee that they would be used. At one Lanham Act Center a supervisor opened a closet and found blocks piled on the shelves, untouched. "They just didn't know what to do with kids and blocks," she reported. As in most child-care arrangements, it was the people, not the setting or the theory, that determined the quality of the program.

Consider the Women

Great uneasiness complicated the obvious need for child care. Since the nineteenth century, Americans have approved women working outside the home, but they were mostly single, usually young, marking time until marriage, or older women whose children were grown. With the notable exception of black women, most mothers did not work outside the home. The experts and common sense agreed that their job was to care for their children. In her survey of research on child care and working mothers, Dr. Louise B. Silverstein of New York University argues that "both governmental policy and psychological research reflect the popular culture's idealized myth of motherhood." A man had a duty to support his wife and children, and a mother's employment was an indication of abject poverty or family failure. Women's jobs and women's wages reflected the expectation that a man supported a family with what he earned, but a woman did not. Neither the suffrage movement nor agitation for women's rights changed this attitude, and in 1940, the percentage of women working was still about the same as it had been in 1920—a little more than 20 percent. It took the needs of a wartime economy to fuel a revolution. But even during the war, although the National War Labor Board supported the position that women should be paid the same money for the same job, in practice they earned only 65 percent of men's wages in factories.

Before almost 2 million mothers entered the labor market, those bent under the double burden of work and child care had been a small minority, hidden in poverty statistics. With mothers flooding into factories, a spotlight was focused for the first time on the exhausted lives of ordinary women. *The New York Times* reported in 1944, "Of late many voices have been raised in defense of the wage-earning mother, carrying a double load of job and home-making." Her backbreaking schedule also became the object of compassionate concern in the popular women's magazines.

Children, too, carried a double load, often forced to be their own parents while their mother and father worked or went into battle. A contemporary observer of the Alabama war industry boom towns warned, "It is an evil situation today and . . . it can and will make a hell of this country, unless we take heroic measures to meet it."

The Lanham Act Centers were as close as the country got to heroic measures. By July 1945, the peak of the war effort, approximately 1.6 million children were in federally funded nursery schools and day-care centers, according to the U.S. Children's Bureau. Others have calculated that a total of about six hundred thousand different children received care through Lanham Act funds during the two and a half years of its existence. The real figure is hard to come by. Depending on when the count was taken, figures could vary widely. Some children could be counted several times, others not at all. The Children's Bureau had a stake in inflating the figures to make the program seem significant; critics had an equal interest in making it seem inadequate. One estimate is that only 10 percent of the children needing care were in the centers. Whatever the specific numbers, more young children were cared for away from their mothers than ever before.

The Slow Start

Ambivalence haunted the experiment. On the one hand were those who saw working mothers as exhausted patriotic heroines on whom the war effort depended; on the other were traditionalists who saw them as a "national disgrace." Women were told their labor was vital; they were also told their place was at home with their children. Paul McNutt, chairman of the War Manpower Commission, tried to clarify the government's stand in August 1942 when he declared, "The first responsibility of women with young children, in war as in peace, is to give suitable care in their own homes to their children." An educator who supervised Lanham Act Centers in upstate New York remembers that "people yelled about the idea of day care. There was antagonism or hostility with a religious undertone. It wasn't the way God intended it. Mothers should take care of their children. The idea of day care was appalling to a lot of people." The implicit assumption was that young children did best when they were cared for by their mothers, and underlying that assumption was the premise that all mothers were, by definition, the perfect caretakers of their children. The National Catholic Welfare Council supported the centers, albeit reluctantly, "because of unavoidable conditions placing mothers in industry," but other Catholic groups continued to oppose them.

An unexpected champion of working mothers was Chicago's Institute for Psychoanalysis. "Employment," said their statement on women in wartime, "saves the woman from a feeling of helplessness; work makes her feel free and independent. If the children are satisfactorily cared for [the statement did not specify the ages], work is a good solution since it decreases the wife's resentment at being left alone in a drab, everyday life, and it protects her children from the resentment she might feel toward them if she were tied down, kept from her own need to go out in the world. Increased income gives her good justification for leaving her children, and if she is not too tired at the end of the day, she makes compensation to them in what time she has." Quality time, not quantity, was what counted.

With so many conflicting attitudes to be reconciled, the centers got off to a slow start. They were a novel idea, not well publicized at first. Reluctance to use them even when they were known reflected the traditional American view that families took care of their own without outside help, and that public facilities were for the poor or those whose kinship ties had broken down. Sometimes money was allotted but not used because not as many children as expected enrolled, and some of the first centers closed quickly because too few children showed up at their doors.

Grandmothers and other relatives took care of children under fourteen for a third to a half of all working mothers in nine war production areas studied in 1944–45. Very few of them used nursery schools. The highest usage—11 percent—occurred in San Francisco, an area with a long tradition of early childhood education. Nation-wide, a Gallup poll in 1943 found that only 29 percent of the women questioned would take war jobs if their children could be cared for without cost in a day nursery; 46 percent said they preferred relatives and friends. They, like many Americans, associated day care with welfare and cruelty. One war worker said she was criticized for leaving her children in a center because "it sounds like the Spartans binding their children over to the state."

Government infighting reflected the dissension in society, with one agency or another grasping for control of whatever child-care program was established. Social welfare agencies warned against leaving the care of infants to others but recognized that whatever care was set up should be considered in the broad context of services to children. War agencies concentrated on the temporary nature of the need and consistently emphasized that the government was not then, and should never be, in the business of intruding into the lives of families with young children.

Difficulties in finding space in overcrowded war production areas and delays in recruiting trained personnel also impeded the centers. In addition, communities hesitated to apply for funds because, as a California report put it, "Many regarded any encouragement to mothers to leave the home for a job as socially undesirable."

The Lanham Act's creaking start prompted the National Council of Jewish Women to warn that "if a community does not provide proper care for its children, it will shortly be faced with even greater problems of disease, illiteracy, and delinquency. By providing child-care facilities, we are not granting special privileges to mothers who suddenly decide they want to work. We are protecting our investment in post-war America by caring for today's children."

Opposition to the centers faded as they became better established and better known. Within a few months, they demonstrated that preschool children could be happy in group care, and mothers who had been struggling with alternative arrangements enrolled their youngsters. Soon, many of the centers had waiting lists. Some that had closed after failing to attract patrons reopened. Studies of 500 California children in two nursery schools between 1943 and 1946 confirmed this success. When they were asked how they felt about their children's experiences, the 173 mothers questioned gave generally favorable opinions in 81 percent of the cases. The researcher concluded: "The child care program for under-fives has reduced tensions, lessened friction in the home and insecurity in non-home situations, and so benefitted the children and strengthened family living." In Detroit a 1945 survey showed that 84 percent of the parents of children in the centers thought they benefited physically, and 94 percent noticed they got along better with other children. Fears that the Lanham Act Centers would hurt children and destroy family life subsided as the realities of the experience became evident.

Mothers endorsed the professional findings. Wilma Thatcher, a welder whose husband was serving overseas, called the centers "the best thing that could happen for working mothers." In Seattle, Edith Brown, a chauffeur at the Navy Yard, said the View Ridge Play Center her children attended was "a marvelous place," and added that "it would be impossible for me to teach them all the things they're learning." Frankie Cooper, a crane operator in a foundry, told an interviewer years later that at first she felt guilty about leaving her two-and-a-half-year-old daughter. But she soon came to see "that sometimes it's good for the child. . . . So when I look back on it now, I think that it was a plus for me, to have her learn about different people and be with them, because she was an only child." Other mothers noticed that their children learned songs, spoke more clearly, and were more cooperative.

Asked how they themselves benefited from having their children in nursery school, the mothers in the California survey most often cited increased patience with their children. They said they also learned to treat their youngsters as individuals and to encourage the sometimes maddening curiosity of their preschoolers. In short, they felt they became better mothers.

The Daily Routine

Children spent twelve hours a day, six days a week at the centers. Mothers or fathers dropped youngsters aged two to five off at about 6:00 or 6:30 A.M. on their way to work and picked them up at 6:00 or 7:00 P.M. after work. The centers were open six days a week, over the summer, and during holidays except for Christmas, and they also adapted their hours to local needs. When it was rush season at the canneries, they stayed open later. Some were regularly open around the clock to accommodate workers at airfields, factories, sugar refineries, and oil depots that had three shifts. Others were open on farming schedules for the children of migrant workers.

In the best of them the children's routine was that of any good nursery school and included indoor and outdoor play, a chance to use paints and clay and musical instruments, and regular naps. With one teacher for every ten children, they met standard recommendations. Since one of the aims of the program was to improve nutrition, the children were fed hot lunches and, if necessary, dinners, and dosed every day with cod-liver oil and orange juice, the precursors of vitamin tablets. The food was included in the fees parents paid.

Centers around the country at first charged fixed amounts, which varied with the locality. In Detroit in 1943 this was six dollars a week per child. In Jacksonville, Florida, it was two dollars a day for whites, one dollar and twenty-five cents a day for Negroes. But with clerical workers earning only twenty-eight dollars a week and workers in war plants forty-seven dollars, it soon became clear that many families could not afford to pay this much. Some communities were hard-pressed to provide the 50 percent matching funds required to get federal money, and when fees were recalculated according to a sliding scale, the situation got worse, not better. Reducing parents' contributions put a greater burden on localities. Some of them decided they could not afford the centers at all. Eventually, in an attempt to keep fees as low as possible and make child care more affordable, the federal government set a uniform fee in 1943 of fifty cents a day; later it was raised to seventy-five cents a day.

By 1944 the program's administrators had answered some criticisms that their services were too narrowly focused by adding information centers for parents, health care (including examination by a physician) for children, and transportation in a few places where distances were great.

A study of five hundred children in two Lanham Act California nursery schools provides a profile of the population using these centers. In 1945, at the height of the war effort, almost half the fathers were in the armed services. About a third were in industry—the draft usually exempted fathers who were in war work. Some of the women were war widows. Most of the children were two years old, reinforcing the observation of others that the greatest need was for the youngest children. About half the children showed no noticeable emotional effects because of the war. But among those who did react, there was a sharp drop in worry and fear about the father when the war had been over for almost a year and many of the servicemen were home.

In some families, the servicemen did not return. In Grand Rapids, Michigan, a survey as the war was ending showed that between 75 and 85 percent of the children receiving care were from homes in which the mother worked because the father had been killed or disabled in the fighting. In Cleveland, Ohio, over 66 percent of women using the centers were the sole wage earners in their families.

Necessity Versus the Experts

Group care for nursery-school-age children might be acceptable, but the experts drew the line at such care for the very young, despite the compelling necessity for women with infants to work—particularly after fathers were eligible to be drafted after October 1943. Millie Almy, who supervised WPA and Lanham Act Centers in California, recalls that "psychoanalysis said, 'No, No,' so public support for infant care was minimal." Lanham Act funds could be used for group care of those under two, but not for care in another home, and local officials were reluctant to place infants in groups. Science, they said, bore them out. Anna Freud summarized the latest thinking with "There is no justification to extend what we recognize as the benefits of the nursery school for the older child to the care of infants, especially not for those between birth and year 2."

But by 1944, Florence Kerr, director of war public services of the Federal Works Agency, was saying, "Although the employment of women with children under 2 years of age has been frowned upon, we know that, realistically, many women with young children have been forced to take war jobs. If a community needs group care for children under 2 years to answer a pressing war need, we shall be glad to provide funds for it." The financial reality was that servicemen's wives received thirty to forty cents a day as an allowance for the support of each child—not even enough to feed them. Women had to work.

As a result some infants were placed in nurseries. The Child Welfare League, in 1945, called this a blunder, pointing out that infants under two needed home care and should not be put in groups. The Children's Bureau, too, warned that such communal arrangements risked the dangers of high infant mortality faced by orphanages and other institutions.

In what Karen Anderson, author of *Wartime Women: Sex Roles, Family Relations and the Status of Women During World War II*, called "a classic example of predetermined conclusions," an FWA (Federal Works Administration) study found that children under two years of age in an experimental infant-care center in San Diego showed (as predicted) "troubling signs of developmental difficulty" although the infants had been in the center for only a short time and could hardly have been seriously affected. The study abruptly ended any attempt in California to fund group care and validated what the Child Welfare League of America and the Children's Bureau had been saying all along: Mothers with young children should stay home or the children would suffer dreadful damage. If mothers did not stay home, the next best thing would be to develop foster homes to provide day care.

A few private agencies did establish what they called "foster family day care"—what we now call family day care. Infants were placed in homes where they could be cared for during the day, then returned to their mothers at night. Foster day care could also be used to handle the temporary emergency of a sick child, or a child who did not do well in group care. Then, too, there was the situation of a large family that might otherwise have to juggle multiple child-care arrangements, and the problem of Texas-sized distances that made getting to a day nursery unreasonable. Wartime working conditions, too, which put women on rotating shifts at different times of the day, made some sort of flexible, individualized day care imperative, as some centers even refused to take children whose mothers worked irregular hours.

Finding foster families was never easy, and wartime conditions made the situation even more difficult, since women who might take in children were working in war factories themselves. In June 1943, only nine areas of the country had programs of this type. The care was expensive and almost entirely in the hands of private agencies or private entrepreneurs.

One successful agency was the Chicago Orphan Asylum, whose program began in 1943 and reflects the general experience of mothers working in war industries. Most of the children were under two, and almost half the women had husbands who were in the armed forces. The agency soon discovered that this kind of day care filled many needs that had little to do with the war. Mothers were working (at war jobs) to help pay the bills, or they were the sole support of their children. Some needed temporary care in a crisis. Some "confessed openly that they preferred outside to domestic chores," a social worker reported. Since it had not developed the program with rigid rules, the agency was able to accommodate this wide variety of needs. Despite this acceptance of the realities of women's lives, wartime or not, the three-year experiment in day care in foster homes ended with the war's end in 1945.

Forgotten Forerunners

What seemed like a shocking departure in the 1940s—taking very young children from their mothers—was really in a long American tradition. Even children under two years of age had been in group care more than a century before the Lanham Act Centers. They went to infant schools that flourished in the 1820s and 1830s and to dame schools in Colonial New England where women taught small groups of small children their ABCs or just kept an eye on them.

No one expressed concern about the effect on their psyches of this early separation until the mid-nineteenth century, when mothers were enshrined as vital and irreplaceable, twenty-four hours a day, in the lives of their young offspring. It was then that motherhood became a full-time profession rather than a role, as Mary Frances Berry pointed out in her book *The Politics of Parenthood*.

Like many other innovations in child care, infant schools originated in Great Britain. In 1815 Robert Owen, a utopian reformer and a partner in several cotton mills, started a school for one hundred children, eighteen months to six years of age, whose mothers worked in the mill in New Lanark, Scotland. By today's standards the school seems both cruel and impossible, since all these children were cared for by one male teacher and a teenage female assistant. Owen's aim was to keep the children healthy and happy until they were old enough to go to work in the mills themselves. At New Harmony, Indiana, his short-lived communal settlement in this country, the first American school based on his model was set up in 1825. His schools are the direct ancestors of the Lanham Act Centers; they were designed to make it possible for women to work in factories, and they evolved from simple caretaking institutions to those that took advantage of the very young child's interest in learning. Like all infant education, Owen's schools owed a debt to Comenius, whose seventeenth-century idea of teaching all children all things so profoundly influenced Moravian boarding and day schools.

The infant-school idea took hold and flourished in this country, first sponsored by churches and other charitable organizations, then absorbed in some places into the public school system. New York had fifty-eight when they were turned over to the public schools in 1853. The New York school on Canal Street served anywhere from fifty to one hundred children from eighteen months to six years of age on any given day, with a staff of two teachers, a principal, and an assistant. Some children came for just the regular school day; others brought their dinners with them and stayed till dark. The schools were seen as a way to counteract some of the deadening effects of poverty and give poor children a "head start" before they entered primary school. New York's Public School Society put it this way: "The infant mind is capable of receiving instruction at the early age of two or three years [and] providing a place in which the younger children of the poor may pass the day comfortably, whilst their parents are engaged in their usual avocations, instead of wandering the streets, exposed to the contamination of vice, is an object worthy the regard of the benevolent."

Infant schools were based on the premise that young children are infinitely malleable rather than fixed at birth in a mold determined by their genetic heritage or programmed to develop according to an inborn timetable. In 1828 Bronson Alcott identified infancy as a time of "great and rapid change" and one of his contemporaries pointed out that "he [the child] can and does learn a great deal more before that age [six] than all he ever learns or can learn in all his after life." Poor children could make up for their disadvantages with early learning that would set them on the path to success in school and in life.

Like other child-care ideas, such as the mid-nineteenth-century kindergarten, these schools were too good to be left to the poor; the standard trickle-up effect soon made them available to all children in privately sponsored facilities. In 1829 the *Ladies' Magazine* commented that the topic of infant schools was becoming more and more popular, and, "We have been told that it is now in contemplation, to open a school for the infants of others beside the poor. If such course be not soon adopted, at the age for entering primary schools those *poor* children will assuredly be the *richest* of scholars. And why should a plan which promises so many advantages, independent of merely relieving the mother from her charge, be confined to the children of the indigent?"

The infant schools, which flourished only for about twenty years starting in the 1820s, owed their quick popularity in part to the fact that children as young as three and four were already in school in the late eighteenth and early nineteenth centuries. Parents did not balk at starting the process even earlier.

The decline of the infant schools is harder to explain than their sudden popularity. The Industrial Revolution, by taking women out of the home to work in factories, created the need for them. Before that time, both work and child rearing took place in the home. But, although the need persisted, thinking changed, and parents were told to return early schooling to the mother's knee. It is always dangerous to credit professional advice with changes in the real world, but Carl F. Kaestle and Maris A. Vinovkis, by examining school records in Massachusetts, found that the percentage of very young children in school declined just as popular and expert opinion were turning against the idea of the intellectual force-feeding of very young children. It seems likely that infant schools died partly in response to the view championed by the Swiss educator Pestalozzi, and embraced by popular advice-givers, that children should be allowed to develop at their own rate. One of them acknowledged that "it is obvious how difficult a task it must be, to persuade parents to let their sprightly little darling alone, till the rain and the sunshine have opened the bud and prepared the way for mental culture." But, he continued, "the fact that a child *can* learn to read when it is three or four doesn't mean it is a good idea to teach him."

The temptation to instruct very young children as soon as they are clearly able to learn has been embraced, then backed away from in a hesitant dance based on the steps of one philosophy or another. In Colonial times, when children were seen as miniature adults, three-year-olds were regularly taught to read, and some of them learned Latin as well as English. By the mid-nineteenth century parents were cautioned about turning their children into prodigies.

Intellectual force-feeding was discouraged then because it was feared that early learning could lead to insanity. Dr. Amariah Brigham cautioned in 1832, "I am forced to believe that the danger is indeed great, and that very often in an attempt to call forth and cultivate the intellectual faculties of children before they are six or seven years of age, serious and lasting injury has been done both to the body and the mind. . . . Early mental excitement will serve only to bring forth beautiful, but premature flowers, which are destined soon to wither away, without producing fruit."

As the infant schools faded, day-care centers that were custodial rather than dangerously intellectual were established for the children of working mothers. In 1838 a day nursery for the children of seamen's wives and widows opened in Boston. In 1854 another was set up at the Nursery and Child's Hospital in New York for children whose mothers had been patients there. Nurses took care of the children when the mothers went back to work. Four years later two women from Troy, New York, who had seen this system went home and established their own version, incorporating a clinic to ensure the health of their young charges. But major impetus for the day-care movement came with the Civil War. As women were needed "to manufacture soldiers' clothing and to clean in hospitals," a day-care nursery was organized in Philadelphia in 1863. By the end of the century, it was estimated that 175 child-care centers, most of them sponsored by settlement houses, were in existence.

Nursery schools descended from the infant schools that had moved from serving only poor children to serving the middle class as well; day care remained the province of the poor, focusing more on custody, cleanliness, and nourishment than on education. A two-tier system had developed by the time the Lanham Act Centers were started, with private nursery schools for the affluent and near-affluent and day care funded by social agencies for poverty-stricken working mothers. Ordinarily, the mothers of children who went to nursery school were at home; the mothers of day-care children were at work. Day care was custodial, nursery school educational. But early nursery schools shared some of the characteristics of later day care; in 1928 a survey showed that 60 percent had school days lasting from 8:30 to 4:30.

Nineteenth-century objections to early childhood education were influential and cast a long shadow. As wartime day-care centers more than a century later moved from the custodial care with which they began to formalized nursery-school training, grave concern was expressed that the experience would harm children. Not only were they to be separated from their mothers, they were to be forced to learn things they might not have learned if they had stayed safely at home. As one observer put it, child care and early childhood education were "unceremoniously united in many communities during the war years." This marriage signaled a social change, giving thousands of children too young for kindergarten group experiences aimed at furthering their physical and intellectual development. "The rumblings against day care went underground during the war," a consultant to the centers recalled in an interview. "There was an upsurge of feeling that it was a good thing to take up the slack. The whole community learned about child care."

Schools as Baby-sitters

The Lanham Act Centers, many of them based in schools, extended the venerable tradition of using schools as caretakers for toddlers and their older brothers and sisters. Since there were no lower age limits for early public schools (a hybrid often supported by public funds plus parents' contributions, as the Lanham Act Centers were), very young children were packed off to the schoolhouse despite protests by local officials that "the practice of sending children, two or three years old, to school, to 'get them out of the way,' cannot be too much deprecated. Every teacher, it should be remembered, is employed to *give instruction*, not to *act the part of a nurse*." Such children were called derisively "trundle-bed trash" throughout the nineteenth century. Very young children were kept in school all day along with their older brothers and sisters, and an official of the Lynn, Massachusetts, system complained that parents felt they had paid to have their children taken care of, and "are annoyed by their presence at home."

When a participant proposed to the New York State Constitutional Convention in 1867 that the law be changed to prohibit children under seven from attending the public schools, a colleague protested that this was part of a movement that would "transcend the decision of parents as to the capacities and needs of their own offspring." Children forced to stay home from school would linger at the corner grocery stores, wander along rural roads, get lost, and be abused by drunken parents. "When [the proposer] sinks at last upon his pillow, the wishes of a host of poor but honest parents will go forth that imps may play all night at mumblety-peg with tiny pitchforks upon his philanthropic breast."

Eventually, and over the objections of parents that continued for fifty years, compulsory education laws were enacted that also included noneducation rules, setting the age at which children might start school at five or six years, and the age at which they might leave at twelve. Parents continued to object that their individual rights and their right to determine what happened to their children were being usurped by the state. But the regulations held, and by 1918 even Mississippi, the last holdout, had adopted them. In 1880 schools in this country stayed in session, on average, for 130 days, but many children attended only sporadically—the average was 86 days. The length of the school year varied widely: In predominantly rural Kentucky, only eight weeks a year were required. Schools adapted to the needs of the communities in which they existed, with some even holding night sessions in the elementary grades for children who worked on farms or in factories and couldn't attend during the day. By the 1940s the school year had stretched to 175 days, and children attended for an average of 152 of them, making schools the primary baby-sitters of the nation's children.

In a persistent pattern, responsibility for children has shifted from home and family to society and government. In the nation's early years children were taught and taken care of at home. Gradually they were sent to school, but parents decided at what age and how long they would stay. Then local and state regulations stripped parents of this choice and put children more and more in the care of teachers. This represented, as Kaestle and Vinovkis put it, "a widespread and seemingly irreversible increase in the extent of state intervention in the rearing of children."

The same sort of thing happened later with child care as a separate entity, rather than as part of the school system. Responsibility for young children shifted from home to child-care centers and nursery schools only in the pressure cooker of the war years. It is not that parents were completely cut out of the process of growing up, but, as in so many other areas, society moved in to play a larger part.

Older Children

If neglect was the propelling force behind providing care for young children during the war, delinquency focused attention on the older ones. Society had a responsibility to protect its citizens from acts that would be considered criminal if they were committed by an adult. Lanham Act funds supported not only child-care centers but before- and after-school and vacation care for children from six to sixteen years of age as a way of keeping youngsters busy and happy, and the streets safe to walk on. In New York City alone, in the first six months of 1942, delinquency rose by 14 percent over what it had been a year earlier. More than five hundred "conflict gangs" were said to exist, using everything from broken bottles to guns as weapons. Even in places where there was not a sharp rise, the kinds of offenses changed. Where there were military camps, what the Child Welfare League of America euphemistically called "teenage problems" rose among girls more than among boys. Sex delinquency, incorrigibility, drinking, and rates of venereal disease shot up. Girls and boys ran away, forming the kinds of gangs the country had seen during the Depression when they roamed from city to city looking for jobs that just weren't there. Now they ran to war production areas where rules against child labor had been relaxed and they could earn more than ever before.

Newspaper editorials in 1943 and 1944 devoted 11 percent of their comment to juvenile delinquency—a term that had just come into common use in 1942. Another word generated by the relative freedom from parental supervision of the war years was "teenager." These youngsters, with their newfound money, developed a separate, antiadult subculture with its own music, dress, and language.

On the other hand, some kinds of delinquency, particularly among older teenagers, decreased as they entered the armed forces or found good jobs. When they joined the military, young men focused attention on the reverse of the problem of maternal neglect— maternal smothering. Three million men were rejected because they had emotional problems—they were too fearful, or unable to live in close quarters, for example—that made them unfit to fight. Overprotective mothers, said many experts, including Dr. Edward A. Strecker, a psychiatric consultant to the army and navy, were to blame. Mothers who were afraid of being seen as rejecting if they sent their children to child-care centers or let the older ones take care of themselves were now accused of hurting their children by holding them too close.

Like the centers, Lanham Act after-school programs were not the first of their kind, but they were the most widespread and got the most national attention. Schools had been providing after-school recreation programs without fanfare as a normal part of their schedules. During the Depression, WPA building efforts enshrined these services architecturally by funding schools with gymnasiums, swimming pools, and playgrounds. The Lanham Act extended-care centers took advantage of these facilities. Most were open a few hours before school (some provided breakfast), at lunch for those who did not eat at school, and after school until 6:00 or 6:30, when parents came home. In communities so crowded that schools were on double sessions, the after-school centers stayed open all day so that children who attended only in the morning or the afternoon would have a place to go.

Other facilities also existed to pick up the after-school slack. Jewish children went to Hebrew School, Greeks studied their culture and so did the Chinese in four- or five-day after-school programs. The public library provided safe, supervised space, and town playgrounds were used for the same reason. Baltimore officials found children dropped off in the morning "stowing away" on the swings and slides waiting for a parent to pick them up after work.

Working mothers were less convinced of the need for after-school Lanham Act services than they were of the need for day care. For one thing, they felt school-age children could look after themselves for a few hours every day. For another, they balked at paying a fee—since schooling was free they felt after-school care should be, too. In Seattle, free after-school centers, provided by social agencies and churches, flourished while Lanham Act Centers were not full.

In California, whose programs reflected the best around the country, the extended-day-care centers were open before and after school, on Saturdays and holidays, and all summer long. They opened between 6:30 and 8:30 A.M. on both school and nonschool days. When there was no school, the children had outdoor play, handicrafts, music and drama clubs, and library reading. In the afternoons, with parental permission, they could be released to go to Cub Scouts or Boy Scouts or similar organizational meetings. From 4:30 to 6:00 on all days they had quiet games, indoor play, and "selected radio programs"—in the era before television. The children were often divided into age groups, with older children helping out with the younger ones as they would have done had they been at home. Good nutrition was an important part of the program, and the youngsters were given hot lunches and morning and afternoon snacks. If necessary, they could receive breakfast and dinner, too, at an extra charge of ten or fifteen cents. Fees for attendance varied and were usually a little lower than for all-day nursery-school care.

Innovative Solutions for Eight-Hour Orphans

Day-care centers were not the whole answer. They were too few, sometimes too far away, sometimes just unacceptable to parents who continued to be ambivalent about having their children in a formal group setting. Young children were still left with grandmothers or neighbors, but even this traditional method felt the strain of the war. People moved to where the war jobs were and left behind families and friends who might have helped out. California alone was inundated with half a million workers from other states within a few months. In Texarkana (twin cities in Texas and Arkansas), shanty towns and tent cities sprouted along highways as the population skyrocketed from thirty thousand to fifty thousand.

Even if parents now had extra money to pay for child care, women who could do this job were in short supply. They, too, could make more money working in war factories, in canneries, or on farms. In 1942 in Jackson, Mississippi, a survey showed that half the children of women working in war factories were cared for by black domestic servants. But many of these black women were later able to get better-paying jobs than had ever been available to them in industry and agriculture, and the improved job market had a domino effect: Their traditional pattern of child care for their own children was disrupted as the caretakers—grandmothers and other relatives—got jobs, too. Requests for foster care and institutional placement increased, as parents tried desperately to find havens for their children. Inevitably, some were left to fend for themselves. A federal study of working mothers in ten defense industry areas in 1944–45 concluded that "the fact stands out . . . from examination of the reports on the care of young children of wartime-employed mothers, that in a substantial proportion of the households no real provision was made for their care while the woman worker was absent." The answer to the question "Who's minding the kids?" seems to have been "No one in particular."

Desperate mothers tried another strategy that had served an earlier generation—they chose the night shift so they could be home with their children during the day. Unions saved the more desirable day shifts for men, so women requesting night work were likely to get it. But for some this proved too taxing. They could not work all night on an assembly line, then shop and cook and clean and care for their children the next day, so they quit. (Paul McNutt, head of the War Manpower Commission, estimated that for every ten women coming into the labor force, eight left it.) In some families with both husband and wife working they arranged for different shifts, so one of them could be home with the children. But this, too, was not a perfect solution. Some children were left alone for the forty-five minutes or more when the shifts changed. Others were cared for by a "daily minder" who stayed with them until a parent came home.

The war emergency also forced larger-scale innovations. In Los Angeles in 1943, the Gale Manor Apartments, occupied only by working parents and their children, developed a comprehensive day-care center on the first floor. The fifty-two families had sixty children needing care. Every morning at 6:30 parents dropped their children off at the center as they left for work, usually in a war factory. The six- and seven-year-olds were later convoyed across the street to school and escorted back for lunch and after-school activities. The eighteen-month-olds to five-year-olds participated in the usual nursery-school activities. After lunch the toddlers took off their shoes and socks (to keep from dirtying the apartments) and were tucked into their own beds for naps, with the woman who ran the center and her helper acting as watchful angels.

By six o'clock parents usually claimed their children. The cost was fifteen dollars per child per month. Sick children were accepted but kept isolated from the other children, and arrangements could even be made if a mother had to work overtime or the night shift. For an extra twenty-five cents youngsters were fed supper, read a story, and again tucked into their own beds, which were patrolled until at least one parent returned home.

One of the problems in encouraging mothers to work during the war was that they had a higher absentee rate than men, staying home twice as often, since they had primary responsibility for the children. In California's San Fernando Valley the Office of Civilian Defense noticed that absenteeism in defense factories was highest on Saturdays, when children were home from school. They started a playground project to keep these children safe and happy so their mothers could still go to work. But they did it against vocal opposition, reflecting the ambivalence of a society that actively recruited mothers as workers but felt, deep down, that they should stay home. One man who opposed the San Diego project said petulantly that if women were really patriotic they would leave the factories and stay with their children. Women were becoming too emancipated anyway, he said, and providing child care would only make things worse.

Women's absenteeism reflected their triple roles as workers, mothers, and wives. They were the ones who stayed home with a young child whose baby-sitting arrangements fell through, or when a school-age child was on vacation or sick; they still had to cook the meals, do the shopping, and stay attractive to the men who were building the bombers or fighting for freedom. A few vital wartime industries addressed these needs as a way to keep production at high speed.

In Portland, Oregon, the Kaiser shipyard's nursery school was the largest in the country, serving fifteen hundred children aged from eighteen months to six years in three shifts. Federal funds paid most of the costs, supplemented by a fee of seventy-five cents a family a day. The nursery school stayed open twelve months a year, twenty-four hours a day, and its kitchen fed not only the children but their parents as well, by providing hot, inexpensive, take-home meals that could be ordered in the morning and picked up at night. The *Saturday Evening Post* commented in surprise on this new awareness of the importance of child care: "Industry may, in fact, find that minding babies is more essential to the production of dive bombers than the inauguration of a speed-up system or any other of the routine things that come under the heading of labor relations."

In addition, since, as a popular magazine put it, "a girl's a girl," whose basic interest is in frills and fashion, another way to improve labor relations and cut down on absenteeism was to bring services that might take a woman away from her lathe right into the war plant. In the Midwest, an electrical company set up a three-person beauty parlor where the paint shop had been, and a cosmetic counter in the toolroom. The Otis Elevator Company's aeronautical division turned Friday lunch hours into shopping time, with a local department store bringing twenty clerks, a pharmacist, and a kaleidoscopic array of merchandise into the factory. Women could choose clothing, foodstuffs, cosmetics, household utensils, and even hats and have them delivered to their homes the next day. Other stores stayed open late. No more wasted days away from work for bargain hunting.

Some women spoke up to support working women. A study of the needs of women war workers by two female Syracuse University students suggested such revolutionary (and "communistic") services as more nursery schools, centralized food preparation and laundries, a five-day workweek, and elimination of overtime to ease their load. (In 1910, Charlotte Perkins Gilman had suggested central kitchens, day care, and professional house cleaners to allow women to work. Her ideas never left the printed page.) After this burst of utopian thinking, the researchers acknowledged that "undesirable standardization" of home life might be the result and recognized that if women had free time they might "waste it."

Catherine Mackenzie, an outraged *New York Times* columnist, reacted with: "The notion that women will get into mischief if they get a minute to relax and take a deep breath is very old indeed. People once said that if women didn't spend the whole day basting and turning things over an open fire they'd be up to no good; it was a strong argument against the introduction of the cooking stove. A threat to the home, that's what it is."

Ambivalence continued to haunt women who had not yet entered the workforce but were faced with that possibility and the threats it might pose to their primary purpose—wifehood and motherhood. In 1944 sociologist Mirra Komarovsky called standards for women "a veritable crazy quilt of contradiction." Half of the young college women questioned in her survey of their expectations for the future said they expected to stop work permanently when they married, and only 10 percent said they hoped to combine marriage and a career. (The war experience did not seem to have altered basic assumptions about women's roles.) Dr. Komarovsky campaigned for greater freedom: "The girl who wishes to marry and have five children should be permitted to do so, and likewise it should be made possible for those who wish to combine marriage and careers to achieve this. At present, the latter path is fraught with difficulties and cruel dilemmas, but it needn't be." On the same page in *The New York Times* in which Komarovsky's survey was reported, Senator Taft of Ohio was quoted as supporting reduced funds for Lanham Act Centers lest they be carried over, surreptitiously, for use after the war and encourage women to leave home.

Despite the acknowledged benefits of day care for the children of working mothers and the hopes of those who had demonstrated their muscle and skills in what were traditionally men's occupations, the country was not yet ready for large numbers of women, particularly mothers, to remain in the labor force. A *Fortune* magazine poll shortly after the war showed that most Americans did not approve of a woman working if her husband could support her and felt that her job was staying home and caring for her children. A New York newspaper labeled the idea of day care "a communist plot." The "Iron Curtain" had succeeded the uneasy wartime alliance, and the evil Soviet Union was a pioneer in providing public nursery schools for working women. There was also economic reality. The boys were coming home and needed whatever jobs would be left when the wartime boom collapsed. In 1945, the year the war ended, 11,650,000 women from twenty to forty-four years of age (the childbearing years) were working; by 1950, there were 10,187,000.

The chairman of the Womanpower Committee of the War Manpower Commission in the Cleveland area foresaw that, after the war, married women with young children would be told to stay home. She saw two reasons for this: "The consciousness of the value of children quickened through war and the belief that the child is best taken care of in the home by his mother" were strengthened. In addition there was the "alarm, already expressed, at the new independence that has come to married women from their experience as wage earners." Women were also told by the magazines they read and believed in that motherhood was their duty and their privilege. It became the expected, full-time job. Between the 1920s and the 1960s the time women spent in child care almost doubled.

The war did not change fundamental attitudes. Yet subtle shifts had occurred that manifested themselves only later. Many women who left the labor force immediately after the war rejoined it. By 1952 almost twice the number of married women were working as had been working in 1940. Day care had been demystified. Young children, so far as anyone could tell, had not been harmed because they had been cared for in groups without their mothers. And middle-class women had become accustomed to unaccustomed independence. Twenty or thirty years after the war, these changes made it routine for middle-class children to attend nursery school, for women whose mothers had not worked to take jobs, and for society to begin to question long-held assumptions about the needs of children.

Support and Dismay

During the war necessity forced governmental funding of child care for young children, and independent psychological research supported this unprecedented move for those from two to five years old. Dr. Leo Kanner, a psychiatrist at the Johns Hopkins Medical School, and R. H. Blank of the Baltimore Child Study Home found advantages for both mother and child if the child was in nursery school while the mother worked. Such children became "social beings" more readily than those who stayed home, and "friction, nagging and quarreling" between mother and child decreased if they had some time apart during the day. When a mother had the "feeling of being a somebody and of doing something worthwhile," family life improved, and so did her relationship with her husband.

This supportive finding, however, did not challenge the basic assumption that a mother's care was necessary for the well-being of the very young child. Anna Freud put it this way: "The needs of the growing child which override all others [are]: the need for intimate interchange with a maternal figure; the need for ample and constant external stimulation of innate potentialities; and the need for unbroken continuity of care." What happened was that the definition of "very young" was subtly transformed. Nursery schools were now laudable for two- to five-year-olds, but mothers of younger children had to stay home or risk serious damage. Before the war, "young children" had been those under school age; now, in response to cultural compulsion, the dangerous age dropped to below the age of two. Above that age, mothers need not feel guilty about leaving their children in someone else's care.

Social workers, taught to see the early mother-child tie as absolutely essential to normal development and traditionally against separating mother and child, were caught in a dilemma. They were reluctant to support or encourage preschool child care, yet this was just what the country needed. The alternatives were no care, or inadequate care, or downright neglect that showed up in their caseloads. As experience demonstrated that the centers were not bad for most children (although, of course, some did not do well), their opposition subsided. Perhaps it was better for children to be cared for by professionals than by relatives such as grandmothers and older siblings who were untrained amateurs. Just as motherhood was professionalized at the turn of the century by the followers of G. Stanley Hall, who warned that parents had to be just as trained as lawyers or doctors, so early child care was professionalized when teachers went into daycare centers, first under the WPA and then under the Lanham Act.

Although Freudian thinking permeated the professional debate about child care, many mothers were still in the practical grip of Dr. Watson and his behaviorist theories as far as everyday living was concerned. Only 9 or 10 percent of the children studied in two Lanham Act California nursery schools had been breast-fed until weaned; almost half had been on a strict feeding schedule, Watson's four-hour regimen. The mothers were concerned about following the best advice they could find, and three-fifths of them read *Parents' Magazine* during their child's first year.

They were asked, "Did you cuddle and love the baby and play

with him as much as you wanted to [during the first year], or did you restrain yourself because of advice someone had given, or for some other reason?" More than 80 percent said they had been affectionate, but some said they avoided too much handling in response to a physician's advice—again, the shadow of Watson's theories. One family that had lost their first child later had a son and "wanted to give him the best—so no one picked him up [unnecessarily] until he was one year old." By nursery-school age the boy was distant and disliked being touched or held.

The bewildering and contradictory advice given to mothers led one of them to conduct her own experiment. "I'm trying various systems," she told the nursery-school researcher. She "was strict with the first, not with the second, and strict again with the third child." The results have not been recorded. As for fathers, almost 20 percent of them neither played with nor took over any of the routine care of their infants. Most of the mothers—and the experts—felt the nursery-school experience had benefited their children.

After the war it was no longer necessary to document the value of care by someone other than the mother: Once again, mothers would harm their children if they left them with other people. In the early 1950s Margaret Mead protested against the increased emphasis on mother and child staying home together: "Under the guise of exalting the importance of maternity [we] are tying women more tightly to their children than has been thought necessary since the invention of bottle feeding and baby carriages," she wrote.

Researchers and theoreticians are as much a part of the culture in which they operate as the people they choose to study, and their conclusions reflect the biases of their time and place. Neither they nor their research exist in a vacuum. During the war the myth of the ever-present mother gave way to the myth of the "supermom" who could juggle home, children, and job without shortchanging any of them. "Supermom" appeared again in the 1960s, a resurrection of Rosie the Riveter, who had to "do it all" with whatever help—public or private—she could find.

After the War

The Lanham Act Centers for both nursery-age and school-age children were criticized because they served only from 10 to 40 percent of the children who needed supervision while their mothers worked.

But when they were threatened with lowered funds as the war came to a close, and then phased out, they were generally praised as having done a good job. *Parents' Magazine* editorialized, "This service to children must not be abandoned."

The centers were to close six months after the war's end, but commonsense protesters pointed out that many men were not yet home and their wives had to continue to work. The closings were postponed until February 1946. A spokesman for nine social agencies protesting the cutoff complained to President Truman, "The Federal Government is without a policy concerning children" and suggested that long-range planning was necessary. This was just what opponents had feared when the centers were first established—that they would be permanent, not temporary, and would make it easier for mothers to do what they should not do—work outside the home. In December 1945, with the war over and the end of federal funds in sight, the California State Department of Education examined its own program and observed that "there has been a rather remarkable change in the public attitude towards group care of children. At its inception three years ago, mothers were inclined to view with suspicion the government suggestion that child care centers could be satisfactory for their children. Now, after several years of experience, and if the loud clamor over the threatened closing of centers may be interpreted as an index of their collective appraisal of the merit of the program, they are surprisingly well pleased, not only that release for employment is possible, but also with respect to the influence on the lives of their children."

California was the only state in which the program survived permanently, although gradually it metamorphosed into publicly funded day care for the children of poor, usually single, mothers. Even today, some prefabricated buildings shipped to school grounds to serve as nursery schools during the Lanham Act era fifty years ago are still in use—although now they house administrators rather than children. The child care takes place in public school buildings

The war and the centers went away, but the questions they raised did not. The nation was not ready to face the implications of the success of the wartime child-care centers. That success challenged basic views of the role of women, the best way to care for young children, and the balance of power within a family in which both parents work. American women have taken on nontraditional jobs in every war since they made musket balls in the Civil War, and after every war they have gone back home, but as a crane operator observed, "Women were different in World War II: They didn't want to go back home and many of them didn't. And if they did go back home, they never forgot, and they told their daughters, 'You don't have to be just a homemaker. You can be anything you want to be.' And so we've got this new generation of women."

But the new generation did not spring up immediately. The great social changes in women's roles during the war faded once the men came back and women were expected to return to their traditional place, despite hopes and predictions that things would be different. Best-selling novelist Margaret Culkin Banning was mistaken when she said in the early 1940s that the idea of women working had moved from a privilege to an obligation and that almost all jobs were open to women, for whom the future was boundless. The near future proved to be more constricting than she had thought. In the 1950s women were once again told to stay home, and many of them followed orders.

Years later, Hanne Sonquist, a California nursery-school administrator who considers the success of the Lanham Act Centers a model for nationally supported, comprehensive child care, told an interviewer, "We've done it and don't choose to look at it. How quickly we repressed that movement after the war. The standard line is 'Mothers should be home with their kids'—the guilt quotient is enormous. The choices in our society to date have never been in support of children, families and women. I personally am unwilling to say society is not able—we are not willing."

Child Care
Revisited

We're a country with no revered past, no yesterday. It's like a national Alzheimer's.

—*STUDS TERKEL*, New York Times *INTERVIEW*

A LOOK AT CHILD CARE today is a look back at the past. It has all been tried before, and the systems society has tended to support are the ones that have met its needs. These systems have been rejected and replaced by others that fit the ethos of a particular time, then resurrected when a new need revived the old situation in slightly different form. Group care away from home, day care, foster care, the schools as baby-sitters, and nanny care have all had previous incarnations, and today's debates about them are echoes of heated discussions of earlier times.

When the "ideal institutions" of the nineteenth century became the "evil warehouses" of the twentieth, orphanages were phased out in favor of the new ideal—foster family care—or transformed into collections of small-scale cottages that hoped to mimic the highest good, family life. The institutions that survived the 1940s and 1950s were mostly for "residential treatment," places where children with emotional problems were cared for temporarily. Even these were hard-pressed when the "deinstitutionalization" movement of the 1970s, aimed at mental hospitals, filtered down to child-care settings. The assumption was that congregate care was bad, community care was good, and best of all was care in a child's own family.

Social work, the professionalization of philanthropy, provided the expert knowledge necessary to decide which parent and which home could best serve the child. But today's reality of essentially parentless children, uncared for because of drug addiction rather than death, desertion, or illness as in the old days, has reawakened the debate about how to care for children who are neglected or abused. Something new (or old) has to be done. Joyce Ladner, professor of social work at Howard University, says bluntly, "We need orphanages, or their modern day equivalent, simply because, for a growing number of children, they offer a safer, better refuge than the current alternatives—foster care or a return to the biological family." She freely admits she used the term "orphanage" because she knew it would get attention. The word conjures up the ghost of places like Junior Village, in Washington, D.C., which closed in 1972 (very late for such an institution) after charges that it separated brothers and sisters and dosed children with tranquilizers to control their behavior. It once housed one thousand homeless, abandoned, neglected, and unmanageable youngsters. What Ladner is proposing is not such a huge, regimented, Dickensian institution but "small-scale caring institutions that can offer children, and their siblings, a place that they can count on to nurture them." She proposes housing five or six children together in a home with salaried foster parents—the same kind of setting proposed at the start of the century as "the cottage plan" to remake the orphanage in more humane terms. "After all," she points out, "most children in families today grow up with some kind of caretaker who isn't their mother—either day care or a baby-sitter. Why should this be so controversial?"

The back-to-the-orphanage movement has met with stiff criticism from experts who concede the child-care system is in a crisis but reject orphanages, however they are set up. E. Kent Hauser, a cofounder of the Menninger Youth Program in Lawrenceville, Kansas, sees the movement as attractive to people who want "simple, cheap answers." (The mid-nineteenth-century orphanages, too, were championed as cost-effective and uncomplicated.) Hauser adds, "These are kind-hearted people who believe that Little Orphan Annie didn't have it so bad, but there is no way to create a nurturing orphanage." His program places small groups of troubled children in homes with substitute parents—a kind of compromise between the old massive orphanages and individualized foster care. A few of the children eventually return home, some move on to other placements, and some stay until they can be on their own.

Ladner's proposal, stripped of the harsh term "orphanage," does not sound very different from the Menninger system. (In 1935 a Northwestern University professor proposed that changing the word can change the reality: "Each time a new phrase is developed," he said, "it seems to bring with it, or at least to be accompanied by, some measure of permanent gain, in standards or in viewpoint, even though much of the old may continue to masquerade as the new. The series, *alms, philanthropy, relief, rehabilitation, case work, family welfare,* shows such a progression from cruder to more refined levels of charity." Perhaps what is needed is a new, gentler word for "orphanage." The professor's suggestions sixty years ago that "treatment" replace "punishment" and "school" replace "reformatory" have already come about.)

Semantics aside, some experts insist, as Helen Borel, a New York psychoanalyst, put it, that "institutions aren't the answer to anything." She grew up in orphanages between the ages of two and seventeen, deprived of the hugs and holding and lap sitting every child needs, she says. No one was cruel, but no one was loving, either.

Shelters for babies are one of the most controversial revivals of the old orphanage idea. In Los Angeles, the private, nonprofit Children's Institute International houses forty-seven children from infancy through the age of four in "families" in homelike settings with one caretaker for every three children. Each "family" has its own nursery, living room, and kitchen. The youngsters have been abandoned, mistreated, or neglected—90 percent come from drug-abusing families. Their stays are planned to be temporary. Despite their benign intent, shelters such as this revive the reluctance of experts to support the group care of very young children—something the Child Welfare League of America branded a "blunder" when it was tried in World War II. Shelters also ignite the skepticism of those who remember that foster care, too, was supposed to be a temporary expedient.

Despite the conviction of most experts that children wither in institutional settings, some children in some orphanages were helped, not harmed, by the experience. Of course, it is tricky to use anecdotal reports from children who were not infants when they went into orphanages, since they often spent some of their early years with their mothers and might therefore have escaped the effects Rene Spitz reported in the 1950s. Nevertheless, the evil effects of living in an orphanage do not seem to have been universal. Anne Whitt Thompson of Gaithersburg, Maryland, wrote to *The New York Times* in 1987 to defend them. "I lived in two orphanages and three foster homes growing up in North Carolina, and I can say nothing but good about my life in orphanages. We did not wonder where we would eat or sleep, because the orphanage was our home." Considering the alternative for many children, the orphanage was better than home. One man at a Florida reunion of "alumni" of the Hebrew Orphan Asylum (HOA) in New York (it closed in 1941) recalled that he ran away from home to go back to the orphanage. His father had placed him there after his mother died and reclaimed him when he remarried. The boy finally convinced the director of the orphanage that he should stay there because he didn't get along with his stepmother. Other "graduates" remember that they felt privileged to be at the HOA—they had music lessons, trips, good teaching, and personal attention that surpassed what the children on the outside were exposed to. It was, in effect, a boarding school that didn't charge tuition.

Girard College is one of the early orphanages that survived to the present day by changing with the times, and is now, as the HOA was, a kind of tuition-free boarding school supported by private funds. So is the Milton Hershey School in Hershey, Pennsylvania. Founded with chocolate candy profits in 1909 to serve boys with only one parent, the school now takes inner-city boys and girls from kindergarten through twelfth grade whether they are orphans or not and helps many of them through college. It has twelve hundred students. Like Girard, which starts with first grade and has about 550 students, it is touted as a model for the future—a way to take children out of damaging environments and give them a better chance in life.

At Hershey, with its endowment equal to that of many Ivy League schools, the children live in houses with house parents who are strict but loving. Birgit Miller, housemother of Birchland, told *The New York Times* that she gives each boy a hug in bed each night, even though "I was told by another housemother once that I shouldn't hug them good night. She said I was just going to get myself hurt. But fortunately we have had pretty good luck doing it this way." The other housemother's warning echoes the cautions to foster parents in the

1920s and 1930s (and continuing today) that they should not love the children in their care too much.

Dealing with rambunctious youngsters is not easy, and Hershey is set up with strict timetables and rules that mimic those of elite boarding schools. Like the theorists and educators who established those institutions for preadolescents and adolescents, the staff at Hershey is convinced of the value of routine for keeping unruly hormones under control.

Today's academies hark back to the environmental theories of the nineteenth century that propelled the Orphan Trains from the evil city streets to the temptation-free countryside. Today, removing children from the drugs, violence, and family disintegration of the inner cities is seen as one way to provide them with better lives. One 1980 graduate of Hershey who is now a television director says what happened to him at the school was that "you reach this point where you suddenly realize a world of opportunity is there for you. . . . And you just want to seize the opportunity and take it as far as you can."

Not everyone believes that private academies, privately funded, with admissions requirements and careful screening, can have a real impact on the problems of many inner-city children whose parents cannot or should not care for them. The approximately six such schools in operation today in various parts of the country are costly attempts to deal with a massive problem on a small scale. But dissatisfaction with the foster-care system that was supposed to deal with these problems has led to a rethinking of what society can do to help children who will be crushed if they stay where they are. Both foster care and the attempt to reconstitute families so that children can safely be returned to them have often fragmented under crushing pressures. With fewer women staying home, good foster parents are harder and harder to find, and families are nonexistent or destructive for many children. Some children in foster care, originally designed as a short-term solution, spend their lives being bounced from one home to another—sometimes as many as thirty or forty times. The children themselves have more problems and are harder to place than those of even thirty years ago, and there are more of them than ever before. Their numbers jumped more than 50 percent nationally between 1987 and 1991.

Yet as Susan Sheehan found in her study of two generations of women in foster care, some children have done well while others have been dreadfully scarred by the system. "The simple remedy one hears proposed most often is that the money spent on foster care—whose wards in New York City have nearly tripled in the past ten years—would be better spent trying to solve its root causes: poverty, drug addiction and homelessness. Yet experience has shown that these social problems are amenable only to slow, expensive, and hard-thought-out measures. In the meantime, something has to be done to take care of the children."

Social agencies are encouraging extended family members to take in the children of their relatives to expand the pool of substitute parents. In the past, informal arrangements were made both inside and outside the child-welfare system, and foster parents who were related to the child were often neither paid nor supervised. In New York City in 1990, under new rules established in 1986, 42 percent of the children in foster care lived in officially designated kinship homes. An estimated 3 million grandparents nationwide—the largest group of relatives acting as substitute parents—now shoulder the age-old burden of caring for the children of their children, and their numbers keep growing. A census report based on 1989 figures showed that 13 percent of black children under the age of eighteen lived in their grandparents' homes, while 5 percent of Hispanic children and 3 percent of white children did so. Half the black children had their mothers in the home, too, repeating a pattern more than a century old.

The new recognition of a folk system that has existed since families began has brought with it both advantages and problems. According to a New York State task force, children feel less stigmatized if they live with an aunt or uncle or grandmother, and brothers and sisters are more often kept together. On the other hand, this system, too, has outrun attempts to police it, and children are sometimes neglected or held on to when they might have been adopted or returned to their biological parents.

Whatever methods have been used to care for children have been distorted and misused to evade well-meaning safeguards. When day care and nursery schools were young at the turn of the century, "baby farms" crowded children into unsanitary quarters and whisked some of the youngsters away when inspectors—a new attempt to regulate them—were due to call. Recently Richard Stolley of Time, Inc., joined the crusade to improve child care after his daughter was hired by a child-care center in Chicago that exceeded the legal ratio of children to caretaker. It was her job to hustle the excess children into a van and drive them around the white middle-class neighborhood when city inspectors were scheduled to visit. Today, as during World War II when the demand of working mothers for child care outstripped the available programs, black-market child care that evades the safeguards exists alongside the regulated system. Despite the rules, children are left in unlicensed homes and centers.

Inspectors and the general public have been misled by orphanages old and new, too. The assertion by one Orphan Train child that the pictures of children dressed in frilly aprons and sitting at neat tables were a come-on for would-be contributors rather than a record of orphanage reality is echoed by a woman who was in a Staten Island orphanage—Mount Loretto Catholic mission—in the 1960s. She told *The New York Times*, "A few days before the inspectors, they'd give you new clothes and right after, they'd take them back." Another woman who had spent five years at Mount Loretto while her father recovered from alcoholism burst into tears as she asked the *Times* reporter, "Do you know how much it would have meant for one of those nuns to hold us, to say they felt sorry for us? They never did. A little girl goes in and all you keep saying is you want your mother. 'Well, you're not going to have her, so forget it.' " Even in the days after Dr. Spock and the recognition of the emotional needs of children, orphans were still deprived of the benefits of psychological knowledge.

Repeating the Past

Comprehensive child care—including sick care, twenty-four-hour care, drop-off care—called for today as if it were revolutionary, is really a throwback. It has been tried before, and it worked. Mothers who can't find adequate child care and try to keep their children with them today are also repeating the past. In 1990, a New Jersey woman who worked in a department store part-time on Saturdays dressed her five-year-old daughter in pajamas, locked her in her Toyota during her shift, and checked on her at every break. The little girl had a book, a flashlight, a blanket, and a stuffed animal to keep her company. At first condemned as heartless by the media, who were quick to seize on her story, the mother was later seen as "a good mother who made a bad decision." She had struggled to support her daughter alone, had had bad experiences with baby-sitters, and finally decided the car was a better and safer place to leave the child. During World

War II children were also left in parked cars while their mothers worked in war plants.

Solutions to the problem of what to do with sick children when a mother works are not new, either. The settlement houses in the early part of the century provided care for sick children, and some of the World War II programs separated children in day-care centers who were not well from those who were, so their mothers could continue to help the war effort. Now, some hospitals and specialized centers provide day care for mildly ill or recuperating children who are not allowed to attend their usual day-care programs. In Massachusetts, St. Joseph's Medical Center in Lowell has a "Sniffles and Sneezes" infirmary, for children as young as six weeks to up to twelve years. About a dozen other hospitals around the country offer similar services. Some employers tackle the problem in a different way. When the National Council of Jewish Women surveyed working mothers in 1989 it found that paid leave to care for sick children was rated the single most important benefit provided by employers. In another approach, seven major New York companies offer emergency child care to their employees, contracting with a health-care agency to send a caretaker into the home when a child is sick. This forward-looking program recalls one proposed by the Child Welfare League of America, which bemoaned the fact that none of its affiliated agencies provided for the care of a child who woke up sick in the morning and whose mother then had to stay home from work during World War II.

Like sick care, round-the-clock care is now being rediscovered as more women with young children are in the workforce, faced at times with long hours or changing shifts. Of course, this kind of care is old, too, having been part of the war program and some settlement house centers long ago.

On-site day care, too, is nothing new. The centers established in war factories and shipyards during World War II did what corporate-sponsored workplace centers are designed to do today—cut down on absenteeism, allow parents to visit their children during the day, and give parents and children more time together, since they share traveling to and from home. Some centers, like those during the war, operate twelve hours a day to accommodate overtime work. Mindful of the importance of day care for two-career families, thousands of companies with more than one hundred employees now provide some child-care services. One of the oldest programs, run by the

Campbell Soup Company, serves about 120 children from seven weeks to six years of age.

Working at home, as the immigrants did in the tenements, is another venerable method now being revived as a way of letting mothers earn money while still caring for their own children. And a new outcry is beginning against an old villain—child labor—that often accompanies women working at home. In Pennsylvania, the state Department of Labor and Industry has ordered a company to stop using home workers to sew its soft sculptures of cuddly cows and cats, because, as a union official—echoing unions a century ago—said, "There is no control. There is no such thing as overtime. Their children help them. Before you know it, children under 12 have become helpers." Yet a movement is growing among professional men and women to work at home, partly so they can be there for their children, and there has been no outcry that the children will be exploited if they staple reports or file papers.

Children are still being reared communally, as they were in the mid-nineteenth-century utopias. Although the hippie communes of the 1960s have faded from the scene, a few religiously based communities such as the Bruderhof in Rifton, New York (producers of Creative Playthings), still survive, but their numbers are small and their influence is minimal. Another, less demanding movement is beginning to attract parents who want to provide their children with a sense of community, yet are not prepared to give up their own individuality. Called cohousing, it is adapted from highly successful experiments in Denmark, which provide common spaces for eating, laundry, cooking, and child care while maintaining separate homes. The communities' facilities are reminiscent of what Charlotte Perkins Gilman suggested in 1898. She proposed central kitchens, community child care, and a trained corps of housekeepers to handle routine tasks and free women to be more than wives and mothers.

Child-welfare programs today are based on the conclusion of the first White House Conference on Children in 1909, which is still struggling to be more than a written statement: Children are best brought up in their own families. And Jacob Riis's declaration of about that time—"Every baby is entitled to one pair of mother's arms"—finds its counterpart in a current psychoanalyst's statement criticizing orphanages: "Every child needs holding and kissing. Every child needs to be special to someone." Riis also said that " 'the more kindergartens, the fewer prisons' is a saying the truth of which the generation that comes after us will be better able to grasp than we." Substitute "Head Start programs" for "kindergartens," and the quotation could be used in a current newspaper.

And the idea that "we can change the way we are in the world through our children," as day-care provider Joan Roemer put it in her 1989 book, *Two to Four from 9 to 5*, is right out of the beliefs of the Progressives, who were optimistically convinced that they could improve man's condition by improving mankind.

The litany of similarities between yesterday and today could go on and on. Even the rhetoric is the same. Just as child care was compared with the care of animals when the Society for the Prevention of Cruelty to Children was founded on the model of the ASPCA in 1875, child care today is measured against what is provided for dogs. The Connecticut Association for Human Services complained in 1990, "We have assigned a higher priority to the supervision of facilities caring for animals than to the supervision of those caring for children." And in another throwback to the past, a 1994 Carnegie Corporation report on the plight of children under three years old suggested dealing with their bleak situation by offering services such as parent education, immunization, prenatal care, and child care "in one place"—as settlement houses did in the early 1890s.

That these methods, statements, and sentiments repeat themselves through the years and could be interchanged despite the passage of time may reflect a basic reality about human nature. They may also reflect the resurgence from time to time of basic conditions—war, economic depression—which demand that society look again at its needs and the needs of children. The new look turns up suspiciously similar circumstances and theories.

Schools for the Future

Even what seems to be a unique way of dealing with the problems of today turns out to have a counterpart in the past. Edward Zigler, one of the architects of the Head Start program, now proposes a "School for the Twenty-first Century," which would take over the care of very young children and provide what would amount to almost cradle-to-college services. "The idea," he says, "is to take a good Head Start–style preschool program and tie it to an institution where the kids will end up anyway. Parents need a reliable place to put their kids, and they trust the schools." This notion has its match in a statement made almost fifty years ago by the Association for Childhood Education: "There still are and always will be working mothers," the association declared. Their children will need care and "logically, the responsibility is that of the public schools."

The idea has been tried before. During World War II, Lanham Act Centers often operated in schools, providing day care, before- and after-school care, and vacation coverage. The public-school system in Independence, Missouri, was the first to put Zigler's plan into effect in the late 1980s as a pilot project, linking twelve-hour child-care, preventive health services, and family counseling for children from preschool to the age of twelve. This is no more than was routinely provided by the WPA nurseries and the school-based Lanham Act Centers. Even earlier, at the turn of the century when tuberculosis killed more children than anything except diphtheria, public schools were in the business of health care. They held fresh-air classes, with the children wearing hats and jackets as they did their lessons outside, the only way known of keeping the dreaded plague from flowering in particularly vulnerable youngsters.

New needs have always stretched the use of the schools. Some expanded services started in the 1960s are a response to an explosion in the number of teenagers with children and anticipate some of Zigler's proposals. The New York City Board of Education's in-school day-care centers for the children of high school students began in the late 1970s and care for more infants than any other program in the city. School officials have also supported year-round schools to care for children in the summer. When *New York Times* columnist Anna Quindlen pointed out to the president of the New York City Board of Education that keeping schools open in the summer would be prohibitively expensive, the president replied, in a modern variant of the old school-as-prison-preventive argument, "I'd rather pay for schools than for detox."

Zigler's plan, too, has run into opposition as too costly. It has also been criticized by those who feel the overburdened public schools are already failing to do a good job and those who are concerned that very young children need skills conventionally trained teachers may lack. Battles over turf and who gets scarce funds as well as debates over who is best equipped to deal with children may delay the start of the twenty-first century.

Head Start

But Zigler certainly had a part in changing the twentieth century with his advocacy of early education for poor children, which became the Great Society's Head Start program in 1965. Changing attitudes about children had laid the groundwork for acceptance of this early intervention. In the 1950s, the pendulum swung again from the interior to the exterior of the child. Change the environment, the thinking went, as it had at the turn of the century, and you can change the child. This was a reaction against the idea that basic endowments and programmed developmental stages propelled a child toward adulthood. In the sixties and seventies, the environmental approach was again modified by a recognition of the importance of genetics and temperament. By the time Head Start came along, the focus was on "the whole child."

By 1993, Head Start had provided a year of comprehensive early childhood education for more than 13 million poor children in approximately thirteen hundred programs. Nationwide it aims to give three- to five-year-olds the skills they need to succeed in school and also provides nutritional and health services. (The Lanham Act Centers, too, had a daily health examination built in.) Like the earlier national experiments in day care, it emphasizes parental involvement, but it goes beyond its predecessors in helping families get social services and even acts as a kind of employment agency.

Head Start has ridden a roller coaster of acclaim and criticism. On the one hand, it has been hailed as "the most successful of the Great Society efforts." On the other, it has been called a sham, several studies showing that the immediate intellectual gains of the children fade after several years. Zigler counters that one year of Head Start cannot be expected to do the job. At least two years, plus follow-up in the regular school system, are needed. He also estimates that 50 percent of the present programs are "excellent," 25 percent are "marginal," and 25 percent are "poor." He suggests better funding and better staffs in order to reach the program's potential. He also freely admits it is hard to prove Head Start's long-term effects—the necessary studies have never been done. But despite this country's perpetual ambivalence about mothers working and children being cared for outside their own homes, Head Start has helped keep day care firmly on the national agenda.

Some argue that Head Start, even if it can be made to work as well as possible, is not enough. Gwen Morgan, of Lincoln, Massachusetts, is recognized as one of this country's experts on day care and the education of young children. She modeled her early pre–Head Start day-care programs on the Lanham Act Centers, which served children who were not necessarily poor, but now says, "I'm pretty scornful of what's happening on a federal level. The biggest error Congress makes is assuming that day care is only for rich people, who can afford to pay for it, and for poor people, who can't. What it doesn't realize is that more than half the people using day care are working people who don't qualify for support but aren't rich enough to solve their own day-care problems."

Her assumption—and Zigler's—that government has a leading role to play in the care of young children reflects the conviction of a large segment of the American people. As in the past, as Stacey G. Goffin, an assistant professor of early childhood education at the University of Missouri–Kansas City, points out, advocates for children believe that child care is both a family and a societal responsibility. Families cannot do it all, and making sure that children get the services they need is a concern that is legitimately in the political arena. On the other hand, the American traditions of individualism and self-sufficiency lead some to believe that families should be able to take care of themselves, and that those who cannot are incompetent. Government support is seen as an invasion of family life. These two streams have crossed each other again and again in the history of child care in this country. When the Federal Children's Bureau was set up in 1912, it was explicitly forbidden to invade the territory of parents. The idea that the poor were responsible for their own condition receded only slowly as the Progressives focused on the social forces behind indigence, and the dictum of the first White House Conference on Children in 1909 that children should not be removed from their families simply because of poverty has been cited (and evaded) through the years. Inexorably, however, government has moved more and more into areas once thought to be exclusively the province of parents—schooling, health, child care—and salutes to American individualism have been tempered by the complex realities of the twentieth century.

Other governments have been even more involved than ours in providing for and regulating the care of children. When Hillary Rodham Clinton was chairman of the Children's Defense Fund, a lobbying and information group in Washington, she visited France in 1989 with a delegation of experts. They came back enthusiastic about the French system, largely funded with tax dollars, that blends education, health, and child care in subsidized, all-day centers and licensed private-care homes. Nearly 90 percent of French children from three to five are served in these facilities. Zigler has also pointed to other countries as places we might learn from. "The Israeli government provides kindergarten for all five-year-olds, and child care is provided for 50 percent of all 3–4 year olds. . . . In China, nurseries are available for virtually all children from the age of 56 days on," he points out. As a matter of fact, in China's major cities, boarding care is available five days a week. Some parents, faced with this ultimate solution to two-career families, cannot tolerate so much separation and take their children home one or two nights a week.

No one is proposing that the United States adopt any of these plans wholesale; our attitudes and circumstances are different. France is intent on encouraging and rewarding births, since its population has not recovered from the decimation of two world wars. The United States is philosophically dedicated to discouraging population growth and encouraging mothers to stay home (ignoring the fact that more and more of them are entering the labor force). China's totalitarian regime can proceed no matter what people think; we in America are bound by democratic dissent.

Despite these serious impediments to sweeping change, Congress did pass the Child Care Development Block Grant of 1990, the most comprehensive child-care bill since World War II. As in the days of Rosie the Riveter when, in 1944, women made up one-third of the workforce, women again rushed into the marketplace between 1975 and 1985. The percentage working or looking for work rose from 46 percent to 58 percent. In one case, necessity produced the Lanham Act. In the other, it belatedly spurred state-sponsored family leave bills and federal block grants. The measure President Bush signed gave 2.5 billion dollars to the states over three years to subsidize child care for mostly low-income working parents. It was expected to benefit about 750,000 children and their parents by supporting day care as well as providing grants for before-school and after-school programs.

This is not as novel as it seems. The federal government has long been in the child-care business, providing subsidies for centers that serve the military, usually on military bases. But that limited involvement has not become a model for widespread funding outside the armed forces.

Nannies Again

Day care of some kind has become a fact of life in today's world, in which more than half the mothers with children under six years of age are in the workforce. Day-care centers, neighbors, relatives, and family home centers take care of most of the children. But a study reported in 1988 that 58 percent of the working mothers surveyed favored "in home" care by a baby-sitter (nanny) for children under the age of five. By 1993, only 3 percent had achieved that preferred goal, and for many parents the search for an affordable, suitable nanny was a consuming quest.

Today's nannies often work in families where both parents are professionals deeply committed to their careers rather than in families caught up in the social whirl. In 1990, 68 percent of women college graduates with infants under one year of age worked outside the home. But the parents, like those of the famous and rich in the twenties and thirties, have to depend on someone else taking total or almost total care of their children so that they can live the lives they have chosen or have been forced to choose. More children today are cared for by someone other than a parent or relative than ever before in our history.

Karen DeCrow, former head of the National Organization for Women, recognized the importance of the nanny in the lives of professional women. She shocked a conference of women lawyers who decided that, at the time of a divorce, a child should live with the person with whom it had spent the most time when she suggested that "if we followed that policy, the babies of women lawyers would be living in the Caribbean. There were some gasps; a few fainted."

The word "nanny" no longer refers exclusively to a woman trained in England but has come to be a generic term for a full-time, home-based child-care worker. Today's nannies are most likely to come from the Caribbean, Mexico, Asia, or the American Midwest. Some of them see the job not as a profession but as a way station, a way of marking time until marriage or higher education. Other nannies come from third-world countries and see themselves as indentured servants, working for low wages so that they can acquire a green card permitting them to stay in this country. Nannies usually work without clear-cut hours or well-defined tasks. The comfortable myth that the nanny is "a part of the family" still persists, and some nannies insist they feel that way. But Dr. Steven Mintz, a professor of history at the University of Houston and coauthor with Susan Kellogg of *Domestic Revolutions: A Social History of American Family Life*, points out bleakly that "slaveholders, too, said that they treated their slaves like part of the family. Nothing disguises exploitation more than the sense that you're doing it for somebody else's good."

In the past ten years, in an attempt to professionalize the occupation and remove it further from the taint of servitude, nanny schools have been established in the United States. The International Nanny Association (dedicated to improving working conditions and status) estimates that more than sixty schools were operating in 1991. Their increasing popularity attests to the fact that nannies answer the need of the new breed of parents—those with two demanding jobs and incomes to match. These parents lack the long tradition of being cared for by servants that buttressed the traditional nannies—their mothers wore aprons, baked cookies, stayed home, and looked after them—and they have had to forge their own attitudes and ways of dealing with shared motherhood without the personal or even societal memory of how it should be done.

In a reflection of changing attitudes about men and child care, some nannies hired today are men. Men as nurturers have a long history—as masters of apprentices, as tutors—but they have not been seen as primary caretakers of young children. Now a few men are moving into that role. The movement is a rivulet rather than a flood, but single mothers have hired them to act as role models, and couples have seen them as particularly good with boys. A complicating factor is what one social worker called "the presumption of perversion"— the fear that boys will be sexually molested—a fear that does not affect female nannies.

One new way of finding nanny care is the au pair system, authorized by Congress in 1986. Eight agencies, officially designated to screen candidates and families, provide European, English-speaking child-care workers who are on a twelve-month cultural exchange program. At the end of the year, the au pair (usually a young woman) leaves to go back home, and the family is faced with replacing her. The nanny is no longer a family fixture, as she often was in the old days, but someone whose departure is built in. What this means in practice is that children have a succession of caretakers, just as Dr. J. B. Watson suggested as a formula for protecting a child against the inept mothering of its own mother and the dangers of close attachment. But this flies in the face of Freudian thinking that one consistent caretaker is necessary for a child's psychological welfare.

Benjamin Spock was the first expert who, in his professional training as both a pediatrician and a psychoanalyst, brought Freudian thinking into everyday child rearing. In a revolutionary move, he battled John Watson and the behaviorists, who had seen children as perfectible mechanisms and warned against too much loving. Perhaps Spock's most revolutionary contribution was to treat parents as capable of bringing up their own children. He was an expert acting as an antiexpert when he began his *Baby and Child Care* in 1946 with "You know more than you think you do." He then proceeded to tell parents how to handle everything from toilet training to upper respiratory infections but made them feel that they had some choice in how to deal with their children. The book has sold more than 40 million copies around the world.

In the immediate postwar period, Spock's child-centered ideas struck a sympathetic chord. With the regimented discipline of the war behind them, Americans could begin to loosen some of the restraints and focus on feelings. Spock has been accused of fostering the "me" generation and championing permissiveness and instant gratification. In a *New York Times* interview celebrating his eighty-eighth birthday he disputed this characterization with "I always believed in giving a child firm, clear leadership. It's not remotely my idea that you give a child what he wants or let him do what he wants." Just as no one can determine what parents actually did by reading advice books, no one can determine how well or how badly they interpreted the advice that was given.

What Recent Studies Show

Most recent studies of children left in the care of someone other than their mother have tended to be less alarming than some of the earlier work, which was based firmly on the idea that a young child needed one person—and that person was its mother. This theory fit the reality of the post–World War II world when women were told to go home and stay there. Spock advised mothers for two decades that, unless a mother was forced by economic necessity to hold a job, she was foolish to "pay other people to do a poorer job of bringing up [her] children." By 1976, he had revised his view to accept the new reality that both parents had an equal right to a career, but he added, "If they want others to do it all, I'd advise against their having children." It is likely he would consider the full-time classic nanny as doing it all.

Yet there is no clear evidence that an infant is harmed by being cared for by someone other than its mother. When Claire Etaugh, a psychologist at Bradley University, reviewed the scientific literature on other than mother care in children before and after the age of two, she cautioned, "Conclusions regarding the effects of nonmaternal care on young children must be considered tentative, given the shortcomings of the research literature," because it is contradictory and based on small samples. "A reasonably cautious conclusion," she went on, ". . . is that high-quality nonmaternal care does not appear to have harmful effects on the preschool child's maternal attachment, intellectual development, social-emotional behavior or physical health."

The time children spend away from their mothers being cared for by someone else can be considerable. Three University of Virginia psychologists calculated that young children in day care (at a center or in a family day-care home) spend 1,715 hours a year during the workweek with their caregivers and only 1,102 hours with their parents. But parents also are with the children an average of 1,274 weekend hours a year, and 455 hours for vacation and sick days. What all this adds up to is that parents spend about a thousand more hours a year—the equivalent of forty days—with their children than do their other caregivers, according to this study. This, of course, assumes that children and parents vacation together, yet many privileged children go from some sort of day care to summer camp and skip the vacation time they might spend with parents. Then, too, when the caregiver lives in the home, or comes to the home every day (more likely in more affluent families), the numbers probably converge even more closely, although firm statistics are not available.

Etaugh's review of the studies dealing with mother-child separation for much of each day was conducted through a different lens from that of the followers of John Bowlby and Rene Spitz. Those two researchers found that infants separated from their mothers and deprived of warm maternal care went into an emotional and physical decline that often led to their deaths. The finding fit in with the belief—held to with the fervor of religious dogma—that the mother-infant relationship could not be disturbed without drastic results. These were, however, institutionalized children, cut off from their parents. Despite this vital difference, the conclusions were extended to apply to children at home, too. Now that more mothers are working than ever before, the question is being reexamined. Researchers have looked again at the data not only with new scientific training but with different cultural attitudes as well. Since women are going to work, why make it harder? Guilt doesn't help. Support does. The psychoanalytic view that a mother's place was in the home, since only she could give an infant the security it needed, endorsed the social reality that mothers stayed home while fathers went out to work; the new view supports today's reality of two working parents.

Of course, there are studies that confirm the notion that a child may be harmed by other than mother care, and a few that indicate that a secure attachment to a caregiver can compensate for unsatisfactory mothering. Much of the laboratory research on the question has been conducted along the guidelines developed in the late 1960s by psychologist Mary Ainsworth, then of Baltimore. Her Strange Situation Procedure provides a framework for assessing mother-child attachments before the child is eighteen months old. Children are observed as they are separated from and reunited with their mothers, their caregivers, and strangers in an unfamiliar environment—a laboratory, not a home or school. They are then classified as "anxious/avoidant," "anxious/resistant," or "secure." Reacting to an unknown person just as the child reacts to its mother (called the absence of "stranger anxiety") indicates poor attachment. Protesting when a mother leaves, recovering quickly, and greeting the mother happily on her return indicate "secure" attachment. The small number of studies using the Ainsworth Strange Situation Procedure that looked at the reaction to the caretaker in contrast to the reaction to the mother indicate, according to the psychologist Claire Etaugh, "that the child can form an attachment to a stable substitute caregiver that parallels the development of attachment to the mother. At the same time, however, children appear to direct more attachment behaviors toward their mothers than toward their substitute caretakers"—another case of science documenting the obvious.

Two of the few studies of in-home nonmaternal care of infants using the Ainsworth approach looked at infants when they were twelve and thirteen months old. The researchers found that children with twenty hours or more of in-home day care showed "significantly more avoidance on reunion with mother." In other words, they seemed less secure and, perhaps, resentful of the mother who had left them with a substitute. And sons whose mothers worked full-time were more likely to be classified as insecure in their attachment to their fathers than other boys. The researchers can't explain the seemingly greater effect of a mother's absence on boys and point out that other studies don't confirm this "bewilderingly contradictory conclusion." Dr. Jay Belsky, a coauthor of this study, continues to feel that mothers should stay home given today's less-than-adequate day care, despite attacks on his findings by other academic experts.

Dr. T. Berry Brazelton, today's Dr. Spock for the psychologically sophisticated, warns that there may be long-term negative effects of separation of mother and child that have not yet been examined and that may not show up in early behavior. He cautions, "We do not have enough studies yet to know about the issues for the infant. . . . We need to know when it is safest for the child's future development to have to relate to two or three caregivers; what will be the effects on a baby's development of a group care situation; when babies are best able to find what they need from caregivers other than their parents; when parents are best able to separate from their babies without feeling too grieved at the loss. In a word, we need information on which to base general guidelines for parents. For it could be that the most subtle, hard-to-deal with pressure on young adults comes indirectly from society's ambivalent and discordant attitudes" about the importance of a mother staying home with her young child. Despite Dr. Brazelton's litany of what is not known, parents are faced with a shelf-full of books of contradictory advice by experts who sound authoritative. Some say staying home for the first year (or six months, or nine months) is vital. Dr. Penelope Leach, the English psychologist and researcher, is convinced that "full-time care for several months is best for a new infant." The cut-off point— when it is safe for a mother to leave her baby with others—keeps going down. The controversy now centers on the first year, rather than, as it had in the past, the first two years or five years or six years. And yet, other experts point out that the effects of the first year of life, although important, are not irrevocable.

The debate continues to rage, despite the fact that social policy and psychological research both reflect a common belief in the myth of the perfect mother as the standard of comparison. Only she—or her exemplary substitute—can provide what a child needs to thrive. Yet this fundamental creed is not supported by a body of respected research. As a matter of fact, when Anthony N. Maluccio, a professor of social work at Boston College, looked at the history of child welfare in this country he concluded, "The choice of one type of substitute care over another has typically been determined by prevailing values and biases more than by validated theories and empirical research." A basic problem in assessing differing views is that no one has yet studied a population brought up by "perfect" mothers—so there is no way of knowing if they do better than children cared for by substitutes.

In the great adventure of caring for this nation's children it has not been the setting that was important, it has been the quality of care and the quality of caring. Children have been helped and hurt by any system, whether orphanages, foster care, upper-class nanny care, or mother care. The best was good; the worst was bad. And in each case, much depended on the age and resilience of the child. Every era has had to find its own way of caring for its children supported by a psychological model that is itself a product of that time.

From Colonial times to the present, children have lived with a bewildering variety of caretaking systems. Some, in the bosom of their families, have been looked after by women other than their mothers. Some have been herded into institutions, or sent away from home, or exposed to substitute mothers in one arrangement or another. America's historical amnesia has let the details of many of these arrangements slip into oblivion, forcing society to make a fresh start again and again. The truth is, we really know both more and less than we think we do about how to care for this nation's children.

NOTES

Abbreviations Used in Notes

CAN: Children's Aid News.

CAS: Children's Aid Society of New York.

CASP: Children's Aid Society of Pennsylvania Collection, Historical Society of Pennsylvania, Philadelphia.

CB: United States Children's Bureau.

CCNY: Oral History Project: Immigrant Women, Tamiment Institute Library, New York University.

CSS: Community Service Society Papers, Rare Book and Manuscript Library, Butler Library, Columbia University.

CWLA: Child Welfare League of America.

DC: Dartmouth College Library, Dartmouth College, Hanover, New Hampshire.

GC: Girard College, Philadelphia, Pennsylvania.

GH: Greenwich House Papers, Tamiment Institute Library, New York University.

IC: Ilka Chase Papers, Billy Rose Theater Collection, New York Public Library for the Performing Arts.

JA: Jane Addams Papers, 1860–1960 microfilm.

LH: Lewis W. Hine, National Child Labor Committee Collection, Library of Congress.

LSRM: Laura Spelman Rockefeller Memorial Archive, Rockefeller Archive Center, North Tarrytown, New York.

LW: Lillian Wald Papers, Rare Book and Manuscript Library, Butler Library, Columbia University.

MA: Moravian Academy, Bethlehem, Pennsylvania.

NYHS: *Indentures of Apprentices, 1718–1727*, in *Collections of The New-York Historical Society for 1909* (1910).

Colored Orphan Asylum Papers, Manuscript Division.

NYPL: New York Public Library.

NYT: *The New York Times.*

RS: Russell Sage Foundation, Rockefeller Archive Center, North Tarrytown, New York.

1. Apprenticeship

Page
17 *"cultural invention"*: Demos (1982), 444.
17 *"natural production"*: Earle, 225.
18 *Lord Chesterfield:* ibid., 179.
19 *poor apprentices in Boston:* Schulz, 70.
19 *Thurlow Weed:* Bremner (1970), vol. 1, 160.
20 *"social liabilities"*: Towner (1955), 9.
20 *"single-woman"*: Ritter, 53.
20 *"Negro lad"*: Bremner (1970), vol. 1, 154.
20 *Peter Jacobson:* NYHS, *Indentures, 1718–1727,* 119.
20 *Freedmen's Bureau:* Williamson, 321.
20 *Virginia in 1748:* Bremner (1970), vol. 1, 263.
21 *"bind out"*: Towner (1966), 424.
22 *"showing their earnestnes"*: ibid., 421.
22 *"shall be consulted"*: Bremner (1970), vol. 1, 266.
23 *"more affectionate"*: Demos (1970), 121n.
24 *John Galway's:* NYHS, *Indentures, 1718–1727,* 120.
24 *Franklin's father:* Franklin, 26.
24 *Daniel Clapp:* Thomas (1971), 35n.
25 *Elizabeth Burgess:* Howard, 6.
25 *Mary Mariot:* NYHS, *Indentures, 1718-1727,* 117.
25 *Judith Shields: Indentures in Philadelphia, 1771-1773,* 23
25 *fee was standard:* Towner (1955), 29.
25 *George Beckwith:* Ritter, 10.
26 *Between 1734 and 1751:* Towner (1955), 84.
26 *"astonishing inaptitude"*: Seabury, 79.
26 *term "master"*: Rorabaugh, 179.
27 *comforted at night:* NYT, February 10, 1993.
27 *Final say:* Norton, 94.
27 *"mother substitute"*: Du Bois, 38.
28 *advice to Laertes:* "A Father's Gift," 87.
28 *"duely Endeavor"*: Seybolt, 37.
29 *"wisdom of the master"*: Rorabaugh, 130.
29 *latter-day Socrates:* ibid., 102.
29 *neglected their obligations:* Bailyn, 30.
29 *"to learn me"*: Thomas (1962), 19.
30 *whip the delinquents:* Demos (1978), 119.
30 *"Jesus Christ"*: Towner (1955), 28.
30 *"choice of opportunity"*: Seabury, 55.
31 *journeyman Samuel Draper:* Thomas (1962), 6.
31 *"Patience and perseverance"*: Garrison, 41.
32 *"little heart"*: ibid., 36.

32 *"younger children"*: ibid., 37.

33 *"garret room"*: Seabury, 61.

33 *"never beat or abused"*: ibid., 66.

33 *"example of wrongdoing"*: Rorabaugh, 15.

34 *"wholesome diet"*: Bremner (1970), vol. 1, 127.

34 *offered him shelter*: Demos (1970), 113.

34 *"Reward 3 shillings"*: Ritter, 18.

34 Pennsylvania Gazette: Bremner (1970), vol. 1, 153–54.

35 *"Better whipt"*: Mintz and Kellogg, 15.

35 *John Robinson*: Calhoun, 112.

36 *"sorest punishment"*: ibid., 113.

36 *"tyrannical treatment"*: Franklin, 33.

36 *"twice whipped"*: Thomas (1962), 7.

36 *"ulcerated leg"*: Bremner (1970), vol. 1, 124.

36 *convicted of manslaughter*: Demos (1970), 114.

37 *"Stripped them Naked"*: Quimby, 113.

37 *"most trying season"*: Seabury, 57.

38 *"long to see you"*: Garrison, 33.

38 *"yearnings of her soul"*: ibid., 34.

38 *"lodged in your hands"*: "A Father's Gift," 87.

38 *"Our disputes"*: Franklin, 33.

38 *"improve my style"*: ibid., 28.

39 *"doleful crying"*: Bremner (1970), vol. 1, 125–26.

39 *idleness was a vice*: ibid., 125.

40 *"departed this life"*: Horne, 39.

40 *"Alas, Alas"*: Earle, 173.

42 *"Father chair"*: Jarcho, 41–42.

42 *separation from their mothers*: Lamb, 5.

42 *"his boys"*: Norton, 95.

42 *"Psychology follows culture"*: Kessen, 819.

43 *"Silver Buckles"*: Bremner (1970), vol. 1, 153.

43 *populous as Philadelphia*: Clarkson, n.p.

44 *"valuable and workable"*: Towner (1966), 433.

2. The Mammy, the Nurse, and the Planter's Wife

45 *"mistresses helped raise the black"*: Genovese (1974), 290.

45 *"motherhood had to be shared"*: White, 128.

46 *"pat him a little"*: Sterling, xi.

46 *"father interchangeably"*: Rawick (1977), vol. 6, part 1, xcv.

47 *supposedly promiscuous black females*: Hymowitz and Weissman, 45.

47 *"had to be sold"*: Picquet, 6.

48 *"eat victuals"*: Sterling, 5.

48 *"got their profits"*: Lerner, 25.

48 *"Hush-a-bye"*: Sterling, 18.

48 *"specially Missus"*: Rawick (1977), vol. 5, part 4, 1561.

49 *"no more to nobody"*: Hymowitz and Weissman, 48–49.

49 *twice the rate:* Jones, 35.

49 *"nigh 'bout busted"*: Rawick (1977), vol. 10, 2014.

49 *"they were well"*: Hurmence, 45–46.

50 *"only mother"*: Rawick, vol. 10, 2212–13.

50 *"superstitious things"*: ibid., vol. 1, 230.

50 *hidden from God:* Lowery, 79.

51 *"with a stick"*: Hymowitz and Weissman, 47.

51 *"whip me"*: Rawick, vol. 6, 25.

52 *"fed right"*: ibid., vol. 10, 2249–51.

52 *"like pigs"*: Sterling, 5.

52 *"baby was sucking"*: ibid., 41.

53 *"watch de babies"*: ibid., 10.

53 *" 'cause he cry so"*: Lerner, 41.

53 *hoed her rows:* ibid., 48.

53 *"as any other child"*: Yetman, 71.

54 *"little slave children"*: Hurmence, 45–46.

54 *Parker Pool:* ibid., 81–87.

54 *"tote the head"*: Botkin, 126.

55 *"I'd play then"*: Lerner, 25.

55 *"get dat goat"*: Yetman, 66.

55 *"aid of she-goats"*: Montaigne, 155.

56 *"children for her"*: Yetman, 71.

56 *"called for the cap"*: Burnett, 245–46.

56 *"wid dey mammy"*: Sterling, 5.

57 *"mistress and mother"*: White, 49.

57 *legendary mammy:* Mitchell, 22.

57 *"people come from"*: Parkhurst, 36.

57 *"little ladies"*: Genovese (1974), 354.

57 *"neighboring gentry"*: Blackford, 3.

58 *Mammy Rose:* Rawick (1977), vol. 9, 1901.

58 *"Mammy's sayings"*: Rawick (1977), series 2, vol. 1, 117.

58 *"Nain was sixteen"*: Percy, 26–27.

59 *she herself died:* Srygley, 41–42.

59 *Charles County:* Carr, 39.

59 *"No stepmother"*: Fox-Genovese, 27.

59 *"Mother Tid"*: Rawick (1977), vol. 10, 2121.

60 *"nursed all the babies"*: Hurmence, 26.

60 *Ellen Betts:* Botkin, 126.

60 *"go without her"*: Genovese (1974), 353–54.

60 *"are suckled"*: Blassingame, 167.

61 *Ellen Cragin:* Rawick (1977), Supplement, series 2, vol. 1, 43.

61 *"sufficient food"*: Jacobs, 14.
62 *Lewis H. Blair:* Genovese (1974), 357.
62 *Klaus, who studied:* Klaus and Kennell, 66.
62 *"mother-infant"*: ibid., 1–2.
63 *white male:* Blassingame, 168.
64 *"auction block"*: Jacobs, 15.
64 *Benjamin L. Hooks, Jr.:* NYT, December 8, 1988.
64 *Jamaica Kincaid:* Kincaid, 54–55.
65 *Jessie W. Parkhurst:* Parkhurst, 349–50.
65 *"Betsy Beagle"*: Wylly, 84.

3. Utopia, U.S.A.: The Nineteenth-Century Vision

67 *"Sectarian utopias"*: Martin, xi.
68 *"sat down to breakfast"*: Brooks, 251.
69 *"wearied of life"*: Bremer, 96–97.
70 *"brilliant talents"*: Cott (1972), 249.
70 *"example of the Shakers"*: Andrews, 130.
71 *"earth is [already] heaven"*: NYT, June 2, 1867.
71 *broadside summarized:* Morse, 93.
72 *Eldress Harriet Hubbard:* NYT, November 23, 1974.
72 *Holy Mother Wisdom:* Andrews and Andrews, 209.
73 *"All are carefully taught"*: Green and Wells, 67.
73 *"round we go"*: Diary of Seth T. Bradford, DC.
74 *Charles Dickens:* Sprigg, 65.
74 *Elizabeth Chandler:* NYPL, Shaker Manuscript Collection, Rare Books and Manuscripts Division, Astor, Lenox and Tilden Foundations.
74 Mother's Word to the Caretakers: ibid.
75 *"Always be lively"*: ibid.
75 *"small twigs"*: Andrews, 192.
75 *public humiliation:* "Mother's Word to Care-Takers," Manuscript, Hancock Shaker Village Library, Pittsfield, Massachusetts, 14.
75 *"to the light"*: Green and Wells, 290.
75 *Nicholas Briggs:* Briggs, 471.
77 *"growing crooked"*: Morse, 40.
77 *"must lie"*: Briggs, 471.
77 *"vice of masturbation"*: Kern, 453.
77 *Mother Ann:* NYPL, Shaker Manuscript Collection, Rare Books and Manuscript Division, Astor, Lenox and Tilden Foundations.
77 *Eleanor Fairs:* Typescript, Hancock Shaker Village Library, Pittsfield, Massachusetts.
78 *"institution rather than a home"*: Briggs, 27.
78 *including novels:* ibid., 63.
78 *"wishing to be a girl"*: ibid., 27.

79 *"In the school"*: Nordhoff, 194–95.

80 *"according to their age"*: Andrews and Andrews, 204–5.

80 *"Extreme peculiarity"*: Pritchett, 148–49.

80 *"wasn't I was unhappy"*: Eleanor Fairs, Typescript, Hancock Shaker Village Library, Pittsfield, Massachusetts.

80 *Luella Carpenter:* NYT, February 22, 1878.

81 *"death unto death"*: Andrews (1963), 129.

81 *Anna White:* NYPL, Shaker Manuscript Collection, Rare Books and Manuscript Division, Astor, Lenox and Tilden Foundations.

81 *"longed for death"*: Briggs, 2.

81 *"Church Family"*: ibid., 28.

81 *Sister Ada S. Cummings:* Collection of the United Society of Shakers, Sabbathday Lake, Maine.

83 *"dark and dirty hut"*: Furnas, 384.

83 *Elder Daniel Hawkins:* NYPL, Shaker Manuscript Collection, Rare Books and Manuscript Division, Astor, Lenox and Tilden Foundations.

84 *"good humor"*: ibid.

84 *"as children hippe"*: ibid.

84 *they ran ads:* Whitworth, 75.

84 *without discrimination:* Halloway, 78.

84 *colored Elder:* Nordhoff, 197.

85 *world as a house:* Hinds, 104–5.

85 *Joseph and Betty Stone:* Aurelia Mace Journal, Collection of the United Society of Shakers, Sabbathday Lake, Maine.

86 *"dutiful children"*: NYPL, Shaker Manuscript Collection, Rare Books and Manuscript Division, Astor, Lenox and Tilden Foundations.

86 *"great big hug"*: Briggs, 56–57.

86 *Eunice and James Chapman:* Blake, 359–78.

88 *"to take monkeys"*: Nordhoff, 211.

88 *"rotten apple"*: Eleanor Fairs Typescript, Hancock Shaker Village Library, Pittsfield, Massachusetts.

88 *"learn the art"*: Collection of the United Society of Shakers, Sabbathday Lake, Maine.

89 *"Morphene pills"*: Prudie A. Stickney and Ada S. Cummings History of the Children in the Church of West Gloucester, Manuscript, Collection of the United Society of Shakers, Sabbathday Lake, Maine.

89 *day began at 6:00:* Eleanor Fairs Typescript, Hancock Shaker Village Library, Pittsfield, Massachusetts.

91 *"influence of a power"*: Nordhoff, 233.

92 *Santa Claus:* Aurelia G. Mace Journal, Collection of the United Society of Shakers, Sabbathday Lake, Maine.

93 *"Social Architects"*: Morse, 92.

94 *John Humphrey Noyes was born:* Parker.

94 *"neither marry":* Matthew 23:30.

95 *to guide parents: Oneida Circular,* January 29, 1863.

96 *Grandparents: Oneida Circular,* May 2, 1864.

97 *193 children:* Dalsimer, 201.

97 *"Victorian exaggeration":* Noyes, 101.

98 *"fire and brimstone":* ibid., 105.

98 *"Biblically educated":* ibid., 107.

98 *fourteen months: Oneida Circular,* July 3, 1871.

99 *"sooner children learn": Oneida Circular,* June 23, 1873.

99 *ideas about diet:* Robertson, 326.

100 *new regimen: Oneida Circular,* November 10, 1873.

100 *"melodramatic scene":* Worden, 9.

100 *"hearing the commotion":* Dalsimer, 176.

100 *"passionate wails":* Kinsley, 16.

101 *death of the child:* Dalsimer, 180.

101 *"passing illness":* Kinsley, 24.

101 *"approved bounds":* Noyes, 32.

101 *"toys which she had":* ibid., 65.

101 *"missing the parental love":* ibid., 72.

101 *"for us individually":* ibid., 130.

102 *doll burning:* Worden, 80.

102 *"harder for a little child":* Nordhoff, 281.

103 *"individuality was much studied":* Kinsley, 20.

103 *"more to my mother":* Noyes, 70.

103 *did not even mention:* Dalsimer, 178.

103 *"no more proof":* Muncy, 178.

104 *mortality rate:* Robertson, 166–67.

104 *"shrewd insights":* Levine and Bunker, 54.

105 *"criticism as their medicine": Oneida Circular,* March 29, 1855.

105 *"indignation meeting": Oneida Circular,* February 7, 1870.

105 *"not going to be sick": Oneida Circular,* March 6, 1871.

105 *"criticism does away with": Oneida Circular,* March 16, 1874.

105 *"tattletale, hang him":* Noyes, 63.

106 *"mental chaos":* Kinsley, 30–31.

106 *building self-esteem: Oneida Circular,* March 19, 1857.

107 *hypothetical question:* Hinds, 121–22.

108 *obstetrician who visited:* Van de Warker, 787–809.

108 *"Women's dress":* Worden, 10.

109 *"vesture of the soul": Britannica,* 1964, 7:677.

109 *"deliverances":* Dalsimer, 291.

109 *"No consistent pattern":* Silverstein, 1027.

110 *"kibbutz group show":* Rabin and Beit-Hallami, 183.

110 *"scientific combination":* Whitworth, 128.

111 *George Bernard Shaw:* Parker, 253.
111 *experiment's existence:* Kern, 250.
111 *"fixed in the blood":* Oneida Circular, December 6, 1875.
111 *"improve humanity":* Eslake, 101.
111 *"moral superiority":* Noyes, 23.
112 *"become a curse":* Oneida Circular, June 8, 1874.
112 *"free love":* NYT, August 4, 1873.

4. The New Immigrants

115 *"toiled and suffered":* Rolvaag, xi.
115 *"walk on top":* Yetta Brier, CCNY.
115 *"indescribable in print":* Beard and Beard, 405.
116 *Tenement House Committee:* Riis (1900), 7.
116 *"This is the place":* Alland, 22.
116 *"One block":* New York Society for the Improvement of the Condition of the Poor, *Annual Report*, 1884, CSS.
116 *Dumbbell tenements:* Howe, 151.
116 *William Waldorf Astor:* ibid., 152.
116 *"seven in the bed":* New York Society for the Improvement of the Condition of the Poor, *Annual Report*, 1884, CSS.
116 *densely populated:* Riis (1890), 8.
117 *fearful the hard-won:* Rosenberg, 68.
117 *"Race suicide," commented:* ibid.
117 *"Mr. Dooley":* Abrams, 256–57.
118 *"get some money":* Abbott (1969), 78.
118 *"House of Have":* Huntington, 121–22.
119 *sewed overalls:* Campbell, H., 207.
120 *"will of God":* ibid., 202.
120 *"morning till night":* ibid., 203.
120 *movies every afternoon:* Smith, Judith E., 212.
120 *1887 study:* Campbell, H., 204–5.
121 *"this poison":* ibid., 206.
121 *"Home industry":* National Child Labor Committee, Leaflet No. 15, 1907, Box 40, LW.
121 *"nursing a dirty baby":* LH.
121 *"True Home Life":* Good Housekeeping, March 2, 1889, 196.
122 *"common scene":* LH.
122 *"I go to bed":* National Child Labor Committee, Pamphlet No. 239 (January 1915), 34, Box 40, LW.
122 *sixty healthy children:* Campbell, H., 207.
122 *Anna Kuthan:* CCNY.
123 *"great grandmother":* Abbott (1910), 323.

123 *"damned rather than born"*: Riis (1900), 7.

123 *"should help the family"*: Ewen, 98.

124 *"manifestation of love"*: Weinberg, 139.

124 *"career of idleness"*: Abbott (1910), 58–59.

124 *Rosa Peccaro: Thirteenth Annual Report, 1913-1914*, GH, 19.

125 *"Mother in shop"*: LH.

125 *"pleasant interval"*: Nasaw, 47.

126 *"pay her rent"*: LW, Box 41.

126 *"No fledgeling"*:LH.

127 *Mrs. William Astor*: Morris (1951), 146.

127 *"great and rich"*: Riis (1900), 6.

127 *"social phalanx"*: Riis (1892), 8.

127 *"to form an exception"*: de Tocqueville, 208–13.

128 *"older children must slave"*: Ewen, 87.

128 *"thoroughly dignified"*: ibid.

128 *"pigmy people"*: McHugh, 37.

129 *twelve hours a day*: Bremner (1970), vol. 1, 596.

129 *"children's labor"*: Abbott (1910), 350–51.

129 *Carding, roving*: ibid., 59n.

130 *"had a chance"*: McHugh, 67.

130 *night work*: Baxandall, Gordon, and Reverby, 160.

130 *smallpox scare*: ibid., 19.

131 *"creature of environment"*: Riis (1892), 8.

131 *"develop freely"*: Adler, 23.

131 *"Declaration of Independence"*: Pamphlet No. 65, 1908, National Child Labor Committee, Box 40, LW.

132 *"domestic nature"*: Commons et al., 281.

132 *position of power*: Ewen, 87.

133 *"From the first"*: Addams (1960), 109.

133 *"experimental effort"*: ibid., 13.

134 *"every scrap of yard"*: Hull-House Maps, 5.

134 *"endure social work"*: Baltzell, 160.

134 *"cultural invention"*: Borstelmann, 35.

135 *Shaw complained*: NYT, May 3, 1992.

135 *"adapt methods and matter"*: Lasch, 81.

136 *college women*: Ryan, 201.

136 *never married*: Davis, A., 29.

136 *"discovery of the self "*: Lasch, xxvi.

136 *"family group"*: Deegan, 48.

138 *"Noblest Mission"*: ibid., 232.

138 *model for her own life*: Davis, A., 266.

138 *"peasant habits"*: ibid., 65.

139 *"change it"*: Addams (1960), 12.

139 *caramel factory:* McCree, 112.

139 *"banish fear":* Polacheck, 52.

139 *"dangerous woman":* Davis, A., 266.

140 *"more unsatisfied":* Pinchot, 26.

141 *"working mothers":* Steinfels, 42.

141 *"baby Marcus":* McCree, 112.

141 *"let me out":* Tims, 142.

141 *crippled him:* Addams (1960b), 168.

141 *"to love me":* Davis, A., 6.

142 *single philanthropy:* Riis (1892), 182.

142 *"out of mischief":* Bremner (1970), vol. 1, 445–46.

142 *"precious material":* Addams (1960b), 174.

142 *"wretched delusion":* ibid., 173.

143 *"keeps them alive":* ibid., 169.

143 *"remarkably healthy": Hull-House Bulletin,* October 1896, JA.

143 *"syphilis":* Minutes of Mary Crane Conference, November 8, 1928, JA, Reel 51.

144 *"truly beloved": Hull-House Maps,* 224–25.

144 *"good looks":* Addams (1960b), 170.

144 *"purely economic":* ibid., 172.

144 *"both father and mother":* ibid., 172.

144 *blown off the roof:* ibid., 173–74.

145 *New York Day Nursery:* Steinfels, 45.

145 *"type of parents":* JA, Reel 51, 198.

145 *"noticeably softened":* ibid.

145 *chocolate pudding:* ibid.

145 *discredit the superstition:* Lasch, 198.

145 *"heart and interest":* JA, Reel 51.

146 *"swamp of bestiality":* Deegan, 297.

146 *Juvenile Protective Association:* Bowen, 7–8.

147 *Dr. Lee J. Frankel:* Steinfels, 51.

147 *Dr. Carolyn Hedger:* ibid., 56.

148 *"problem of the children":* Riis (1892), 181.

148 *number of kindergartens:* Rothman, D., 1990, 9.

148 *New York Kindergarten Association:* Polster, 42.

149 *"race problem":* Giddings, 100.

149 *"jail deliverer":* Riis (1892), 181.

149 *"to prevent it":* Ross, E., 21.

149 *Ethical Culture Society:* Friess, 64.

149 *truant officer:* Riis (1892), 181–82

149 *Ragamuffin Jim:* LW.

150 *"soap bubble":* Riis (1892), 174–75.

150 *Milton Bradley:* Shea, 108–10.

150 *Game of Life: Seventeen* magazine, June 1992, 27.

151 *"so does every immigrant"*: Hoffman, 209.

151 *"Italian wine"*: Lasch, 103.

151 *"gentle with them"*: Rothman, S., 102.

151 *In 1891 there were six:* Davis, A., 92.

152 *"love of service"*: Polacheck, 75.

152 *"go back on them"*: Addams (1910), 33.

152 *"five children"*: ibid.

153 *"neighbor took care of them"*: Zinsser, 98–99.

153 *"under one roof"*: Smith, Judith (1979), 399.

153 *"golden age"*: Gordon and McLanahan, 97–115.

154 *specialists in ethnicity:* Rotunno and McGoldrick, 343.

156 *Desertion Bureau:* Glanz, 62.

156 *"Worthy Editor"*: Berkow, 6–7.

157 *"intimate things"*: Covello, 272.

157 *"stay away from your relatives"*: Nelli, 135.

157 *"desired and valued"*: Gabaccia, 3

158 *"mother died"*: Smith, Judith (1979), 209.

158 *"close-knit domestic network"*: Mancuso, 316.

159 *warm certainty:* Johnson, 243.

159 *"never another mother"*: ibid., 40.

159 *"very close"*: Canteura, 95.

160 *"Dr. Spock"*: Johnson, 242.

160 *"cried during the interview"*: Strom, 214.

160 *school-age children:* Vecchio, 77.

161 *"write her own name"*: Krase, 257.

162 *ten extended black families:* Aschenbrenner, 28.

162 *"matrifocal black family"*: Furstenberg, 233.

164 *complete strangers:* Billingsley, 31.

164 *crusading newspaper reporter:* Wells, 10–18.

165 *"close female kinsmen"*: Stack, 83.

165 *"depend on"*: Hines and Boyd-Franklin, 91.

166 *"Do You Know Them?"*: Kuyk, 60.

166 *fourteen Southern cities:* Davis and Haller, 127.

166 *In Boston, too:* Holloran, 145.

167 *In 1900, a look:* Gordon and McLanahan, 104.

167 *Fanny Kemble's daughter:* Gutman, 304.

167 *"first child"*: ibid.

167 *"destructive conditions"*: Furstenberg, 232.

168 *"unfortunate condition"*: Sterling, 224–25.

168 *"conflict and disorganization"*: Campisi, 315.

168 *"first-generation family"*: Pecorini, 318.

169 *"Black family structure"*: Sterling, 145.

169 *"migrants, and nonmigrants"*: Gordon and McLanahan, 99.

169 *"support networks"*: Letter, NYT, January 16, 1993.

171 *Bridget Malone:* Gilje, 115.

171 *"my more than father":* Fischer, 76.

172 *"inducement for them to labor":* Bremner (1970), vol. 1, 642.

173 *Dickens approved:* ibid.

173 *New York State Senate:* ibid., 663.

174 *"best method":* Fink, 164.

174 *"State institutions":* Holloran, 15.

174 *"many temptations":* Girard (will), GC, 11.

175 *"begin with the child":* Tyson, 15.

176 *"Near the city":* Rupp, 68–69.

176 *"fatherless boys":* ibid., 100.

177 *Daniel Webster:* Herrick, 189

177 *John Quincy Adams:* ibid., 341–42.

178 *Early feminists:* Grossberg, 245.

178 *"two respectable male citizens":* Application, GC.

179 *pilloried and a sign:* Allan, 8.

179 *"loneliness of a boy":* Rupp, 100.

179 *Ernest Cunningham:* Cunningham, 134–36.

180 *cost three hundred dollars:* Herrick, 92.

180 *"silence at meals":* Cunningham, 142.

181 *ten-foot wall:* Girard (will), GC, 18.

181 *"discontent and truancy":* Herrick, 269.

181 *"strange sights of the dining room":* Cunningham, 142.

182 *"all the filial":* First Annual Report, GC, 9.

182 *Miss Jane Mitchell:* Rupp, 103.

182 *"best mother":* Huntington, 181n.

183 *astronomy, experimental philosophy:* Girard (will), GC, 20.

183 *"discipline of the institution":* Herrick, 42.

184 *Mother at Home:* Strickland, 37.

184 *"rewards for good conduct":* Twelfth Annual Report, GC, 9.

184 *"better outlook":* Rupp, 100–101.

184 *surveyed the graduates:* ibid., 181.

184 *"typical Girard product":* Beers, 40.

185 *"more like a family":* Herrick, 48.

185 *Anna H. Shotwell:* NYHS, *From Cherry Street*, 6.

187 *1,257 children:* Sappol, 4.

187 *Before the Civil War:* ibid., 16.

188 *"black seamen":* ibid., 18.

188 *single mothers:* ibid., 24.

188 *George Jemison:* ibid., 18.

189 *French ship foundered:* NYHS, Minutes, COA, June 8, 1855.

189 *Jacob Beckett's:* NYHS, Admissions, COA, n.p.

190 *Francis Martin:* ibid.

190 *discipline (as at Girard):* Sappol, 60.

190 *Mary Ann Lyons:* ibid., 26.

190 *John Tomata:* ibid., 13.

190 *"Ill health":* NYHS, *From Cherry Street*, 8.

191 *"extra provisions":* NYHS, *Report of the COA*, 1837, n.p.

191 *"superior to [those in] equivalent":* Sappol, 38.

191 *"rage of the mob":* Harper's Weekly, July 25, 1863, 38.

191 *troops:* MacPherson, 607–10.

191 *rescued and transferred:* Bremner (1980), 88.

191 *"exemplary institution":* Sappol, 38.

192 *Oberlin College:* Sappol, 38.

192 *W. E. B. Du Bois:* Mabee, 66.

192 *Josephine Satters:* Sappol, 33.

194 *"evil environment":* CAS, 1910.

194 *"offscouring from the poorest":* CAS (1945), 1–2.

194 *"good homes":* CAS, *Annual Report*, Appendix, 1864.

194 *"representations should be made":* ibid.

195 *"real home":* Clara Comstock, Report, 1911–1928, unpublished, CAS, 3.

195 *"gemmules":* Clark, 171.

195 *"God's Reformatory":* Jackson, 96.

196 *"three cheers":* CAS (1910), 12.

196 *down with the measles:* Langsam, 23.

197 *Maggie Dickenson:* CAS (1910), 17.

198 *"he had to do":* Crossroads (Orphan Train Heritage Society), January 1990, 2.

198 *Eliza Clements's:* ibid., November 1990, 9.

198 *"On my first trip":* Clara Comstock, Report, 1911–1928, unpublished CAS, 6.

199 *"the babies always called":* ibid., 2.

199 *"Home Sweet Home":* Crossroads, January 1990, 3.

199 *Noah Lawyer:* Jackson, 95.

199 *Sara Hunt:* Crossroads, January 1990, 12.

200 *"that Italian Boy":* CAS unpublished, 1878.

200 *"lonely in the world":* CAS unpublished, 1878.

200 *"wedding ring":* CAS unpublished, 1863.

200 *"would lick me":* CAS unpublished, 1878.

200 *"roving disposition":* CAS unpublished, 1878.

201 *its notable successes:* CAS (1910), 11.

201 *John G. Brady:* Fry, n.p.

201 *Andrew H. Burke:* CAS, unpublished, April 29, 1891.

201 *"respectable men and women":* CAS (1910), 12.

202 *"Human events":* Shengold, 320.

202 *three dolls:* Anthony, S., 389.

203 *"wished to return":* Clara Comstock Report, 1911–1928, unpublished, CAS.

203 *society's records:* Bellingham, 145.
203 *"begged for the return":* CAS (1910), 33.
203 *"great poverty":* ibid., 18.
203 *took in washing:* CAS, unpublished, 1878.
207 *Care of Destitute:* Langsam, 66.
208 *Henry W. Thurston:* ibid., 67.
208 *later social critic:* Hutchinson, 18.
208 New York Sun: Fry, n.p.
208 *"profoundly detrimental":* Goldfarb (1945), 30–31.
208 *"typical family experience":* ibid., 18.
209 *"demanded affection":* Goldfarb (1947), 251.
209 *Theodore Roosevelt:* CAS, unpublished, January 25 and 26, 1909.
209 *"pride of one generation":* Rothman, D. (1990), 17.

5. The Rich and Not So Rich Between the Wars

211 *"nothing natural":* Cookson and Persell, 23.
212 *"not dead, but selfish":* McLachlan, 3.
212 *rapid growth:* Baltzell, 22.
212 *costly enough:* McLachlan, 240.
213 *number of cities:* Cremin (1977), 93.
213 *more millionaires sat:* Baltzell, 110.
216 *"substantial merit":* "Twelve of the Best American Boarding Schools," 51.
216 *"decent, humane":* Hersey, 9.
216 *"sense of alliance":* ibid., 8.
216 *"gift of his example":* ibid., 9.
217 *"neckties will be worn":* Fuess, 50.
217 *"or what not, undesirable":* McLachlan, 214.
218 *softball game:* "Twelve of the Best," 49.
218 *Bo Goldman:* NYT, February 25, 1993.
218 *"the likes of them":* Dunne, 22.
218 *"vicious incidents":* Fuess, 50.
219 *"loss of autonomy":* Cookson and Persell, 19.
219 *"sinkers are silent":* Fuess, 45.
219 *"golden glow":* ibid., 49.
219 *one of the largest:* McLachlan, 3.
219 *"provide a remarkable education":* Fuess, 50.
220 *"depraved nature":* Kraushaar, 62.
220 *"and secret vice":* Hall, xiv.
221 *"metropolitan life":* ibid., 22.
221 *Von Fellenberg:* McLachlan, 60.
221 *Woodrow Wilson:* ibid., 3.
222 *commissioner of Indian affairs:* ibid., 241.
223 *more marriageable women:* Woody, vol. 2, 1.

223 *Catherine Beecher's:* Cremin (1980), 144.

224 *"destiny as a wife":* "Ten Fashionable Boarding Schools," 110.

224 *"does its worst":* Blair, 434.

224 *"haven and confidant":* ibid., 431.

224 *"despots":* ibid., 436.

226 *seven thousand pupils:* Woody, vol. 1, 330.

227 *president of Harvard:* Spinka, 85–86.

228 *"go to college":* Swasta and Krohn, 63.

228 *school spoke English:* ibid., 21.

228 *"mother's love":* MA, Catalogue, 1910–11, 12.

229 *"inspires it is encouraged":* ibid., 11.

229 *"rational creature":* Swasta, 3.

229 *"horses in their stalls":* Swasta, 63.

229 *"never left alone":* Recollections of Mrs. Harriet Gould Drake Tinkam, student, 1817, 1.

229 *"duty teacher":* MA, Catalogue 1910–11, 11–12.

230 *"most fashionable school":* Recollections of Mrs. Harriet Gould Drake Tinkam, student, 1817, 1.

230 *first symphony orchestra: Boston Evening Transcript* magazine, May 23, 1936.

230 *Great Spirit:* MA, Catalogue, 1910–11, 8.

231 *Tuition in 1925:* MA, Comparison of Rates, 1923–24, 25–26.

231 *In 1817: Philadelphia Inquirer,* May 2, 1936.

231 *seven elite boarding schools:* McLachlan, 216.

231 *Supervision was unbending:* MA, Catalogue, 1924–25, 39.

231 *"timid at night":* MA, Catalogue, 1910–11, 18.

232 *"sitting room":* Recollections of Mrs. Harriet Gould Drake Tinkam, student, 1817, 2.

232 *"use alarm clocks":* MA, Handbook, 1939, 3.

232 *"scrunching of the crumbs":* MA, *The Rocket,* 1938, 7.

233 *was shocked:* Pogrebin, 22.

233 *"loving sacrifice":* ibid.

234 *"preventorium":* Simpson, 53.

235 *convent in Seattle:* McCarthy, 92.

236 *her daughter Kathleen:* Hamilton, 92.

236 *looking up words:* McCarthy, 100.

236 *"heiresses of the Chevrolet":* ibid., 104.

237 *"Girls' Reformatory":* Trahey, 7.

238 *"one billiard table": Golden Jubilee Yearbook,* 1912–62, School of the Holy Child, Suffern, New York, 35.

238 *"corner pocket":* Chase, 12.

239 *"like a man": New York Herald Tribune,* April 19, 1914.

240 *"screamed bloody murder":* ibid.

240 *"Homesickness seems to me":* Chase, 10.

240 *"I implore you"*: IC, Letter, Series 1, Box 28,071, Folder 1.

240 *"girls have socks"*: IC, Letter, May 1916, Series 1, Box 28,071, Folder 1.

241 *"new dresses"*: IC, Letter, December 11, 1916, Series 1, Box 28,071, Folder 1.

241 *"should have known"*: Chase, 10.

243 *"perfect nanny"*: Plant, 12.

244 *"love and discipline"*: Gathorne-Hardy, 62.

245 *common courtesy:* ibid., 45.

245 *"princely classes"*: Fitzgerald, 38.

247 *Hyde Park:* Casson and Grenfell, 1.

247 *four baths:* Trager, 64.

247 *safety elevators:* ibid., 91.

248 *"Park Avenue"*: Fitzgerald and Fitzgerald.

249 *"good nursemaid"*: Sutherland, 93.

249 *"no formal training"*: Casson and Grenfell, 1.

250 *"child's first relationship"*: Scarr, 103.

251 *"different routes"*: Gathorne-Hardy, 143.

251 *"My contemporaries"*: Fitzgerald, NYT, September 18, 1933.

252 *"Becoming a mother"*: Milford, 86.

252 *Lillian Maddock:* Mellow, 202–3.

252 *"at the plage"*: ibid., 120.

253 *"child was unhappy"*: ibid., 143.

253 *"don't know them"*: NYT, September 18, 1933.

253 *"I was alone"*: Bergman and Burgess, 233.

253 *in the* Social Register: Goldsmith, 572.

254 *"mostly going out"*: Vanderbilt, n.p.

254 *inability to distinguish:* ibid., 7.

255 *"really goes away"*: Goldsmith, 594.

257 *"by a different nurse"*: Watson, 83.

257 *"rotate mothers"*: ibid., 84.

257 *"really hard to leave"*: Terkel (1975), 628.

258 *"they are friends"*: NYT, July 5, 1990.

258 *"devoted friend"*: Plant, 66.

259 *"beloved Nanny"*: NYT, November 14, 1990.

260 *Mary Poppins:* NYT, book review, August 27, 1989.

260 *"smother-love"*: Casson and Grenfell, 2.

260 *survey of magazine articles:* Davis, G., 135.

260 *"child's character"*: Watson, 70.

261 *"never be played with"*: Holt, 20.

261 *"first week of life"*: ibid., 119.

261 *Toilet training:* ibid., 183.

261 *"The less kissing"*: Davis, G., 135.

262 *Anna Eleanor:* Roosevelt, E., 60.

262 *"is facing failure"*: Watson, 11.

262 *"laboratory methods":* ibid., 13.
262 *"serious question":* ibid., 5–6.
263 *"everybody was leaving":* Bergman and Burgess, 224.
263 *Eleanor Roosevelt:* Roosevelt, E., 58.
263 *"charmed to have me":* Liebling, 42–43.
264 *"She became the weather":* Raines, 90.
266 *"Modern Manner":* CWLA, *Bulletin,* vol. 10, no. 2, February 1931.
267 *"talkin' about love":* Childress, 134.
267 *"in their food":* ibid., 133.
268 *"cultural transmission":* McConahay, 37.
268 *"precious gift":* Raines, 50.
268 *"thinking of Spanish":* McConahay, 23.
269 *"talk patchy":* ibid., 49.
269 Strange Fruit: Tucker, 17.
269 *"surrogate mother":* Rollins, 99–100.
270 *"go a long way":* Silverman, 330.
270 *"from the colored":* Tucker, 131.
270 *"live a treadmill life":* Katzman, 25.
271 *"around the premises":* ibid., 25.
271 *"on to work":* Tucker, 154.
271 *"strength of black women":* ibid., 108–9.
272 *"do for them":* ibid., 156.
272 *"making hardly anything":* ibid., 157.
272 *"miss my girls":* NYT, January 19, 1991.
272 *"know she's a maid":* Rollins, 104–5.
272 *"go I did":* Katzman, 10.
273 *"alone so much":* Rollins, 96.
273 *gravestone lists her name:* Tucker, 14.
273 *"polite lie":* Childress, 2–3.
274 *"front or back":* Katzman, 188.
274 *"an angel":* Liebling, 44.

6. Borrowed Mothers

275 *"social being":* U.S. Children's Bureau (1930), n.p.
275 *"nursing, keeping and relieving":* Bremner (1970), vol. 1, 58.
276 *first child-care institutions:* Slingerland, 27–29.
276 *In 1875:* Bernard, 14.
276 *"over the objection":* Steiner, 5.
277 *New York Foundling Hospital:* Letter, Hastings Hart, July 1, 1910, RS Series 3, Box 14, Folder 122.
277 *"both types of care":* Wolins and Piliavin, 8.
278 *"boarding-home project":* CAS (1910), 41.
278 *actually making them available:* Steiner, 6.

278 *"skimmed milk":* White House Conference, 1929–30, 18.
278 *animal shelter:* Terkel (1970), 387.
279 *"under par": Brooklyn Times Union,* July 29, 1933.
279 *filling and nutritious:* NYT, May 22, 1933.
279 *"Gold Spoon":* CWLA, *Bulletin,* February 1930, 4.
279 *Ray Lyman Wilbur: Brooklyn Eagle,* May 22, 1932.
280 *homeless women:* NYT, May 22, 1933.
280 *"absence of the wage":* White House Conference, 1929–30, 18.
280 *"for bread two meals":* McElvaine (1983), 57.
280 *"potential delinquent":* CAS, *Annual Report,* 1930, 31.
281 *boys as foster children:* State Charities Aid Association, *Annual Report,* 1933, LSRM, Series 3, Box 87, Folders 911–16.
281 *temporary care:* CAS, *Annual Report,* 1934, 41.
281 *"in fact so insulting":* Bremer, 56.
282 *"A hungry man":* NYT, May 13, 1932.
282 *" 'adequate' family":* Keniston, 457.
282 *pay for the layette:* ibid., 457.
282 *"plain HUNGER":* McElvaine, 181.
282 *"increasing steadily":* NYT, October 31, 1933.
283 *"would be abnormal":* Terkel (1970), 387.
283 *"part with her children":* CB (1936), 2.
283 *"population increased":* Pelton, ix.
283 *"direct cause":* CAN January, February, March 1932, CAS of Pennsylvania.
283 *1927 study:* CB (1927), 48.
284 *Adopt-A-Family:* NYT, April 20, 1933.
284 *Deloria:* NYT, April 20, 1933.
284 *"children's own homes:"* CWLA *Bulletin,* vol. 11, no. 5, June 1932, 6.
285 *eligibility was widened:* Pelton, 17.
285 *"not the child":* ibid., 10.
286 *"this kind of assistance":* White House Conference, 1940, 129–30.
286 *children of widows:* CB (1927), 48.
286 *"pay you back":* CAS, note, unpublished.
287 *Charlie Bertram:* CAS (1929), 7.
287 *"American family life":* "What Are Foster Parents?" CAS (n.d.), 2–4.
288 *"empirical knowledge":* Maluccio (1973), 13.
288 *"moral influence":* Wolins, 14.
288 *"reasonably good mother":* CB (1936), 2.
289 *needs of black children:* Slingerland (1915), 40.
289 *beginning to serve:* CAS, *Eighty-eighth Annual Report,* 1940, 17.
289 *"foster home finders":* CWLA, *Bulletin,* vol. 11, no. 4, May 1932, 2.
290 *"under such circumstances":* Dudley, 159
290 *North Carolina girls:* Whitt, 30.
290 *"reasons of poverty":* White House Conference, 1909.
290 *"try to finance it":* CWLA, *Bulletin,* May 1932, 4.

290 *family of five:* White House Conference, 1929–30, 18.

290 *wage homes:* CAN, CAS of Pennsylvania, January, February, March 1930, 4.

291 *"said of own parents":* CWLA, *Bulletin*, vol. 9, no. 4, April 1930, 4.

291 *"faults vanished":* CB (1936), n.p.

291 *"three classes":* CAS (1929), 5.

292 *"with contempt":* Slingerland (1915), 41.

293 *poignant appeal:* CB (1936), 4.

293 *"The fine art":* ibid.

293 *organized by Macy's:* Leach, 232.

293 *deserved an allowance:* CAS, *Foster Parents' Manual*, 5.

294 *"Big Brown Bag":* CWLA, *Bulletin*, vol. 9, no. 8, October 1930, 2.

294 *in the long run: How Foster Children Turn Out*, 15.

295 *"better man":* CAN, CAS of Pennsylvania, May, June 1934, 7

295 *roundtable discussion:* CWLA, *Bulletin*, January 1931, 2.

296 *What Is Malnutrition?:* CWLA, *Bulletin*, May 1930, 2.

296 *"Sometimes parents":* CAN, CASP, April, May, June 1930, 5.

296 *"her own reward":* CWLA, *Bulletin*, May 1930, 2.

297 *"payments on the home":* White House Conference, 1930, 18.

297 *impersonal agency:* CWLA, *Bulletin*, July 1934, 5.

298 *"failure to visit":* McAdams, 309.

298 *"legs became numb":* Whitt, 32.

298 *photographing the children:* CWLA, *Bulletin*, October 1930.

299 *deeply depressed:* McAdams, 309.

299 *"child's worth":* ibid., 311.

300 *"love and respect":* Whitt, 173.

300 *"hard time":* Malcolm X, 23.

300 *"come to see him":* CAN, CASP, May, June 1934.

300 *"was my revenge":* Wexler, 175.

300 *"rejection and abuse":* NYT, October 14, 1992.

301 *painful loss:* Kates et al., 587.

301 *"bad for sprouts":* Slingerland (1919), 121.

302 *"take you away":* CAN, CASP, January, February 1933, 5.

302 *"free to feel":* CAN, CASP, April, May, June 1930.

302 *"care so much":* ibid.

302 *"do you love me?":* Wexler, 22.

303 *study done in 1922:* SRM Homer Folks to Arthur Woods, January 19, 1923, Folder 912, Box 87, Series 3.

303 *"overcome deprivation":* Columbia University Alumni Newsletter, Spring/Summer 1991, 6.

303 *Dr. Warner Bridger: Harvard Mental Health Letter*, August 1991, 4.

303 *Jules R. Bemporad: Harvard Mental Health Letter*, September 1991, 5.

304 *"to forgive and to forget":* U.S. Congress, Hearing (1975), 9.

304 *broken homes:* CB (1927), 48.

306 *parental rights:* ibid.
306 *"preserve and support":* U.S. Congress, Hearing (1975), 41.

7. Rosie the Riveter and Her Sisters

307 *"welfare of children":* NYT, March 1, 1946.
307 *One and a half million women:* Chafe, 135.
308 *chained to trailers:* U.S. Congress, Hearing (1943), 95.
308 *"waiting out on the streets":* Lingeman, 86.
308 *2 million youngsters:* Chafe, 162.
308 *52 million dollars:* Mintz and Kellogg, 163.
309 *segregated centers:* U.S. Congress, Hearing (1943), 74.
309 *relief rolls:* Pope, 105.
310 *children of working Negro mothers:* "Federal Programs for Children of Working Mothers," 5.
311 *"idealized myth":* Silverstein, 1025.
311 *percentage of women working:* Chafe, 135.
311 *same money for the same job:* ibid., 158.
312 *"voices have been raised":* NYT, October 15, 1944.
312 *1.6 million children:* Bradbury, 61.
312 *six hundred thousand different children:* Baxandall, Gordon, and Reverby, 295.
312 *children needing care:* Chafe, 170.
313 *"first responsibility":* Bradbury, 60.
313 *Catholic groups:* U.S. Congress, Hearing (1943), 81.
313 *"what time she has":* ibid., 45.
313 *The highest usage:* U.S. Department of Labor (1946), 22.
314 *preferred relatives:* Chafe, 164.
314 *"Spartans binding":* Anderson, 133.
314 *"socially undesirable":* California State Department of Education (1945), 1.
314 *"post-war America":* U.S. Congress, Hearing, (1943), 54–55.
314 *Studies of 500 California children:* Koshuk, 148.
315 *In Detroit:* U.S. Congress, Hearing (1943), 7.
315 *"best thing":* Anderson, 145.
315 *"all the things they're learning":* Koshuk, 14.
315 *"only child":* Harris, Mitchell, and Schecter, 133.
316 *Detroit in 1943:* U.S. Congress, Hearing (1943), 7.
316 *Jacksonville, Florida:* ibid., 25.
316 *clerical workers earning:* ibid., 91.
316 *uniform fee in 1943:* California State Department of Education (1945), 17.
316 *drop in worry:* Koshuk, 139.
317 *sole wage earners:* NYT, January 1, 1946.
317 *"no justification":* Freud (1974), xxi.
317 *"provide funds for it":* NYT, May 1, 1944.

317 *allowance for the support:* U.S. Congress, Hearing (1943), 106.

317 *high infant mortality:* NYT, March 8, 1944.

318 *"classic example":* Anderson, 139.

318 *develop foster homes:* U.S. Congress, Hearing (1943), 32.

318 *individualized day care:* ibid., 91–92.

318 *Chicago Orphan Asylum:* McCausland, 151.

319 *Robert Owen:* Potter, 149.

320 *New York school:* ibid., 150.

320 *"regard of the benevolent":* ibid.

320 *Bronson Alcott:* Palmer and Andersen, 433.

320 *"of the indigent?":* Kaestle and Vinovkis, 54.

321 *"good idea to teach him":* ibid., 60.

321 *"without producing fruit":* ibid., 59.

322 *Troy, New York:* Beer, 35.

322 *175 child-care centers:* Kadushin and Martin, 338.

322 *school days lasting:* Fein and Clarke-Stewart, 18.

322 *"unceremoniously united":* Koshuk, 134–47.

323 *"part of a nurse":* Kaestle and Vinovkis, 60.

323 *"trundle-bed trash":* Clifford, 17.

323 *"are annoyed":* ibid., 65.

323 *"philanthropic breast":* New York World, June 24, 1867.

324 *length of the school year:* Potter, 331.

324 *"state intervention":* Kaestle and Vinovkis, 45.

324 *"conflict gangs":* Mintz and Kellogg, 165.

325 *Newspaper editorials:* Campbell, D., 20.

325 *Dr. Edward A. Strecker:* ibid., 164.

325 *extended-care centers:* California State Department of Education, 11.

327 *In Texarkana:* Flater, 7–11.

327 *Jackson, Mississippi:* "Federal Programs," 4–5.

327 *"no real provision":* U.S. Department of Labor (1946), 22.

327 *Paul McNutt:* Zucker (1944), 169.

327 *"daily minder":* CWLA, *Bulletin*, October 1943.

328 *Gale Manor Apartments:* Pope, 24.

328 *higher absentee rate:* Chafe, 159.

328 *San Diego project:* U.S. Congress, Hearings (1943), 95.

329 *Kaiser shipyard's:* Chafe, 162–63.

329 *"minding babies":* Fisher, 90.

330 *"threat to the home":* NYT, October 11, 1943.

330 *Mirra Komarovsky:* NYT, March 29, 1944.

330 *Fortune magazine poll:* Chafe, 178.

331 *"alarm, already expressed":* Zucker (1944), 49.

331 *almost doubled:* Vanek, 503.

331 *Dr. Leo Kanner:* Anthony, S., 126.

332 *"unbroken continuity":* Freud (1974), xx.

333 *More than 80 percent:* Koshuk, 138.

333 *As for fathers:* ibid., 139.

333 *"importance of maternity":* Mead, 477.

334 *"service to children":* Owen, 20.

334 *long-range planning:* NYT, September 17, 1945.

334 *"lives of their children":* California State Department of Education, 23.

335 *"new generation of women":* Harris, Mitchell, and Schecter, 133.

335 *Margaret Culkin Banning:* Morris (1947).

8. Child Care Revisited

336 *"national Alzheimer's":* NYT, May 4, 1992.

337 *"We need orphanages":* Washington Post, October 29, 1989.

337 *"small-scale caring institutions":* Chicago Tribune, April 22, 1990.

337 *E. Kent Hauser:* Gannett News Service, June 15, 1989.

338 *"permanent gain":* Mencken, 292–93.

338 *"aren't the answer":* NYT, November 17, 1988.

338 *Children's Institute International:* Gannett News Service, June 14, 1990.

339 *"nothing but good":* Forer, 19.

339 *Milton Hershey School:* Cohen, 31–34.

341 *"to take care of the children":* Sheehan, 79.

341 *kinship homes:* NYT, December 16, 1990.

341 *3 million grandparents:* National Association of Social Workers News, March 1992, 5.

341 *Richard Stolley:* Larson, 11.

342 *Mount Loretto:* NYT, November 22, 1992.

342 *"good mother who made":* Bergen Record, October 28, 1990.

343 *St. Joseph's:* NYT, February 26, 1989.

343 *paid leave:* NYT, March 20, 1989.

343 *send a caretaker:* NYT, September 7, 1989.

344 *Campbell Soup:* NYT, March 16, 1989.

344 *"children under 12":* NYT, June 19, 1989.

344 *Called cohousing:* U.S. News & World Report, April 6, 1992, 82.

344 *Charlotte Perkins Gilman:* Chafe, 9.

344 *Jacob Riis's:* Alland, 37.

344 *"needs to be special":* NYT, November 17, 1988.

344 *"fewer prisons":* Riis (1892), 181.

345 *"change the way we are":* NYT, August 13, 1989.

345 *"facilities caring for animals":* Boston Globe, November 18, 1990.

345 *"in one place":* NYT, April 12, 1994.

345 *"trust the schools":* Shell, 51.

346 *Childhood Education:* NYT, March 26, 1946.

346 *pilot project:* NYT, October 4, 1990.

346 *care for more infants:* NYT, January 19, 1990.

346 *Anna Quindlen:* NYT, July 8, 1990.

347 *13 million poor children:* NYT, July 23, 1993.

347 *thirteen hundred programs: Time* magazine, March 8, 1993, 43.

347 *"most successful":* NYT, April 18, 1993.

347 *estimates that 50 percent:* ibid.

347 *long-term effects:* NYT, July 23, 1993.

348 *"aren't rich enough":* Shell, 50.

348 *Government support is seen:* Polstrel, 27.

348 *Clinton was chairman:* NYT, April 7, 1990.

349 *"In China, nurseries":* Polstrel, 27.

349 *Child Care Development Block Grant:* NYT, October 7, 1992.

350 *only 3 percent:* NYT, January 28, 1993.

350 *Karen DeCrow:* NYT, February 26, 1993.

351 *"disguises exploitation":* NYT, September 16, 1993.

351 *"presumption of perversion":* NYT, August 5, 1990.

351 *au pair system:* NYT, January 28, 1993.

352 *"firm, clear leadership":* NYT, March 5, 1992.

352 *"pay other people":* Spock, 570.

353 *"nonmaternal care":* Etaugh, 313.

353 *University of Virginia: Washington Post* Health, March 6, 1990, 15.

354 *"stable substitute":* Etaugh, 311.

355 *"contradictory conclusion":* Belsky and Rovine, 157.

355 *"enough studies":* Brazelton, 15.

355 *Penelope Leach:* Leach, 13.

356 *"prevailing values":* Maluccio, 13.

BIBLIOGRAPHY

Abbott, Edith. *Historical Aspects of the Immigration Problem: Select Documents.* New York: Arno, 1969.

————. *Women in Industry: A Study in American Economic History.* 1910. Reprint. New York: Arno, 1969.

Abrams, Richard M., ed., *The Issues of the Populist and Progressive Eras, 1892–1912.* Columbia: University of South Carolina Press, 1970.

Addams, Jane. *Jane Addams: A Centennial Reader.* New York: Macmillan, 1960a.

————. *Spirit of Youth and the City Streets.* New York: Macmillan, 1910.

————. *The Subjective Value of the Settlement.* New Haven: Research Publications, 1977. Text-fiche.

————. *Twenty Years at Hull-House: With Autobiographical Notes.* New York: Macmillan, 1960b.

————, ed. *Philanthropy and Social Progress: Seven Essays.* New York: Thomas Y. Crowell, 1893.

Adler, Felix. *American Civilization.* National Child Labor Committee Pamphlet No. 70, 1908.

Admissions and Short Histories of the Association for the Benefit of Colored Orphans 1837–1867. Colored Orphan Society Papers, 1836–1936. The New-York Historical Society.

Allan, George A. T. *Christ's Hospital.* London: Blackie and Son, 1937.

Alland, Alexander, Sr. *Jacob A. Riis Photographer and Citizen.* Millerton, N.Y.: Aperture, 1974.

Anderson, Karen. *Wartime Women: Sex Roles, Family Relations and the Status of Women During World War II.* Westport, Conn.: Greenwood Press, 1981.

Andrews, Edward Deming. *The People Called Shakers: A Search for the Perfect Society.* New York: Dover Publications, 1963.

Andrews, Edward Deming, and Faith Andrews. "Shaker Children's Order." *Winterthur Portfolio* 8, Winterthur, Del. Henry Francis du Pont Winterthur Museum. 1973.

Anthony, E. James. "The Vulnerable Child in Retrospect." In Anthony, E. James, Cyrille Douropernik, and Collette Chiland, *The Child in His Family: Vulnerable Children. Yearbook of the International Association for Child Psychiatry and Allied Professions,* vol. 4. New York: John Wiley and Sons, 1978.

Anthony, Susan Brownell. *Out of the Kitchen—Into the War: Women's Winning Role in the Nation's Drama.* New York: S. Daye, 1943.

Aschenbrenner, Joyce. *Lifelines: Black Families in Chicago.* New York: Holt, Rinehart and Winston, 1975.

Bailyn, Bernard. *Education in the Forming of American Society: Needs and Opportunity for Study.* Chapel Hill: University of North Carolina Press, 1960.

Baltzell, E. Digby. *The Protestant Establishment: Aristocracy and Caste in America.* New Haven: Yale University Press, 1964.

Bane, Mary Jo. *American Families in the Twentieth Century.* New York: Basic Books/Harper Colophon Books, 1976.

Baxandall, Rosalyn, Linda Gordon, and Susan Reverby, eds. *America's Working Women.* New York: Random House, 1976.

Beard, Charles A., and Mary R. Beard. *A Basic History of the United States.* New York: The New Home Library, 1944.

Bedell, Madelon. *The Alcotts: Biography of a Family.* New York: C. N. Potter, 1980.

Beer, Ethel S. *Working Mothers and the Day Nursery.* New York: Whiteside and Morrow, 1957.

Beers, Paul. "Stephen Girard's College—Home and Hope for Generations of 'Orphans.' " *Pennsylvania Magazine,* June 1989.

Bellingham, Bruce. "Waifs and Strays." In *The Uses of Charity,* Peter Mandler, ed. Philadelphia: University of Pennsylvania Press, 1990.

Belsky, Jay, and Michael J. Rovine. "Nonmaternal Care in the First Year of Life and the Security of Infant-Parent Attachment." *Child Development* 59 (1988).

Ben-Or, Joseph. "The Law of Adoption in the United States: Its Massachusetts Origins and the Statute of 1851." *New England Historical and Genealogical Register* 130 (October 1976).

Bergman, Ingrid, and Alan Burgess. *Ingrid Bergman, My Story.* New York: Delacorte Press, 1980.

Berkow, Ira. *Maxwell Street: Survival in a Bazaar.* Garden City, N.Y.: Doubleday, 1977.

Bernard, Jacqueline. *The Children You Gave Us.* New York: Jewish Child Care Association of New York, 1973.

Billingsley, Andrew. *Climbing Jacob's Ladder: The Enduring Legacy of African American Families.* New York: Simon & Schuster, 1992.

Blackford, L. Minor. *The Story of a Virginia Lady.* Cambridge: Harvard University Press, 1954.

Blair, Emily Newell. "Why I Sent My Children Away to School." *Harper's,* March 1926.

Blake, Nelson M. "Eunice Against the Shakers." *New York History* 41, no. 4 (October 1960).

Blassingame, John W. *The Slave Community: Plantation Life in the Antebellum*

South. New York: Oxford University Press, 1972.

Bogen, Hyman. *The Luckiest Orphans: A History of the Hebrew Orphan Asylum of New York.* Urbana: University of Illinois Press, 1992.

Borstelmann, Lloyd J. "Children before Psychology: Ideas about Children from Antiquity to the Late 1800's." In *Handbook of Child Psychology,* vol. 1, Paul H. Musser and William Kessen, eds. New York: John Wiley & Sons, 1983.

Boswell, John. *The Kindness of Strangers: The Abandonment of Children in Western Europe from Late Antiquity to the Renaissance.* New York: Pantheon, 1989.

Botkin, B. A., ed. *Lay My Burden Down: A Folk History of Slavery.* Chicago: Phoenix Books, University of Chicago Press, 1945.

Bowen, de Koven Louise. *Fighting to Make Chicago Safe for Children.* Chicago: Juvenile Protective Association of Chicago, 1920.

Bowlby, John. *Maternal Care and Mental Health,* 2d ed. Geneva: World Health Organization, 1952.

Boyer, Paul. *Urban Masses and Moral Order in America, 1820–1920.* Cambridge: Harvard University Press, 1978.

Bradbury, Dorothy E. Five *Decades of Action for Children: A History of the Children's Bureau,* rev. ed., Publication 358. Washington, D.C.: GPO, 1962.

Brazelton, T. Berry. "Issues for Working Parents." *American Journal of Orthopsychiatry* 56, no. 1 (January 1986).

Bremer, William W. *Depression Winters: New York Social Workers and the New Deal.* Philadelphia: Temple University Press, 1984.

Bremner, Robert H. *The Public Good: Philanthropy and Welfare in the Civil War Era.* New York: Alfred A. Knopf, 1980.

———, ed. *Children and Youth in America: A Documentary History,* 3 vols., Cambridge: Harvard University Press, 1970.

Bridenbaugh, Carl. *The Colonial Craftsman.* New York: New York University Press, 1950.

Briggs, Nicholas. "Forty Years a Shaker." In *The Granite Monthly,* January 1921.

Brooks, Van Wyck. *The Flowering of New England.* New York: E. P. Dutton, 1937.

Burnett, Lerone, Jr. *Before the Mayflower: A History of Black America.* New York: Penguin Books, 1984.

Butler, Samuel. *Erewhon.* New York: E. P. Dutton, Everyman's Library. 1969.

Calhoun, Arthur W. *A Social History of the American Family from Colonial Times to the Present,* vol 1. Cleveland: Arthur H. Clark, 1917.

California State Department of Education, Child Care by California School Districts. Sacramento: California State Department of Education, December 1945.

Campbell, D'Ann. *Women at War with America: Private Lives in a Patriotic Era.* Cambridge: Harvard University Press, 1984.

Campbell, Helen. *Prisoners of Poverty: Women Wage-Earners, Their Trades and Their Lives.* Westport, Conn.: Greenwood Press, 1970. Boston: Roberts Brothers, 1887.

Campisi, Paul J. "Ethnic Family Patterns: The Italian Family in the United States." In *The Italians: Social Backgrounds of an American Group,* Francesco Cordasco and Eugene Bucchioni, eds. Clifton, N.J.: A. M. Kelley, 1974.

Canteura, Linda Graudi. *Growing Up Italian.* New York: William Morrow, 1987.

Carden, Maren Lockwood. *Oneida: Utopian Community to Modern Corporation.* Baltimore: Johns Hopkins Press, 1969.

Caroli, Betty Boyd, ed. *The Italian Immigrant Woman in North America.* Toronto: Multicultural History Society of Ontario, 1978.

Carr, Lois Green, and Lorena S. Walsh. "The Planter's Wife." In *A Heritage of Her Own: Toward a New Social History of American Women,* Nancy Cott and Elizabeth H. Pleck, eds. New York: Simon & Schuster, 1979.

Casson, Hugh Maxwell, Sir, and Joyce Grenfell, eds. *Nanny Says: As Recalled by Sir Hugh Casson and Joyce Grenfell.* Diana, Lady Avery, ed. London: Dennis Dobson, 1972.

Cath, Stanley H., et al., eds. *Father and Child: Developmental and Clinical Perspectives.* Boston: Little, Brown, 1982.

Chafe, William H. *The American Woman: Her Changing Social, Economic and Political Roles, 1920–1970.* New York: Oxford University Press, 1972.

Chase, Ilka. *Past Imperfect.* Garden City, N.Y.: Doubleday Doran, 1942.

Children's Aid News. Children's Aid Society of Pennsylvania.

Children's Aid Society of New York. *Crusade for Children: Its Placing Out System and Its Results* (1910).

———. *Mending Broken Homes* (1929).

———. *The Society of Firsts* (1945).

———. *What Are Foster Parents?* (n.d.).

Childress, Alice. *Like One of the Family: Conversations from a Domestic's Life.* Brooklyn: Independence Publishers, 1956. Boston: Beacon Press, 1986.

Child Welfare League of America Bulletin. Child Welfare League of New York, 1930–1946.

Clark, Ronald W. *The Survival of Charles Darwin.* New York: Random House, 1984.

Clarkson, Matthew. *An Address to the Citizens of Philadelphia.* Philadelphia: Ormrod and Conrad, 1795. Text-fiche.

Clifford, Geraldine Jonçich. "Home and School in 19th Century America: Some Personal-History Reports from the United States." *History of Education Quarterly* 7, no. 3 (Spring 1978).

Cohen, Mark. "Uncle Miltie's Lost Kids." *New York Times Magazine*, August 1, 1993.

Columbia University Alumni Newsletter. Spring/Summer 1991.

Commons, John, et al., ed. *Documentary History of American Industrial Society.* 1910–1911. Reprint. New York: AMS Press, 1988.

Cookson, Peter W., Jr., and Caroline Hodges Persell. *Preparing for Power: America's Elite Boarding Schools.* New York: Basic Books, 1985.

Cott, Nancy F. "Eighteenth Century Family and Social Life Revealed in Massachusetts Divorce Records." In *A Heritage of Her Own: Toward a New Social History of American Women*, Nancy Cott and Elizabeth H. Pleck, eds. New York: Simon & Schuster, 1979.

————, ed. *Root of Bitterness: Documents of the Social History of American Women.* New York: E. P. Dutton, 1972.

Covello, Leonard. "Autobiography." In *The Italians: Social Backgrounds of an American Group*, Francesco Cordasco and Eugene Bussioni, eds. Clifton, N.J.: Augustus M. Kelley, 1974.

Cremin, Lawrence. *Traditions in American Education.* New York: Basic Books, 1977.

————. *American Education: The National Experience.* New York: Harper & Row, 1980.

Cunningham, Ernest. *Memories of Girard College.* Philadelphia: Girard College, 1942.

Dalsimer, Marilyn Haltzell. "Women and Family in the Oneida Community, 1837–1881." Ph.D. diss., New York University, 1975.

Davis, Allen F. *American Heroine: The Life and Legend of Jane Addams.* New York: Oxford University Press, 1973.

Davis, Allen F., and Mark H. Haller, eds. *The People of Philadelphia: A History of Ethnic Groups and Lower-Class Life.* Philadelphia: Temple University Press, 1973.

Davis, Glenn. *Childhood and History in America.* New York: The Psychohistory Press, 1976.

Deegan, Mary Jo. *Jane Addams and the Men of the Chicago School, 1892–1918.* New Brunswick, N.J.: Transaction Books, 1988.

deMause, Lloyd, ed. *The History of Childhood.* New York: The Psychohistory Press, 1974.

Demos, John. "The Changing Faces of Fatherhood: A New Exploration in American Family History." In *Father and Child: Developmental and Clinical Perspectives*, Stanley H. Cath et al., eds. Boston: Little, Brown, 1982.

————. "Children in the New England Family." In *Turning Points: Historical and Sociological Essays on the Family*, John Demos and Sarane Spence Boocock, eds. Chicago: University of Chicago Press, 1978.

————. *A Little Commonwealth: Family Life in Plymouth Colony.* New York: Oxford University Press, 1970.

Dickens, Charles. *American Notes for General Circulation*. New York: Fawcett, 1961.

"Do You Know Him?" *Negro History Bulletin* 42, no. 3 (July, August, September 1979).

Dreiser, Theodore. *The Color of a Great City*. New York: Boni and Liveright, 1923.

Du Bois, Cora. *The People of Alor: A Social-Psychological Study of an East Indian Island*. Minneapolis: University of Minnesota Press, 1944.

Dudley, Virginia. "Foster Mothers: Successful and Unsuccessful." *Smith College Studies in Social Work* 3 (December 1932).

Dunne, John Gregory. "The Death of a Yale Man." *New York Review of Books*, April 22, 1993.

Earle, Alice Morse. *Child Life in Colonial Days*. Williamstown, Mass.: Corner House Publishers, 1984.

Ernst, Robert. *Immigrant Life in New York City, 1825–1863*. New York: King's Crown Press, Columbia University Press, 1949.

Eslake, Allan. *The Oneida Community: A Record of an Attempt to Carry Out the Principles of Christian Unselfishness and Scientific Race Improvement*. London: George Redway, 1900.

Etaugh, Claire. "Effects of Non-Maternal Care on Children." *American Psychologist* 35 (1980).

Ewen, Elizabeth. *Immigrant Women in the Land of the Dollar: Life and Culture on the Lower East Side, 1890–1925*. New York: Monthly Review Press, 1985.

"Father's Gift to His Son on His Becoming an Apprentice, A." New York: Samuel Wood and Sons, 1821. Quoted in Ian M.G. Quimby, *Apprenticeship in Colonial Philadelphia*. New York: Garland Press, 1985.

"Federal Programs for Children of Working Mothers as They May be Related to Negro Women and Children in Local Communities," unpublished. Washington, D.C., Bethune Museum and Archive.

Fein, Greta, and Alison Clarke-Stewart. *Day Care in Context*. New York: John Wiley & Sons, 1973.

Fink, Arthur E. *The Field of Social Work*. New York: Henry Holt, 1949.

Fischer, Christiane, ed. *Let Them Speak for Themselves: Women in the American West 1849–1900*. Hamden, Conn.: Archon Books, 1977.

Fisher, Austin M. "Absenteeism Can Be Licked." *Saturday Evening Post*, May 22, 1943.

Fitzgerald, F. Scott. *Tender Is the Night*. New York: Bantam Books, 1951.

Fitzgerald, Zelda, and F. Scott Fitzgerald. "The Changing Beauty of Park Avenue." *Harper's Bazaar*, January 1928.

Flater, Ruth Louise. "Day Care of Children of Working Mothers." *Child Welfare League of America Bulletin*, October 1943.

Forer, Lois G. "Bring Back the Orphanage: An Answer for Today's Abused Children." *The Washington Post Monthly*, April 1988.

Fox-Genovese, Elizabeth. *Within The Plantation Household: Black and White Women of the Old South.* Chapel Hill: University of North Carolina Press, 1988.

Franklin, Benjamin. *The Autobiography of Benjamin Franklin and Other Writings.* New York: New American Library, 1961.

Freud, Anna. "Families and Reports on the Hampstead Nurseries." In *The International Psycho-Analytical Library,* no. 96, M. Masud R. Khan, ed. London: Hogarth Press, 1974.

Freud, Anna, in collaboration with Dorothy Burlingham. *Infants Without Families: The Case for and Against Residential Nurseries.* New York: International University Press, 1944.

Freud, Anna, and Dorothy T. Burlingham. *War and Children.* New York: Medical War Books, 1943.

Friess, Horace. *Felix Adler and Ethical Culture.* New York: Columbia University Press, 1981.

From Cherry Street to Green Pastures: A History of the Colored Orphan Asylum at Riverdale-on-Hudson, New York. Colored Orphan Asylum Papers, 1836–1936. The New-York Historical Society.

Fry, Annette Riley. "The Children's Migration." *American Heritage,* December 1974.

Fuess, Claude M. *In My Time: A Medley of Andover Reminiscences.* Andover, Mass.: Phillips Academy, 1959.

Furnas, J. C. *The Americans: A Social History of the United States, 1587–1914.* New York: G. P. Putnam's Sons, 1969.

Furstenberg, Frank F., Jr. "The Origins of the Female-Headed Black Family: The Impact of the Urban Experience." In *Philadelphia: Work, Space, Family and Group Experience in the Nineteenth Century. Essays Toward an Interdisciplinary History of the City,* Theodore Hershberg, ed. New York: Oxford University Press, 1981.

Gabaccia, Donna R. *From Sicily to Elizabeth Street: Housing and Social Change Among Italian Immigrants, 1880–1930.* Albany: State University of New York Press, 1984.

Garrison, Wendell Phillips. *William Lloyd Garrison: The Story of His Life Told by His Children, 1805–1879.* 4 vols. New York: Century, 1885.

Gathorne-Hardy, Jonathan. *The Unnatural History of the Nanny.* New York: Dial Press, 1973.

Genovese, Eugene D. "Life in the Big House." In *A Heritage of Her Own: Toward a New Social History of American Women,* Nancy F. Cott and Elizabeth H. Pleck, eds. New York: Simon & Schuster, 1979.

———. *Roll, Jordan Roll: The World the Slaves Made.* New York: Pantheon Books, 1974.

"Getting Smart about Head Start." *Time* magazine, March 8, 1993.

Giddings, Paula. *When and Where I Enter.* New York: William Morrow, 1984.

Gilje, Paul A. "Infant Abandonment in Early Nineteenth-Century New

York." In *Growing Up in America: Children in Historical Perspective*, N. Ray Hiner and Joseph M. Hawes, eds. Chicago: University of Illinois Press, 1985.

Gilligan, Carol. *In a Different Voice: Psychological Theory and Women's Development*. Cambridge: Harvard University Press, 1982.

Glanz, Rudolf. *The Jewish Woman in America: Two Female Immigrant Generations*. New York: KTAV Publishing House, 1976.

Glazer, Nathan, and Daniel Patrick Moynihan. *Beyond the Melting Pot: The Negroes, Puerto Ricans, Jews, Italians and Irish of New York City*. Cambridge: MIT Press, 1963.

Goldfarb, William. "The Effects of Psychological Deprivation in Infancy and Subsequent Stimulation." *American Journal of Psychiatry*, July 1945.

———. "Variations in Adolescent Adjustment of Institutionally Reared Children." *American Journal of Orthopsychiatry*, June 1947.

Goldsmith, Barbara. *Little Gloria . . . Happy at Last*. New York: Alfred A. Knopf, 1980.

Gordon, Linda. "Black and White Visions of Welfare: Women's Welfare Activism, 1890–1945." *Journal of American History*, September 1991.

Gordon, Linda, and Sara McLanahan. "Single Parenthood in 1900." *Journal of Family History* 16, no. 2 (April 1991).

Green, Calvin, and Seth Y. A. Wells, eds. *A Summary View of the Millennial Church or the United Society of Believers*. Albany: Packard and Van Benthuysen, 1823.

Grossberg, Michael. *Governing the Hearth: Law and the Family in Nineteenth-Century America*. Chapel Hill: University of North Carolina Press, 1985.

Gruber, Alan R. *Destitute, Neglected, . . . Betrayed*. New York: Human Sciences Press, 1979.

Gutman, Herbert G. "Marital and Sexual Norms Among Slave Women." In *A Heritage of Her Own: Toward a New Social History of American Women*, Nancy F. Cott and Elizabeth H. Pleck, eds. New York: Simon & Schuster, 1979.

Hall, G. Stanley. *Adolescence: Its Psychology and Its Relations to Physiology, Anthropology, Sociology, Sex, Crime, Religion and Education*. New York: D. Appleton, 1905.

Halloway, Mark. *Heavens on Earth: Utopian Communities in America 1680–1880*. London: Turnstile Press, 1951.

Hamilton, Nigel. *JFK: Reckless Youth*. New York: Random House, 1992.

Handlin, Oscar. *The Uprooted*, 2d ed. Boston: Little, Brown, 1973.

Harris, Mark, Franklin Mitchell, and Steven Schecter, eds. *The Homefront: America During World War II*. New York: G. P. Putnam's Sons, 1984.

Harvard Mental Health Letter 8, no. 2 (August 1991).

Harvard Mental Health Letter 8, no. 3 (September 1991).

Hawes, Joseph M., and Ray N. Hiner, eds. *American Childhood: A Research*

Guide and Historical Handbook. Westport, Conn.: Greenwood Press, 1985.

Herrick, Cheesman A. *History of Girard College.* Philadelphia: Girard College, 1927.

Hersey, John. *Life Sketches.* New York: Random House, 1991.

Hinds, William A. *American Communities,* rev. ed. Chicago: C. H. Kerr, 1902.

Hines, Paulette Moore, and Nancy Boyd-Franklin. "Black Families." In *Ethnicity and Family Therapy,* Monica McGoldrick, John K. Pearce, and Joseph Giordano, Jr., eds. New York: Guilford Press, 1982.

Hoffman, Eva. *Lost in Translation: A Life in a New Language.* New York: E.P. Dutton, 1989. New York: Penguin, 1990.

Holloran, Peter C. *Boston's Wayward Children: Social Services for Homeless Children 1830–1930.* Rutherford, N.J.: Fairleigh Dickinson University Press, 1989.

Holt, L. Emmett, Jr. *The Care and Feeding of Children: A Catechism for the Use of Mothers and Children's Nurses,* 4th ed. New York: D. Appleton, 1929.

Horne, Field, ed. *The Diary of Mary Cooper: Life on a Long Island Farm 1768–1773.* New York: Oyster Bay Historical Society, 1981.

Howard, James. *The Little Victims: How America Treats Its Children.* New York: David McKay, 1975.

Howard, Louise Ogier, and Mildred McKenney Trice, eds. *Guardianships and Indentures Involving Orphans of Baltimore County.* Baltimore: Genealogical Publishing Co., 1975–76.

Howe, Irving. *World of Our Fathers.* New York: Simon & Schuster, 1976.

How Foster Children Turn Out. New York State Charities Aid Association. New York: State Charities Aid Association, 1924

Hull-House Bulletin, October 1896.

Hull-House Maps and Papers. New York: A. S. Holbrook, 1895.

Huntington, James O. S. "Philanthropy—Its Success and Failure." In *Philanthropy and Social Progress: Seven Essays,* Jane Addams, ed. New York: Thomas Y. Crowell, 1893.

Hurmence, Belinda, ed. *My Folks Don't Want Me to Talk About Slavery: Twenty-one Oral Histories of Former North Carolina Slaves.* Winston-Salem, N.C.: John F. Blair, 1984.

Hutchinson, Dorothy. *Cherish the Child: Dilemmas of Placement.* Metuchen, N.J.: Scarecrow Press, 1972.

Hymowitz, Carol, and Michaele Weissman. *A History of Women in America.* New York: Bantam Books, 1978.

Indentures, 1718–1727. Collections of the New-York Historical Society for 1909. New York: The New-York Historical Society, 1910.

Indentures in Philadelphia, 1771–1773. Baltimore, Md.: Genealogical Publishing Company, 1973.

Jackson, Donald Dale. "It Took Trains to Put Street Kids on the Right Track Out of the Slums." *Smithsonian Magazine,* August 1986.

Jacobs, Harriet Brent. *Incidents in the Life of a Slave Girl: Written by Herself.* New York: AMS Press, 1973.

Jarcho, Julius. *Postures and Practices During Labor Among Primitive Peoples: Adaptions to Modern Obstetrics, with Chapters on Taboos and Superstitions and Postpartum Gymnastics.* New York: Paul B. Hoeber, 1934.

Jelliffe, D. B., and E. F. P. Jelliffe. *Human Milk in the Modern World: Psychosocial, Nutritional, and Economic Significance.* New York: Oxford University Press, 1978.

Jernegan, Marcus Wilson. *Laboring and Dependent Classes in Colonial America, 1607–1783.* Westport, Conn.: Greenwood Press, 1980.

Johnson, Colleen A. L. "The Maternal Role in Contemporary Italian-American Life." In *The Italian Immigrant Woman in North America,* Betty Boyd Caroli, ed. Toronto: Multicultural History Society of Ontario, 1978.

Jones, Jacqueline. *Labor of Love, Labor of Sorrow: Black Women, Work and the Family from Slavery to the Present.* New York: Basic Books, 1985.

Kadushin, Alfred, and Judith Martin. *Child Welfare Services,* 4th ed. New York: Macmillan, 1988.

Kaestle, Carl F., and Maris A. Vinovkis. *Education and Social Change in Nineteenth-Century Massachusetts.* Cambridge, England: Cambridge University Press, 1980.

Kates, Wendy Glockner, et al. "Whose Child Is This? Assessment and Treatment of Children in Foster Care." *American Journal of Orthopsychiatry,* October 1991.

Katzman, David M. *Seven Days a Week: Women and Domestic Service in Industrializing America.* New York: Oxford University Press, 1978.

Keniston, Kenneth. "Children and Families." In *Family in Transition,* 3d ed., Arlene Skolnick and Jerome H. Skolnick, eds. Boston: Little, Brown, 1979.

Kern, Louis J. *An Ordered Love: Sex Roles and Sexuality in Victorian Utopias.* Chapel Hill: University of North Carolina Press, 1981.

Kessen, William. "The American Child and Other Cultural Inventions." *American Psychologist,* October 1979.

Kessler-Harris, Alice. *Women Have Always Worked: A Historical Overview.* Old Westbury, N.Y.: The Feminist Press/New York: McGraw-Hill, 1981.

Kincaid, Jamaica. "If Mammies Ruled the World." In *The Village Voice Anthology: 25 Years,* Geoffrey Stokes, ed. New York: William Morrow, 1982.

Kinsley, Jessie Catherine. *A Lasting Spring: Jessie Catherine Kinsley, Daughter of the Oneida Community.* Syracuse: Syracuse University Press, 1983.

Klaus, Marshall H., and John H. Kennell. *Maternal-Infant Bonding: The Impact of Early Separation or Loss on Family Development.* St. Louis: C. V. Mosby, 1976.

Klaw, Spencer. *Without Sin: The Life and Death of the Oneida Community.* New York: Viking Penguin, 1993.

Koshuk, Ruth Pearson. "Developmental Records of 500 Nursery School Children." *Journal of Experimental Education* 26, no. 91 (1944).

Kostelnik, Marjorie J., et al., eds. *Child and Nurturance,* vol. 2, *Patterns of Supplementary Parenting.* New York: Plenum Press, 1982.

Krase, Jerome. "Italian-American Female College Students: A New Generation Connected to the Old." In *The Italian Immigrant Woman in North America,* Betty Boyd Caroli, ed. Toronto: Multicultural History Society of Ontario, 1978.

Krause, Azen. *Grandmothers, Mothers and Daughters: Oral Histories of Three Generations of Ethnic American Women.* New York: American Jewish Committee, 1978.

Kraushaar, Otto F. *American Nonpublic Schools: Patterns of Diversity.* Baltimore: Johns Hopkins University Press, 1972.

Kuyk, Betty M. "Seeking Family Relationships." *Negro History Bulletin,* July, August, September 1979.

Lamb, Michael E., ed. *The Role of the Father in Child Development.* New York: John Wiley and Sons, 1976.

Langsam, Miriam Z. *Children West: A History of the Placing-Out System of the New York Children's Aid Society.* Madison: State Historical Society of Wisconsin, 1964.

Larson, Paul. "Dick Stolley Loves Kids." *The Medillian,* Fall 1993.

Lasch, Christopher, ed. *The Social Thought of Jane Addams.* Indianapolis: Bobbs-Merrill, 1965.

Leach, Penelope. *The First Six Months.* New York: Alfred A. Knopf, 1986.

Leach, William. "Child-World in the Promised Land." In *The Mythmaking Frame of Mind: Social Imagination and American Culture,* James Gilbert et al., eds. Belmont, Calif.: Wordsworth, 1993.

Lerner, Gerda. *Black Women in White America: A Documentary History.* New York: Vintage Books, 1973.

Levine, Murray, and Barbara Benedict Bunker, eds. *Mutual Criticism.* Syracuse: Syracuse University Press, 1975.

Liebling, A. J. *Between Meals: An Appetite for Paris.* New York: Simon & Schuster, 1962.

Lingeman, Richard R. *Don't You Know There's a War On? The American Home Front 1941–1945.* New York: G. P. Putnam's Sons, 1970.

Lowery, I. E. *Life on the Old Plantation in Ante-Bellum Days.* Columbia, S.C.: The State Co., 1911.

Lundberg, Emma O. *Public Aid to Mothers with Dependent Children: Extent and Fundamental Principles.* U.S. Department of Labor, Children's Bureau. Washington, D.C.: GPO, 1928.

Mabee, Carleton. "Charity in Travail: Two Orphan Asylums for Blacks." *New York History* 55 (1974).

MacPherson, James. *Battle Cry of Freedom*, New York: Oxford University Press, 1988.

MacNamara, Charles. "Stephen Girard: The Will." *Greater Philadelphia*, January 1966.

Malcolm X, with the Assistance of Alex Haley. *The Autobiography of Malcolm X*. New York: Ballantine Books, 1973.

Maluccio, Anthony N. "Foster Family Care Revisited: Problems and Prospects." *Public Welfare* 31, no. 2 (Spring 1973).

Mancuso, Arlene. "Women of Old Town." In *The Italian Immigrant Woman in North America*, Betty Boyd Caroli, ed. Toronto: Multicultural History Society of Ontario, 1978.

Mandelker, Ira L. *Religion, Society and Utopia in Nineteenth Century America.* Amherst: University of Massachusetts Press, 1984.

Mandler, Peter, ed. *The Uses of Charity: The Poor on Relief in the Nineteenth-Century Metropolis.* Philadelphia: University of Pennsylvania Press, 1990.

Martin, David. Introduction to *God's Blueprints: A Sociological Study of Three Utopian Sects,* by John McKelvie Whitworth. London: Routledge & Kegan Paul, 1975.

McAdams, Phyllis. "The Parent in the Shadows." In *Parents of Children in Placement: Perspectives and Programs*, Paula A. Sinanoglu and Anthony N. Maluccio, eds. New York: Child Welfare League of America, 1981.

McCarthy, Mary. *Memories of a Catholic Girlhood.* New York: Harcourt Brace Jovanovich, 1957.

McCausland, Clare L. *Children of Circumstance: A History of the First 125 Years (1849–1974) of the Chicago Child Care Society.* Chicago: Chicago Child Care Society, 1976.

McConahay, Mary Jo. "The Ultimate Experiment." *Los Angeles Times Magazine*, February 19, 1989.

McCree, Mary Lynn. "The First Year of Hull House." *Chicago History*, new series 1, no. 2 (Fall 1970).

McElvaine, Robert S. *The Great Depression: America, 1929-1941.* New York: Times Books, 1984.

———, ed. *Down and Out in the Great Depression: Letters from "the Forgotten Man."* Chapel Hill: University of North Carolina Press, 1983.

McHugh, Cathy L. *Mill Family: The Labor System in the Southern Cotton Textile Industry, 1880–1915.* New York: Oxford University Press, 1988.

McLachlan, James. *American Boarding Schools: A Historical Study.* New York: Charles Scribner's Sons, 1970.

Mead, Margaret. "Some Theoretical Considerations on the Problem of Mother-Child Separation." *American Journal of Orthopsychiatry*, 24, 1954.

Mellow, James R. *Invented Lives: F. Scott and Zelda Fitzgerald.* Boston: Houghton Mifflin, 1984.

Mencken, H. L. *The American Language, Supplement 1.* New York: Alfred A. Knopf, 1945.

Metzker, Isaac, ed. *A Bintel Brief.* Garden City, N.Y.: Doubleday, 1971.

Milford, Nancy. *Zelda: A Biography.* New York: Harper and Row, 1970.

Mintz, Steven, and Susan Kellogg. *Domestic Revolutions: A Social History of American Family Life.* New York: Free Press, 1988.

Mitchell, Margaret. *Gone with the Wind.* New York: Macmillan, 1936.

Montaigne, Michel de. *Essays.* New York: Penguin Books, 1958.

Morris, Lloyd. *Incredible New York: High Life and Low Life of the Last Hundred Years.* New York: Random House, 1951.

———. *Postscript to Yesterday.* New York: Random House, 1947.

Morse, Flo. *The Shakers and the World's People.* New York: Dodd, Mead, 1980.

Muncy, Raymond Lee. *Sex and Marriage in Utopian Communities: Nineteenth Century America.* Bloomington: Indiana University Press, 1973.

Nasaw, David. *Children of the City: At Work and at Play.* Garden City, N.Y.: Anchor Press/Doubleday, 1985.

Nelli, Humbert S. *From Immigrants to Ethnics: The Italian Americans.* New York: Oxford University Press, 1983.

New York Society for the Improvement of the Condition of the Poor: *Forty First Annual Report,* 1884.

———. *Forty Second Annual Report,* 1885.

New York Street Kids: 136 Photographs. Selected by the Children's Aid Society. New York: Dover, 1978.

Nordhoff, Charles. *The Communistic Societies of the United States.* 1875. Reprint, New York: Dover, 1966.

Norton, Mary Beth. *Liberty's Daughters: The Revolutionary Experience of American Women, 1750–1800.* Boston: Little, Brown, 1980.

Noyes, Pierrepont. *My Father's House: An Oneida Boyhood.* Gloucester, Mass.: Peter Smith, 1966.

Nye, F. Ivan, and Lois Wladis Hoffman. *The Employed Mother in America.* Chicago: Rand McNally, 1963.

Oakley, Ann. *The Housewife, Past and Present.* New York: Pantheon, 1974.

Owen, Monica B. "Save Our Child Care Centers." *Parents' Magazine,* March 6, 1946.

Palmer, Francis H., and Lucille Woolis Andersen. "Long-Term Gains from Early Intervention: Findings from Longitudinal Studies." In *Project Head Start: A Legacy of the War on Poverty,* Edward Zigler and Jeanette Valentine, eds. New York: Free Press, 1979.

Parker, Robert Allerton. *A Yankee Saint: John Humphrey Noyes and the Oneida Community.* New York: G. P. Putnam's Sons, 1935.

Parkhurst, Jessie W. "The Role of the Black Mammy in the Plantation Household." *Journal of Negro History* 23, no. 3 (July 1938).

Patri, Angelo. *Talks to Mothers.* New York: D. Appleton, 1923.

Pecorini, Alberto. "The Italians in the United States." In *The Italians: Social Backgrounds of an American Group*, Francesco Cordasco and Eugene Bucchioni, eds., 153–65. Clifton, N.J.: A. M. Kelley, 1974.

Pelton, Leroy H. *For Reasons of Poverty: A Critical Analysis of the Public Child Welfare System in America*. New York: Praeger, 1989.

Percy, William Alexander. *Lanterns on the Levee*. New York: Alfred A. Knopf, 1941.

Picquet, Louisa. *Louisa Picquet, the Octoroon; or, Inside Views of Southern Domestic Life*. In *Collected Black Women's Narratives, The Schomburg Library of 19th-Century Black Women Writers*. New York: Oxford University Press, 1988.

Pinchot, Amos. *The Meaning of the Progressive Movement*. Jane Addams Papers, 1912.

Plant, Ruth. *Nanny and I*. London: William Kimber, 1978.

Pogrebin, Letty Cottin. *Deborah, Golda and Me: Being Female and Jewish in America*. New York: Crown Publishers, 1991.

Polacheck, Hilda Satt. *I Came a Stranger: The Story of a Hull-House Girl*. Urbana: University of Illinois Press, 1989.

Polster, Gary Edward. *The Cleveland Jewish Orphan Asylum 1868–1924*. Kent, Ohio: Kent State University Press, 1990.

Polstrel, Virginia I. "Who's Behind the Health Care Crisis?" *Reason*, June 1989.

Pope, Vernon. "Eight Hour Orphans." *Saturday Evening Post*, October 10, 1942.

Potter, Robert E. *The Stream of American Education*. New York: American Book Co., 1967.

Pritchett, V. S. *The Living Novel and Later Appreciations*. New York: Vintage Books, 1964.

Quimby, Ian M. G. "Apprenticeship in Colonial Philadelphia." Master's thesis, University of Delaware, 1963. New York: Garland Publishing, 1985.

Rabin, A. I., and Benjamin Beit-Hallami. *Kibbutz Children Grown Up*. New York: Springer, 1982.

Raines, Howell. "Grady's Gift." *New York Times Magazine*, December 1, 1991.

Rawick, George P., ed. *The American Slave: A Composite Autobiography*, 19 vols. Contributions in Afro-American Studies, no 2. Westport, Conn.: Greenwood, 1972.

———. *The American Slave: A Composite Autobiography. Supplement*, 12 vols. Westport, Conn.: Greenwood, 1977.

Rexroth, Kenneth. *Communalism: From Its Origins to the Twentieth Century*. New York: The Seabury Press, 1974.

Riis, Jacob A. *The Children of the Poor*. New York: Charles Scribner's Sons, 1892.

———. *How the Other Half Lives*. New York: Charles Scribner's Sons, 1890.

———. *A Ten Years' War: An Account of the Battle with the Slums in New York.* Boston: Houghton, Mifflin, 1900.

Ritter, Kathy A. *Apprentices of Connecticut, 1637–1900.* Salt Lake City, Utah: Ancestry Publishing, 1986.

Robertson, Constance Noyes, ed. *The Oneida Community: An Autobiography, 1851–1876.* Syracuse: Syracuse University Press, 1970.

Roemer, Joan. *Two to Four from Nine to Five: The Adventures of a Day Care Provider.* New York: Harper & Row, 1989.

Rollins, Judith. *Between Women: Domestics and Their Employers.* Philadelphia: Temple University Press, 1985.

Rolvaag, O. E. *Giants in the Earth,* New York: Harper and Brothers, 1927.

Roosevelt, Eleanor. *Autobiography.* New York: Harper and Brothers, 1962.

Roosevelt, Theodore. *Call for a Conference on the Care of Dependent Children.* New York: Children's Aid Society, January 25 and 26, 1909.

Rorabaugh, W. J. *The Craft Apprentice: From Franklin to the Machine Age in America.* New York: Oxford University Press, 1986.

Rosenberg, Charles E. *No Other Gods: On Science and American Social Thought.* Baltimore: Johns Hopkins University Press, 1976.

Ross, Catherine J. "Early Skirmishes with Poverty: The Historical Roots of Head Start." In *Project Head Start: A Legacy of the War on Poverty,* Edward Zigler and Jeanette Valentine, eds. New York: Free Press, 1991.

Ross, Elizabeth D. *The Kindergarten Crusade: The Establishment of Preschool Education in the United States.* Athens, Ohio: Ohio University Press, 1976.

Rothman, David J. *The Discovery of the Asylum: Social Order and Disorder in the New Republic.* Boston: Little, Brown, 1971.

———. *Conscience and Convenience: The Asylum and Its Alternatives in Progressive America.* Boston: Little, Brown, 1990.

Rothman, Sheila M. *Woman's Proper Place: A History of Changing Ideals and Practices 1870 to the Present.* New York: Basic Books, 1978.

Rotunno, Marie, and Monica McGoldrick. "Italian Families." In Monica McGoldrick, John K. Pearce, and Joseph Giordano, eds. *Ethnicity and Family Therapy.* New York: Guilford Press, 1982.

Rupp, George P., ed. *Girard College: Its Semi-Centennial, 1848–1898.* Philadelphia: Lippincott, 1898.

Ryan, Mary. *Womanhood in America: From Colonial Times to the Present.* 3d ed. New York: F. Watts, 1983.

Sanders, Ronald. *The Downtown Jews: Portraits of an Immigrant Generation.* New York: Harper & Row, 1969.

Sappol, Michael. "The Uses of Philanthropy: The Colored Asylum and Its Clients." Master's thesis, Columbia University, 1990.

Scarr, Sandra. *Mother Care/Other Care.* New York: Basic Books, 1984.

School of the Holy Child. *Golden Jubilee Yearbook,* 1912–1962. Suffern, New York.

Schulz, Constance B. "Poor Apprentices in Boston." *In Children and Child-hood in Eighteenth Century America*, Joseph M. Hawes and Ray N. Hiner, eds. Westport, Conn.: Greenwood Press, 1985.

Seabury, Samuel III. *Moneygripe's Apprentice*. Robert Bruce Mullin, ed. New Haven: Yale University Press, 1989.

Seifer, Nancy. *Nobody Speaks for Me: Self-Portraits of American Working Class Women*. New York: Simon & Schuster, 1976.

Seixas, Peter Carr. "From Juvenile Asylum to Treatment Center: Changes in a New York Institution for Children 1905–1930." Master's thesis, University of British Columbia, 1981.

Seybolt, Robert Francis. *Apprenticeship and Apprenticeship Education in Colonial New England and New York*. 1917. Reprint, New York: AMS Press, 1972.

Shea, James J., and Charles Mercer. *It's All in the Game*. New York: G. P. Putnam's Sons, 1960.

Sheehan, Susan. "A Lost Motherhood." *New Yorker*, January 18, 1993.

Shell, Ellen Ruppel. "The Advocate." *Boston Globe Magazine*, October 18, 1990.

Shengold, Leonard. *Soul Murder: Persecution in the Family*. New York: Fawcett Columbine, 1989.

Shields, Judith. *Indentures in Philadelphia, 1771–1773*. Baltimore: Genealogical Publishing, 1973.

Shipton, Clifford K. *Isaiah Thomas, Printer, Patriot and Philanthropist, 1749–1831*. Rochester, N.Y.: Printing House of Leo Hart, 1948.

Shorter, Edward. *A History of Women's Bodies*. New York: Basic Books, 1982.

Silverman, Doris K. "What Are Little Girls Made Of?" *Psychoanalytic Psychology* 4, no. 4 (1987).

Silverstein, Louise B. "Transforming the Debate about Child Care and Maternal Employment." *American Psychologist*, October 1991.

Simkhovitch, Mary Kingsbury. *The City Worker's World in America*. 1917. Reprint, New York: Arno and the New York Times, 1971.

Simpson, Eileen. *Orphans, Real and Imaginary*. New York: New American Library, 1987.

Skolnick, Arlene, and Jerome Skolnick. *Family in Transition: Rethinking Marriage, Sexuality, Child Rearing and the Family Organization*, 3d ed. Boston: Little, Brown, 1980.

Slingerland, W. H. *Child-Placing in Families: A Manual for Students and Social Workers*. New York: Russell Sage Foundation, 1919.

———, ed. *A Child Welfare Symposium*. New York: Russell Sage Foundation, 1915.

Smith, Judith E. "Italian Mothers, American Daughters: Changes in Work and Family Roles." In *The Italian Immigrant Woman in North America*, Betty Boyd Caroli, ed.. Toronto: Multicultural History Society of Ontario, 1978.

————. "Our Own Kind: Family and Community Networks in Providence." In *A Heritage of Her Own: Toward a New History of American Women*, Nancy F. Cott and Elizabeth H. Pleck, eds. New York: Simon & Schuster, 1979.

Smith, Julia Floyd. *Slavery and Rice Culture in Low Country Georgia 1750–1860*. Knoxville: University of Tennessee Press, 1985.

Spinka, Matthew. *John Amos Comenius: That Incomparable Moravian*. Chicago: University of Chicago Press, 1943.

Spitz, Rene A. "Hospitalism: An Inquiry Into the Genesis of Psychiatric Conditions in Early Childhood." In *The Psychoanalytic Study of the Child*. New York: International Universities Press, 1954.

Spock, Benjamin. *Baby and Child Care*, Cardinal ed. New York: Pocket Books, 1957.

Sprigg, June. "Out of This World." *American Heritage Magazine:* April/May 1980.

Srygley, F. D. *Seventy Years in Dixie*. Nashville: Gospel Advocate, 1891.

Stack, Carol B. *All Our Kin: Strategies for Survival in a Black Community*. New York: Harper & Row, 1974.

Steiner, Gilbert Y. *The Children's Cause*. Washington, D.C.: The Brookings Institution, 1976.

Steinfels, Margaret O'Brien. *Who's Minding the Children?: The History and Politics of Day Care in America*. New York: Simon & Schuster, 1973.

Sterling, Dorothy, ed. *We Are Your Sisters: Black Women in Nineteenth-Century American Life*. New York: W. W. Norton, 1984.

Stern, Daniel. *The Interpersonal World of the Infant: A View from Psychoanalysis and Developmental Psychology*. New York: Basic Books, 1985.

Strickland, Charles. "A Transcendentalist Father." In *Perspectives in American History*, vol. 11. New York: Cambridge University Press, 1969.

Strom, Sharon Hartman. "Italian-American Women and Their Daughters in Rhode Island, 1900–1950." In *The Italian Immigrant Woman in North America*, Betty Boyd Caroli, ed. Toronto: Multicultural History Society of Ontario, 1978.

Stroyer, Jacob. *My Life in the South*, 4th ed. Salem, Mass.: Newcomb and Gauss, 1898.

Sullivan, Mark. *Our Times: The United States, 1900–1925*. New York: Charles Scribner's Sons, 1926.

Sutherland, Daniel E. *Domestic Service in the United States from 1800–1920*. Baton Rouge: Louisiana State University Press, 1981.

Swasta, Susan M., and Richard D. Krohn. *Mind, Body and Spirit: Moravian Academy 1742–1992*. Bethlehem, Pa.: Moravian Academy, 1991.

"Ten Fashionable Boarding Schools for Girls." *Fortune*, April 1936.

Terkel, Studs. *Hard Times: An Oral History of the Depression*. New York: Pantheon Books, 1970.

————. *Working*. New York: Avon Books, 1975.

Thomas, Isaiah. *Diary of Isaiah Thomas, 1805–1828*, 2 vols. Edited with an introduction by Benjiman Thomas Hill. Worcester, Mass.: The American Antiquarian Society, 1909; New York: Johnson Reprint Corp., 1971.

———. *History of Printing in America: With a Biography of Printers and An Account of Newspapers*. 1810. Reprint, edited by Marcus A. McCorison. New York: Weathervane Books, 1970.

———. *Three Autobiographical Fragments*. Worcester, Mass.: The American Antiquarian Society, 1962.

Thomas, John L. *The Liberator: William Lloyd Garrison*. Boston: Little, Brown, 1963.

Tims, Margaret. *Jane Addams of Hull-House*. New York: Macmillan, 1967.

Tocqueville, Alexis de. *Democracy in America*, rev. ed. Henry Reeve, transl. New York: Colonial Press, 1889. Quoted in Nancy F. Cott, *Root of Bitterness: Documents in the Social History of American Women*. New York: E. P. Dutton, 1972.

Towner, Lawrence W. "A Good Master Well Served: A Social History of Servitude in Massachusetts, 1620–1750." Ph.D. diss., Northwestern University, 1955.

———. "The Indentures of Boston's Poor Apprentices: 1734–1805." *Colonial Society of Massachusetts*, 43, 1966.

Trager, James. *Park Avenue: Street of Dreams*. New York: Atheneum, 1990.

Trahey, Jane. *The Trouble with Angels*. New York: Dell, 1962.

Trattner, Walter I. *Homer Folks: Pioneer in Social Welfare*. New York: Columbia University Press, 1968.

Tucker, Susan. *Telling Memories Among Southern Women: Domestic Workers and Their Employers in the Segregated South*. Baton Rouge: Louisiana State University Press, 1988.

"Twelve of the Best American Boarding Schools." *Fortune*, January 1936.

Tyson, Job R. *Discourse on the First Anniversary of the Girard College for Orphans*. Philadelphia: Crissy and Markley, 1849.

U.S. Children's Bureau. *The ABC of Foster-Family Care for Children*. Publication No. 216. Washington, D.C.: GPO, 1936.

———. *Public Aid to Mothers with Dependent Children*. Washington, D.C.: GPO, 1926.

———. *The Work of Child Placing Agencies*. Publication No. 127. Washington, D.C.: GPO, 1927.

U.S. Congress. House. *Joint Hearing before the Subcommittee on Children and Youth*, 94th Cong., 1st Sess., December 1, 1975. Part 1.

U.S. Congress. Senate. Committee on Education and Labor. *Hearing on Care and Protection of Children of Employed Mothers*. 78th Cong., 1st sess., June 8, 1943.

———. *Report on the Condition of Women and Child Wage-Earners*. Report prepared by Helen Sumner. 61st Cong., 2d Sess., 1910.

U.S. Department of Commerce, Bureau of the Census. *Historical Statistics of the United States from Colonial Times to 1970.* Washington, D.C.: GPO, 1975.

U.S. Department of Labor, Women's Bureau. *Women Workers in Ten War Production Areas and Their Postwar Employment Plans.* Washington, D.C.: GPO, 1946.

Vanderbilt, Gloria. *Once Upon a Time: A True Story.* New York: Alfred A. Knopf, 1985.

Van de Warker, Ely. "A Gynecological Study." *American Journal of Obstetrics and Diseases of Women and Children* 18, no. 8 (August 1884).

Vanek, Joann. "Time Spent in Housework." In *A Heritage of Her Own: Toward a New Social History of American Women*, Nancy F. Cott and Elizabeth H. Pleck, eds. New York: Simon & Schuster, 1979.

Vecchio, Diane C. "Italian Women in Industry: The Shoeworkers of Endicott, New York, 1914–1935." *Journal of American Ethnic History* 8, no. 2 (Spring 1989).

Watson, John B. *The Psychological Care of Infant and Child.* New York: W. W. Norton, 1928.

Weinberg, Sydney Stahl. *The World of Our Mothers: The Lives of Jewish Immigrant Women.* Chapel Hill: University of North Carolina Press, 1988.

Wells, Ida B. *Crusade for Justice: The Autobiography of Ida B. Wells.* Alfreda M. Duster, ed. Chicago: University of Chicago Press, 1970.

Wertheimer, Barbara Mayer. *We Were There: The Story of Working Women in America.* New York: Pantheon Books, 1977.

Wexler, Richard. *Wounded Innocents.* Buffalo: Prometheus Books, 1990.

White, Deborah Gray. *Aren't I a Woman? Female Slaves in the Plantation South.* New York: W. W. Norton, 1985.

White House Conference on Children. *Care of Dependent Children.* 60th Congress, 2d. Sess., 1909.

———. *Child Health and Protection*, Supplement, U.S. Daily, vol. 5, November 28, 1930.

———. *Children in a Democracy: 40 Preliminary Statements.* U.S. Department of Labor, Children's Bureau Publication no. 266. Washington, D.C.: GPO, 1940.

Whitt, Anne Hall. *The Suitcases.* Washington, D.C.: Acropolis Books, 1982.

Whitworth, John Mckelvie, *God's Blueprints: A Sociological Study of Three Utopian Sects.* London: Routledge & Kegan Paul, 1975.

Williamson, Joel. *After Slavery: The Negro in South Carolina During Reconstruction, 1861–1877.* Chapel Hill: University of North Carolina Press, 1965.

Wolins, Martin, and Irving Piliavin. *Institution or Foster Family: A Century of Debate.* New York: Child Welfare League of America, 1964.

Woloch, Nancy. *Women and the American Experience.* New York: Alfred A. Knopf, 1984.

Woody, Thomas. *A History of Women's Education in the US*, 2 vols. New York: Science Press, 1929.

Worden, Harriet M. *Old Mansion House Memories: By One Brought Up in It.* Oneida, N.Y.: Kenwood, 1950.

Wright, Louis B. *Everyday Life in Colonial America.* New York: G. P. Putnam's Sons, 1965.

Wylly, Charles Spalding. *The Seed That Was Sown in the Colony of Georgia: The Harvest and the Aftermath 1740–1870.* New York: Neale, 1910.

Yetman, Norman, ed. *Voices from Slavery: The Life of American Slaves.* New York: Holt, Rinehart and Winston, 1970.

Zigler, Edward, and Jeanette Valentine, eds. *Project Head Start: A Legacy of the War on Poverty.* New York: Free Press, 1979.

Zinsser, Caroline. *Raised in East Urban: Child Care Changes in a Working Class Community.* New York: Teacher's College Press, 1991.

Zucker, Henry L. "Cleveland's Program of Community Service for the Care of Children of Working Mothers." *The Child* 8, no. 11 (May 1944).

———. "Working Parents and Latchkey Children." *Annals of the American Academy of Political and Social Science* 236 (1944).

INDEX

PICTURE CREDITS

Children's Aid Society of New York: 22
Girard College: 6
Harper's New Monthly Magazine, June 1880: 10
The Historical Society of Pennsylvania: 1
Kansas State Historical Society: 8
Prints and Photographs Division, Library of Congress: 13
Maryland State Archives, MSA SC 4905: 18
Moravian Academy, Bethlehem, Pennsylvania: 21
The Byron Collection. Museum of the City of New York: 17
National Archives: 20; Federal Works Agency Collection: 23, 24;
    Lewis W. Hine photograph: 14, 15
The New-York Historical Society: 7
General Research Division, The New York Public Library, Astor,
    Lenox and Tilden Foundations: 5 (*Frank Leslie's Illustrated Newspaper*, April 9, 1870), 11 (*Frank Leslie's Illustrated Newspaper*, March 4,
    1882), 16 (*Harper's Magazine*, May 16, 1868)
Oneida Community Mansion House: 4
Kirk Pearce, Lebanon, Missouri: 9
Photographs and Prints Division, Schomberg Center for Research
    in Black Culture, The New York Public Library, Astor, Lenox and
    Tilden Foundations: 2
Society of the Holy Child Jesus: 19
Wallace Kirkland Papers, Jane Addams Memorial Collections, Special Collections, The University Library, The University of Illinois at Chicago: 12
Williams College Archives and Special Collections: 3